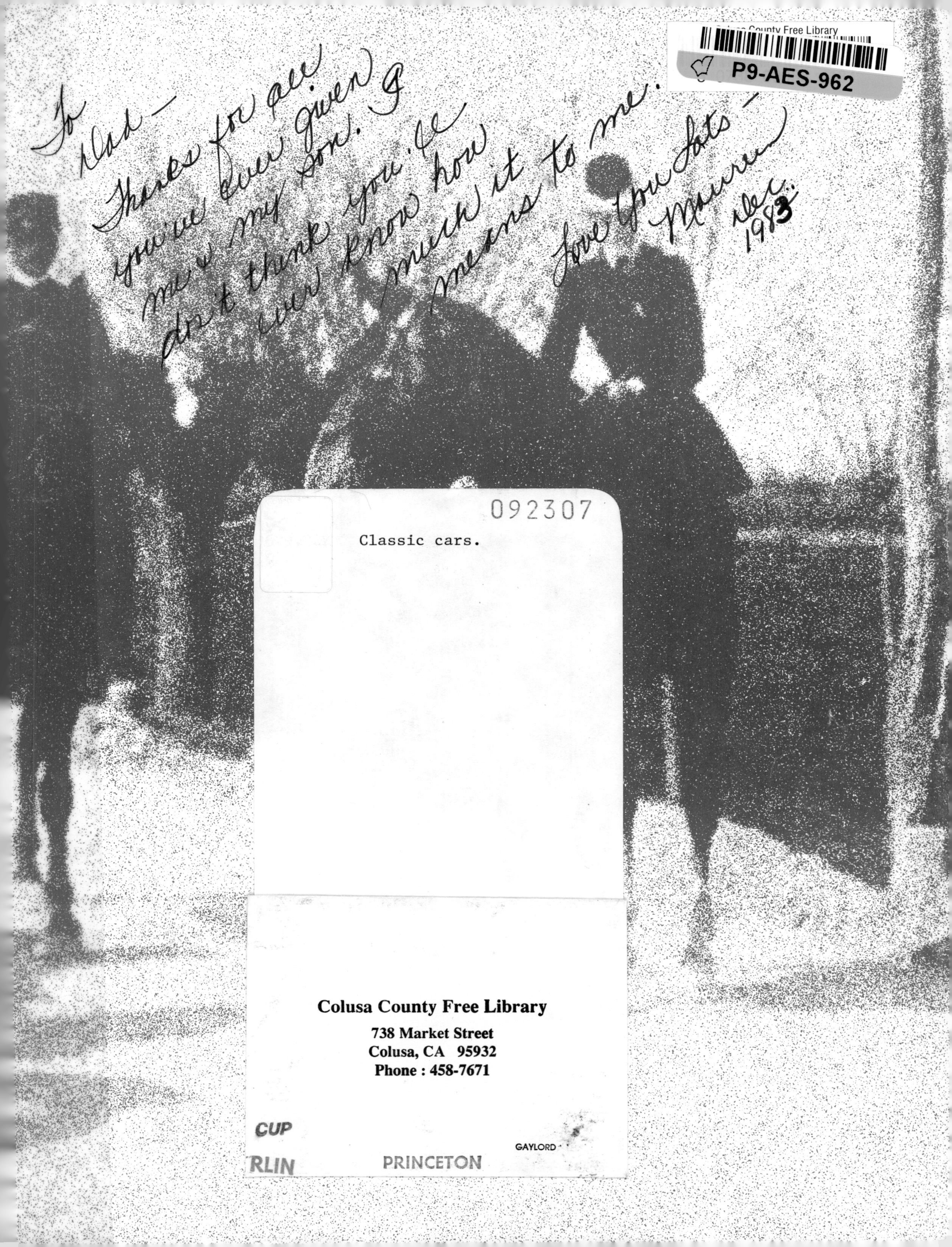

To
Dad —
Thanks for all
you've ever given
me & my son. I
don't think you'll
ever know how
much it
means to me.
Love you lots,
Maureen
Dec.
1983

Classic Cars

Classic Cars

Fifty Years of the World's Finest
Automotive Design

Edited by
Kevin Brazendale and Enrica Aceti
Introduction by Brian Laban

Exeter Books

NEW YORK

Title page *the 1910 Swift, which was fitted with an Austin radiator*

PICTURE ACKNOWLEDGMENTS
Illustrations were supplied by the following:
Alisi, Anselmi, Belli, Betti, Bisconcini, BMW,
Boschetti, Briggs-Cunningham Museum, Ceci,
Cherrett, Chrysler, Coluzzi, Crawford Museum,
Daimler Benz, Cesare De Agostini, Farabola,
Fiat, Ford, Graham, Hanus, Hornet, ICP,
IMS, Italfoto, Mairani, Marka, Marzolla,
Moity, Musée de Val de Loire, Musée Nationale
des Techniques, Museo dei Trasporti di Lucerna,
Museo dell'Automobile di Torino, Museo di
Caramulo, National Motor Museum, Papetti,
Peugeot, Pininfarina, Pozzoli, Price, Quattroruote,
Renault, Smithsonian Institution, Strinati,
Von Fersen, Zagari.

96B5944

First published in USA 1981 by Exeter Books
Exeter is a trademark of Simon & Schuster, Inc.
Bookthrift is a registered trade mark of Simon & Schuster, Inc.
Distributed by Bookthrift, New York, New York
This edition reprinted 1983

ISBN 0-671-05103-2
Printed in Spain

GRAFICAS REUNIDAS. S. A.
Av. de Aragón, 56.—Madrid-27

Contents

Introduction

Love it or hate it, it is impossible to ignore the motor car. Since Gottlieb Daimler replaced horse power with horsepower, the car has stuttered, roared and purred its way into almost every life. In less than a century, the motor car has changed the world; it has broadened horizons and shrunk continents. From inventor's dream through rich man's toy, to providing mobility for the masses, the car has reshaped society.

Throughout its existence the car has eschewed uniformity, as a thousand would-be Henry Fords have left behind their own statements to the motoring world while millions of ordinary people have worshipped their exquisite or improbable creations. *International Classic Cars* looks at the reasons why.

It is necessary to start at the beginning, when the wheel enabled man to trundle more than he could carry, and harnessing the horse and the ox allowed him to ride where once he had pulled. The age of horse-drawn transport was an essential backdrop to what would follow, because in the early days the car was very much a cart without the horse. For thousands of years the horse served its purpose and might be serving the same purpose still, but for man's ambition and the animal's limitations of stamina, speed and strength.

The more man travelled the more he wanted to travel, and the quicker he went the quicker he wanted to go. The story moves on through the industrial revolution, when stationary steam engines and electric power made their bow and the visionaries saw, not for the first time but now perhaps with some real hope, transport free of the vagaries of the horse. The steam and electric vehicle may look odd and amusing to us, but they were the precursors of the internal combustion engine – and may, ultimately, be its successors.

Even more than the horse, steam and electricity had their drawbacks. They were neither so far-ranging nor so fleet and only the most monstrous of steam engines could beat the horse as a beast of burden, but they marked the faltering beginning of the new age.

Just before the turn of the twentieth century, the advent of the internal combustion engine heralded the real birth of the motor car and this book describes, in all its contexts, the early days of its history. Part One of this book depicts the two first great ages of motoring, from the very earliest days until 1904 – the 'veteran' era – and from then until the end of the 'Edwardian' era, in 1918. This second period was dominated by World War 1 and just as that terrible conflict left its indelible mark on world power, so did the role of motor transport in the war years forever change society's attitude to the car. Men went to war never having touched a motor car and came back seasoned drivers. They had fought for their freedom and now they would enjoy it, and that freedom included the right to see the world they had fought to save. The car also overcame the barriers of class and brought transport, and jobs, to millions.

The book tells the story of the coming of mass production, a direct result of the huge new markets that opened up for motorised transport as the designers learned their lessons. The days when every car was built as an individual came to an end with Ransom Eli Olds, who as early as 1904 could turn out his Curved Dash model at the rate of 4000 a year. He was followed by the much emulated but inimitable Henry Ford. Ford perhaps remains the most famous name in motoring legend; his introduction of the moving production line made his dictum 'bring work to the people and the people to work' a reality. The burgeoning motor industry brought work, work brought prosperity and prosperity brought the demand for more and better cars.

As the masses took to the roads it was no longer enough for the smart young thing to be seen in a motor car, now it was necessary to be seen in the *right* motor car. Individuality, at a price, was the *raison d'être* of the grand marques which now proliferated to satisfy the fickle rich or the knowledgeable connoisseur. Great names like Hispano Suiza, Daimler, Rolls-Royce, Panhard and Mercedes brought

Opposite *a Peugeot vis-à-vis of 1895 with canopy roof (Peugeot collection)*

1907 Duhanot (Du Pasquier collection). The Paris company only remained in business for two years (1907–1908) and its production was somewhat limited

to the world of the motor car an elegance and extravagance which has seldom been surpassed. Part Two of this book looks at many of those cars, at how they were greeted by their contemporaries and how they influenced the new industry which they were a product. They are the individual pieces in the jigsaw of the growing motor industry and the developing history of motoring. They are also the products of the companies which flourished as a result of the new passion for motorised transport. This section of the book looks beyond the overall picture of the industry and examines country by country the fortunes of the individual companies which came and went from the motoring scene during the 1920s and 1930s. As a whole their stories *are* the story of motoring, but individually they are stories of unimaginable success and abject failure, engineering excellence and entrepre-

neurial absurdity. Exquisite concepts have met with public scorn and rejection while the most mundane designs have laid the foundations of vast fortunes and political power. The motor car however was everything, and it was the constant striving to bring it to perfection, or more universal public acceptability, that dominated its early days.

But the road to total acceptance was by no means smooth. To many elements of society, the coming of the motor car was not progress but an unspeakable evil, to be discouraged at all costs. To those who loved the new invention, it became a way of life, an extension, as it remains for some to this day, of its owner's character – or perhaps more accurately, the owner's fantasies. Then, to drive was an adventure. The pioneers did not take to the motor car for an easy option. It soon became apparent that the new invention was a real danger to life and limb and it was not only to protect the innocent bystander but also to shield the amateur from his own enthusiasm, that motoring soon came to be the subject of the first of a seemingly endless outpouring of legislation. Traffic laws, some obvious, some patently absurd, soon bedevilled the would-be carefree driver; vehicle licencing, motor insurance, traffic signs and the development of roads more suited to the new-fangled horse-less carriage than to its equine ancestors all quickly followed.

The rigours of early motoring are also reflected in the weird and wonderful fashions which were promoted to protect the intrepid 'automobiliste' from his own follies and the not inconsiderable hazards of the rudimentary roads of the day. As the motor industry itself grew, so too did its satellites: the clothing manufacturers, the makers of 'puncture-proof' tyres, a myriad manufacturers of every conceivable adjunct to the new craze. They are all part of the same fantastic story.

Another familiar aspect of motoring – motor racing – was an almost inevitable consequence of the second car. When man rattled along the road in his first creation he had beaten all the odds; when the next car came along his natural instinct dictated that he must beat that interloper too. To a world which had yet to come to terms with the motor car itself the early motor races must have seemed titanic struggles, and even now the achievements and heroic bravery of the first racing drivers seem formidable. Not for them the luxury of racing a car designed with but a single role, around a purpose-built circuit and for the huge rewards which racing brings today. Their machinery was more down to earth, usually the most monstrous contrivance to be found, stripped of all its creature comforts and dispatched with impressive faith to do battle over distances which today would suffice for a dozen Grands

Prix or more. From Paris the most famous drivers of the day raced to Bordeaux, to Madrid, even to Peking. The motor car was still a fragile infant but now it was being forced to grow into a useful member of society, more quickly by the stress of competition than perhaps by any other stimulus. To bask in the glory of winning, the car and driver had to go faster and last longer, and the lessons learned in racing were soon to be seen on the everyday roads. Tyres, pitifully vulnerable on the rock-strewn roads of the day, grew ever more robust; brakes became more of a fact and less of a promise; steering gradually became more appropriate to the 100 mph speeds soon being achieved than to the less heady pace of the horse or the bicycle. Motor racing had its triumphs and its tragedies, and it was not without its detractors. Thousands of people lined country roads to cheer these heroes, but thousands more fought to outlaw forever the crazy new sport. Yet motor racing survived and flourished, and has frequently been instrumental in pushing back the frontiers of motoring knowledge.

In many ways that too is the story of the development of the car throughout its early years. The motor car met the world head on and it was the world which had to give way. Nowadays the car is so much a part of every-day life and so much taken for granted that it is difficult to appreciate that it was so recently feared and reviled. It is a product of the twentieth century and it may not even survive in its present form until the end of the century, but it has changed all our lives.

This book is intended to evoke the past but it is also intended to put the motor car of today into perspective. It is a history, a social history, an economic history, a history of failure and achievement. What comes after does not matter; this is the way the motor car came into the world, so recently. Love it or hate it, it is impossible to ignore.

Part 1
The Pioneers

When Benz created his petrol-driven three-wheeler in 1886 men had already been working to perfect a 'horseless carriage' for over 100 years. In fact, the first recorded run in a self-propelled steam vehicle was as early as 1769, by Frenchman Nicholas Cugnot. Although sometimes of curious and cumbersome appearance, these ingenious attempts at speed and ease of movement were the true parents of the motor car. Many of the principles of their design and mechanics are the basis of the early internal combustion engined vehicles, and it was not until the establishment of mass production at the end of the second decade of the twentieth century that the motor car had changed enough for us to regard the first era in its history as complete.

Left *a steam car – the 1906 Stanley Model EX*

Wheels into Motion

The term 'locomotion' implies movement from one place to another and therefore the origins of locomotion begin with the dawn of man himself who, from his first appearance on earth, has had to move from place to place. For thousands of years he was a 'self-propelled machine' *par excellence* and had to rely solely upon himself for transportation. Gradually he learned to tame and domesticate certain species of animals, such as the ox, ass and the mule, the camel and the elephant, and finally the most important of all, the horse. All were used to transport both people and goods. Contrary to what one might think, the horse was used at first as a pack animal, only later was it used for human transport. This was because two essential elements for horse riding, namely the saddle and stirrups, had not been invented; in fact, the first extant example of a saddle is in China and is believed to date from around 2000 BC, while stirrups did not appear for another eight hundred years.

In its role as a pack animal the horse was the most important protagonist in the history of transport until the advent of mechanized locomotion at the end of the eighteenth century relegated it to second place.

Long before this, however, there was an extraordinary invention which revolutionized transport. This was the wheel. Where and when the wheel was invented has never been established, and so in the absence of concrete information, we must assume that its discovery was the result of a number of casual observations, ranging from the most banal, namely that a round object rolls more easily, to the more complex such as the reduction of friction that can be achieved by pulling an object on logs rather than simply along the ground. This system, which was first used at the very dawn of civilization, transforms surface friction into rolling friction by interposing elements which roll easily, and leads into the most commonly cited theory about the origin of the first wheel, as a full disc sawn from a tree trunk. The first examples of a wheel date back to the fourth millenium BC and belong to the Elamite, Sumerian and Chaldean civilizations. The oldest record there is comes from a bas-relief which came to light during the excavations of Ur in Lower Mesopotamia in 1928 and which represents a cart drawn by two animals and dates back to 3500 BC.

Whatever its origin, the wheel presupposes

This reconstruction of a four-wheeled, Italian, ornamental chariot, from the Iron Age, is in the Como Museum

a degree of civilization and inventiveness in the people who first used it – in other words, the ability to develop a true 'science'. This is corroborated by the fact that, while developed peoples had been using the wheel for thousands of years before Christ, it was, for instance, quite unknown to the Australian Aborigines when they first came into contact with western civilization more than five thousand years later.

The evolution of the wheel and the cart was, naturally enough, parallel, but was accompanied by another essential element; this was the road. Road networks were first developed by the Persians, the rulers of the Assyrian empire, then the Etruscans and finally by the Romans. According to the German linguist, Osthoff, the total road network in Europe constructed during republican and imperial Rome was 180,000 miles (300,000 km), but a more modest estimate was given as 87,000 miles (140,000 km) by the historian, Schmoller, at the beginning of this century. Assuming the second estimate to be more accurate, it is still an impressive figure, and the tunnels, road-beds, bridges and viaducts of Roman roads, excellent examples of which still remain, reveal the extremely advanced engineering of our forefathers and, considering the means at their disposal, their construction can even be regarded as an art.

The first carts were fairly light and could not carry heavy loads because of the fragility of the wheels and the inefficient method of harnessing the animals to the vehicle, which restricted their performance. In the early days the first harnesses consisted of a collar and pectoral belt; when the animal pulled the cart, the collar pressed against its neck, causing it to lift its head to avoid suffocation and thus transfer the weight to its hind legs, which inevitably hampered traction. Centuries were to pass before this was finally corrected and, in fact, the first example of a modern harness in the West did not appear until the beginning of the tenth century, at the height of the Middle Ages.

In 1700 BC the Egyptians introduced a wheel with four spokes which the Romans later adopted and developed in the third century BC, preceding the modern spoked wheel by more than two thousand years. Since its first appearance, the evolution of the wheel has been primarily aesthetic; structurally it remained unchanged for a long time and consisted of a wooden rim with wooden

spokes although sometimes the rim and hub were reinforced with a metal band.

The two- or four-wheeled cart drawn by two, three or four horses was developed mostly for travelling and sport; it was always very light and able to carry one or two people. The Etruscans, and later the Romans, introduced different types of carts for different uses; thus there were military, travelling, postal, racing, agricultural and transport carts. There were even special chariots for the exclusive use of the imperial family and the higher ranking members of the state.

However absurd it may seem, the appearance of different types of vehicles, together with the increase of the Roman population as the empire expanded, caused considerable traffic problems which led the authorities to apply special urban traffic regulation by introducing the famous Lex Julia of the first century BC, which contained precise rules and restrictions governing the use of vehicles in towns.

With the decline of the western Roman empire and the first barbarian invasions, the development of vehicles and road networks came to an abrupt halt and, with a few exceptions, was not resumed until the end of the Middle Ages, a period which is considered by many, either rightly or wrongly, to be the darkest age of all for the arts and sciences.

Traffic problems continued throughout the Middle Ages, however, especially during the

A light, elegant Hansom Cab from the English coachbuilders Forder & Co Ltd, built around the middle of the nineteenth century (Quattroruote collection)

crusades in which thousands of people took part and travelled by horse instead of by carriage; also in that era sedan chairs, which had been used in ancient times, returned to fashion.

Despite the lack of vehicles the late Middle Ages saw an important innovation in the first carriages with suspension, in which the frame was suspended by belts to reduce the vibration from the very rough road surfaces. A further advance came with the introduction of springs in the seventeenth century, one of the results of metallurgical progress, and this completed the belt suspension system. The problem that remained unsolved, however, at least until the sixteenth century, was that of steering; in medieval carts and carriages steering was by means of a tiller directly connected to the frame of the vehicle.

The re-emergence of coaches was slow but sure and they became firmly established once again in the second half of the sixteenth century, with Italy leading the field in coachbuilding. Florence, Ferrara and Venice were the most famous centres and their craftsmanship was highly esteemed in all the courts of Europe for the structural solidity of their carriages, their elegance and magnificent decorative work. In time technological, and particularly metallurgical, progress led to many important innovations, one of which was the introduction of brakes for every type of vehicle. Carriages became the common means of transport, ceasing to be the prerogative of princes and church dignitaries, and public transport services gradually came into being. The coach as a form of transport was not rivalled until the twentieth century, when the internal combustion engine revolutionized road transport.

A classic example of a Mailcoach from the Milanese coachbuilders, Ferrari (Quattroruote collection)

An elegant berlina,
built by the Turin
coachbuilders
Forzano Brothers at
the end of the last
century (Quattroruote
collection)

Long before steam or internal combustion engines, however, inventors of previous centuries had faced the problem of mechanized locomotion, not the least of whom was Leonardo da Vinci whose scientific inventions were astounding. In the *Codice Atlantico* there is a design by him for a motor carriage propelled by springs set into the frame and, among other things, he also had very clear ideas about roads and even advocated underground and two-tier roads which can be seen in some American cities today.

During the Renaissance military carts abounded, because it was fashionable in European courts to hire so-called military architects. One of these was an Italian called Agostini Ramelli who, in 1558, was in the service of Henry III of France when he designed the first amphibian cart, propelled by two paddle-wheels operated by men inside when on the water; on the land it was drawn by animals. There were numerous and interesting ideas, most of which never came to fruition, including Albert Durer's study of nine mechanized carts which is described in a commemorative work, published in 1526, dedicated to the Emperor Maximilian I. Hans Hautsch, one of the most famous engineers of the time, did however build a coach which worked perfectly.

In addition to vehicles with various types of power plants driving the wheels, at the end of the sixteenth and throughout the seventeenth centuries there was a great number of different vehicles which attempted to exploit wind power. Although many of them were ingenious, results were rather poor as wind tends to be a rather unreliable source of power on land, unlike the open sea where it can blow uninterrupted for hundreds of miles.

After wind-powered vehicles, human energy was used as a means of propulsion for quadricycles, tricycles and bicycles, the precursors of the modern bicycle. One of the oldest examples of a bicycle, if such it could be called, astounded Parisians in the summer of 1791 when it appeared in the gardens of the Palais-Royal. It was ridden by the eccentric Count of Sivrac who was astride a wooden bar placed on two wheels and he propelled it simply by walking. In time, less rudimentary vehicles were built which were easier to ride thanks to the introduction of handlebars for steering; eventually, around 1860, the French engineer, Ernest Michaux, invented pedals to solve the problem of propulsion, at least for early two-wheeled vehicles.

All the vehicles mentioned can be regarded as having rudimentary self-propelling engines, however tenuous is their connection with the motor car as we know it, which can be considered as a completely self-sufficient, self-propelled vehicle powered by combustion. Nevertheless, today's efficient motor car does owe something to the crude but often fantastic early attempts at mechanized transport.

However, locomotion had another fascinating period to live through before the era of the internal combustion engine. This was the age of steam.

Steam Locomotion

In tracing the history of locomotion, albeit in general terms, it is important to know that before steam power was exploited there had been experiments with thermal energy. With this system power was supplied by the pressure of a fluid which would expand when heated. The aeolipyle, described in the *Pneumatica* of Hero of Alexandria, was in fact the basis of the first experiments in steam locomotion which were carried out later, in the seventeenth and eighteenth centuries. It was basically a hollow globe pivoted on a tube; the steam supplied through the tube escaped through two tangentially mounted pipes, thus spinning the globe. A design for a steam carriage fitted with large aeolipyle is attributed to Newton, and the same principle may also have inspired Papin, who made the first cylinder and piston steam engine, to build his small steam carriage around 1698.

However, the first real example of a steam-powered vehicle is without doubt the so-called 'Cugnot Carriage' of 1769. The first one was badly damaged during a test run and was later destroyed, but the second carriage, which was ready two years later, can still be seen at the Conservatoire National des Arts et Métiers in Paris, where it was placed after its discovery in a shed in the Paris Arsenal where it had been abandoned.

It was built by Joseph Nicolas Cugnot who, on completing his studies in military engineering at Mérières, enlisted in the French army. He was subsequently transferred to Vienna where he became an officer in the Austrian army, probably at the request of Francois III, Duke of Lorraine who subsequently became Francois I, Emperor of Austria, in 1745 and who loved to be surrounded by his compatriots. In Vienna, Cugnot, who had a natural flair for engineering, particularly military engineering, was able to continue his studies. He also made the acquaintance of Gribeauval, the Artillery General, and the Duke of Choiseul, the French King's ambassador, all of whom were interested in Cugnot's research and helped him to build his steam carriage. Having finished his military service in 1763, Cugnot returned to Paris and dedicated himself completely to his dream of building a steam-powered cart for transporting artillery. However, the problems involved in such a feat were enormous as each part had to be made by hand with rudimentary tools and at a very high cost. An individual without substantial private means could not undertake such a risky project and only the State could provide the necessary financial backing. Accordingly, Cugnot turned to Gribeauval, who had also returned to

A drawing of Cugnot's steam vehicle, showing its rudimentary structure. Built in 1769, Cugnot's wagon was the first automotive vehicle in history

G.Betti

Two views of Cugnot's second steam vehicle built in 1770.
Above *the front section, with the boiler attached to the single wheel.*
Right *the huge wooden frame resting on the back axle. The vehicle is now preserved in the Conservatoire des Arts et Métiers in Paris*

Paris where he was Inspector-General of the French army, and submitted his idea to him.

At the same time, a Swiss officer called Planta suggested to the Duke of Choiseul that he, Planta, should build a steam carriage of his own design; hearing of this, Gribeauval proposed that their two designs should be compared with each other. The decision went in favor of Cugnot whose design was judged superior even by his own rival, and so the French engineer was finally able to finance the building of a steam carriage. By the end of 1769 the 'fire-operated machine' was complete.

It consisted of a massive oak frame with three wheels, the front one being the driven wheel. A huge iron subframe, connected to the frame by a vertical rod, supported the steam boiler which was suspended at the front. The engine had two vertical and parallel bronze cylinders with a total displacement of 50,000 cc. It was intended to carry four people at a speed of $2\frac{1}{2}$ mph (4 kph), but the lack of a water tank greatly restricted its range and the weakness of the vertical rod, which was the only link between the engine and the frame, compromised its integrity.

Nevertheless, despite the disappointing results of his first model, Cugnot obtained the Duke of Choiseul's permission to build another one, which was given to the Paris Arsenal. By July 1771 the vehicle was ready for testing, but at this point Cugnot's problems began. The Duke of Choiseul had in the meantime become Minister of War but, for political reasons, had to resign and was therefore not in a position to authorise the test runs and his successors either would not, or could not, handle the problem, and eventually the French Revolution put an end to Cugnot's work. However, this in no way invalidates the achievement by the French engineer to whom the first tentative steps in modern motoring can be attributed.

As has been seen, the story of steam propulsion began in France, but it was in England that the use of steam power became widespread. Later the French regained their lead with the internal combustion engine; although it was created in Germany, it was developed and exploited in France.

In 1765 James Watt invented the steam condenser which worked the piston by steam alone. Watt also designed a double-acting steam engine fitted with a steam condenser, which his colleague, William Murdock, used in various experimental vehicles between 1782 and 1793.

In 1786 William Symington, a Scotsman, made a name for himself when he built a steam carriage which he successfully demonstrated in the streets of Edinburgh. However, the most outstanding character of this pioneering age was undoubtedly Richard Trevithick, although he is better known for his work in the field of rail locomotion. From the outset he was also interested in road locomotion and by 1796 had already built a steam-powered carriage which was followed four years later with a sort of omnibus. In 1802 he produced a third vehicle which, after running well on short journeys at a speed of 5–7 mph (8–11 kph), was almost destroyed in an accident. After this, disappointed with the set-back, Trevithick abandoned his work on road vehicles and dedicated himself to rail locomotion with much greater success.

Although steam power found its greatest supporters in England, it was also being researched and experimented with in other countries. In America, for instance, as far back as 1773, the young Oliver Evans, who is considered the father of the American automobile, had designed a high pressure, steam engine which he intended for road transport. It was not until 1787, however, that Evans succeeded in obtaining a patent for it from the Maryland authorities after being refused one the year before in Pennsylvania. The American engineer later improved his engine considerably, reducing its size and increasing its power. In 1805 Evans astounded the citizens of Philadelphia by producing an extraordinary amphibian dredger which was powered by a steam engine of his own construction. This strange vehicle was named *Orukter Amphibolos*. The propulsion unit drove both the wheels for land use and a large paddle wheel at the rear for travel on water.

Evans, however, was not the only American to tackle the steam question at that time; in 1791 Nathan Read, one of his contemporaries, invented a multi-tubular steam generator which could be adapted for use in automotive vehicles (it was patented bearing the signature of both George Washington and Thomas Jefferson). James Rumsey and John Fitch, who were the first Americans to apply steam

propulsion to a boat in 1785–86 are also worthy of mention.

However numerous and interesting they may be, all the experiments in steam locomotion which were carried out on both sides of the Atlantic in the second half of the eighteenth century revealed the defects of an extremely rudimentary engineering which did not reach its peak until the nineteenth century, rightly called 'the age of steam'. The development of steam propulsion owed much to England where it was widely used for road and rail locomotion. One problem confronting engineers at that time was the public's distrust; although steam was accepted for locomotives, its use in road vehicles was regarded with scepticism. Such prejudice was partly due to the dubious aesthetic value of the first steam-powered stage coaches to appear on English roads; they looked as though they

Above and far left
Virginio Bordino's third steam vehicle, built in 1854
Left *detail of the two-cylinder engine which drove the back axle which was in the form of a crankshaft. An officer in the Engineers of the Sardinian army, Virginio Bordino is remembered as the designer of the first Italian steam vehicle, in 1852*

L'Obéissante, *a twelve-seater omnibus unveiled in Paris by Amédée Bollée in 1875. The steam vehicle was technically advanced, with geometrically precise steering and a differential on the driven wheels (Conservatoire des Arts et Métiers)*

Although Amédée Bollée was primarily concerned with public transport, his 1878 Mancelle *is regarded as a private carriage*

Below left *side view and plan view of* La Mancelle, *a six-seater break with a front-mounted, vertical-cylinder engine, shaft transmission and front suspension with wheels moving independently of each other*
Below right *the 1881* Rapide, *another vehicle by Amédée Bollée, capable of a maximum speed of 37 mph*

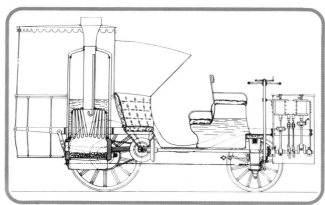

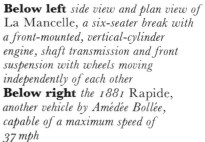

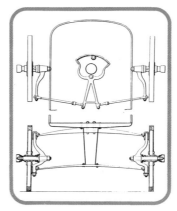

should belong in a collection of prehistoric monsters rather than be allowed to circulate freely on quiet country roads. The public's reserve was not altogether unjustified, especially when one considers vehicles like Jules Griffith's colossal stage coach, which he had designed and built in 1821; it was a cross between a locomotive and a coach. From a technical viewpoint, however, Griffith's vehicle did have interesting technical innovations, such as a device for changing engine speed, the first of its kind in the history of mechanized locomotion.

Another outstanding character of this period was the eclectic Goldsworthy Gurney, who was a surgeon by profession but an engineer by vocation and this undoubtedly gave him more pleasure than the science of Aesculapius for which he showed no inclination. Before 1820 Gurney had already assembled an efficient thermosiphon and he later became interested in road locomotion and designed a steam-powered stage coach.

His vehicle was presented to the public in November 1827. It was a large coach designed to carry eighteen passengers and was driven by a twin-piston engine with a very efficient boiler. As the grip of the wheels was insufficient on steep hills, Gurney fitted two 'legs' which were driven by a complex rotating mechanism and provided extra thrust by pushing on the ground. However, this device proved useless and was abandoned.

The following year Gurney's steam-powered stage coach succeeded in climbing Highgate Hill and in 1829 it made its first journey from London to Bath, arriving safely at its destination, despite a number of unforeseen stops on the way. Gurney then abandoned stage coaches and turned to the construction of much simpler and lighter steam engines for driving two-seater gigs.

At this time there was a growing demand for better inter-city communication, especially to and from London, and many public transport companies seriously considered replacing their horse-drawn coaches with the new steam vehicles. It was largely the work of Walter Hancock, who built the first real road locomotive which remained unrivalled for about sixty years, that did so much to convince them. After studying different types of boilers, Hancock tested his first steam vehicle, a sort of large tricycle with the propulsion system at the rear and the driving seat very far forward. The single front wheel was for steering and was controlled by a round steering wheel. A second model followed, called the *Infant*, with which a regular public service was established between Stratford and London in 1831. The following year the *Era* appeared and in 1833 there were two new types of coach, the *Enterprise*, which ran between Moorgate and Paddington, and the *Autopsy* which ran from Finsbury Square to Pentonville. In 1836 the omnibus *Automaton* superseded the earlier models.

Hancock, however, was also interested in private transport and in 1834 he built a small, steam-powered carriage for a Viennese client, and four years later built a second one for himself. It was a light, silent vehicle with three seats and was the closest design to a motor car that had ever been built.

The increasing popularity of steam omnibuses for public transport met with firm resistance from the owners of horse-drawn stage coach companies, who saw steam locomotion as their greatest enemy. In some cases opposition degenerated into acts of outright sabotage. In the summer of 1834 a carriage built by John Scott Russel, which was in regular service on the Glasgow–Paisley route, was the victim of one such deliberate act. The coach hit a large stone on the road, which had been put there deliberately, as an obstruction. A wheel broke and, with the sudden lurching of the coach, one side of the boiler hit the ground, causing the boiler to explode and killing five passengers. The accident provoked such an outcry that the Scottish authorities banned steam engines throughout the country, while in England such severe, restrictive measures were introduced that traffic came to a virtual standstill. These measures were consolidated in the 'Locomotive Act' of 1861 which, among other things, imposed a speed limit of 4 mph (6½ kph) on all automotive vehicles, the requirement for at least three drivers, and instruction that the vehicle itself 'should be preceded by a pedestrian waving a red flag'. The act caused a major set-back to the development of steam propulsion in England until its repeal in 1896 which was celebrated by a race, known as the 'Emancipation Run' from London to Brighton, in which about thirty cars took part.

Other countries, however, were not affected by England's restrictive traffic laws and the development of locomotion continued unhampered both in Europe and America. After Cugnot's experiments nothing was done in

France for some time, but work gradually resumed, gathering momentum and self-confidence. In 1803 Charles Dallery patented a steam boat, and a steam carriage which had a very interesting tubular boiler which first saw the light of day in France. There was also Charles Dietz, born in Germany of a French family, who began to build road and towing locomotives in his Paris workshop in the Rue Marbeuf. In 1834 he submitted a steam train with a trailer to the Academy of Sciences for their opinion. The vehicle made its inaugural journey between the Champs-Elysées and the park at St Germain. The following year Dietz's road train went into service on the Paris–Versailles route and in 1840 a modified version was used on the Bordeaux–Libourne route.

In Italy the introduction of steam carriages was much later than in more industrially developed countries like France, England and America, and these coincided with the country's first railways. In the first half of the nineteenth century Italy lacked raw material and heavy industry, and was desperately poor, but despite these problems something was achieved. In 1830 Luigi Pagani designed, but probably never built, the first Italian steam carriage, while Virginio Bordino actually built steam-powered vehicles which worked. Bordino was born in Turin and eventually became an officer in the Engineers. He was sent to England in 1833 to study the possibility of using steam locomotion in the transport service of the Sardinian army. On his return to Italy two years later, he designed and built a steam engine but there is no trace of it left. After repeated experiments, Bordino built a three-wheeled steam gig around 1852, using the engine and other parts of his first vehicle. His third vehicle, which is now in the Museo dell'Automobile in Turin, was completed in 1854. This was a standard landau which had been modified to include rack and pinion steering, double leaf spring suspension and more robust wheels; it also had a good range. The boiler was coal-fired and fitted with a thirty-eight tube steam generator at the rear. The engine, which was located under the carriage, consisted of two horizontal cylinders with pistons operating directly on the back axle, which was joined to the crankshaft by means of connecting-rods; four water tanks were mounted under the seats. The carriage could run for two hours during which time it would consume approximately sixty kilogrammes of coal and reach a maximum speed of 4–5 mph (6–8 kph). Continuing his studies and experiments, Bordino patented two other steam vehicles, one for public and the other for private use; these never progressed beyond the design stage.

With England obliged to mark time, Italy doing very little and Germany waiting to produce a trump card in the form of the internal combustion engine, France and the United States were the only two participants in the story of steam locomotion, with Bollée and Serpollet representing France, and the Stanley brothers representing America. From the second half of the nineteenth century onwards, a number of engineers put their faith in steam locomotion, even after the internal combustion engine had become established, while others, like De Dion, Peugeot, Olds and White, began with steam but later changed to the new system. In fact, steam propulsion made a brave stand against its powerful enemy, and even won a few battles before losing the war.

In both Europe and America huge steam commercial vehicles gradually gave way to the safer and more powerful rail locomotives, but for private use steam was successfully applied to lighter vehicles. From 1863 to 1894 an American, Sylvester Howard Roper, built at least ten steam-powered buggies which were light four-wheel carriages for two people, fitted with a small rear boiler and 2hp engine. Among the numerous American pioneers of steam were Henry House, Rev J. W. Carhart, George Alexander Long, Lucius D. Copeland, James H. Bullard and Ransom Eli Olds. The last named is, perhaps, the best known, not so much for the superior quality of his carriages as for the establishment of Oldsmobile in 1896, then called Olds Motor Works, one of the oldest American automobile companies and now a division of General Motors.

The story of Ransom Olds, however, goes back to 1883 when he began work in his father's workshop doing basic mechanical repairs, and also building steam engines in his spare time. The young Ransom, twenty years old at the time, was more interested in the engines than the repairs and in 1887, after personally designing two new models, initiated large-scale production. It was a short step from engines to complete vehicles and in that same year, 1887, Olds was ready to present his first carriage to the public, but the little 2 hp engine was not powerful enough and the test runs were rather disappointing. With his second model, which appeared in 1892, Olds

The 1890 Secretant break, a curious steam vehicle with tiller steering (Rochetaillée-sur-Saône Museum)

skillfully overcame the problem of insufficient power by installing two engines, giving a total output of 4 hp, and the result was so satisfactory that the young entrepreneur soon found a buyer for his rudimentary vehicle in the shape of the Francis Times Company, which sent it to its branch office in Bombay. It is not known if it ever arrived, but it was nevertheless the first American self-propelled vehicle to be exported.

Despite his undoubted success, Olds was not fully convinced about the future of steam propulsion. He was more a business man than an engineer or inventor and was one of the first to appreciate the great commercial potential of self-propelled vehicles. He saw the need for a light easy-to-build vehicle which he could launch on the market at a reasonable price. He therefore began experimental work on the internal combustion engine designs of the Germans, Otto and Daimler, and, to keep his options open, electric propulsion.

In contrast to Olds, the Stanley twins, Francis and Freeland, continued building steam carriages until the 1920s. They ran a prosperous business selling photographic material in Newton, Massachusetts, but around

1895 decided to broaden their scope by turning to other business ventures. All they needed was a good idea, and this came to them while watching the disappointing performance of a steam carriage at the Brockton Falls fair in 1896. This stimulated their competitive spirit; convinced that they could do better they set to work immediately. For their first vehicle they used components of different origin, but all of excellent quality. The result was a light, two-seater buggy powered by a vertical engine with two side cylinders, with the crankshaft in unit with the back axle. The boiler was placed under the seats and heated by a number of petrol burners; the engine had no clutch and no gearbox. The little carriage made its first official test runs in July 1897, but made its debut in October at the Brockton Falls fair where it aroused such enthusiasm that the Stanley brothers found themselves with their first orders.

The 1899 models were modified and as a result were heavier and more reliable with a range of about 25 miles (40 km). Their success was now guaranteed, but for some reason the Stanley brothers did not protect themselves by patenting their invention and A. Lorenzo

23

Barber took advantage of their negligence when, after buying several Stanley vehicles, he patented the design and founded a company, Locomobile, to build them. Despite its unethical beginning, Locomobile grew to a considerable size in the space of a few years with enviable financial stability. In the meantime the Stanley brothers, faced with this *fait accompli*, had no choice but to accept Barber's terms and they undertook not to build similar steam carriages for a period of two years, although the blow was softened somewhat by a payment of $250,000.

In spite of this, 1899 was a particularly good year for the Stanleys. They sold their photographic business to Kodak on very favourable terms and at the same time established their supremacy in the newly-born field of motor sport. On 31 August Freeland and his wife successfully made the first automobile ascent of Mount Washington in two hours, ten minutes; this record was not broken until 1905, by Francis Stanley, and he did it in only twenty-eight minutes. These achievements reveal the high performance attained by steam-powered cars in the short space of only six years. Furthermore, at Ormond Beach in 1906 the Stanley brothers set a world land speed record with an aerodynamic Stanley, driven by Fred Marriott, at a speed of 121·569 mph (195·647 kph). The same driver made another attempt the following year, but was less fortunate; his car was completely destroyed and he was lucky to escape with his life. After this misfortune, the Stanleys abandoned all their sporting ambitions and turned to the manufacture of tourers, varying from 10 to 30 hp. In 1917 they retired from business, but their steam cars continued in production, at a reduced rate, until the end of the 1920s.

The European counterparts of the Stanley brothers were undoubtedly the great French steam enthusiasts, Amédée Bollée and Léon Serpollet. The importance of Amédée Bollée's achievements does not lie in the means of propulsion, which had already been established, but in a number of his structural techniques which later became standard in the modern car.

The son of a bell maker in Brévannes, near Le Mans, Amédée Bollée set up his own workshop in 1867 near his father's business, with whom he collaborated, and there he began experimenting with carriages, producing an automotive steam vehicle for road use in 1872. His work was interrupted by the Franco—

Prussian war of 1870 which caused a set-back both in construction and demand. However, in August 1873 Bollée patented a design for a carriage with a steering mechanism which kept the wheels perpendicular to the radius of the curve. This was a fundamental improvement in design and represented the first practical application of a device invented as far back as 1828 by the watchmaker Onésiphore Pecqueur, better known as the inventor of the differential. The name of Bollée's vehicle, *L'Obéissante (the Obedient One)*, symbolized this steering precision, which was impossible to attain in a coach with an axle rotating on a central swivel ring.

Neither the twelve-seater omnibus, *L'Obéissante*, nor another of Bollée's vehicles, the six-seater break, *La Mancelle*, were cars in the modern sense, but his designs favoured the demands of private owners and he gradually reduced the dimensions of his vehicles, a process cultimating in the light two-seater which he built in 1885.

After obtaining a traffic permit, probably the first in history, *L'Obéissante* was presented in Paris in 1875 and collected about seventy-five traffic infringements on its first journey. It aroused considerable interest because of its technical innovations, such as its novel steering mechanism and the differential between the driven wheels, but it did not bring forth orders from the public.

With *La Mancelle*, which was presented as a prototype in 1878 and only later being

The small, steam-powered Stanley of 1898, a light two-seater carriage with a vertical, two-cylinder engine (Museo dell'Automobile, Turin)

Opposite *the Scotte steam omnibus of 1892, which could attain a speed of 7½ mph*

25

Above *a 1904 Stanley (Grandson Museum). At the beginning of the century, Stanley cars were at the height of their success, although petrol cars had already become established by that time*

Right *a 1904 steam-powered White, with the characteristic third door for access to the rear seats. Rollin White began building steam vehicles in 1900 in his sewing-machine factory in Cleveland, Ohio*

built as a series, Amédée Bollée made an important step towards producing a vehicle suitable for private use. Apart from its steam propulsion, *La Mancelle* bore many similarities to the conventional car of twenty years later in that it had a front engine with vertical cylinders, transmission through a longitudinal shaft, and independent front suspension by means of double transverse leaf springs.

Even though Bollée did not abandon his smelting work at the foundry he continued to build steam vehicles, with the collaboration of his son Amédée, almost until the end of the nineteenth century, but they never succeeded in making the company profitable. Among his last productions were two racers, *Rapide* and *Nouvelle*. By this time, however, the fate of steam propulsion seemed to be sealed and the future of motoring lay with the internal combustion engine, but for Amédée Bollée *père*, who was already an old man, it was too late to change and it was his two sons, Amédée and Léon, who were to gain fame and fortune with the new system.

With the cars of Léon Serpollet, steam enjoyed its golden age on the road and at the turn of the century enjoyed great prestige, being easily the most serious rival of the internal combustion engine. There were, in fact, numerous occasions when Serpollet's racing cars proved considerably more powerful than the more famous contemporary petrol-powered cars.

Besides being a good engineer – in the course of his career he patented sixteen steam vehicles – Serpollet is remembered as one of the first people to industrialize the production of his steam cars. In approximately eight years, from 1899 to 1907, the factory produced a hundred examples, an impressive number given the artisan labor and the methods of the time.

Léon Serpollet built his first steam tricycle as early as 1885, and five years later Armand Peugeot, who had recently bought the manufacturing rights for the tricycle, successfully made the journey from Paris to Lyons on a similar vehicle. At that time, however, mainly due to Gottlieb Daimler's development work, the internal combustion engine was becoming widely used in France, to the detriment of both steam and electric propulsion. To stem Daimler's onslaught, backed by a business which had already reached respectable industrial dimensions, Serpollet came to an agreement with an American financier, Frank Gardner, in 1899 and founded Usines d'Automobiles Gardner, later changed to Gardner-Serpollet.

At the factory in the Rue Stendhal in Ménimontant in the suburbs of Paris, production began at a steady pace from the first year and grew as the range of models increased. The engines varied, with two, four or even eight pistons, with the boiler positioned either at the front or back, although in the former case it was mounted under a conventional hood with a false radiator. Serpollet invented a light, compact, generator which produced steam instantly and he used steam condensers which considerably reduced the water requirement while increasing the power. As a result of these innovations, the French company's cars performed competitively, especially on uphill stretches. Compared to their rival internal-combustion-engine cars, they

*From 1906 to 1908
Serpollet steam
carriages were also
manufactured in Italy
by the Italian
Serpollet subsidiary.
This model 12/15 hp
of 1906 is of
Italian construction
and belongs to the
Quattroruote collection*

could also boast other qualities; they were quieter and did not require the use of a clutch or gear change.

Serpollet's success was not limited to France, but spread to England, Italy and even Germany and in 1902 Daimler himself was interested in coming to an agreement with him to manufacture his cars under licence, but it was never drawn up.

His many international sporting successes contributed much to the popularity of the cars. At Nice in 1902 a racing model, driven by Léon Serpollet himself, set the world land speed record at 75·06 mph (120·797 kph). Known as *Oeuf des Paques* (the *Easter Egg*), the car had a front-engine with four cylinders and had a power output of 100 hp. A second racing model was entered for the Deauville meeting in August of the same year and it appeared that this could easily produce 180 hp. The car was by far the fastest in the race, but

was forced to retire because of a breakdown. At other events, too, such as the Paris–Madrid in 1903 and the Gordon Bennett Cup in 1904, the performance of Serpollet's cars proved awe-inspiring.

The Serpollet cars represented the swansong of steam power, at least in Europe – in the United States it continued for another thirty years thanks to the Stanley Brothers and Abner Doble. Before concluding this brief history of steam propulsion, however, it is worth mentioning De Dion-Bouton, the great French car manufacturers, which began with steam engines, but owed its fame to their later success with petrol-powered cars.

The company was created in 1883 following a meeting between the then Count Albert De Dion, who became a marquis on his father's death, and George Bouton, co-inheritor with his brother-in-law, Trépardoux, of a factory making steam-powered toys in the Rue de la

The 1909 White O Touring, one of the American company's last steam carriages before the company changed allegiance to petrol propulsion in 1911 (Harrah collection)

Chapelle in Paris. After forming a partnership with De Dion, the two brothers-in-law moved to new premises and the firm took the name of De Dion, Bouton and Trépardoux, and began the business of producing steam-powered vehicles for adults rather than children. In 1883 the company's first steam boiler was designed and built; it was notable for its light and simple construction. In the same year a steam quadricycle was built, with two drive wheels at the rear and belt transmission. This rudimentary vehicle, driven by a twin-cylinder engine, was considered a great symbol of progress of the time. The following year a second, improved, vehicle was built as a tricycle-tandem. A similar model was entered for a race on 28 April 1887, which was the first recorded competition of its kind, organized by the journal *La Vélocipède*, and the strange vehicle managed a speed of 37 mph (60 kph).

After this exploit, the three partners became interested in the design of marine steam engines, but in spite of some praiseworthy results, the venture was a commercial disaster. De Dion, the most enterprising of the three, was convinced that the future of motoring lay with the internal combustion engine, but Trépardoux remained faithful to steam propulsion and the disagreement between the two led to a split. Bouton stayed with De Dion and founded a new company in 1893, De Dion Bouton to produce petrol-powered cars.

Thus ended what was in many ways the heroic age of steam locomotion, an age which revolutionized transport and gave motoring its initial impetus. With the introduction of steam propulsion man finally had an alternative to the animal as a form of transport. This must certainly be considered a turning-point in the march of progress.

Steam Technology

Even after the invention and establishment of the internal combustion engine, steam propulsion continued to play a major role in motoring. The reasons for the steam engine's surprising longevity were two-fold. The first lay in the degree of progress in steam technology that had been made before its application to motor vehicles, and the second was that, even in its automobile application, it was more efficient than the internal combustion engine for many years.

By the turn of the century the steam car engine had ceased to be a 'monster' and had become the most important means of locomotion. In practice, the steam engine represented the state of the art in vehicle propulsion; its main rival, the internal combustion engine, was still beset by difficult technical problems. This superiority was in spite of the fact that the steam engine did not lend itself to light, popular vehicles and was structurally complex.

Most important of all, the principle of the steam engine was understood perfectly and its mechanism was easy to control, from the heating of the water to its vaporization, from the expansion of the steam in the cylinders to its condensation. In addition, heat was produced in a traditional manner, in that there was a naked flame inside the boiler, similar to a domestic stove, and it is easy to realize how important this was for the drivers of the time who were totally unfamiliar with 'technical' matters and who were somewhat diffident about novelty. The type of combustion used in steam engines had other advantages too, in that it permitted the use of different fuels, such as wood, coal, vegetable and mineral oils, all of which were readily available and cheap.

From a functional point of view, the steam engine did have one great drawback in that there was a rather long wait for the boiler to come to pressure, but once the steam was up, the engine worked without missing a beat, and was silent and reliable.

It must be remembered that the steam engine was a very important part of the technology of the time and had benefited from hosts of early experiments and subsequent improvements. Development had started in an age when steel technology and smelting techniques were still being perfected, the use of malleable materials like copper, brass and bronze made engineering precision easier to achieve and, in spite of rudimentary manufacturing methods, were sufficiently robust for the job.

A cutaway drawing of the 1906 Serpollet (Quattroruote collection). The boiler, with water pipes, was under the front hood while the double-acting, two-cylinder engine was under the seats and drove the rear wheels by chain transmission. The two tanks under the back seat could hold either water or oil. The carriage had a top speed of 50 mph

From the point of view of mechanical stress, the steam engine had several advantages, there were fewer and more simple working parts, compared to the internal combustion engine where many components were subject to violent and irregular stress. Brass, bronze and copper were not prone to corrosion to the extent of iron and steel, and also there were no lubrication problems with the more delicate parts such as the cylinders, pistons and valves as they worked at a low speed and were not subjected to high temperatures. But it was quite a different story with the internal combustion engine where the lubricated parts came into direct contact with flame and hot gasses, and were polluted by burnt fuel residues.

Initially the growth of steam-powered vehicles was rather slow and did not reach maturity until the internal combustion

car had become a firm and obvious rival. The first steam vehicles were essentially hybrids between coaches and locomotives and their weight and size made them more akin to coaches than cars. The transition to smaller, more functional vehicles marked the end of the old vertical boilers and the move to smaller ones which were more efficient and burned 'cleaner' fuels like paraffin and refined oil.

Regarding the engine itself, the change to double-acting pistons, that is with cylinders in which the steam exerted its pressure alternatively on the upper and lower part of the piston, was rapid and followed the example of larger engines. They usually had twin cylinders placed side by side, resulting in a powerful and compact engine which could be easily mounted low down in the centre of the vehicle.

Favoring this arrangement, which was not, however, suitable for the internal combustion engine, was the absence of a clutch, gearbox and cooling system (the air alone was quite enough for the cylinders). At this point it is perhaps worth mentioning that, odd though it seems at first sight, the lack of gears was irrelevant; in the early days of motoring, no one considered the possibility of using gears to improve the engine's performance, and for a long time travelling by car meant working up to a given speed (usually the only one available), and maintaining it for the entire journey. Indeed, the absence of a clutch, besides being a technical simplification, was a particularly good thing for 'operators' – they had not yet come to be known as 'drivers' – as the clutches of the time did not always work very well.

Another advantage of the steam engine which cannot be overlooked, especially in the context of the period, was that once the boiler reached pressure, 'it went on its own'. At the turn of the century it must have been very tedious to have to start a recalcitrant internal combustion engine with a crank, compared to the simple task of opening a valve in a steam engine. Steam was thus much more popular with aspiring drivers, who frequently lacked any technical or motoring know-how. Another interesting aspect of steam engines was the transmission. In Cugnot's carriage, for example, the front drive wheel was moved by a ratchet gear operated directly at each stroke of the piston.

Another system, and for a long time this was the most common of all, consisted of attaching the piston connecting-rods directly to the axle of the drive wheels so that it operated like

a crankshaft. In principle, this arrangement was similar to that used in railway locomotives and, besides being extremely simple, eliminated the need for intermediary mechanisms, which were unreliable and noisy.

Among the more complex transmission systems was that used in Bollée's carriage of 1878, *La Mancelle*. This vehicle had an engine with four vertical cylinders arranged in-line ahead of the front wheels. The engine was then connected to the differential (an exceptional feature for the time) by a drive shaft. Final drive to the rear wheels was by means of two chains.

Chain final drive was, however, the most commonly used because steam engines, being mounted with the cylinders running fore and aft, would naturally have a transverse crankshaft, which was therefore parallel to the back axle.

After Amédée Bollée's massive steam vehicles, machines more suited to public than private transport, came the light carriages of De Dion, Bouton & Trépardoux, and Serpollet. It was Serpollet's company in particular, more than any other in Europe, which did most to improve the steam engine for road use and for many years its conservative but tried and tested technology competed equally with the internal combustion engine.

Among Léon Serpollet's most prestigious inventions was the strange aerodynamic vehicle, *Oeuf des Paques* (the *Easter Egg*), with which the French manufacturer set a world land speed record at just over 75 mph (120 kph) in 1902. This machine was a special example of a racing model built in three versions from 1901 to 1903. To break the record, the vehicle was lightened as much as possible and had a very neat shape with a rounded bonnet and a long, tapering tail. The four single-acting pistons were mounted longitudinally under the carriage and operated directly on the back axle via connecting-rods.

There was another impressive record breaking performance four years later by an American firm, Stanley, which produced a rather unusual vehicle with a tapering wooden body and faired-in wheels. Drive was conventional, the boiler was reinforced to resist a pressure of approximately seventy atmospheres, and the engine had two very simple, compact cylinders weighing only 85 lb (38·6 kg). Its estimated power was 120 hp at only 800 rpm; the vehicle was very light (about 1550 lb or 700 kg), and very fast; driver, Fred Marriott, managed to reach a speed of 121·6 mph (195·6 kph) in it. These records show how much steam propulsion had improved by the turn of the century when the internal combustion engine was still unreliable.

Even after steam propulsion was replaced by the internal combustion engine, it was not completely abandoned and experiments are still being done today, especially in the United States. In fact, the two Americans, Stanley and Doble, resisted the internal combustion engine longer than anyone else and kept steam cars in production until the 1930s. The Dobles were undoubtedly better and attained an extraordinary degree of efficiency and because their design permitted conventional bodies, they were aesthetically almost indistinguishable from petrol-driven cars.

Electric Propulsion

In our age of technological progress in which nuclear power has been mastered and used as energy, and in which man can travel in space at over 25,000 mph (40,000 kph), there is one slight flaw, namely that it is not yet possible to build an electrically powered car equal in performance with a petrol-run car.

In the electric car the equivalent of the fuel tank consists of storage batteries containing the power required to drive the motor, but unfortunately the power in a 1 kg lead battery, the only reliable type available, is approximately five hundred times less than that in 1 kg of petrol; consequently, a car with a total weight of 1000 kg requires about 300 kg of batteries to cover 30 miles (50 km) at a speed of only 30 mph (50 kph).

The history of electric propulsion, however, has much to be proud of and, in some cases, proved superior to petrol. In 1899, the first car to break the speed record of 60 mph (100 kph) was electric, although the origin of

A light, electric vehicle built by Jeantaud and Raffard in 1893. At the time electric motors were as a rule better than petrol engines

electric propulsion dates back to 1837 and was first experimented with in America where the first electric motor was patented by Thomas Davenport in that year. The idea had come to him four years earlier when he saw a rudimentary electromagnet which was capable of lifting an anvil. Following this, Davenport continued to study electric propulsion and designed a carriage driven by an electric motor which ran on rails. In 1847, another American, Moses Farmer, succeeded in making a vehicle work with two people on board. Considerable progress was made by Professor Charles G. Page whose vehicle, equipped with a 16 hp motor, travelled from Washington to Bladensburg at a speed of 19 mph (30 kph). As with earlier models, Page's vehicle also ran on rails because at the time every attempt was being made to find an alternative to steam locomotives which were noisy and dirty, on account of the smoke and coal. The insurmountable obstacle to the exploitation of electric railways, however, was the problem of the inefficient, primitive and extremely costly batteries. For this reason, railway companies soon abandoned the idea of using batteries and turned instead to electric power fed by a third rail or wire. Having failed with rail locomotion, supporters of electric propulsion applied it to road transport, although a few decades were to pass before the first electric cars worthy of the name appeared.

In the United States, where electric traction was without doubt more widespread than in Europe, one of the most important names was that of William Morrison who, in 1890, built an electric vehicle of considerable efficiency. It had an ingenious steering system and could travel for thirteen hours at a speed of 14 mph ($22\frac{1}{2}$ kph). Morrison's electric carriage enjoyed great success, largely due to the publicity campaign organized by Harold Sturges, secretary of the American Battery Co in Chicago. The carriage, in fact, went on a promotional tour of the major cities and gave practical demonstrations in city streets. In this way, the public had the opportunity of seeing and touching the vehicle which helped to overcome their natural suspicion which was very strong towards any type of automotive vehicle.

As is often the case, many similar vehicles followed in the wake of Morrison's success although, being imitations, they made no progress in electric propulsion. However,

Clyde J. Coleman made a positive and original contribution: after inventing a new type of dry battery, he built a number of small motors, one of which was mounted on a two-seater vehicle in 1892. Other positive results were obtained with the Electrobat model, built in 1894 by Henry Morris and Pedro Salom.

Towards the end of the century, the electric car had attained a range and efficiency which led to large-scale production, and its distribution was also favored by the development

A Baker electric of 1899, now in the Frederick C. Crawford Auto-Aviation Museum in Cleveland, Ohio

The 1897 Bersey, an English carriage driven by two electric motors with chain transmission

of public tramways in numerous European and American cities. From 1897 onwards, the first electric taxis appeared alongside electric trams on the streets of the major cities in the Western world. The electric motor also found an unexpected ally in the female members of the public who preferred it to petrol-powered cars because of its silence and cleanliness. At the beginning of the century, Queen Alexandra, the wife of Edward VII, used an electric carriage for short drives in the grounds of Sandringham House. It was a model from Columbia Electric, the American company whose electric vehicles were manufactured under licence in Great Britain and France with the respective names of City & Suburban and Electromotion.

One of the most famous names in electric locomotion is that of Baker, a company which was founded in Cleveland, Ohio, in 1899 by Walter C. Baker and the industrialist Fred R. White. The first Baker prototype was laid down two years earlier and from it came a succession of models which were mass-produced with a wide range of body styles and an even wider range of prices. Their one weak point was obviously the distance they could travel as the batteries had to be recharged after six to eight hours. In 1902 Baker built the *Torpedo*, a cigar-shaped racing car with the engine installed behind the seats, which were in the centre of the car and were protected by a canopy. Baker and his engineer tried to break the mile and kilometre records with this machine, but the venture ended in disaster. The *Torpedo* left the road, overturned, killed two spectators and came to a halt in a field, and was almost completely destroyed. The following year, Baker produced a smaller version of the *Torpedo*, called the *Torpedo Kid*, which won several national awards.

Having concluded its racing interlude, the Cleveland company resumed production of runabouts with greater enthusiasm. The vehicles were fitted with electric motors which were then very popular, and in 1915 Baker took over another firm, Rauch and Lang, creating the group Baker, Rauch & Lang. One of the directors of the new company, Ray Owen, decided to adapt the Entz magnetic transmission for the motor car, a device which at that time was only used in ships. This gave birth to a luxury model, the Owen Magnetic, in which the necessary power was generated by a dynamo operated by a standard six-cylinder engine. At the end of World

War I, the demand for electric cars decreased substantially, although production continued at the Cleveland factory for another few years before stopping completely.

Between 1900 and 1915, there were more than a hundred American manufacturers engaged in constructing electric cars. As in the case of steam propulsion, some companies were dedicated to it and nothing else, while others experimented with electric motors before turning to petrol engines, including famous names like Oldsmobile and Studebaker, although their work in the field of electric locomotion was negligible.

In 1915 Henry E. Dey and Steinmetz also designed an electric car. It had no differential, but the motor was so designed that the armature and field windings were both connected to a driveshaft and could rotate in relation to

Top *the* Jamais Contente, *the electric-powered* torpedo *in which Camille Jenatzy became the first man to exceed 100 kph in a motor vehicle, in 1899* **Above** *Victor Emmanuel III and his wife in a Kriéger electric*

each other. In this way, the power was distributed between the two shafts which could turn corners at different speeds (although one shaft would need its direction of rotation reversed). Going downhill, the motor became a dynamo to recover some electricity and also worked as a brake.

In the meantime, Europe was also developing electric locomotion, especially in Austria, Italy, Great Britain and France. In Austria, the coachbuilder, Jacob Lohner, one time supplier to the Austro-Hungarian imperial family, began building cars in 1896 using French Pygmée engines. At that time, however, petrol cars presented numerous problems and the Austrian industrialist soon opted for electric propulsion. He had a meeting with the young engineer Ferdinand Porsche who, at only twenty, held a responsible position at Bela-Egger (now Brown-Boveri), the well known electrical firm. Porsche then went to work for Lohner. Convinced that the weak point of the internal combustion engine lay in the complexity of its drive, Porsche thought of solving the problem by fixing electric motors directly onto the wheels. In 1900, at the Salon de Paris, he presented a car with four wheels and a storage battery powering two electric motors on the front wheels. His achievement caused a sensation, especially the later racing version with which he campaigned in numerous competitions, obtaining results which were formerly considered inconceivable in an electric car. However, the young engineer was soon confronted by the two most difficult problems of electric propulsion, the weight of the batteries and the limited range. To overcome the problem, Porsche chose mixed propulsion, that is, so-called electro-propulsion in which a petrol engine was used which, connected to a dynamo, produced the necessary current to the electric motors on the wheels. Porsche's solution, which consisted in separating the propulsion and transmission units and in using electric final drive, represented an important technical innovation in the field of mixed propulsion which had first been experimented with in 1897. In 1900 a Belgian company, Pieper, fitted some vehicles with an electrical unit coaxial with the petrol engine which could act as a dynamo or as an electric motor according to the need. It differed from Porsche's system in that the internal combustion engine was directly connected to the wheels by electromagnetic friction and a standard drive shaft. While travelling on flat ground, the generator unit, working as a dynamo, charged a number of batteries; going uphill or starting, current was supplied by the batteries to the generator unit which, acting as a motor, helped the rotation of the internal combustion engine. The superiority of Porsche's system was recognized by Daimler who hastened to buy the manufacturing licence and inspired other manufacturers of petrol-electric engines such as the French company, Kriéger and Mildé, the American Columbia, the Belgian Auto-Mixte and the Italian STAE.

Returning to the subject of pure electric vehicles, one of the very first cars to be built in Italy was electric-powered and was built by the Friulian engineer and inventor, Arturo Malignani, in 1891. It was, in fact, a carriage with wheels of different diameters – the back wheels being the larger – and was propelled by electricity. Another pioneering attempt was the light, three-wheeled carriage built in 1894 in the textile factory owned by Count Giuseppe Carli di Castelnuovo. In this, the power came from ten Verdier accumulators which each had a capacity of 200 watt-hours; the tricycle could travel for four to five hours at an approximate speed of 9 mph (15 kph). Carli's light carriage was also entered in one of the first car races, the 1894 Paris–Rouen. The outcome is not known, but it is likely that, along with many other carriages, it never succeeded in starting.

In 1902 the Milanese company Camona, Giussani, Turrinelli & Co, which later adopted the name Ausonia, began production of electric vehicles. In addition to carriages for private use which used two electric motors each of 5 hp, there were larger versions which were mostly used for delivering mail and as coaches for clients of the big Milan hotels. One of the last Ausonia electric vehicles was the model *Silencieuse*, built between 1909–1910, in which the characteristic silence of electric propulsion was further improved.

Another Italian firm which began production of reliable electric carriages was STAE in Turin, which was founded in 1905 to manufacture the French Kriéger cars under licence. Two years later, however, the French company was no longer able to honour its commercial agreements with the Turin firm which was then obliged to manufacture its own cars. STAE produced two types, one of which was petrol-electric and the other plain

Opposite the 1901 Columbia Electric which belonged to Queen Alexandra, wife of Edward VII. The chassis was American, but the bodywork was made in Great Britain (National Motor Museum)

37

electric. The first type, which was available with a limousine or tonneau body, was equipped with a front-mounted, four-cylinder petrol engine of about 20 hp which, coupled to a dynamo, formed the generator; propulsion, however, was by two electric motors mounted on the rear wheels. Its speed was about 45 mph (75 kph). The second, smaller model also had two electric motors mounted on the rear wheels, each of about 5 hp, which were fed by accumulators. Its speed was lower than that of the petrol–electric carriage and its range was also somewhat limited. STAE eventually ceased production in 1912.

In Great Britain, where the development of locomotion had been abruptly checked by severe traffic restrictions, there were few examples of electric carriages, but there were two which are worth mentioning, the Bersey and the Electromobile. The first was developed by a small London firm owned by W. O. Bersey who began by building an electric traction autobus in 1888. It was not until 1895 that the first carriage appeared, fitted with two electric motors, chain drive and two speeds. In spite of good results, Bersey soon found it difficult to sustain production on his own and in 1899 ceased manufacturing and turned to representing foreign makes. Bersey's place was taken by the Electromobile company which, after a number of years of distributing foreign makes on the English market (BGS, Columbia, Kriéger, Lohner-Porsche), began designing and constructing its own electric vehicle in 1902. Its Greenwood and Batley engine had a power output of 5 hp with a maximum speed of $15\frac{1}{2}$ mph (25 kph) and a range of 40–50 miles (70–80 km). Later, Electromobile offered electric vehicles for hire but in 1908 they ceased production to represent Opel. In 1919 they made a brief return to electric cars with the Elmo, a seven-seater model with an 8 ft 9 in (2·67 m) wheelbase, but its distribution was limited.

Despite experiments in other countries, France unquestionably led in reaping the benefits of the automobile. She led in the development of steam-powered vehicles and also played an important part in the improvement of the petrol engine. It was the French engineer Planté who invented the lead battery in 1859 and this was subsequently perfected by another Frenchman, Faure, in 1881, who increased its power and effective life. Another leading French designer was Charles Jeantaud, one of the most famous and

brilliant specialists in the growing field of electric propulsion.

Jeantaud was born in Limoges in 1843 and began studying locomotion around 1880, and a year later produced a carriage with an electric motor, although regular production of Jeantaud carriages did not get under way for another ten years. One of the first models to be built was a six-seater break which took part in the Paris–Bordeaux–Paris race of 1895. The motor was based on the design of a certain Rechniewsky, and had a maximum power output of 7 hp and was fed by 300 Ah batteries; it had a top speed of 15 mph (24 kph). Jeantaud himself entered the carriage in the race, but was forced to retire after fifty miles (80 km), having achieved an average speed of 11 mph (18 kph).

It was Jeantaud who initiated the first

record-breaking events. In 1898 a 'speed test' was organized in Paris and it was won by a Jeantaud vehicle. Later record attempts, organized by Count Gaston de Chasseloup-Laubat, who drove a Jeantaud, gave rise to the famous challenges with the Belgian, Camille Jenatzy, which were sponsored by the French newspaper *La France Automobile*, with the aim of breaking the 66 second per kilometre record set by the cyclist Albert Champion. Jenatzy, too, drove an electric car, the famous *Jamais Contente*. which he had designed himself, and which used an aerodynamic torpedo-shaped body.

After a number of attempts, on 4 March 1899, Chasseloup-Laubat reached a speed of 57·5 mph (92·698 kph), but on 1 May his record was broken by Jenatzy with a speed of 65·8 mph (105·878 kph), travelling the kilometre in 34 seconds. This run by the Belgian driver-constructor was of particular importance in that it was the first time that 100 kph had ever been exceeded.

Having lost the contest, Jeantaud abandoned racing and continued manufacturing conventional cars, trying to improve their efficiency and, above all, their range. The bodyline, too, which until then had imitated the horse-drawn carriage, was altered by the addition of a hood in front where the batteries were grouped. The Jeantaud cars were also fitted with a special five-speed gearchange and were steered by a wheel and tiller bar; an interesting detail was that the brakes on the rear wheels, were powered electrically.

Competition with internal-combustion-engine cars was growing constantly, and at one point Jeantaud tried to apply single and two-cylinder petrol engines to his cars, but he only did it as an experiment as he was a firm believer in electric propulsion. In 1905 the French manufacturer built his last creation – in fact, he committed suicide a year later – which was a new and more modern car with front-wheel drive, but which still had an electric motor. Besides Jeantaud, electric propulsion was used successfully by two other French makers, Kriéger from 1897 to 1909 and Mildé whose business was begun in 1900 and continued with varying fortune until the 1920s.

Of the two, undoubtedly the most important was Kriéger whose cars were exported or built under licence in a number of European countries. From the outset, Kriéger used techniques which were original and avant-

garde. His first vehicle, for instance, which was built in 1897, is considered one of the finest examples of front-wheel-drive technology in the field of motoring – the two electric motors acted in unison on the front wheels to which they were directly coupled – and was one of the first cars with four-wheel braking. Kriéger had fitted brakes on the rear wheels, which was customary at the time, but in addition had designed the two electric motors so that they provided not only the drive but also braking. This method of construction remained substantially unchanged until Kriéger ceased production in 1909.

After World War I, the electric car rapidly lost ground to the internal-combustion-engined machine which triumphed everywhere, although it was revived briefly during World War II, but again fell into oblivion afterwards. Midway through the 1960s, however, electric traction was re-examined for a number of reasons connected with oil crises and, above all, pollution. There are still many people who believe that the future of motoring lies in electric propulsion; if their hopes come to fruition, perhaps the car of 2000 will be electrically powered.

A 1909 two-seater STAE with two 5 hp electric motors mounted on the back wheels (Museo dell'Automobile, Turin)

The Electric Car: For and Against

It is natural to wonder why the electric motor enjoyed such popularity in the early years of motoring, and played such an important role, when today it is beset by problems. Indeed, it may seem a contradiction in terms that a system which was held to be practical and efficient at the turn of the century has not benefited from the technical evolution, at least to a degree sufficient to maintain its viability.

In fact, the technology of electric traction has developed a great deal since then, but at the same time the other widespread system of propulsion, the internal combustion engine, has developed and been perfected to such an extent that no other form of traction compares. On the other hand, at the turn of the century the electric motor was far behind today's technology, but the internal combustion engine was at such a primitive stage of development that, practically, it was much worse.

The reasons for the success of the electric motor, however, are much more complex, the principal one being, of course, that it was exceptionally easy to drive thanks to the number of extremely simple and natural manoeuvres, at least compared to the complexity of driving other types of motor vehicles. Furthermore, apart from purely technical reasons, there were others which cannot be ignored, such as the lack of smoke, smell and especially noise which made this type of vehicle extremely popular.

The construction of electric traction vehicles was extraordinarily simple and was reflected both in production methods and the use of the vehicles. The absence of a clutch allowed very simple and reliable transmission systems, such as a chain or belt, to be used. In many cases, a further simplification was made by placing the engine directly on the wheels. This led to two important advantages which were the elimination of any obstruction inside the vehicle and the complete isolation of the motors from the chassis, so that there was no noise and little vibration was transmitted to the driver's seat.

It is interesting to note that placing the motor (or motors) directly on the wheel is an idea which has been taken up several times, even recently, for different types of traction (electric, hydraulic or pneumatic), for the many advantages it entails and primarily for the elimination of all mechanical transmission (including the differential). In practical terms, however, this system, although theoretically simple, creates problems through the motor's bulk and the increase of total unsprung mass. At the turn of the century, the presence of a huge electric motor rigidly fixed to a wheel was not of any consequence as far as the car's acceleration, top speed or road-holding were concerned.

The tendency to use two engines, even when both were fitted to the chassis, was common because the bulk and weight of two small motors was less than one large unit, providing the same power. Furthermore, the two motors had independent drive chains for each wheel so that it was unnecessary to use a differential unit.

The simplicity of the electric car also allowed the production of light carriages with all the comfort of the large ones. Compared to vehicles run by other types of propulsion, which in most cases were manufactured by the same builders of steam and internal combustion engines, the electric car could be assembled without any consideration other than the space and robustness required for carrying the batteries. For this reason, electric cars seemed much more practical and modern than their rivals and were readily accepted by the public. Even in those days, not all motorists were devotees or skilled mechanics and in the eyes of a normal driver it was a great relief to have a simple, reliable and extremely comfortable car.

The structural simplicity and the absence of numerous mechanical parts which were subject to wear and tear, eliminated the majority of possible breakdowns, avoided the need for complex controls and reduced maintenance to a minimum. The simple, rugged

STANHOPE WITH OPEN TOP

$1600

The Baker Motor Vehicle Co. Cleveland, O.

Above *a 1906 model Ausonia*
Top left *an Ausonia omnibus used to convey clients of a big Milanese hotel. From 1902 to 1910 Ausonia was the trade name applied to electric vehicles made by the Società Vetture Elettriche Camona, Giussani, Turrinelli & Co in Milan*

Centre and below left *two models in the 1903 range from the American Baker company, one of the most important manufacturers of electric carriages*

Below *an old advertisement from Dora, a Genoese company which made lamps and storage batteries and built several prototype electric carriages in 1906*

THE BAKER RUNABOUT

$850

The Baker Motor Vehicle Co. Cleveland, O.

electric motors only required bearing lubrication and the brushes were the only parts which were subject to wear and had to be cleaned and replaced.

The main problem of the electric vehicle, and the reason why it was abandoned, was its limited travelling range: the lead batteries could not store the energy required for a distance comparable to that of an internal combustion engine car, and even small vehicles were enormously weighed down by their accumulators.

Manufacturers often claimed a range of 18·25 miles (30–40 km), but this was only possible under ideal conditions and with new batteries. After a period of not being used, or after a certain number of complete discharges, recharging rapidly decreased their efficiency, forcing the driver to recharge them frequently or even to replace the entire set of accumulators.

The fact that electric vehicles were particularly suited to short runs, established their superiority in speed tests. Indeed, the first speed records were easily broken by light carriages with electric motors, which also had the advantage of good acceleration over short distances.

The first 'official' speed record was set in December 1898 in Achères by a Jeantaud electric car driven by Chasseloup-Laubat who reached 39·3 mph (63·150 kph). The vehicle was fitted with a 36 hp motor, fed by non-rechargeable battery cells, placed in series and which weighed around 3,100 lb (1400 kg). A few months later, in March 1899, the same driver in the same car, which had been modified by the addition of a primitive streamlined body, reached a speed of 47·5 mph (92·698 kph). The second vehicle to hold the world speed record was also electric. This was the famous Camille Jenatzy's *Jamais Contente* which in May 1899, exceeded 100 kph for the first time ever and retained the record for three years.

From a technical point of view, *Jamais Contente* was a true sports car and was much more refined and efficient than the earlier Jeantaud. The body, in particular, with its torpedo shape, was built entirely of light-alloy panels riveted together, and it was powered by two relatively small motors mounted directly on the wheels; here, too, the motors were driven by non-rechargeable batteries.

Regarding the early records, it is interesting to note that they were achieved by vehicles which developed less power than other contemporary systems of propulsion. The technical reasons which determined the success of the electric motor for road vehicles for private use were good acceleration and the fact that the motor would run reliably at maximum power.

After years of oblivion, due to the supremacy of the internal combustion engine, the electric motor became news again during the 1970s when there was concern about pollution and the possible exhaustion of world oil reserves. In this field, too, the United States is in the lead and already has an industry which is ready to be developed and expanded; however, the widespread use of the electric car is still a dream and will remain so for some time.

The Rise of the Internal Combustion Engine

The story of motoring, which began in the eighteenth century, divides with one route developing more rapidly, leading to the progressive development of steam engines, and the other leading to the internal combustion engine which was initially fed with gas and then, at the end of the nineteenth century, with liquid fuels. In the former case, it was possible to attain high temperatures with relatively low pressure, but the increase in temperature was restricted by the availability of materials resistant to combustion without rapid deterioration. In fact, by heating water to only 300°C (572°F) it is possible to obtain steam pressure of about 100 atmospheres, which is sufficient to set a vehicle in motion; by heating air it would be necessary to exceed 2000°C (3664°F). It was not until 1856, when

Bessemer established the first industrial process for the production of steel on a vast scale, a product able to resist more than 1000°C (1832°F), that the internal combustion engine could become a reality, although all the structural theories had already been in existence for some time.

In 1777, for example, Alessandro Volta loaded a toy pistol with a mixture of methane and air, plugged the muzzle and lit the charge with a powerful spark from a Leyden jar, causing an explosion which blew out the plug. In theory he had already discovered the principle of the internal combustion engine, that is, the mixture of air and fuel and a spark to ignite it in order to move a solid mass.

In the wake of Volta's experiments, in 1807 the Swiss–French lawyer, Isaac de Rivaz,

This, the first internal combustion engined car in the world, was patented on 29 January 1886 by the German engineer, Karl Benz

Above *an impressive picture of the first Panhard & Levassor carriages of 1892* **Opposite page** *three Peugeot models of 1892. From the top: the original vis-à-vis with ornate inlay work, the Victoria, with a 1282 cc twin-cylinder engine, and another vis-à-vis* **Below** *in 1886 Daimler and Maybach produced this, their first four-wheeled vehicle*

patented an internal-combustion-engine vehicle which was driven by the energy produced from the explosion of gas. De Rivaz's *char mécanique* was made entirely of wood, had four wheels and was driven by an engine consisting of a long, vertical cylinder with two pistons inside it. The first piston, which was very big and heavy, had a longer stroke than the second, smaller piston which was positioned in the lower part of the cylinder; the second piston also controlled the inflow of the explosive mixture to the combustion chamber. A metal tip, acting as an electrical contact, produced the spark to ignite the mixture of hydrogen and oxygen. The explosion pushed the main piston upwards and, rebounding against the cylinder head, was then forced

downwards, and it was this downward stroke which was the essential part of the engine cycle. The piston, drawing a cord, drove the front wheels by means of a special pulley. In 1813 de Rivaz built a second, bigger vehicle with an internal combustion engine, called the *grand char mécanique*, which was tested in Vevey, in the canton of Vaud, on 18 October 1813. It was $19\frac{1}{2}$ ft (6 m) long, had two wheels, each $6\frac{1}{2}$ ft (2 m) in diameter, and had a top speed of approximately 2 mph (3 kph); the engine produced an explosion every four seconds.

These early experiments involving the explosive power of a gaseous mixture were soon followed by those of the Englishmen, Brown (1823 and 1835), and Wellman Wright (1833). In 1842 the American Alfred Drake devised an engine with an incandescent ignition tube, and applied for a patent in Great Britain. A working prototype of Drake's engine was displayed in Philadelphia in 1847, but he was not granted the British patent until 1855, that is after the issue of the same patent to Eugenion Barsanti and the engineer, Felice Matteucci, dated 13 May 1854, concerning 'the manner in which the explosion of gas is used to generate motor power'. This principle was applied to a prototype engine with twin cylinders, built in 1856 in Florence and with which the Italian inventors attained a thermal efficiency of fourteen per cent, which was much higher than anything obtainable in engines of the time. Finally, on 24 January 1860, Etienne Lenoir, a Franco-Belgian engineer of great ability, was granted a French patent for an engine which worked on a mixture of gas and air, and was duly proclaimed the inventor of the gas engine by the French Academy of Sciences, who disregarded the earlier work of Barsanti and Matteucci.

45

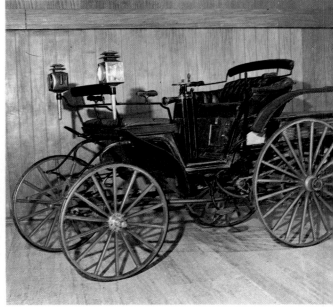

Nevertheless, the work of Barsanti and Matteucci was of fundamental importance in the history of the internal combustion engine. If a criticism can be made of the two Italian inventors, it is for not being able to exploit their achievements on a practical level. This 'fault' however, is more environmental than personal as Italy in the nineteenth century still lagged behind France in all aspects of engineering. In short, the Barsanti-Matteucci case is just one of many examples where a potentially good invention was made in one country, but was then established and exploited in one of the more highly developed industrial countries. At that time the centers of industrial power were France and Germany and consequently the success which should have gone to Barsanti and Matteucci went instead to Etienne Lenoir in France and Otto and Langen in Germany.

Lenoir's engine, however, was different from that of Barsanti and Matteucci; it appears that Lenoir was inspired by the engine patented by Pierre Hugon in 1858, thereby arousing the indignation of the latter. Nevertheless, it is a fact that the Franco-Belgian inventor did have good technical assistance and was helped by an advanced technology which enabled him to exploit his invention commercially and to distribute it abroad, which was perhaps one of his greatest achievements.

On 18 April 1860 Lenoir lodged a second patent which proposed the use of oil-based fuels, rather than gas, mixed with oxygen. The patent took up an idea first applied by Luigi de Cristoforis, who was the first to suggest using liquid fuel as well as gas in the internal combustion engine in 1841. Lenoir, however, foresaw the phenomenon of compression that occurs in modern engines and had designed a rudimentary carburettor, the second in history following that patented by Levêque in 1859. Lenoir's contribution to motoring was more than just designing the abovementioned engine and extended to its practical application in a motor vehicle. Although the production of the carriage, which appeared in *Le Monde Illustré* on 16 June 1860, is very doubtful (the engine's very limited power of little more than $\frac{1}{2}$ hp would certainly not have driven such a large vehicle), it has been proved, at least by Lenoir's own declaration, that in 1862–63 a vehicle was built which made the journey from Paris to Joinville-le-Pont and back several times, averaging 6 kph (4 mph). The test runs, however, were unsatisfactory because of the engine's excessive weight, limited power and poor speed.

Of much greater efficiency were the engines made by the German Nikolaus Otto, the father of the four-stroke engine which he patented in 1876. The origin of the idea is perhaps due to the French engineer, Alphonse Beau de Rochas, who described it in detail in a memorandum published in Paris as early as 1862. This was the year in which Otto, while continuing his work to improve Lenoir's engine of which he had built a smaller version, manufactured an engine which foreshadowed that with four strokes, that is, the intake of fuel, its

These two 1894 Peugeot carriages show how the shape of the early cars still closely resembled that of horse-drawn coaches
Left *a five-seater break (Peugeot collection)*
Right *a light buggy (Museo dell'Automobile, Turin)*

compression, its combustion and power and the expulsion of burnt fuel. This engine proved so inefficient, however, that Otto abandoned all further experiments in that direction and turned to the construction of atmospheric engines similar to the Barsanti one. In 1864 Otto formed a partnership with the engineer Eugen Langen and founded the Gasmotoren-fabrik Deutz to produce his engines, production of which began in 1867.

It was not until 1875 that he resumed his research into the four-stroke engine, where compression occurred inside the cylinders, and the following year presented his first prototype, which worked perfectly. This success was no doubt partly due to the presence at Deutz, from 1872 onwards, of two of the most famous engineers of the time, Gottlieb Daimler and Wilhelm Maybach, who will be discussed in detail later.

The efficiency of Otto's engines constituted a fundamental stage in the development of the internal combustion engine car which was destined in the course of a few decades to dominate the world of public and private transport which until then had been monopolized by horse-drawn and steam carriages. However, at the close of the 1870s, it was not yet ready to launch its attack and almost ten years were to pass before the appearance of the light tricycles and quadricycles of Benz and Daimler, considered by all to be the legitimate ancestors of the modern car. The two Germans, however, had rivals to the title of the originators of the automobile, among whom the most aggressive was undoubtedly Siegfried Marcus whose vehicle, now at the Technisches Museum in Vienna, was reputedly built in 1882. This date now seems improbable, however, as it is fitted with a four-stroke engine built by Marcus himself, and a carburettor patented in 1882. Moreover, it is certain that Marcus's four-stroke engines, which were mostly of the stationary variety, were not the subject of conversation in the Austrian capital until 1888. In the light of these observations, the most reliable biographies of Marcus set the design period of his carriages at around 1888 and their presentation at 1890, which was later than those of Benz and Daimler. It must be pointed out, however, that Marcus's vehicles did set a precedent by running on petrol fired by electromagnetic ignition (a primitive electromagnet with low tension contact breakers). Otto's engines, on the other hand, ran on town gas, as did Edouard Delamare Deboutteville's carriage of 1883, which was one of the first internal combustion engine vehicles.

All the examples that have been examined up to this point belong to the purely experimental period of motoring and the leap forward in terms of quality was primarily due to Karl Benz and Gottlieb Daimler who were the first to construct and sell complete carriages. The fact that they both achieved the same results simultaneously but independently has made the two German pioneers be remembered together and, by some strange twist of fate, this symbolic union later became

Two views of a Bernardi tricycle built around 1894–95. The Veronese designer pioneered several technical innovations, such as the detachable cylinder head, valves in the head, filters for oil and air, the exhaust pipe and ignition by a platinum 'sponge'

reality when, in 1926, the companies which they founded merged into one industrial complex, Daimler Benz AG, which continued, and still continues, the great motoring tradition of the two founders.

Karl Benz, the head of Benz and Cie of Mannheim, had already been building two-stroke stationary engines for some time and had also been studying their application to a four-wheeled vehicle. Those engines were not suited to the purpose, however, and the steering of a four-wheeled vehicle still presented difficult problems, even though Ackerman had already pointed the way with his system, patented in 1818. So it was that Benz's first vehicle only had three wheels. The problem of the engine was solved as soon as the German engineer installed a four-stroke engine with a crankshaft rotational speed of 300 rpm, which was capable of providing 2–3 hp.

In the autumn of 1885, after the first uncertain trials in the courtyard of his workshop, Benz ventured onto the streets of Mannheim with his vehicle, gradually increasing the distance travelled; it caused a great sensation. The press seized upon the creation, either praising the invention or, as often happens when confronted with revolutionary events, conjecturing about the disastrous results which would follow such progress.

Karl Benz patented his tricycle on 29 January 1886. The engine had a single cylinder and ran on Ligroin, a liquid fuel which was easy to vaporize. The piston stroke was 70 mm and the cylinder bore was 150 mm. The engine drove the big, cycle-type rear wheels by means of a flat belt, a cross shaft fitted with a differential, and side chains. A heavy flywheel was also used but was mounted horizontally rather than vertically. Lubrication was by oil reservoirs and ignition was by means of a Ruhmkorff coil, fed by a battery which was replaced every six miles (10 km). A spark plug, made by Benz, was used, while the single cylinder was fed by a carburettor of very simple design. The volatile petroleum spirit was kept in a tank and was sucked, together with the requisite amount of air, into the cylinder. The

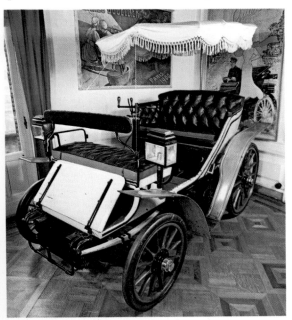

Above *a Rochet-Schneider* vis-à-vis *of 1895 (Musée de Rochetaillée-sur-Saône). The company, based in Lyons, began business in 1890 – manufacturing bicycles. It then changed to car production and brought out a number of models which were very similar to other makes, especially Panhard, Benz and Daimler, though the end products were often superior*
Left *the 1895 Panhard & Levassor, built in the year when the French company replaced the Daimler V-twin engine with the in-line, twin-cylinder Phönix engine (Deutsches Museum, Munich)*

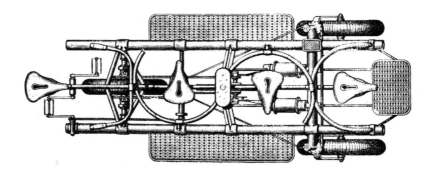

The Tricar was one of Edward Pennington's first creations. It was made in 1896 after the American inventor had moved from the United States to England

engine speed was regulated by the simple expedient of regulating the amount of air taken in.

The chassis was made of steel tubes and the wheels, of large diameter, had fine spokes similar to those of a bicycle. Steering was controlled by a tiller-rod and longitudinal flat springs formed the suspension unit.

In addition to the engine's extraordinary novelty, it must be stressed that the entire Benz carriage was of an entirely original design. Benz, in fact, did not limit his experiments to installing an engine in a carriage, but from the outset was concerned with the mechanical working of the vehicle as a whole.

Karl Benz continued his experiments and during the course of 1886 he built a second,

more powerful engine capable of 500 rpm, which was mounted on a carriage shown at the Munich Fair of 1888 where it was awarded a gold medal.

Although Benz was primarily an academic and an inventor, he also firmly believed in the practical application of new systems and consequently it was not long before he tried to exploit his vehicles commercially. His carriages had interested many people and sales began well, and even abroad the name of Benz did not remain in obscurity for very long. In Paris in 1888, Emile Roger, who represented the Benz stationary engines in France, bought a carriage from the German company for his private use. Immediately realizing its enormous potential, he hastened to order

original engines and components from Mannheim, which he then assembled locally, selling the completed vehicles under the name of Roger-Benz.

In the meantime, the mother company required new investment and new managers to organize and administer the firm so that production could get under way and leave Benz to his research. Both problems were solved in 1890 when Friedrich von Fischer and Julius Gauss-Fischer joined the staff. Benz was at last free from administrative duties and devoted himself full-time to experimenting, and in 1893 patented a driving device for four-wheeled vehicles. In fact, he placed the steering axle on the chassis by utilizing a revolving double leaf spring arrangement.

In the same year a new Benz model, the Victoria, appeared with a choice of a 3 or 5 hp engine, of 1730 and 2920 cc respectively, which, from 1897 onwards, had an epicyclic gearbox. The Victoria marked a return to the stylized lines of horse-drawn carriages, which were still the customary shape and this was a skilful manoeuvre on Benz's part to overcome the public's conservatism. Unlike other contemporary manufacturers, Karl Benz was against high speed and considered that his vehicles were fast enough. In 1893 he designed the Velo with a 1·5 hp engine, which was the

first carriage in the world to be mass-produced, and this was the basis of the more powerful Comfortable model which appeared a few years later.

The increase in sales and the progressive distribution of the car led the German company to offer a greater number of models to satisfy different requirements. This enabled the firm to produce 603 cars in 1900, a record figure for the time. By the following year, however, business had got noticeably worse with only 226 cars sold and deteriorated even more in 1902 with just 176 cars produced. The fluctuation was largely due to the public's preference for faster and more powerful cars, a demand which was satisfied by Daimler, Peugeot and Panhard & Levassor. However, Benz was convinced that the efficiency of his cars would prevail over speed, but Julius Gauss-Fischer, one of the Benz directors, was of a different opinion, and on his own initiative employed a group of French engineers, including Marius Barbarou. Under the latter's leadership, a new series of models was designed with one, two and four cylinders; at the same time Karl Benz was pursuing another line of experimental work using his own designs. The two engineers, one French and the other German, worked in competition, although at least one of the models, the Parsifal,

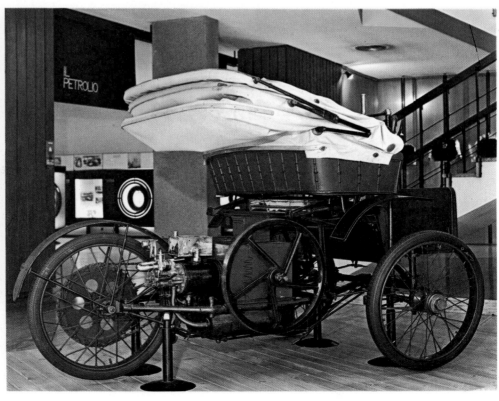

An 1896 Bernardi tricycle, built by Miari & Giusti, the company set up in the same year to exploit Bernardi's patents. In spite of the Veronese engineer's praiseworthy designs, the company was unsuccessful

Opposite page *the first four-cylinder Coventry Daimler and the first British car to race on the Continent – it gained first place in the Tourist Class of the 1899 Paris–Ostend race. It subsequently competed in the Thousand Miles Trial of 1900 (National Motor Museum)*

Right *a Delahaye vis-à-vis of 1898, a fairly conventional design of small car with a rear-mounted engine (Chateau de Grandson)*

Below *the amazing Pennington Autocar Torpedo of 1896. This machine was supposed to be able to carry nine people and travel at up to 40 mph*

which appeared in that period, encompassed the experiments of both. Following a dispute about the origination of that design, first Benz and then Barbarou left the company in 1904, though Karl Benz was subsequently brought back as a director.

In 1882 Gottlieb Daimler and his friend Wilhelm Maybach left Deutz to form their own business building gas engines of Daimler's design. In 1883, after devising the *brûleurs* – or 'hot tube' – ignition system, he produced his first internal combustion engine. Initially, Daimler intended to use his engine in the different forms of transport, but Maybach pushed for its use in motor cars and in the end his opinion prevailed.

The Daimler motor cycle of 1885 and the *Motorkutsche* (motor coach) of 1886 were fitted with these engines which differed considerably from any other of the time.

At Maybach's insistence, Daimler agreed to present a completely new vehicle at the Paris Universal Fair of 1889. This was a *Stahlradwagen* (a carriage with steel wheels), for which Maybach made a chassis of steel tubes which could house the engine and transmission unit, abandoning the old ideas connected with horse-drawn carriages, just as Karl Benz had done three years earlier.

In 1890 the two partners founded Daimler Motoren Gesellschaft near Cannstatt to begin the production of engines and complete cars for the German market; manufacturing licences were also granted to Panhard & Levassor and Peugeot.

The first car for sale was the Riemenwagen (a belt driven vehicle), available with different body styles, such as a Victoria and a coupé, all with twin cylinders in line-and-belt transmission. Following the example of the French licensees, Daimler also placed the engine in front in the model Phoenix, initially fitted with 4 and 6 hp twin-cylinder engines, and from 1898 with four-cylinder engines in which the racing version had a power output of 23 hp.

Unlike Benz, Daimler immediately realized the importance of entering and winning competitions, as did his French colleagues, and his business therefore turned towards fast and powerful cars which were designed to rout his rivals. His ideas were fully shared by both Maybach and Emil Jellinek, the Consul-General of the Austro-Hungarian empire in Nice and a devotee of motoring, who played a decisive role in the development of the Cann-

statt company's cars for which he very soon acquired the exclusive sales for France, Austria and Hungary.

Jellinek is also remembered as the man who inspired a range of Daimler models which went by the name of Mercédès, a name destined to have a very important place in world motoring. Mercédès was the name of Jellinek's daughter, and was used for the first time on a Daimler Phönix which he drove at a race in Nice in 1899. Daimler's first car built expressly for competitions was also called Mercédès. This was a very interesting and original machine which can be regarded as the first modern car.

Designed by Maybach, it was fitted with a four-cylinder engine of 5900 cc, which produced 35 hp at 1000 rpm. One of its characteristics was its honeycomb radiator placed in front of the engine; the car had a sleek, streamlined appearance, a shape that would soon become universally accepted as the norm. Gottlieb Daimler however, was not to see his company's eventual outstanding success, as he died in 1900. The company continued to be run by Wilhelm Maybach until 1907 when he retired. His replacement as chief executive was Paul Daimler, son of Gottlieb, who had previously been running the Austro-Daimler company, set up in 1899 as an off-shoot of the German parent company.

Following the first 35 hp Mercédès, other models appeared but they were of little importance. The later series, the Mercédès Simplex models, with lower outputs of 18/22, 28/32, 40/45 and 60/70 hp, were more successful. A 60 hp model won the Gordon Bennett Cup in Ireland in 1903, driven by Camille Jenatzy; this victory, with an average speed of over 56 mph (90 kph) for 375 miles (600 km), was considered the most important factor for the car's success, both as a racing model and a tourer.

The names of Benz and Daimler are undoubtedly the leading ones in the history of motoring, but they did not find enough support in their own country to conquer the entire European market at a stroke. Indeed, they had the opportunity as the first producers of cars, but innate Teutonic diffidence regarding novelty won the day and the development and distribution of the new means of transport proceeded slowly. The French were the first to master the German invention and to take advantage of the uncertainty and set out to conquer the world's roads. Their sense of

The Benz Velo of 1898 was based on the model of the same name of 1893. Below is the horizontal, single-cylinder engine, of 1140 cc, and a detail of the steering wheel with controls and horn (Museo dell'Automobile, Turin)

timing proved highly successful and the results were better than the most optimistic expectations. This meant that, although motoring was born in Germany, it was France that made it into an industrial phenomenon.

Companies like Panhard & Levassor, Peugeot and De Dion-Bouton, to name just a few of the most important firms at the end of the last century, contributed to its success. The name of Renault was added in 1899 and before the end of the century, the French motoring industry numbered at least twenty firms, including that of the Bollées, the sons of the steam engineer who later changed to petrol cars, Darracq, Rochet-Schneider, Clément, Berliet, Mors and others. In Germany during the same period, besides Benz and Daimler, there were only about ten motor companies among which were Opel, Horch, Gaggenau, Protos, Stoewer and Adler.

One of the first Renault carriages, of 1899. It is a light quadricycle with a 273 cc De Dion engine, cooled by air and mounted at the front of the car (Renault collection)

Left from the outset, the French motoring industry developed in two well defined areas, around Paris, in the north, and around Lyons, in the south. Here is an 1898 Rochet-Schneider vis-à-vis (Musée de Rochetaillée-sur-Saône), a product of one of the oldest companies in the south, which began production in 1894

In France, Panhard & Levassor shared first place with Peugeot in construction of cars with an internal combustion engine. The firm grew from a small carpentry workshop founded in 1845 by a certain Périn who, in 1867, hired the young engineer René Panhard. In 1872 Emile Levassor, who was a student friend of Panhard, joined the company and at the death of Périn in 1886, the two men took over the firm.

At this point their interests led the company towards motor engineering. The two partners were friendly with Edouard Sarazin who held the exclusive licence in France for an internal combustion engine designed by Gottlieb Daimler, and they were engaged to build some examples of the propulsion unit. Sarazin died in 1887 and his widow, who inherited the licence, married Emile Levassor shortly afterwards. As Levassor now had a suitable engine at his disposal, he immediately thought of applying it to road vehicles.

In 1889 he persuaded Armand Peugeot, another famous motoring pioneer, to build a prototype quadricycle, and then in the same year decided to build a complete vehicle himself. This was how the first Panhard & Levassor came into being. It turned out to be a light carriage with a centrally-mounted propulsion unit of poor design. However, after numerous attempts, in January 1891 the carriage succeeded in travelling $12\frac{1}{2}$ miles (20 km) of the route from Ivry to Point-du-Jour without stopping and this earned the company its first orders. In the course of that same year six vehicles were sold, four of which

had their engines mounted at the front. They were vee-twin-cylinder engines designed by Daimler, which were replaced by the in-line, twin-cylinder unit as used in the Phönix of 1895. This was available in two versions, one developing 3 hp and the other 4 hp. The following year the first four-cylinder engine was installed in carriages taking part in the Paris-Marseille-Paris race. Unfortunately, Emile Levassor was very seriously injured in the race and died the following spring from the after effects of his injuries.

His place as technical director of the company was taken by Arturo Krebs who later developed the Phönix engine the final version of which had four cylinders and a cubic capacity of seven liters. Until the appearance of Maybach's Mercédès at the beginning of the twentieth century, Panhard & Levassor manufactured the most advanced cars from a technical point of view.

The French company was also heavily involved in racing cars from the beginning, entering all the major races of the time, from the very first race for non horse-drawn carriages, the Paris–Rouen in 1894, to the Paris–Amsterdam in 1898 and the Gordon Bennett Cup which was disputed from 1900 to 1905. Panhard & Levassor was also one of the first European companies to take an interest in the American market. After an unlucky start – the first vehicle to be exported was confiscated by American customs and became the subject of a law suit – the French company succeeded in becoming firmly established in a short time and its reputation was later consolidated by its victory in the first Vanderbilt Cup in 1904. This was the ultimate success for the French firm, which then completely abandoned the production of racing cars, with the exception of record-breaking events, and turned to large-scale production.

A contemporary of Panhard & Levassor was Peugeot, founded by the initiative of Armand Peugeot who came from one of the oldest and most powerful French families of Franche-Comté, owners of foundries and rolling-mills. Abandoning family tradition, and relying on his own faith in the development of private transport, Armand Peugeot began producing bicycles in Beaulieu in 1881. He then passed naturally to in-depth studies of achievements in the field of steam locomotion and highlighted the problems and limitations. Peugeot then met the Bollée family and later Serpollet who had created a generator which seemed very promising.

However, Armand Peugeot, although recognizing the theoretical merits of the cars built until then, judged them severely on their practicality. He wanted a car that was easy to build and to drive, and the right opportunity soon presented itself through his excellent relations with Panhard & Levassor. It was this firm which commissioned the construction of a quadricycle with a Daimler engine, for which it held the exclusive licence, the machine being structurally similar to those built in Germany. Armand Peugeot soon realized that he had found what he had been looking for. After tests with Serpollet, he came to an agreement with Panhard to supply the engine, at the same time buying the manufacturing rights for the quadricycle, which he instructed the engineer Rigoulot to perfect.

The first Peugeot quadricycle was introduced in July 1890, but turned out to be unreliable. The second model of 1891, fitted with a vee-twin engine of 565 cc producing 2 hp at 1000 rpm, also proved ineffective. At this point Armand Peugeot decided to stake everything on a desperate gamble for publicity. In September 1891 he entered a mark three quadricycle, a four-seater with mudguards and headlights, in the Paris–Brest–Paris race, held over a distance of around 750 miles (1200 km). His gamble proved successful and the event aroused considerable interest with the result that from 1891 to 1894, 64 examples of the quadricycle were constructed. For the Paris–Bordeaux race of 1895, Peugeot entered an historic vehicle; developed in con-

This 'horseless carriage' is an 1898 Peugeot with four seats, 8 hp rear engine, with two horizontal cylinders, 'hot tube' ignition, four-speed gearbox (plus reverse) and a leather disc clutch (Musée de Rochetaillée-sur-Saône)

In 1898 the Swiss engineer Lorenz Popp built two carriages, with financial help from the Swiss agent for Benz. One of these was the two-seater model illustrated (right), now in the Lucerne Transport Museum

junction with the Michelin brothers, it was the first motor car in the world to be fitted with pneumatic tyres.

From that moment onwards, automobile construction acquired a regular rhythm and until 1896 different versions appeared with Daimler engines in which the cubic capacity rose from 565 cc to 1645 cc and the power output from 2 to 4 hp. Armand Peugeot was not very satisfied with the efficiency of the Daimler propulsion units, however, and he charged his technical department, which comprised the engineers Rigoulot, Doriot and Michaux, with developing a horizontal-twin-cylinder engine of 1645 cc with automatic inlet valves, centrifugal governor, ignition by 'hot tube' or, from 1899 onwards, by electric batteries and a coil. From 1897 to 1902 more than 1400 carriages with every type of body were fitted with this engine. Unlike other companies of the time which installed engines into bare chassis that were then 'dressed' by specialist firms, Peugeot cars were delivered complete with body and, upon request, with Michelin tyres in place of solid rubber tyres.

Although they changed to the petrol engine a few years after Panhard and Peugeot, the De Dion-Bouton company, already known for their steam tricycles, made up for lost time very quickly and towards the end of the cen-

tury equalled the fame gained by their two rivals. As has already been mentioned in the preceding chapter, De Dion-Bouton dissolved the company with Trépardoux in 1893 and founded a new one, De Dion-Bouton & Co, to produce internal-combustion-engine cars. In the same year the two partners patented a revolutionary rear suspension system, the famous de Dion axle, still considered one of the best. The following year the first De Dion–Bouton petrol engine appeared. It had a single cylinder cooled by air and a power output of $\frac{1}{2}$ hp. However, it presented a number of problems, especially concerning the crankshaft, but these were brilliantly overcome by Bouton who eventually succeeded in making the engine rev to 1500 rpm with perfect regularity. It soon became the company's most popular model and was produced in thousands.

After building a number of tricycles of little commercial appeal, De Dion and Bouton found the winning formula with a 3 hp model which was particularly simple, light and elegant. This was followed by the famous vis-à-vis in 1899 with a chassis made of steel tubes, semi-elliptic leaf spring suspension, a de Dion rear axle, drive shaft, clutch, gearbox and a horizontally-mounted engine. This light, four-wheeled carriage was produced in

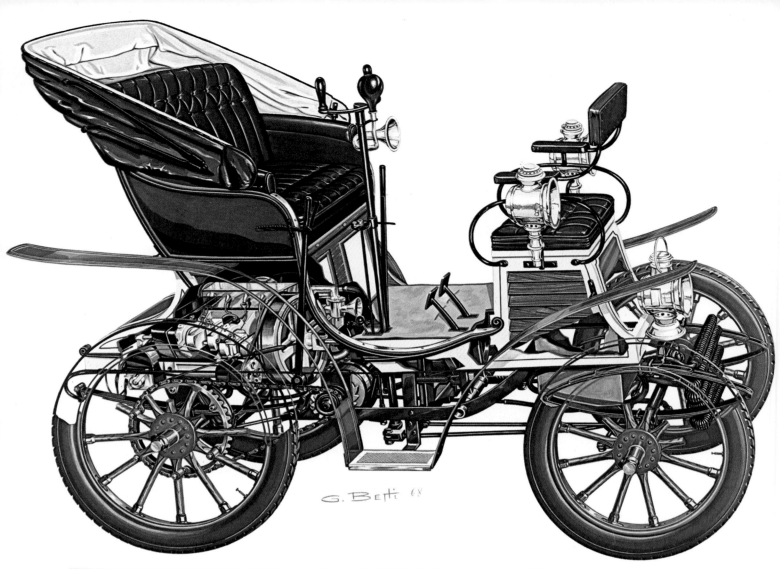

Top *a cutaway of the 3·5 hp Fiat of 1899, the first Fiat carriage, following the traditional design of the time, ie a vis-à-vis with the engine at the rear*
Above *the 3·5 hp now in Fiat's Centro Storico*
Right *the Fiat 3·5 hp engine with two horizontal cylinders. Curiously, the pistons did not move together, as in other four-stroke, in-line, twin-cylinder engines, but moved one behind the other with two successive power strokes followed by a pause*

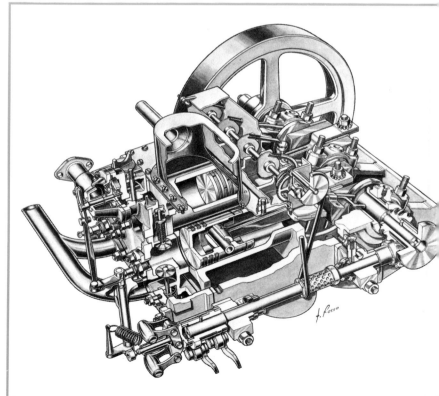

The first Renault quadricycle worked quite well and led its constructor to try exploiting it commercially. To do this, however, he needed a workshop and capital to get the venture under way. Louis Renault, therefore, persuaded his brothers, Fernand and Marcel, to be a part of his company and between the three of them they managed to raise the 60,000 gold francs required to fit out the first factory. So, on 25 February 1899, the Société Renault Frères was registered with its office in Billancourt, and from the outset it showed itself capable of gaining first place in the dawning motoring industry.

In that same year, besides initiating the production of the quadricycle with a De Dion engine, Louis Renault made an important innovation by designing the first saloon car in the world, the construction of which was entrusted to the famous coachbuilder Labourdette who adapted a hansom cab to suit motoring requirements. The choice of a covered carriage, which was so tall, was determined by the fashion of the period which required a chauffeur to wear a top-hat while driving the vehicle.

In 1900 the Renault car was improved and the power increased (348 cc, 3·5 hp). The engine was the standard single-cylinder De Dion, but with a cooling system using water instead of air. It was not until 1902 that the French company began making its own engines. This coincided with the growth of Renault in the sporting field, an activity begun by Marcel and Louis Renault in 1899 when they drove their vehicles personally at races. The highlight of the 1902 season was the Paris–Vienna race, which was an endurance test for drivers and cars alike to be run in four stages, covering a total of 1,057 miles (1700 km). Billancourt prepared for the race very seriously and two new engines were built for the occasion. One was a twin-cylinder unit of 1728 cc, which was later to be used in a series of models until 1920, and a four-cylinder example of 3800 cc. The event was a success for Renault because it was the four-cylinder engine, in a racing car driven by Marcel Renault, that was first over the finishing line in Vienna. This was the car in which Renault's distinctive long bonnet first appeared and this remained a design feature of the French make for many years.

If 1902 was a good year, 1903 was one of the most tragic in the short history of the Billancourt company. During the Paris–Madrid

The 1899 two-seater Prinetti & Stucchi, was the most popular model produced by this small Milanese company which was in business from 1898 to 1906. It had a 4 hp, twin-cylinder De Dion engine, two-speed gearbox and belt transmission (Museo dell'Automobile, Turin)

numerous versions and was finished in different ways by several coachbuilders. In 1900 the Populaire met with instant public acclaim. Of slender line, light and reliable, the Populaire was produced until 1907 with three different engines with one, two and four cylinders. In all, twenty-seven models of the Populaire, all slightly different from each other, were made. The car signified an important stage in the development of the firm which by then was growing into a big industrial company; by 1906, in fact, it had about three thousand employees.

Completing the picture of the French motoring industry of that time was Renault, a company founded in 1899 by Louis Renault. He began by tinkering with engines in a tool shed in the garden of the Renault family's villa in Billancourt, in the suburbs of Paris. Here, in 1898, the young Louis, assisted by a friend and his brother Marcel, changed a De Dion tricycle into a quadricycle. Renault, however, added something of his own, namely a driveshaft unit featuring a three-speed gearchange and a reverse gear. This unit was silent, light and neat and was patented the following year. At a single stroke it solved the serious inconveniences of chain drive and oscillation of the back axle.

race, one which was beset by accidents to such an extent that it was stopped at Bordeaux, Marcel Renault crashed off the road at the village of Couhé-Vérac and was killed.

Deeply affected by his brother's death, Louis Renault decided to abandon racing and to concentrate his efforts on building up his company. He was again crowned with success. In 1903 there were 600 employees with an output of about 1000 cars; two years later these figures had risen to 800 and 1179 respectively.

During this period France dominated the European motoring scene, followed some way behind by Germany, but this does not mean that other countries stood idly watching although their output in no way matched that of France. In Austria, between 1895 and 1897, the Gräf brothers built one of the first cars to use front-wheel drive. In 1902 the two brothers became associated with Willi Stift, thus giving birth to the Gräf and Stift company, which specialized in the construction of large-capacity luxury cars. Still in Austria, Austro-Daimler had been operating since 1899. This

was a subsidiary of the German Daimler company and became an independent organization in 1911. In Switzerland there were two prototypes produced in 1898 by the engineer Lorenz Popp. To this can be added the Berna make of 1902 and the Turicum of 1904, while the Dufaux brothers, whose first racing car was built in 1904, were concerned with sports vehicles. In Czechoslovakia Tatra began production in 1897, to which was added Laurin & Klement, the future Skoda, in 1905. In northern Europe, in Sweden, there was Vabis from 1891 onwards and Scania from 1901; later, in 1911, these two companies merged into Scania-Vabis. Of greater interest, because of their technical originality, were the cars produced by the Dutch company Spyker, which built the first motor vehicle with four-wheel drive in 1903. From the turn of the century, the little country of Belgium counted four motoring marques of considerable importance, the Métallurgique (1898), the FN (1899), the Minerva (1900) and the Excelsior (1901). In Spain the Spagna company had to

The 1899 four-seater Panhard, with tonneau bodywork, was one of the first carriages with a steering wheel. It had a slightly inclined steering column and pneumatic tyres (Musée de Rochetaillée-sur-Saône)

Front and rear views and the engine of the small, elegant carriage built by Georges Richard in 1899, with a characteristic, asymmetrical tiller-rod. There is a curious umbrella holder, originating from the whip holders on horse-drawn carriages

wait until 1904 before being recognized in the world of motoring; it was a worthwhile wait, however, because it produced the Hispano–Suiza.

In this brief panorama of the motoring industry in Europe at the end of the nineteenth century and the beginning of the twentieth century, there are still two countries to be mentioned, Italy and Great Britain, whose contribution to the motoring cause is worth studying in more detail.

In Italy the development of motoring was rather slow, not from any lack of interest but from a lack of the raw materials required to set up industrial production. In the beginning, therefore, Italy's cars were either imported from France or Germany or assembled in Italy from imported parts. The first person to

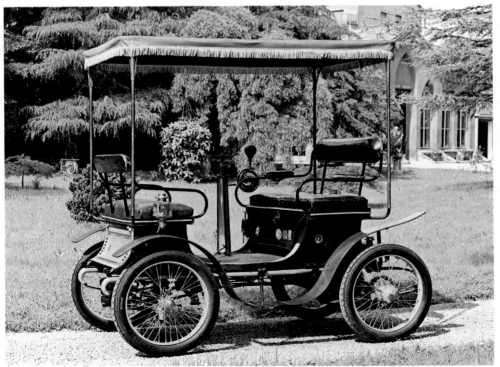

Above *the 1900 Adler vis-à-vis, one of the first cars built by the Frankfurt company which had only changed to car manufacturing the previous year; it had been making bicycles since 1886*
Left *a perfectly preserved example of the De Dion-Bouton vis-à-vis, the French company's first commercial production, produced in two versions from 1899 to 1901 (Longoni collection)*
Right *Adolphe Clément, besides being a manufacturer himself, held shares in other motoring companies which allowed him to use his name in conjunction with theirs for some models. This was the case, for example, with the carriage illustrated opposite, which dates back to 1901 and was sold under the name of Clément-Panhard (National Motor Museum)*

After playing an important part in the founding of Fiat, which was created after the dissolution of his previous company, Giovanni Battista Ceirano established his own company, Ceirano Brothers, with his brother Matteo in 1901. Production began in the same year with this 5 hp model, fitted with single-cylinder Aster or De Dion engines (Museo dell'Automobile, Turin)

attempt the construction of an entirely Italian car was Michele Lanza, from Turin, who ran a wax candle factory which subsequently became the chemical company Mira Lanza. In July 1895 he designed a small six-seater with the assistance of Giuseppe Stefanini, who later joined Isotta Fraschini. The construction of the vehicle was entrusted to Giovanni and Giuseppe Martina. The carriage was ready in the spring of 1896 and is regarded as the first four-wheel Italian car with an internal combustion engine, although the first prototype was really built by Bernardi in 1893–94, but that was a tricycle.

The public's reaction to Langa's rudimentary vehicle was not lacking in scepticism, but he did not give up and in 1897 brought out a new model which was much more advanced. With this model Michele Lanza went into business, albeit on a very small scale, and in 1898 founded the Michele Lanza Fabbrica di Automoboli in Turin. The company remained in business until 1903, but produced few cars as Michele

Lanza was more of an inventor than a businessman. The same spirit also permeated the work of Enrico Bernardi, one of the most ingenious precursors of Italian motoring, with the same disappointing results on the commercial front.

A firm advocate of the three-wheel carriage, Bernardi produced his first tricycle in 1893–94 which already contained all the original features which earned him a reputation as the creator of the most modern vehicle of the time. In 1896 Miari, Giusti & Co was founded at Padua to develop Bernardi patents and manufactured tricycles and later quadricycles designed by the Veronese engineer. The commercial enterprise, however, did not produce the expected results and Miari & Giusti was dissolved in May 1899. The company was reborn a little later as the Societa Italiana Bernardi but it in turn went into liquidation in June 1901.

Of quite a different temperament was Giovanni Agnelli, the only real entrepreneur

66

in the group of partners who, on 1 July 1899, created Fiat which from its beginning revealed its promise. It was Giovanni Agnelli who made a number of decisions that ensured the immediate success of Fiat. The most important decision concerned the size of the company; the second was the plan not to develop inventions and new devices when this time could be put to better use in the company's production output. In doing this, Giovanni Angelli persuaded the group of Turin financiers to back his venture of car production. Agnelli, however, could not wait for the first Fiat to be designed in-house as this would have required months during which the production gap which separated Italy from France and Germany would never have been bridged.

The first Fiat, therefore, was one based on a machine which had already been developed by the Ceirano brothers who had produced a number of models, designed by Aristide Faccioli, and called Welleyes. However, before bearing the name Fiat, the light carriage underwent some modifications. Initial production got under way in the courtyard of the Lancia house, where the Ceirano brothers had their workshop for building bicycles and small carriages, however, only eight months after its foundation, Fiat found new premises between the Via Chiabrera and Corso Dante.

The original 3·5 hp Fiat only remained in production for a few months, less than ten

models being built. In motoring circles there was a tendency developing for heavier vehicles which were more comfortable and powerful, although the formula of the light, small carriage of French origin had not yet died. For Fiat the change to larger cars was very gradual; in 1900, and for part of 1901, the 6/8 hp model kept the same basic design at the 3·5 hp version with a rear-mounted engine with horizontal cylinders and chain drive, and only the chassis became longer.

A real step ahead came in 1901 when the engine, now with two vertical cylinders, was placed in front. A second step, the importance of which was more aesthetic than functional, occurred in 1902. The engine of the new 8 hp model, with a considerably increased cubic capacity (1884 cc instead of 1082 cc), was fitted with a honeycomb radiator based on the Mégevet system. In the same year Fiat also introduced its first four-cylinder vehicle, of 3768 cc, while in 1903 the twin-cylinder models were eventually abandoned.

The engines of the 1903 and 1904 cars showed a maturity of design equal to that of other European countries, which meant that the team of designers led by the engineer Enrico, who replaced Aristide Faccioli in 1901 as the technical director of the company, had nothing more to learn from their rivals across the Alps.

In 1904 there was a new series including two different types of models, the 16/20 hp,

A 1901 Dürkopp model (National Motor Museum). The design was loosely based on that of Panhard & Levassor. It had a twin-cylinder engine and chain drive

Left *the 1902 12/16hp Fiat tonneau (Museo dell'Automobile, Turin). It was in this year that the honeycomb radiator replaced the tubular radiator and the front assumed a trapezoidal shape, constituting the first stylistic innovations on the Turin models* **Below** *an example of the E line of the tonneau version of the 1902 10 hp Marchand*

mainly for urban use, and the sporting 24/32 hp version. Thus began a range of cars destined to last, with few modifications, until the end of 1906. Production, too, became consistent. In 1904 Fiat delivered 268 vehicles as opposed to 134 the preceding year. Part of this output was exported, first to France, then to England and

the United States. At this point the Turin company was in a position to compete with the major European countries.

During this period Britain's contribution to the motoring scene was fairly limited. It must be remembered, however, that until 1896 motoring was practically outlawed in Britain

The 1902 De Dion K, fitted with a front-mounted, single-cylinder, 864 cc engine

The 1902 Berna vis-à-vis (Transport Museum, Lucerne). The Swiss company's emblem was the bear, the symbol of the country's capital

and it was only after this date that anything positive could be achieved. To complicate matters, there was a certain Mr Henry Lawson, a businessman of few scruples and great foresight, who rightly thought that the motoring industry would one day become big business, and organized the British Motor Syndicate which acquired British rights to the continental patents. In practice, he tried to monopolize the developing industry, his only objective being personal gain. To this extent he imposed royalties for every car built or im-

ported by the few companies who managed to remain independent. All of this certainly did not encourage the development of motoring in Britain, which did not begin until after 1903, the year in which Lawson's group collapsed. In addition, the majority of the cars appearing on the English market at the end of the century were imitations of German or French models, Lanchester and Wolseley being the only exceptions to build original 'completely English' cars.

Frederick Lanchester had turned his attention to petrol engines as early as 1893 and in 1895 began building his first vehicle which was tested the following year. From that first prototype, Lanchester made unconventional technical innovations, such as the epicyclic two-speed gearchange which avoided the irritating noise of the clutch, starter unit with a bendix and an ingenious carburettor with a wick. In a second prototype of 1897 Lanchester proposed a pedal accelerator and cantilever leaf springs. Production, although limited, only began in 1900 with 10 and 20 hp models, both based on the second prototype. The first vertical four-cylinder engine appeared in 1904 in a new 20 hp model which had no connection with the preceding model, except the name. The 101 x 76 mm engine had a power output of 25 hp at 2000 rpm and was fitted with two oil pumps, one for the engine and one for the gearbox. Proof of Lanchester's constant search for advanced techniques was the fact that the three-speed gearchange with preselector, which returned to fashion in 1929, was already present in all Lanchester cars from 1901 to 1914.

Wolseley's success, on the other hand, was created by another great name in British motoring, Herbert Austin, better known perhaps for founding the motoring company of his own name in 1906. Austin originally served Wolseley as chief designer. Founded in Birmingham in 1889, as the English subsidiary of an Australian company manufacturing machines for sheep-shearing, Wolseley set up a motoring division in 1895, entrusting its direction to Herbert Austin. The latter produced two prototypes of tricycles with engines in the autumn of 1896. The first was a vehicle, similar to a Bollée, with a twin-cylinder engine of 1255 cc, while the second was characterized by independent rear suspension, which was very advanced for its day.

At the end of 1899 Austin presented his first four-wheeled car, a 3.5 hp model with a single-

cylinder, front-mounted engine of 1300 cc with automatic chain drive. Some changes were made to the models in production such as the adoption of complete chain drive and a steering wheel in place of the tiller.

In 1901 Wolseley was taken over by the Vickers brothers who appointed Herbert Austin managing director of the firm. In the meantime sales had reached considerable figures, from 323 cars in 1901 to 800 in 1903, while the range of models was increased to include single-cylinder, twin-cylinder and four-cylinder engines with cubic capacities from 1·3 to 5·2 litres.

Although Europe pioneered motoring, it certainly did not retain its lead. In fact, across the Atlantic the United States was to launch the car in grand style, making it a popular object within everyone's reach. In popular jargon it can even be said that America was responsible for making it 'democratic'. From the outset production reached inconceivable figures compared to Europe. Oldsmobile alone, the first American company to introduce mass-production, built 2500 models of the Curved Dash in 1902 which increased to 5500 in 1904.

In America, as in Europe, the first experiments on the internal combustion engine date back to the first half of the nineteenth century, the highlights of which include the patents by Samuel Morey in 1826, Stuart Perry in 1844 and 1846, Alfred Drake in 1857 and George Bailey Brayton in 1872. It was Brayton's

engine, in fact, that was the starting point for the shrewd lawyer George Selden to cause one of the most extraordinary events in the history of the motor car. Selden, seeing Brayton's engine, was convinced that the future of non-horse-drawn vehicles would depend on the internal combustion engine, and by a skilful strategy managed to patent the principle of the car, as a vehicle fitted with an engine and all the other parts required to set it in motion. These elements were already known and were the subject of numerous patents, but each one separately. Selden, however, regarded them as a whole and therefore as scope for a patent which he obtained in 1895. As a result he could impose a levy on each car built by every American manufacturer.

This absurd duty was not lifted until 1911 after a legal battle lasting eight years, which was brought by Henry Ford, the great industrialist of Detroit, who was intolerant by nature to any kind of imposition. In some ways this resembled the case of Lawson in Britain, and conditioned the development of American motoring, discouraging many promising inventions.

There was a further complication which arose from the controversy as to who was the first American constructor of a petrol engine car. For a long time this was attributed to the Duryea brothers, Charles and Frank, whose first vehicle was tested in 1893, but it was later discovered that two years earlier John William Lambert and Henry Nadig had already built prototypes of an internal combustion engine. However, even if the Duryea brothers were not the first Americans to build a car, they were the first to set up production, which they did in 1895.

Ransom Eli Olds was another pioneer of American motoring at the turn of the century who enjoyed great commercial success with his mass-produced models. He had been constructing steam carriages since 1887, and in 1899 went into partnership with Samuel Smith and established the Olds Motor Works in Lansing, Michigan, at the same time setting up a new plant in Detroit. It was here that a new series of experimental vehicles was produced with electric motors and petrol engines which was put on sale in 1901. Unfortunately, in March of that year a fierce fire destroyed nearly all of the Detroit factory, but Olds did not become disheartened and immediately resumed work in the few parts of the building left standing. The only vehicle to escape the fire

Left *the 1902 Oldsmobile Curved Dash (Harrah collection)*
Below *Isotta-Fraschini, one of the most prestigious Italian makes, began by assembling foreign, especially French cars. The example illustrated, dating from 1902, is almost identical to Renault models of the same period (Caproni collection)*

was a light runabout, built at the end of 1900, and the entire production was centred around it.

Simple, economic and functional, this carriage was an immediate success, and so the famous Curved Dash model was created, almost by accident. This, as time subsequently proved, was the first American car to be mass-produced. Olds was a firm advocate of the utilitarian formula for cars and this was why, in 1904, he decided to leave the company he had founded, rather than accept the new direction towards better quality cars, set by his partner Samuel Smith.

Henry Ford, a character in the forefront of the motoring scene in America as well as throughout the world, was much closer to the ideas held by Olds. Officially, the story of the

Ford Motor Company began in 1903 when a group of twelve people decided to start a company to implement Ford's ideas.

The firm was situated in a narrow area on Mack Avenue in Detroit where production began on the first Ford car, the Model A. It was the first to be produced, but not the first to be built by Henry Ford who had already made a quadricycle with a petrol engine in 1896, followed two years later by a decidedly more modern version. Twice he had tried to direct his productions towards commercial exploitation, but had failed. At the beginning of 1903 he built two large racing cars with four-cylinder engines, the *999* and the *Arrow*, with the help of his friend Tom Cooper. The *999* was awarded the Diamond Trophy and this success enabled Henry Ford to find financial

Right *the 1903 Ford A runabout, a light, two-seater (Ford Museum)* **Below** *a 1903 Wolseley from the Harper collection. Like all this British company's models up to 1905, it was designed by Herbert Austin*

The 1903, single-cylinder, Type 18 Thomas (Harrah collection)

An impressive 16/20 hp Fiat of 1903 (Fiat's Centro Storico)

backing to establish his company. Eight days after his victory, he founded the Ford Motor Company.

Ford overturned the commercial practice in vogue at the time which was to begin production only after receiving a given number of orders. He started work on his Model A with his only guarantee that of 'hoping' to find buyers. His decision risked bringing the com-

pany to a rapid end and within barely a month of being established, the company had only $233 available in the kitty. Fortunately the first car was sold for $850 and the buyer, Dr Pfennig of Chicago, can therefore be regarded as the saviour of Ford. From then on sales climbed steadily and after fifteen months of production more than 1700 examples of the Model A had been sold.

The first Cadillac, of 1903 (National Motor Museum). It had a 1610 cc, single-cylinder engine and two-speed gearbox

The 1903, 10 hp Florentia, with 1400 cc, twin-cylinder engine with a power output of 15 hp at 1200 rpm (Museo dell'Automobile, Turin)

In 1904 this first model was replaced by the Model C, which was produced for two years; at the same time the first mass-produced four-cylinder Ford engine appeared. This was used in the Model B, an unsuccessful de luxe car, and the intermediate Model F.

During this period Henry Ford was not free to guide production towards popular, low-priced cars as he had to work with his partners whose ideas were opposed to his. Only in 1906 did he succeed in obtaining a majority sharehold in the company and this allowed him to act as he thought best. That his intuition was correct was proved by the outstanding success of the small, popular Model T, the car produced for almost nineteen years (1908–1927), with more than fifteen million being built, which 'put America on four wheels'.

Early Automobile Technology

Technically, it is impossible to pinpoint the 'invention' of the motor car because in the beginning the car was merely a development of the horse-drawn vehicle. In practice, the first experiments on automotive vehicles were limited to substituting mechanical traction for animal traction without any change to the general structure of the carriage.

The first motor carriages – which, naturally, were steam-powered – retained the shape, general line, steering and suspension systems of contemporary horse-drawn carriages. In some cases even the tiller-rod, which controlled the steering of the main axle, was retained. Driver-controlled steering, in addition to being complicated, was also a novelty in the last century and it must be remembered that in the case of horse-drawn carriages it was the horse that 'steered', by obeying the driver's commands and exercising the necessary force to move the front axle.

The transition from a centre-pivoting front axle to two front wheels which steered independently of one another was fairly rapid and answered the need for precise control imposed by the advent of the engine and higher speeds. The centre-pivoting axle demands a great effort to set it in motion and creates problems of instability for large steering angles. Also of course, the lower part of the vehicle must be completely uncluttered to allow movement of the whole axle. On the other hand, a system with its wheels steering independently and mounted on a fixed axle demands less force and the only free space needed is to allow the wheels to turn through a relatively small angle.

The adoption of this system, and development of geometrically correct steering linkages, largely solved these difficulties but the driven wheels presented another problem as, in a corner, the inner and outer wheels of a vehicle travel at different speeds; if the wheels move at the same speed while turning a corner, the outer ones will drag against the ground.

The need for a differential, that is a device to control the driven wheels so that they can follow perfectly concentric arcs, remained for many years one of the main problems for car manufacturers and was the basis of innumerable designs, some of which were extremely complicated and never found any practical application. Even today, the problem has not been fully solved.

In the case of a vehicle with only one front wheel, the problem of steering is much simpler and it was this factor which, for a while, favored the 'tricycle', a design used for smaller, lighter vehicles. Besides permitting a very simple steering system (usually controlled by a long lever called an 'ox tail') the tricycle permitted other structural simplifications such as

The motorized 'trailer' made by the Italian inventor, Bernardi, in 1895, which was undoubtedly one of the first and most extraordinary examples of a motor cycle

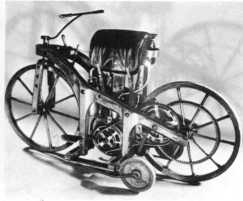

the elimination of complicated front suspension and lightening of the chassis. For a long time the typical chassis was made of wood and even in larger, four-wheeled carriages complete transition to metal construction was gradual, though this was due to practical considerations rather than any prejudice towards steel.

The early car manufacturers, in fact, used artisan methods of building, whereas working with metal presupposed work on an industrial level. It was logical, therefore, for manufacturers to use simple, traditional technology and any modifications or repairs had to be carried out by mechanics who were frequently untrained.

Contrary to what might seem to be the case, the main contributions to the development of motor vehicles came initially from the smaller carriages because they were light, structurally simple and relatively easy to drive; they were therefore much closer to the modern concept of a car than were the early, huge motor coaches. Because of their reduced weight and size, smaller carriages were easier to drive, were more adaptable, suffered fewer brake failures and proved to be both faster and more practical.

Although the problem of performance was not a serious one when the main preoccupation was safety and reliability, as soon as the chassis and suspension systems improved, it was obvious that the 'race for power' would get under way with the development of the internal combustion engine.

In contrast to other types of engines used in road vehicles, the internal combustion engine, after being tested and developed in other applications, improved at much the same rate as the motor car. Even Daimler's, Maybach's and Bernardi's earliest models were quickly applied to rudimentary vehicles after brief workshop tests, showing how suitable this type of propulsion was for road transport.

The internal combustion engine, of course, presented new technical problems, but these were not insoluble even in the last century. The development of smelting enabled the main parts of the engine to be made with precision and robustness, albeit in a simple form.

In a short time a number of the more ingenious and experienced, or simply better equipped, manufacturers began producing, in small quantities, engines which could be installed in a wide variety of motor vehicles. These were often built by a completely different group of craftsmen, usually former coachbuilders. Among the most famous names are Daimler, Aster, Panhard and De Dion–Bouton. The typical engine at the end of the nineteenth century had a single cylinder with side valves and the combustion chamber extended laterally to where the valves and ignition unit were fitted. It was the ignition unit that was the most thorny problem for engineers of the time as it had to be able to cope with fuels of varying quality and low grade.

One of the first ignition systems was the so-called 'brûleur' or 'hot tube' system which was very simple and consisted of a small tube, made of a platinum alloy, passing into the combustion chamber. The outer end of the tube was kept alight by two burners fuelled by either petrol or gas. When the air-fuel mixture in the cylinder was compressed, it was pushed into the tube, reached the hotter end and ignited. The flame then spread to the entire mixture contained in the combustion chamber. This system, lacking as it did any fine timing, was obviously only suited to very slow engines, but on the other hand it presented no mechanical complexities of any kind.

Above left *one of the first internal combustion engines to be built by Bernardi was this single-cylinder example built in 1884. On the right is the rudimentary tank-radiator for cooling the water* **Above** *the 'motor cycle' built by Daimler and Maybach in 1885*

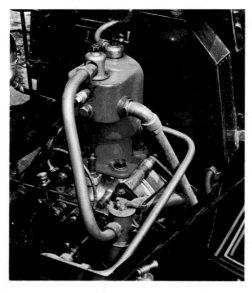

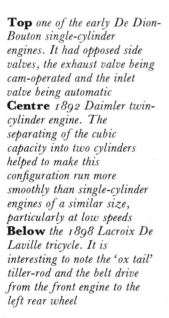

Top *one of the early De Dion-Bouton single-cylinder engines. It had opposed side valves, the exhaust valve being cam-operated and the inlet valve being automatic*
Centre *1892 Daimler twin-cylinder engine. The separating of the cubic capacity into two cylinders helped to make this configuration run more smoothly than single-cylinder engines of a similar size, particularly at low speeds*
Below *the 1898 Lacroix De Laville tricycle. It is interesting to note the 'ox tail' tiller-rod and the belt drive from the front engine to the left rear wheel*

Systems giving ignition by a spark followed immediately afterwards, at first by the so-called 'disconnector switch' and later by devices similar to modern sparking plugs. The disconnector was a unit which consisted of a pair of electrical contacts placed inside the combustion chamber and having a fairly high current running across them to earth. When the piston reached (or approached) top dead centre, the contacts were opened and thus caused a spark which was sufficient to ignite the mixture compressed in the cylinder.

With other systems the spark might be produced by a battery circuit and contact breaker (a simple device to increase the electric current, similar in effect to present-day coils), or by a magnet moved within a coil by the engine shaft itself. With systems such as these, the ignition could be co-ordinated with the engine turning over, so besides being much more efficient, they also constituted a very important contribution to the smooth running and easy starting of the engine.

For a long time all the engine's mechanical parts were simplified as much as possible, which meant, for example, that only the exhaust valve was controlled by a cam (usually connected to the crankshaft by gears), while the inlet valve opened automatically; the valve head was kept in position on its seat by the action of a rather weak spring so that the depression caused by the piston in the cylinder during the induction stroke was sufficient to make the valve open. The most common layout had the exhaust valve flanking the cylinder and directly controlled, while the automatic inlet valve was placed above and facing the exhaust valve.

The fact that the valves were opposed was also very important for a practical reason. In those days, because of the poor quality of materials, burning of the valves and deterioration of their seating was very common and therefore regular maintenance was necessary to replace the valves and restore the seating. By placing the valves in two ports parallel to the cylinder and to each other, construction and maintenance were enormously simplified.

Engine speeds, of course, were very low (typically, under 1000 rpm), which also helped maintain the condition of the mechanical parts and reduced wear and tear. The pistons were made of cast iron and were very heavy, and the compression stroke was very slow because of the large volume of the combustion chamber. Even the connecting-rods

Top *the small, efficient De Dion-Bouton single-cylinder engine came with either water or air cooling in the smallest versions*
Below *the 1899 De Dion-Bouton* vis-à-vis *with the two directors of the company in the driver's seat*
Bottom *back view of a De Dion-Bouton carriage with the characteristic rear suspension*

were very long to reduce the lateral stress of the piston against the cylinder (which is proportional to the angle of the connecting-rod during the engine cycle). Consequently, the inertia of the system was extremely high.

Another factor which limited the rotational speed was lubrication which in the early engines was by a number of oilers installed to act on the main areas of friction. Considering the lack of mechanical precision and the quality of the available lubricants (mostly low grade oils and animal and vegetable fats), it is easy to understand how an engine's performance was restricted.

The inertia of the very heavy flywheels, which were used to counter the chronic lack of smoothness of cars, enabled the crankshaft to rotate more or less independently of the irregular power pulses. With the demand for greater power and cubic capacity, the usual method to improve the engine's performance was to increase the number of cylinders, even at the expense of greater mechanical complexity. The first Daimler twin-cylinder engine, of 1890, had its cylinders in a very narrow vee, so that the two connecting rods acted on one journal (in this way the crankshaft was kept virtually identical to that of a single-cylinder engine), but subsequently more complex engines were built with in-line cylinders and extended crankshafts.

To eliminate, or at least reduce the terrible vibration typical of the early internal combustion engine, complex and sophisticated balancing systems were studied and tested. These became increasingly necessary with higher engine speeds and the demand for improved comfort, especially in the early cars with the engine rigidly fixed to the chassis.

At the beginning of the twentieth century Lanchester patented and built an engine with perfect balancing and with opposed twin cylinders; the two pistons moved in opposite directions and were connected to the crankshaft by two pairs of connecting rods. In this way the inertia of the pistons and their two connecting-rods offset each other perfectly. The system worked quite efficiently, but was too complex and was therefore only used by Lanchester himself in his vehicles.

The power delivering characteristics of the internal combustion engine also posed other problems regarding transmission of power to the wheels; in particular, a clutch was required to start and stop the vehicle with the engine running. The first clutches were very

Metal chassis first appeared on small, light vehicles
Right *the entire chassis, with all its components, of the 1900 Albion*
Below *a Noël Bennet carriage built around the turn of the century and which the French regard as the first front-wheel-drive car. It had a De Dion engine, mounted horizontally at the level of the top of the front wheels and was driven by jointed half-shafts with cardan joints, similar to those used in modern cars*

rudimentary and certainly did not give the same degree of control as the pedal clutches of modern cars. They usually consisted of two conical surfaces, one inside the flywheel and the other on a component connected to the drive shaft; when declutching, the cone slipped off the flywheel and when in motion remained pressed against its seating. The moveable cone was usually covered with leather which, before the introduction of asbestos compounds, was the material which gave the best friction and wear properties. The conical shape of the two contact surfaces had the dual purpose of generating high friction between the surfaces for a given contact pressure and of ensuring perfect alignment between the engine and transmission.

In smaller, lighter vehicles, such as motor cycles, the system of direct belt drive was very common. By using a strong piece of leather to connect the drive shaft directly to the axle of the driven wheel or wheels, it was possible to eliminate the friction clutch and the engine was disengaged by varying the tension of the belt between the pulleys. However, since the friction between belts and pulleys was not so much as that in a friction clutch, the system could not be applied to heavy or powerful vehicles.

The Cars of the Edwardian Era

By the turn of the century the car had reached a relatively high degree of technical efficiency and car manufacturers multiplied in Europe and America to meet the challenge of an ever-increasing demand. Production, of course, was not on a large scale and the high prices prevented all but the wealthy from buying a car and motoring therefore remained a privilege of the upper classes. However, in the early years of the twentieth century, output reached considerable figures and it was accepted that eventual general mass-production of cars was just a matter of time.

There was a growing number of potential motorists waiting for the industry to produce low cost models which they could afford. To do this manufacturers had to modernize their factories and change from artisan to industrial labor methods which alone could reduce production costs and therefore selling prices to the public. Henry Ford was to point the way towards this with a strict organization of labor to avoid time wastages, and the adoption of the assembly line, however rudimentary. The first car to benefit from the new system was the Ford Model T, the world's first real

economy car. More than 10,000 examples of the Model T were manufactured in 1909, and this figure rose to 100,000 in 1913. Mass-production, a very low retail price (it dropped to $260), extraordinary reliability, which was very rare for those times, and considerable robustness made the Model T the car for everyone, earning it the affectionate nickname of 'Tin Lizzie'.

The first Model T tourer, that is, an open four-seater with a hood, cost $850, and was designed by J. Galamb and C. H. Wills under the direction of Henry Ford. It had a four-cylinder, 2880 cc engine with side valves with non-adjustable tappets, a head that could be removed, sparking plugs with a tapered seat, a two-speed epicyclic gearbox, low tension magnetic ignition on the fly-wheel, two transverse leaf springs, one front and one rear, and no shock-absorbers. It had a power output of 20 hp at 1800 rpm and a maximum speed of 45 mph (70 kph). Electric ignition and lighting were introduced in 1915.

The popularity of the Model T, which in 1916 alone sold more than half a million, was such that some American states introduced

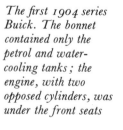

The first 1904 series Buick. The bonnet contained only the petrol and water-cooling tanks; the engine, with two opposed cylinders, was under the front seats

Left *a curious 1904 Larroumet and Lagarde tricycle with a front-mounted, single-cylinder engine of 8 hp (Grandson Museum)*

The small Populaire model, launched in 1902 by Cottereau and updated and relaunched in 1905

two types of licence, one for cars with a pedal clutch (Ford T) and one for all the others. Its popularity was only excelled after World War II by the now legendary Volkswagen Beetle. One of its numerous merits was that it made motoring possible in rural areas of America for the first time as no car could survive for long on the terrible country roads of the early twentieth century and the Ford T only succeeded because of its robustness and reliability. To make it even more adaptable to 'rustic' use, it could be fitted with rear wheels with steel grips, which made it into a sort of tractor. As a result, the small, indestructible Ford Model T was also one of the first cars to travel in remote areas.

Initially the Model T was built by the same methods used for all the other cars which preceded it, that is, the workers took individual parts which they assembled to form the various components and then mounted them on the chassis to complete the car. Henry Ford was shrewd, however, and had observed that this system wasted a considerable amount of time and he was convinced that an increase in the daily output of his Detroit workshop would justify the introduction of the system

advocated by the American, Taylor, fifty years earlier. This was based on the idea that the workers should have a supply of parts to be assembled and mounted and that the vehicle should pass slowly in front of them, rather than having the vehicle in one place, thereby obliging the workers to make frequent trips to the storeroom for parts.

Each worker would always assemble the same part or parts, with a great saving of time once the operation had become automatic and at the end of the line the car was complete and ready to leave.

The results of the first tests were surprising. The new system began with the assembly of magnetos, increasing productivity by about 300 per cent, then passed to the engines and was finally applied to the entire car. At the beginning, twelve hours were required to assemble a car but, when the line was perfected, this was reduced to $1\frac{1}{2}$ hours. Previously, ten workers were needed for each chassis as opposed to fifty or sixty under the new system, but in return output was a good eight times higher.

This makes it easy to understand how Ford could sell cars, however simple they may have

Opposite page *the 1908 Austin 100 hp Grand Prix car was, like many of its contemporaries, loosely based on a road-going car. The impressive looking 9677 cc straight-six was, however, not as powerful as it looked* **Below** *a well-preserved 1903 Peugeot from the National Motor Museum*

The 1904 Franklin Light Car, a two-seater which had an air-cooled engine, as did all the cars manufactured by the American company for over thirty years between 1902 and 1934

been, at low prices but get good returns. In fact, by the time it was discontinued in 1927 the Ford Model T had made about six hundred million dollars for the American company.

The overwhelming success of the Ford Model T, besides proving the validity of Henry Ford's formula for economy cars, also gave the insecure American motoring industry the incentive to become more positive and to abandon the useless and dangerous flights of fancy which had brought about one of its first and deepest crises in 1907–08.

Many people had set up as car manufacturers in a wave of enthusiasm for the new means of transport, but they either lacked the technical knowledge or the capital to back the venture which, in most cases, ended in collapse. During that period more than fifty companies shut their gates permanently and their failure discouraged the growth of new enterprises. Even the few companies who did manage to survive were not in a very healthy position. As they produced almost identical models, which were very costly and for which the market was very limited, competition had become ruthless. The problem had to be solved and solved quickly so that the situation would not deteriorate into a more serious and irreversible crisis. Someone was needed who had sufficient enterprise, business sense and courage to counteract

the lack of confidence, and that someone turned out to be William Crapo Durant, one of the most ingenious and brilliant entrepreneurs the American motoring industry has ever known.

Durant, who had made his fortune with the Durant-Dort Carriage Work, a prosperous coachbuilding firm in Flint, Michigan, was not new to rescue operations of companies in difficulty, although what he had achieved until then was not even remotely comparable to what he now set out to accomplish. By 1904 he had taken over Buick, founded the previous year by David Dunbar Buick – an able engineer but a hopeless businessman – thus saving it from a premature end. Four years later he was planning the creation of a national trust which all American car manufacturers would be obliged to join. Showing no concern for the criticism which rained on him from all directions, Durant immediately set about contacting the major manufacturers of the time to persuade them to accept his idea. Negotiations continued throughout the Summer of 1908 between Durant, Benjamin Briscoe and George Perkins of Maxwell-Briscoe Motor Co, Henry Ford and Ransom Olds who, after leaving Oldsmobile in 1904, had founded the Reo Motor Car, and were concluded when Ford announced that he would

never agree to a merger but, at most, would be prepared to sell his factory. Olds was of the same opinion and both decided not to pursue the matter. Durant did not give up, however, and decided to change his plans. He began buying companies in difficulty, offering them shares in the company he was setting up by way of payment. This was how he acquired control of

Top *a 1904 tonneau with its twin-cylinder engine of 1817 cc*
Above *the 1905 Bébé, with its single-cylinder engine and contact-breaker ignition (San Martino Museum, Rio)*
Left *an experimental quadricycle made by Peugeot in 1905 with rear engine and tiller-rod steering (Peugeot collection)*

Above *the Ford Model B
of 1905, a large, de-luxe
car with four-cylinder engine*
Above right *the Model F
of the same year
Both these cars belong to the
Ford Museum*

Centre and below *1906
saw the appearance of two
new Ford models, the
Model K (shown here are
the touring version, centre,
and the roadster, below
right), which introduced the
six-cylinder engine, and the
four-cylinder Model N,
below left (Ford Museum)*

Pope, the American group, comprised three motoring companies, Pope-Hartford (Connecticut), Pope-Tribune (Maryland) and Pope-Toledo (Ohio). The car illustrated was the product of the last-named company and is the 1906 Type 12 (Long Island Auto Museum)

Dow, Ewing, Elmore and Cartercar and, on 16 September 1908, he founded the General Motors Company in New Jersey with an initial capital of barely $2000.

Twelve days later, however, on 28 September, the company's capital rose to $12\frac{1}{2}$ million dollars and the following day General Motors bought the Buick Motor Company for approximately four million dollars and soon afterwards took over the coachbuilding works of Stewart, which already belonged to Buick. Another takeover was that of Oldsmobile on 12 December in a transaction involving little more than three million dollars. Before the end of 1908, the company's board of directors increased from three to seven and W. M. Eaton, an influential business man, was elected president; Durant was appointed vice-president, a position he held until 1915.

The growth of General Motors continued unabated. In January 1909 the acquisition of the Oakland Motor Company was authorized; this was later to become the Pontiac Motor Company. A few months later Cadillac was added to the GM stable for a record sum of $4\frac{1}{2}$ million dollars in addition to 275,000 preferential shares in General Motors. William Durant had also persuaded Albert Champion to leave the company in Boston founded under his name by the Stranaham brothers (this company subsequently became Ford's exclusive supplier), to found a new company in 1908 for the production of sparking plugs and feed-pumps. Called AC, after his initials, the company was owned by General Motors.

The growth of General Motors developed around famous names to which it owed a great deal of its rapid success. It also narrowly failed to absorb Ford in October 1909 in a deal worth one million dollars. Durant approached the National City Bank of New York to obtain the money he required, but his application was refused. The rapid, convulsive growth of the car industry was regarded with suspicion in American banking circles as they understood speculation only too well.

The economic crisis, which began in 1909, began to hit the motoring industry which was forced to submit to its consequences. Banks suddenly withdrew their money and refused loans, especially substantial ones. Until the early months of 1910 the sales of General Motors, which had by now acquired about thirty companies of its own besides its shares in numerous smaller companies, were going well, but during the summer matters got progressively worse. Durant feverishly set about looking for money; he needed at least twelve million dollars and finally found it in New York and Boston, but on condition that he changed the top men in his company, a demand which was an explicit criticism of his operation. He remained vice-president, but the real control of the company now passed into other hands. Furthermore, the General Motors Company was organized in such a way that it effectively owned the property of its associate companies and this gave his financial backers the opportunity to mortgage them.

The new management's policy was to strengthen the position of the various companies within the group rather than to buy new ones. For this reason there was no further attempt to buy Ford and car production was concentrated on four makes, Buick, Cadillac, Oakland and Oldsmobile.

Durant, however, was not a man to accept being cast to one side. His position as vice-president demanded collaboration with the new group of directors, although he did not share their ideas, but this did not prevent him from trying to buy a greater number of shares in the company he had created. To this end he was helped by powerful friends, the DuPont family, who put twenty-seven million dollars at his disposal. In September 1915 Durant proposed the acquisition of Chevrolet to General Motors, but was flatly refused. It was at this point that he laid his cards on the table.

Directly or indirectly he now held a majority of shares in General Motors and thus became head of the company for the next five years, during which the group's assets reached the sum of 514 million dollars. Pierre S. DuPont became president of the board to be followed by Charles Nash from 1910 to 1916 when he was replaced by Durant himself.

On 13 October 1916 the name was changed to The General Motors Corporation and in August of the following year it bought all the shares of the General Motors Company in New Jersey. Once again at the head of the company, Durant continued his policy of expansion and in a short time bought numerous other companies. Among the more significant acquisitions were those of Chevrolet in 1918 and Fisher Body, one of the most important American coachbuilders, in 1919. The growth of General Motors was to continue in the following decades, becoming established in the European market as well, following the takeover of the German Opel Company in 1921 and the English Vauxhall organization in 1925.

In spite of his controversial business methods, William Durant succeeded in creating what is today, seventy years later, the most impressive car manufacturing company in the world, by being the first to introduce a policy of extensive market penetration which later found many imitators worldwide.

Although the companies within the General Motors group – Buick, Cadillac, Oakland, Oldsmobile and Chevrolet – were foremost in

the American market from the first decade of the century onwards, many others who remained independent contributed as much to the enormous popularity of the American automobile both nationally and internationally. The first of these was, naturally, Ford, followed by the Reo of Ransom Olds, Studebaker, Winton, Peerless, Pierce-Arrow, Packard and Willys–Overland, to name just a few of the best known on a list which included more than a hundred and fifty at the beginning of the second decade of the century. Of these the most prestigious was undoubtedly Packard, the closest rival to Cadillac in the exclusive field of luxury cars. It was created by

The 40/50PS Adler of 1907, shown here in a special exhibition version which was commissioned by Kaiser Wilhelm II; the car was painted with the Hohenzollern colours of ivory and blue

A large sports car built by the Belgian company Métallurgique in 1907

A tonneau version of the 1907 Gladiator. It had a four-cylinder, in-line engine with a power of 12/14 hp; the back wheels were driven by a cardan shaft and the engine had a four-speed gearbox

James Ward Packard, owner of the New York & Ohio Co of Warren, Ohio, a manufacturer of electrical apparatus.

The first Packard appeared in November 1899 and was very similar in structure to most of the other American cars of the period. It had very high, slender wheels, tiller-steering and a single-cylinder, centrally-mounted engine situated under the seat. Priced at $1250, the Model A was commercially successful and led Packard to establish a motoring division.

In 1901 Packard was one of the first American companies to adopt the steering wheel, a feature which only later became universal. By 1902 production had reached the Model F, but each model contained innovations which made it unique. They were all, however, single-cylinder cars as Packard thought that by increasing the number of cylinders he would also increase the likelihood of breakdowns. The transition to engines with more cylinders came only after Henry B. Joy, a wealthy Detroit industrialist, had bought all the shares in the Packard Motor Car Company.

James Packard remained president of the firm until 1909 and was managing director until 1912, but he chose to stay in Warren when the Packard factory moved to new premises in Detroit in 1903. Here, in the same year, the first four-cylinder Model K was produced. It was designed by Charles Schmidt, a French engineer who had been employed by Joy.

From the outset Packard had a sales policy which was rather unusual in the United States and was based on factory-owned distributor-ships established in strategic areas, rather than independent agents. Whereas other companies were paid for a car the moment it left the factory, Packard deferred collection of payment until the car had been sold. This policy required the investment of a large amount of capital in addition to that already allocated to production, but resulted in high standards of quality, uniformity of price and excellent service facilities throughout the country, which served to boost Packard sales.

In the Packard company's history the Model L, designed and built by Schmidt, was a landmark as it was the first model to have a radiator with raised shoulders which formed the wings of the bonnet, a distinctive design feature of Packard cars for years to come.

In 1910 Alvan Macauley took over the general management of Packard, contributing in a big way to making the name an internationally respected one. It was Macauley who was responsible for the presentation of the first six-cylinder Packard engine in 1912. In 1916, when Henry Joy resigned, he became president of the company. Joy, Macauley and Jesse Vincent then created the model which earned Packard a leading position in the history of motoring. This was the sensational Twin Six of 1915. While other manufacturers were discussing whether a four-, six- or eight-cylinder engine was best for a luxury car, Packard outstripped them all by presenting a car with a V12 engine in May 1915.

Although it was not the first car to be designed with twelve cylinders, Packard's was so

successful that it was installed in almost half of the 18,572 cars sold in 1916 and remained in production until the end of 1922.

Between 1915 and 1916, Packard also built two special racing cars, fitted with V12 engines. The smaller version, driven by Ralph DePalma, won several local races and was awarded sixth place in the Indianapolis 500 in 1919. The larger version, a single-seater strictly for racing, set a world land speed record at Daytona in 1919 with an average speed of 149·9 mph (241·99 kph). Even more impressive was the 92·71 mph (149·2 kph) average achieved over the standing-start mile, a record that stood for over thirty years in the United States.

Taking part in racing events was still a point of honour for motoring companies and a source of good publicity which could be exploited in various ways. More and more frequently manufacturers launched models onto the market which had won a particular race and buyers were attracted by the prestige of owning a real racing car, even if its urban use was obviously limited. This was the case, for example, of Mercer which was founded in 1911 in Trenton, New Jersey, and which was one of the great names in American sports cars that were popular in the second decade of the century. Mercer enjoyed the same prestige between 1911 and 1915 as Duesenberg at the end of the 1920s.

The most successful Mercer model was the 35R Raceabout of 1911, designed as a racing car but used for normal road transport. The aim of the Trenton company was to offer its customers a car of exceptional performance to give the average American motorist the exhilaration of speed. With a top speed of 75 mph (120 kph), the 35R was one of the fastest American cars of the time. It also boasted a pleasant appearance of extreme simplicity. There was no bodywork as such because the chassis, besides containing the mechanical parts and the essential controls, just had a hood over the engine, two collapsible seats and a fuel tank at the rear. It had a curious windscreen which was round and was mounted in a metal frame on the steering column.

The engine was a large, in-line, four-cylinder unit of 4949 cc, with side valves and a power output of approximately 50 hp at 1600 rpm. Because of its lack of weight, the Raceabout, besides being fast, also had good acceleration – for the time – and could cover one mile in 51 seconds from a standing start.

Above *the racing version of the 1908 Alpha model, the first Lancia, with a four-cylinder, twin-block engine, of 2543 cc (Lancia Museum)*
Below left *a 1908 Austin, now in the Cheddar Motor Museum, England*

Opposite
top *the Packard 30, a touring model of 1908 (Long Island Auto Museum)*
below *a Sizaire-Naudin of the same year (Musée de Rochetaillée-sur-Saône)*

Mercer was not the only company to take an interest in racing. Stutz and Marmon were its keenest rivals. Stutz succeeded in excelling the Mercer Raceabout with their Bearcat model, a speedster with a four-cylinder, 6·5-litre engine and a power output of 60 hp. Introduced in 1912, the Bearcat was in the market until the beginning of the 1920s. From the purely technical point of view, the Marmon cars, produced from 1902 onwards by Walter and Howard Marmon in Indianapolis, were superior. A Marmon car won the first Indianapolis 500 in 1911 with a car built expressly for the big American races. It used a powerful, in-line, six-cylinder engine, and was driven by Ray Harroun. The car was interesting in that it had an interior mirror, probably the first ever to be fitted.

Towards the end of the decade the American motoring industry had caught up with Europe technically and in terms of output had far outstripped it. Of course, it was still a mark of distinction to import a car but this was a luxury reserved for a small circle of enthusiasts with particularly refined tastes. Generally, however, the American public was satisfied, and justifiably, with what the domestic market was able to offer.

During this time, however, Europe had not been a passive spectator and the car had come to play a more important role in the social and economic life of the continent. Even Italy though still lagging behind the industrialized countries of Europe, had an expanding motor industry which had become recognized as excellent business and capital flowed readily into the various companies (in 1906 there were about thirty), as they were able to pay higher dividends than other industries. This allowed the motoring industry to offer its employees higher salaries, but this was an exception in an otherwise very depressed industrial climate and the situation later deteriorated with the rise in the cost of living. Consequently, in 1906 strikes and riots broke out all over Italy, the spark being set off by those industries, like the textile industry, which were more severely hit by the crisis. Soon even the large Turin car factories were involved. The disturbances began in spring and continued until the autumn when the situation gradually returned to normal, but not for long. Towards the middle of 1907 a new crisis erupted and this time it was the car industry that suffered the most severe consequences. What was happening in Europe was later to happen in the United States where shares fell so low that companies were unable to pay dividends resulting in dismissals and collapse. In Italy, as elsewhere, only the strongest companies

1908, 10 hp Zedel with a 1692 cc, four-cylinder, side valve engine and shaft drive (Bonfanti collection)

The 1908 torpedo version of the four-cylinder Grégoire. The twin-block engine developed approximately 18 hp

Another 1908 Grégoire model, this one a two-seater racing car of 14/20 hp

Left *the 1908 Lancia Alpha, also known as the 18/24 hp in its touring version* Below *the 1909 Beta was fitted with Lancia's first single-block engine. Both cars are in the Lancia Museum in Turin*

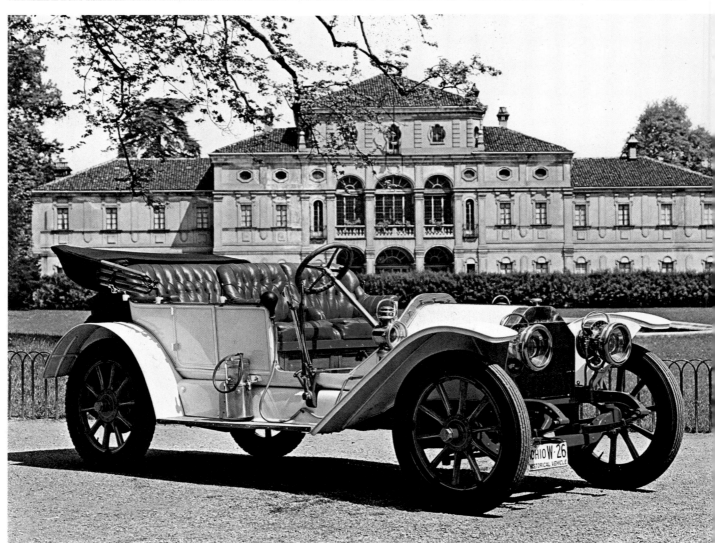

*The Pierce, which became the Pierce-Arrow in 1909
(until then 'Arrow' had simply been a model name).
This model is the 1909 version of the six-cylinder Great
Arrow introduced in 1906 (Harrah collection)*

1909 Rolland-Pilain racing car, with a four-cylinder, 2200 cc engine (Musée de Rochetaillée-sur-Saône)

such as Fiat, Itala, Isotta-Fraschini, SPA and Züst, managed to survive while many others were swept away in the crisis.

Yet at this very moment there was somebody with enough faith in the future of the car to set up a new business. This 'somebody' could only have been an exceptional person, as indeed Vincenzo Lancia was. He had been with Fiat since its founding, together with his friend Felice Nazzaro, and had been one of the creators of the Turin company's major successes. His intense passion for motoring, however, led to a desire to build motor cars bearing his own name. Thus, in 1906, he took the step. The separation from his patron caused no ill feeling and the fact that Lancia was to continue to run a racing team under the Fiat colours for another two years bears this out. The new company was registered in November 1906 but the first car, which was built by Vincenzo Lancia and his partner, Claudio Fogolin, did not appear until September 1907 and was not put into production until the beginning of 1908, at the height of the crisis in the car industry.

However, as though to reward Vincenzo Lancia's courage, that first model was very successful. More than a hundred examples were built until 1909 and the first one, which was exhibited at the Salone di Torino in 1908, was bought by Lancia's friend and colleague, Felice Nazzaro.

It was fitted with a side-valve, four-cylinder engine of 2·5 litres which produced 30 hp at 1800 rpm. By comparison, Fiat only reached this performance level four years later with the Zero. It also had a respectable maximum speed of 55 mph (90 kph). First marketed as the 18/24, it later became known as the Alpha,

thus establishing the Lancia company's policy of naming its models after the letters of the Greek alphabet.

In 1908, the Dialpha appeared (the prefix 'di' indicated a sports version of the basic model), the only six-cylinder Lancia built in the long period before 1950, the year in which the V6 Aurelia appeared. Then followed the Beta of 1909, the Gamma of 1910, the Delta, Epsilon and the Eta of 1911, all with four-cylinder engines, cubic capacities of between 3·1 and 5 litres and power outputs of 30 to 50 hp. The tendency to increase the cubic capacity was inevitable for people like Vincenzo Lancia who wanted to become established in the luxury car market.

With commercial success, industrial growth naturally followed. After the expansion of the first factory in the Via Ormea in 1909, the company moved in 1911 to larger premises in the Via Monginevro. 1911 also saw the appearance of the classic Lancia symbol, designed by Count Carlo Biscaretti di Ruffia, featuring a raised flagstaff.

The following year the first truck emerged from the Turin company. Known as the 1Z, it was similar in size to a large car. It was from the 1Z that one of the most successful Lancia models was created in 1913. This was the Theta, the first European car with electric lighting. It had a 5-litre, 70 hp, four-cylinder engine and a maximum speed of 75 mph (120 kph). It remained in production until 1919 and 1700 examples were built.

Vincenzo Lancia's cars came to occupy a special sector of the Italian market. They were good, average-sized cars for members of the public whose ideal vehicle was somewhere between the popular and robust Fiats and the

An elegant cabriolet featured in the 1909 Rochet-Schneider catalogue (Musée de Rochetaillée-sur-Saône)

Below right *the 1909 45PS Mercédès (Long Island Auto Museum)*
Below left *1909 Peugeot double phaeton with a 12 hp, twin-cylinder engine (J. J. Belet collection)*

extremely refined cars of Isotta-Fraschini. At Fiat, in fact, Giovanni Agnelli's ideas were being implemented more and more in matters of car production and in many ways were very similar to Henry Ford's. Like Ford, Agnelli believed in mass-production, but unlike his transatlantic colleague, who was an inveterate supporter of one model, Agnelli favoured wide distribution of as many models as could be manufactured.

Although less affected by the 1907 crisis than other companies, Fiat did not emerge unscathed. To accommodate its own growth, it had prepared, the year before, for the dissolution of the company and its immediate reforming with a capital of nine million lire. It was subsequently accused of feigning a profit in order to maintain its share value; a court case ensued in which the directors were acquitted. However, there remained an interesting contrast between the racing achievements of a triumphant year (1906)

which saw Fiat win all the important events, thereby gaining an international reputation, and the administrative situation which was one of the most precarious in its history. There were complex financial problems concerning the extent of the debts which were not solved until 1911, bringing arguments about the company's management in their wake.

With regard to production, Fiat's range was radically changed in 1908 with the replacement of a number of models and a general decrease in the engine size of its cars.

The early Fiat models are somewhat difficult to catalog. Because of the imperfections of the six-cylinder engines, the six-cylinder type 5 models of 1908 were quietly replaced by a new type 5 in 1909 with an almost identical cubic capacity but with a four-cylinder engine. This created some confusion in the enumeration of models, the number of which in the catalogue indicated the number of cylinders in the engine; a much less ambiguous system

prevailed with the series of models produced between 1910 and 1911.

At that time the smallest Fiat was the type 1B, produced in a variety of economy versions. This was followed by the type 2, a classic car of average size destined to become very popular. Finally there was the type 3 model with an engine of 3964 cc which in 1912 evolved into models 3A, 3C, and 4, still with an engine of 5·7 litres. The type 5 reappeared in 1912 with an enormous engine of more than 9 litres which had a power output of 60 hp. At the same time, its twin model, the type 6, was introduced. There then followed the little known type 7 with six cylinders in separately cast blocks.

However, the real novelty of 1912 was the 12/15 hp model which utilized the 1844 cc engine of the type 1B model but with a shorter, lighter chassis and a torpedo-shaped body. There just remained the Zero model, smaller than the type 1 model and part of the new 15 hp range; despite its unusual name, it was well received by customers. It was well finished and, above all, very solid, but certainly not an economy model in the French style, except perhaps in its price, which was one of the lowest on the Italian market at 8000 lire. The Zero

never sold well (only about 2000 examples were built before World War I put an end to production in 1915), but it was nevertheless an important step in the standardization of car production and in this sense a single body design, the torpedo-shape, was a decisive factor.

Between 1913 and 1914 all the cars in the range were subjected to radical cosmetic surgery. The body design was completely re-worked using oval-shaped radiators which were incorporated within the line of the hood. The streamlined effect was also accentuated by the paintwork. Fiats of that period had an economy of style hitherto unknown and this was undoubtedly a very important factor in making them so popular in Europe.

Fiat retained this range until the outbreak of World War I but, once the war was under way, kept only the 2B in production for civilian use, while some examples of the 4 were built for use by army staff. The extent of Fiat's war effort is shown by the 35,000 vehicles of various types which were supplied to the allied armies in 1918. In addition to cars, various trucks and special artillery caterpillar trucks and aero engines were built. The production

Above *a 1910 Rolls-Royce Silver Ghost, with a six-cylinder, 7·4-litre engine (Harrah collection)*
Right above *the Fiat Model 4, one of the Turin company's most popular pre-war models (Fiat Centro Storico)*
Right below *the model AB 8, made by Louis Delage in nine versions from 1910 to 1913 (Museo dell' Automobile Turin)*

Above *the Limited model, a large, six-cylinder,*
11.5-litre car made by Oldsmobile in 1910 (Harrah
collection)
Below *the 20/30 hp Bianchi landaulet of 1910*

of civilian cars reached a total of 16,542 in
1918, although sales to the public had virtually
stopped.

By now Turin had become the capital of the
Italian car industry and a number of other
companies gradually set up manufacture
there. Though not equal in status to Fiat,
many went on to make names for themselves.
Typical of these were Lancia, based in Turin
from 1908, and Itala, which had been established some years earlier. Itala came into
being through the enterprise of one of the
prolific (in the motoring field) and restless
Ceirano brothers. In this instance it was Matteo Ceirano who, in 1903, left Ceirano
Brothers, the company founded in 1901 with
his brother Giovanni Battista, and together
with other partners, founded Matteo Ceirano
& Co. Production was concentrated on the
4562 cc, 24 hp model with four cylinders, a
solid car probably inspired by the 16 hp model
designed by F. Ceirano Brothers, with which
Matteo Ceirano himself won first place in the
light car class at the Susa–Mont Cenis race of
1904.

Sporting success, soon followed by commercial success, led the directors to seek new
financing to enable expansion and to put the

company on a more secure footing, as Fiat had done. So, in September 1904 a group of Genoese men, headed by G. B. Figari, a director of the Bank of Liguria, took over the management of the company and changed the name to Itala Fabbrica Automobili SA. Matteo Ceirano stayed on as chief designer, but his position with the company did not last long and he left Itala a year later to found the SPA company with Michele Ansaldi. Despite the restlessness of the Ceirano brothers, which constantly drove them to new ventures, they were both experts on cars and all their companies were highly successful. So it was for Itala and so it was to be for SPA which soon became one of the major Turin manufacturers of cars, aircraft engines and industrial vehicles with a reputation for quality and robustness.

Meanwhile at Itala, the new management returned immediately to the building of racing cars. After reorganizing the sports division in 1905, the technical department, led by the engineer Alberto Ballocco who succeeded Ceirano as chief designer, introduced a 100 hp model with four cylinders, of almost 15 litres cubic capacity, with which Giovanni Battista Raggio won the Coppa Florio event.

In 1906 Itala employed Alessandro Cagno as its principal driver. He had come from Fiat where he had already proved his undoubted ability as a racing driver but where he was almost swamped by the strong personali-

ties of Vincenzo Lancia and Felice Nazzaro. This was the year of the first Targa Florio, an event dominated by Itala with four cars in the first five places; Cagno took first place, second position went to Graziani, fourth to Rigal and fifth to De Caters. 1907 was even more successful when the Itala 35/45 hp model, belonging to Prince Scipione Borghese, won the epic race from Peking to Paris, one of the most extraordinary motoring events of all time.

Above *An Isotta-Fraschini torpedo, model BN 30/40 hp of 1910 (Museo dell' Automobile, Turin)*

Below *The Léon Bollée double berlina of 1911*

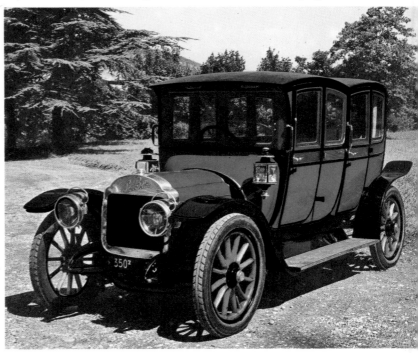

The 1910 four-cylinder Hansa, a small sports car built by Hansa Automobil Gesellschaft. The German company, founded in 1905, merged with Lloyd Motoren Werke of Bremen in 1914, becoming Hansa-Lloyd AG

From 1905 onwards the construction of tourers developed alongside the sports division under the energetic guidance of engineer Ballocco. This section of production was also favoured by an agreement with Fiat, their keenest rival, in 1906 whereby the two companies undertook to inform each other about their respective programmes for a period of four years. So, until 1909, Itala could work in peace, planning its output without risks. It was largely due to this situation of relative tranquillity that enabled Itala to survive the economic crisis of 1907 without serious harm and its recovery was quick and efficient. In 1911 a catalog published by the company read: 'As with all great international companies, Itala can offer its vast clientele not only the most extensive range of tourers and racing cars from 12 to 120 hp, but also a practical range of industrial vehicles, omnibuses,

After building steam cars for ten years, White changed to building petrol cars in 1910. The first White with an internal combustion engine was the model GA Touring which is illustrated here (Harrah collection)

trucks and air and marine engines of all types.' Even bearing in mind the inevitable exaggeration of a publicity statement, it was not really too far from the truth. Production was, in fact, very varied and included new models of cars ranging from the 2235 cc, 14/18 hp model to the 60 and 75 hp models with engines of 11,148 and 12,930 cc respectively.

At the Salone dell'Automobile in Turin in 1911 a new and original technical novelty was presented. This was the 'valveless' engine – which had rotary or sleeve valves – designed by Alberto Ballocco, and was the first of its kind to be built in Italy. Its reliability and silence were its main characteristics and the results were so favorable that the engine was installed in the cars prepared for the 1913 season.

The outbreak of war saw Itala still producing models with sleeve-valve engines in four versions with different cubic capacities, as well as

the Model 39 which remained in production until 1917. These activities were soon curtailed, however, and then almost completely set aside in favour of war production. Although Itala remained in existence until 1934, its golden age was now over; a series of unfortunate circumstances prevented the company from repeating its excellent pre-war results.

Even though Turin represented the greatest centre of the Italian car industry, Milan also made its contribution to motoring from the beginning of the century. Bianchi, Isotta-Fraschini and Alfa Romeo were all Milanese. Of the three, Isotta-Fraschini was undoubtedly the most aristocratic and the only Italian company manufacturing machines comparable to the most exclusive car in the world, the Rolls-Royce. The model which put it on the same level was the fabulous type 8, designed by Giustino Cattaneo between 1916 and 1918

The 1911 20 hp Empire. Built by the Indianapolis company of the same name from 1909 to 1912, the model was promoted as the 'Little Aristocrat'

Right *the 1911 Rolls-Royce Silver Ghost roi-des-Belges, with bodywork by Barker. The famous winged figure, called the 'Spirit of Ecstasy' can be seen on the radiator and first appeared in that year*

Right *an original spider built in 1911–1912 by the French coachbuilder, Labourdette on a Delaunay-Belleville chassis and featuring wickerwork panelling*

The Mercer 35-R Raceabout designed by Finlay R. Porter in 1911, offered to American motorists as a racing car for touring

and then launched on the market around 1920. Isotta-Fraschini was not exclusively identified by this dream car, however, and all its business before World War I was characterized by ingenuity of design, precision of workmanship and the kind of quality which made its cars superior to the average car of the time.

Founded in January 1900 by a group of partners including the lawyer Cesare Isotta, the Vincenzo brothers, Oreste and Antonio Fraschini, Riccardo Bencetti, Paolo Meda and Ludovico Prinetti, Isotta-Fraschini began in the motoring business by representing the French Renault cars, then passed on to assembling foreign cars and finally imported engines from France which were then mounted on to chassis of their own design. Unfortunately, the cars which resulted were still too similar

to the Renault to avoid accusations of plagiarism and Isotta-Fraschini soon set about building original models.

At this point the enterprise could have faded into obscurity. Many other similar companies had tried to produce their own type of vehicle without being able to find the market to sell it. Fortunately, the Milanese company was able to rely on a number of favorable factors, including the relative abundance of capital, continuity of credit, the excellent social standing of its directors (especially Vincenzo Fraschini), the ability of its designers who made timely innovations destined to become standard in modern motoring, and finally the personalities of its engineers, among whom were Trucco, Maserati and Chiribiri.

The creator of the initial success of the Milanese make was the designer Giuseppe Stefanini who designed all the Isotta-Fraschini cars from 1903 to 1905. Also designed by him was the overhead-camshaft 100 hp model of 1905, and the FE model of 1908, a 1200 cc single-cylinder-engine car, which in itself would have made a designer's name.

In 1905 Stefanini was assisted by Giustino Cattaneo who later replaced him as head of the technical department. Cattaneo came from the Venetian school of motoring run by Enrico Bernardi and Vittorio Rossi and then worked for Florentia and Züst. He left his personal mark on the final version of the three tourers, models A, B and C, and he designed the winning cars in the Coppa Florio of Brescia in 1907 and the Targa Florio of 1908. These machines followed conventional design but produced an exceptional amount of power. He designed a brake control system on the front wheels which he patented in 1910 and which later became standard on cars worldwide.

When the 1907 crisis hit the European motoring industry, which had become inflated by too many companies competing for a small market, Isotta-Fraschini was hailed by the press as an example of good management in difficult times; it ended the year with a small profit of 9532 lire. Together with Itala, on which orders had rained since their victories in the year's major races and also the incredible Peking–Paris race, the Milanese company was one of the few Italian firms to enjoy a degree of financial stability. The profit was in fact counteracted by heavy debts for which provision had to be made.

In spite of an uncertain future, Isotta-Fraschini's capital rose to four million lire in 1907 (double that of 1906). The money was found by means of an agreement with the Société Lorraine des Anciens Etablissements De Dietrich et Cie. It bought half of Isotta's shares with an undertaking to place its own European sales network at Isotta's disposal, to buy at least 500 Milanese chassis a year, and to produce cars designed in Milan in its own factories at Lunéville and its associate factory in Marseille.

As a result of this alliance with Lorraine-De Dietrich, Isotta-Fraschini developed driveshaft transmission which was at first used only for less powerful engines in town cars.

One of the most famous Austin models was the Seven of the 'twenties and 'thirties, but Austin had previously built 7 hp cars. The model illustrated is the 1911 version which was an updated version of the original 7 hp of 1909 (National Motor Museum)

The golden period in the field of racing for Isotta-Fraschini was between 1907 and 1908, at the height of the agreement with Lorraine-De Dietrich. Besides winning Italian races, Isotta-Fraschini was triumphant in America and all these successes resulted in putting Lorraine-De Dietrich in the shade. However, at the Coppa Florio in Bologna in 1908 the French company insisted that the cars to be driven by the Isotta-Fraschini drivers carry the Lorraine-De Dietrich name only and that the Italian company should not be present at the awards.

Between 1909 and 1910, the Milanese company, no longer able to tolerate the alliance with Lorraine-De Dietrich, broke with them. Fortunately the company had access to exclusively Italian investment which enabled it to regain its financial stability and continue in business. The operation was successful and by 1911 the company was in a position to pay a dividend of 6 per cent. In the meantime, the factory had begun building aero engines and airships and in this field, too, Giustino Cattaneo was outstanding. Besides his aero-

nautical engineering achievements, he designed an extremely advanced engine, the so-called 100/120 hp unit – which had an actual power output of 140 hp. The engine had four cylinders and an overhead camshaft which operated the four valves per cylinder. This engine, with minor modifications, was installed in three large tourers, the KM, TM and IM models, which would have achieved great things if the arrival of World War I had not intervened.

The post-war period saw Isotta-Fraschini enter the restricted market of luxury car manufacturers. On this level there were only two main rivals in Europe, Rolls-Royce and Hispano-Suiza. By a strange coincidence all three were rivals not only in motoring but also in aeronautics and in many ways their histories are very similar.

Hispano-Suiza was one of the few Spanish motoring companies and the only one to achieve fame. The creator of Hispano-Suiza's success was the Swiss engineer Marc Birkigt. Birkigt arrived in Barcelona in 1899, after

The 1911 12 hp Alfa Romeo. The following year it's power output was increased and it was renamed the 15 hp. Further modified in 1914, it was given the designation 15/20 hp

working for a Swiss watch company, at the invitation of a college friend who had worked out a design for the construction of electric omnibuses. While working for his friend's company, named De La Cuadra after one of the directors, Enrique De La Cuadra, Birkigt took over responsibility for the design department and technical direction. He soon completed work on a large vehicle with an electric motor which in 1900 had an unfortunate test run in the square of Barcelona. Birkigt then took to the internal combustion engine and, abandoning the idea of building omnibuses, began designing a car.

By this time, however, De La Cuadra was in severe financial trouble and was taken over by J. Castro who confirmed Birkigt's appointment as technical director. In 1903 he built two cars, one with a 4 hp, single-cylinder engine, the other with a twin-cylinder engine of 8 hp, but neither progressed beyond the prototype stage. Soon after, two other models appeared, one a 10 hp twin-cylinder model, the other using a 14 hp four-cylinder engine,

both designed by the Swiss engineer for Castro. They were good cars and revealed the engineer's meticulous attention to detail, a characteristic which was later to appear in his better-known creations. At that time, however, Birkigt's designs were not commercially successful. The Castro company duly found itself in financial difficulties and was taken over by Damian Mateu in 1904. Once again, Birkigt retained his position as technical director, while the company's name was changed to Hispano-Suiza.

The first car to carry the new name was a 20 hp, four-cylinder model similar to the machine which had appeared the previous year under the Castro name. It was also vaguely inspired by a Décauville model which Birkigt had bought in order to study its technical secrets (the same type of car was bought at about the same time by Frederick Henry Royce for the same purpose).

At the Salon de Paris in 1907, Birkigt exhibited a 40 hp, four-cylinder model while the following year saw a refined six-cylinder model

Left a 1905 20 hp Rolls-Royce, the body of which is an exact replica of one of the Tourist Trophy cars of that year. This car was built from two identical chassis found at Brae Cottage, Knutsford, where Sir Henry Royce lived for many years (National Motor Museum)
Below two views of the 1903 60 hp touring car. A similar machine won the 1903 Gordon Bennett Cup at the hands of Camille Jenatzy

make its appearance. This marked the first step in the production of luxury cars, later to become a characteristic of the Spanish company. However, before definitely going in that direction, Birkigt chose to continue making conventional four-cylinder cars for another few years.

The jump up market came in 1911 with the introduction of the Alfonso XIII model. Named in honour of the King of Spain, and based on the car which won the Coupe de l'Auto competition of 1910, it established Hispano-Suiza in the European market. An excellent car which was comfortable, luxuriously finished and with an exceptionally high standard of engineering, the Alfonso XIII was soon being sold throughout Europe and was the Spanish company's best model in the period preceding World War I.

In the meantime, in 1911, Hispano-Suiza opened a French subsidiary in Levallois, in the suburbs of Paris, which was to prove very important for the future of the company. This initiative had been taken by Birkigt himself during a trip to Paris in 1910 when he won the Coupe de l'Auto. The Swiss engineer realized that only a firmer foothold in the French market would enable Hispano-Suiza to gain international recognition. In those days world motoring still revolved around France and the Salon de Paris, the most famous international

trade fair. The intuition proved correct and it was at Levallois that Birkigt's most prestigious cars were made.

In 1914, after the construction of an aluminium-bodied racing car, called *The Sardine*, which only won a few prizes in minor Spanish events, the indefatigable Swiss engineer began work on a new car which was to replace the Alfonso XIII. The idea came to him after he had had an opportunity to test a Rolls Royce which he judged to be decidedly superior to his own designs, and which stimulated his pride as an engineer to attempting to equal, if not excel, the quality of the British cars. The outbreak of the war, however, forced Birkigt to postpone his idea and to concentrate on aero engines exclusively. In this field, too, his talents as an engineer were proved in the construction of excellent engines with eight and twelve cylinders which were installed in the fastest French fighter planes of World War I; and, as had happened to Cattaneo, Birkigt's aeronautical constructions were an inexhaustible well of inspiration for future cars.

The first Hispano-Suiza to benefit from the engineer's aeronautical experience was the extraordinary H6B, which appeared in 1919 and with which Birkigt achieved his ambition of creating a Franco-Spanish equivalent of the Rolls-Royce. For style and quality the

Above *the impressive Winton 17B Touring with seven seats, built in 1911. It was one of the most expensive American de-luxe cars of the period and had a six-cylinder, three-block engine, of 9500 cc and 45 hp (Harrah collection)*
Opposite Above right *an elegant 1911 racing torpedo on a 20 hp Renault chassis (Renault collection)*
Below right *the Oakland model A of 1911, in runabout guise.*

H6B was really able to stand alongside its aristocratic Anglo-Saxon rival.

At this point, to complete the triad of aristocratic makes, comes Rolls-Royce which, compared to its two European competitors, can boast a much longer tradition. Of the

three, in fact, it is the only one which has survived, maintaining its high standard until the present day. Indeed, many enthusiasts regard the Rolls-Royce as 'the best car in the world'.

It has already been shown how in the course of the history of these three companies it is easy to find similarities, at times even in the smallest details. This was the case, for instance, of the Décauville bought second-hand by Frederick Henry Royce which served as a starting point for his first car in 1904. In the same year, and some thousands of miles away, Marc Birkigt had also bought a Décauville and had used it as a basis for the first Hispano-Suiza car. For what reason both chose the French car as their inspiration will never be known, especially as the Décauville did not offer any particular technical or structural characteristics superior to those of other cars. However, Royce's prototype retained a certain similarity to the French car and shared its twin-cylinder, front-mounted engine, conical clutch, three-speed gearbox and final drive by helical gear.

Frederick Henry Royce ran a small company in Manchester where he produced cranes and winches. His entry into the field of car manufacturing could have been limited to one experimental car had it not attracted the attention of Charles Stewart Rolls, one of the founder members of the British Automobile Club and owner of a London agency for the sale of French and Belgian cars. So, from the meeting between the two men, Rolls-Royce was to be born in 1906 for the production of cars designed by Royce.

Four models based on Royce's original prototype were manufactured. They were a twin-cylinder 10 hp version, a 15 hp, three-cylinder model with a cubic capacity of three litres, a 20 hp example with four cylinders and a 30 hp model with six cylinders. The output of these cars remained modest, and by 1907 less than a hundred examples had been built.

On the other hand only three examples were built of a special car, fitted with a futuristic 90° V8 cylinder engine of around 3·5 liters, which was designed either as a brougham with the engine under the floor of the car, or as a two-seater phaeton. The second version, apart from its appearance, was not built as a sports car; indeed, it was fitted with an automatic speed control unit which prevented it from exceeding 30 mph, the maximum allowed in most parts of England.

In 1905 a private 20 hp car was awarded second place in the Tourist Trophy. Rolls, who had to withdraw from that race because of gearbox failure, gained his revenge the following year by an absolute victory with an average speed of 39·22 mph (63·25 kph). Claude Johnson, already a partner of Rolls in his previous business and who remained in the company after it had changed its production, was against the company's sports policy, but he sponsored a contest, the so-called 'battle of cylinders', between a 30 hp, six-cylinder Rolls-Royce and a powerful Martini four-cylinder car. The Rolls-Royce won the contest.

At the London Fair of 1906 the first Rolls Royce was presented, as the two partners had by then consolidated their agreement of 1904 and formed a company. The model in question was the 40/45 hp with six cylinders, later called the Silver Ghost and bearing all the characteristics of a luxury car which made and still make Rolls-Royce cars the best.

From the beginning Rolls-Royce were distinguished by their exceptional flexibility, silence and robustness, in addition to their elegance and comfort. Even then their indestructible engines were able to travel more than 185,000 miles with simple and ordinary maintenance. In 1907, a car which was tested by officers of the Automobile Club ran continuously for 15,000 miles (24,000 km) and the repairs necessary at the end of the experiment were so negligible that they only amounted to £3. Four years later a Silver Ghost successfully completed what is perhaps the most famous test undertaken by a Rolls-Royce when it was driven from London to Edinburgh and back in direct third and overdrive fourth gears and, upon arrival, registered an average consumption of one gallon every 17·8 miles (11·6 litres per 100 km). This sensational performance allowed the British company to dethrone the rival model, the Napier, from its traditional position as leader of luxury, six-cylinder cars.

In the meantime, the increase in demand had outstripped production capacity in the small Manchester factory and in 1907 the company moved to new premises in Derby.

Two views of the Chevrolet Classic Six of 1912, powered by a six-cylinder engine of 4·9 litres capacity
Opposite page
Top *the Fiat Model 2 (Fiat Centro Storico)*
Below *the NAG K2, a double phaeton. Both cars date from 1912*

Soon after, Johnson, who had assumed responsibility for commercial direction, realized that it was not enough just to produce an excellent car and that it was also necessary to establish a close rapport with clients. So, a system was introduced whereby the company's mechanics carried out regular after-sales service at the client's home; a driving school was also set up. The success of this venture was considerable both at home and abroad, and by 1913 there were official service stations in five European capitals. From the beginning of 1908 there was a single model policy and until the end of 1922 the Silver Ghost remained alone to defend the prestige of the British company. Of course, it underwent improvements to conform to technical progress which was slowly being introduced to the industry. The installation of electric lighting dated from 1914, while the self-starters did not appear until 1919 because of Rolls-Royce's extreme caution in introducing novelties.

During World War I, the Derby company increased its output of aero engines, a field in which it had excelled since 1908. Civil production was resumed in 1919 and still continues, maintaining its high level of quality and defending a tradition and prestige which has lasted more than seventy years.

Rolls-Royce is undoubtedly the jewel of the British motoring industry but its contribution to the popularity of the car is minimal. The public in general could only dream of owning a Rolls-Royce, but at the moment of choosing had to opt for less grandiose products, and particularly less expensive ones, like the Humber, Austin and Morris. Of these three companies the oldest is Humber, dating back to 1868 when Thomas Humber began building bicycles in Beeston, Nottinghamshire. Nineteen years later a new plant was established in Coventry where experimental work began on the internal combustion engine. For a time, Humber was part of Harry Lawson's syndicate and was engaged in the production of vehicles of dubious design like the Pennington Tricar, the Motette Coventry and the MD.

The first real car appeared in 1901. This was an extremely simple vehicle with either a single or twin-cylinder engine and cardan-shaft transmission. The following year the 12 hp in-line four-cylinder engine appeared, and in 1903 there were more efficient models with blocks cast in pairs and side valves.

When production reached a substantial level, the Coventry plant concentrated on economy models while the superior vehicles were constructed at Beeston. The first mass-produced model from Coventry was the Humberette of 1903, a single-cylinder 613 cc vehicle, of which at least five hundred were sold in just six months. Production of Humberettes continued in various forms until

Opposite *the 1912 Hispano-Suiza Alfonso XIII in racing guise, which combined excellent performance with a luxurious finish (Le Mans Museum)* **Right** *two Delaunay-Belleville six-cylinder models of 1912, the Victoria Touring model and the Roadster model (far right)*

1905, some of which featured twin-cylinder engines.

In 1906 the company's profits exceeded £100,000 and so further expansion was discussed with the closure of both small plants and the installation of one larger and more modern complex in Coventry. In the euphoria of the moment, even an aeronautical division was set up. However, all this culminated in a financial crisis in 1909, aggravated by the failure of a new 1525 cc car with which it had been hoped to renew the popularity of the marque instigated by the Humberette. This was resumed in 1913 with a successful, low-cost model which enabled the Coventry company to regain its lost position. The new Humberette had a vee-twin-cylinder engine, cooled by air, of 998 cc and 11.5 hp. Its main attraction lay in its price, which was only £120, and for this reason it was possible to produce them at the rate of seventy cars per week in the first year. However, despite its undoubted success, this model was not sold after the war when

Humber chose to move up market and build medium-priced cars, well made and with elegant bodywork. Even with the higher price, sales remained constant at about 3000 a year for the whole of the following decade.

In 1906 when Humber was already an established concern, another company, destined to become one of the biggest in Britain, appeared to contend first place in the section of popular cars. This was the Austin Motor Company, founded by Herbert Austin, who had been managing director of Wolseley. With an initial capital of only £5000, the new company had to be content with buying and equipping an old disused canning factory, near Longbridge, seven miles south of Birmingham.

The design of the first Austin car was shown at the London Fair in November 1905, with the announcement that deliveries would begin in March 1906 at a price of £650. Several orders were taken for a car which only existed on paper and which had to be manufactured

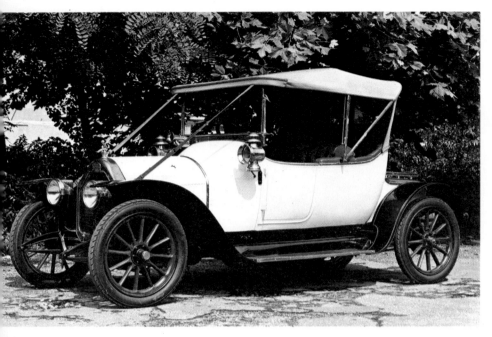

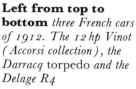

Left from top to bottom *three French cars of 1912. The 12 hp Vinot (Accorsi collection), the* Darracq *torpedo and the* Delage R4

by a company not yet formed. However, Herbert Austin and his partner kept their promises made at the Fair and in April 1906 (one month late being quite acceptable), they presented their first creation to the trade press. This was the 15/20 hp with four vertical cylinders and opposed side valves and, consequently, two camshafts. All this was conventional, but the crankshaft, made of nickel-chromium steel, was not in the least conventional and rotated on five main bearings while the valves were controlled by an interposed oscillator. Other parts included an automatic Krebs carburetor and two ignition systems which could be used alternately, a low voltage magnet and a coil and battery system. The engine was lubricated under pressure and fed from a rear tank and had a power of 32 hp at 900 rpm and a capacity of 4400 cc.

The 15/20 hp, although a middle-upper market car, became popular with the public and 106 examples were built, thus giving Austin the incentive for mass-production. A characteristic from the beginning was a certain conservatism of structure, accompanied by very precise workmanship and occasionally enlivened by original innovations from Herbert Austin himself.

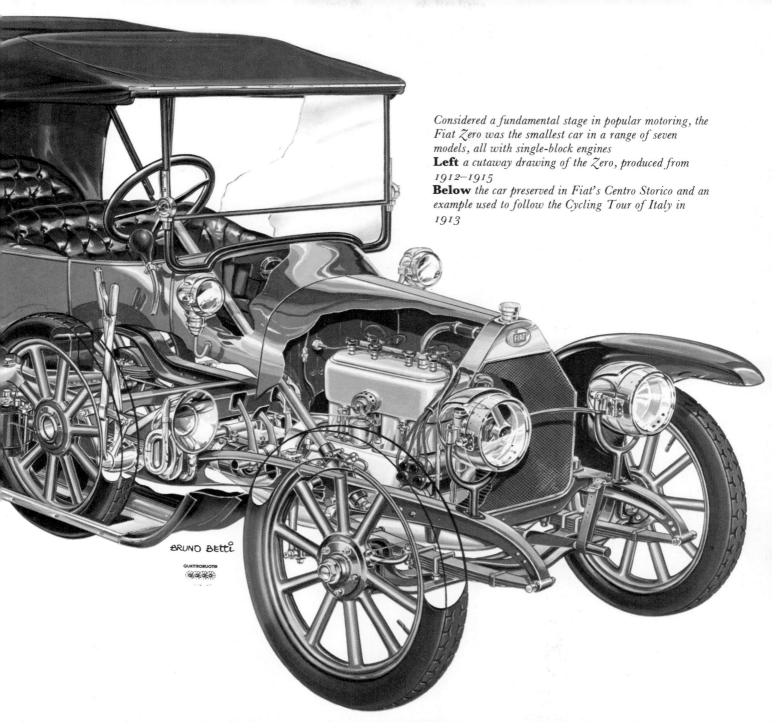

Considered a fundamental stage in popular motoring, the
Fiat Zero was the smallest car in a range of seven
models, all with single-block engines
Left a cutaway drawing of the Zero, produced from
1912–1915
Below the car preserved in Fiat's Centro Storico and an
example used to follow the Cycling Tour of Italy in
1913

BRUNO BETTI

QUATTRORUOTE

The two-seater Peugeot Bébé of 1912, designed by
Ettore Bugatti (J. J. Belet collection)

At the end of the first decade of the century, Austin occupied an important place in the home market as well as in the colonial market; it employed about one thousand workers and the Longbridge plants operated a tight schedule with three daily shifts. The range of models had increased and went from the small single-cylinder 7 hp to the four-cylinder 10/60 hp and the six-cylinder, 50 hp model. The smallest car in the range was renamed and became immortalized as the Seven, and it was considered by many to be the British equivalent of the Ford T. Even though production figures were on a completely different scale (300,000 as opposed to 15 million), the Seven had a similar impact as the T on the promotion of mass-production.

However, before finally turning to popular cars, Austin introduced the Twenty, an intermediate car of American inspiration. In the immediate post-war period, the English market was invaded by a large number of American cars which were spacious, not very well finished but at prices which were so low as to indicate possible ruin for British manufacturers. Austin, like the others, at first thought that the public liked this sort of car and so presented the Twenty as a similarly spacious, easy to drive and fairly cheap car, but with a better finish than its American rivals. It soon transpired that the Americanized productions were unsuited to English motorists who had simpler and more traditional tastes. As a result, Austin opted for a popular, robust and efficient car, without frills and of sound construction. Thus, the Seven came into being, a typically British model with its only 'American' feature being in its mass-production.

Like Austin, William Morris was also a firm believer in the economy car, built by American methods and sold at a very low price. But unlike his colleague, Morris was not a designer in the full sense of the word, although he had a sound engineering mind. For this reason, when in 1913 he decided to add car manufacturing to his car sales and service business, he presented a car which was the product of various parts of different origin. Called the Morris Oxford, this model compensated for its lack of originality by its very attractive price of only £175, so much so that it quickly became established on the English market with approximately 1500 examples produced. Even cheaper was the following model, the Cowley, which was an-

nounced shortly after the declaration of war. As Morris was not yet in a position to introduce a mass-production assembly line system in his plant in Oxford, he compromised and imported eighty per cent of the parts for the Cowley directly from the United States, which he then assembled with the remaining twenty per cent which came from Britain. Mobilization permitted an output of only 1450 cars out

The Rambler Cross Country of 1912, with four-cylinder engine (Harrah collection)

The 1912 Delahaye model 32 with four-cylinder engine

of a proposed 3000.

The car in Great Britain had many obstacles to overcome before reaching the level of popularity in other European countries, and in this negative atmosphere it is easy to understand how racing cars were also rather limited, although Brooklands was the first European race track when it was built in 1907. However, this arose from the simple fact that in those days racing on public roads was forbidden. For this reason, one of the few English companies to build racing cars in the period before World War I was Napier which succeeded brilliantly and achieved international fame. It is significant that the Napier's green color which appeared in 1902, later became the official color of English racing cars, British Racing Green. In addition to racing, Napier was also successful in the production of standard tourers and in particular luxury six-cylinder-engined cars which were only excelled by Rolls-Royces.

Napier was created in 1808 as an engineering company for the production of guns, scales and machines for coining and printing money. Towards the end of the century, the factory, which was in Lambeth, South London, was directed by the founder's nephew, Stanley Napier, who was a friend of another motoring enthusiast, Selwyn Francis Edge. So, when in 1899 Edge bought an 1896 Panhard, Napier immediately tried to make it more powerful and designed a vertical twin-cylinder engine with automatic inlet valves. It was this engine which was installed in the first Napier car, introduced in 1900 and built according to traditional techniques, that is with a chassis of reinforced wood, four forward and four reverse speeds, an LT coil and magneto ignition system and elliptical leaf spring suspension.

From the beginning, the two friends showed a keen interest in racing and in the first year of business as car manufacturers entered one of their cars in the Paris–Toulouse race. The following year, they produced a huge four-cylinder engine of 17,157 cc with a power output of 107 hp at 800 rpm. It weighed almost two tons (2000 kg) which caused rapid wear of the tyres, and the car was withdrawn from the Gordon Bennett Cup of that year.

After these unfortunate experiences, Edge and Napier finally hit upon the winning formula with a small four-cylinder car of 6·6 liters with which Edge himself won the Gordon Bennett Cup in 1902. This victory prompted the company to increase considerably production which rose from 100 to 250 units that year and decided the transfer of the plant to larger premises in Acton in West London in 1903.

The 1904 Napier catalog included a small four-cylinder car of 12 hp, the 15, 20 and 24 hp, all with four cylinders but of great power and cubic capacity, and the 18 hp, with a revolutionary six-cylinder engine with inlet valves in the cylinder head and the exhaust valves at the base. On the other hand, the 15,100 cc L48, the first Napier racing car with six cylinders, was built exclusively for racing and Napier felt that a two-speed gearbox was sufficient as the engine had enormous flexibility. His conviction proved erroneous, however, and was shown up at the 1905 Gordon Bennett Cup. The car got better results in competitions of pure speed such as the world record for the mile set by Arthur Macdonald in 1905 at 104·4 mph (168·417 kph) and the national record for the kilometre at 97 mph (156·51 kph).

In 1908 the car, by this time named *Samson*, was modified by increasing the stroke (178 mm) which brought the cubic capacity to over 20 liters and the power to 212 hp at 2500 rpm. It was with this car that Frank Newton took part in the contest with the Fiat SB4 of Felice Nazzaro on the Brooklands circuit. Although the Fiat won, the contest was excellent publicity for Napier.

Among Napier's other speed achievements was the twenty-four hour record broken by Edge at Brooklands in 1907 at an average speed of 65·8 mph (106·08 kph), while William Watson's victory in the 1908 Tourist Trophy should also be remembered.

Later, Napier thinned out its own participation in the big international races and increased its output of conventional cars which reached its height between 1901 and 1911. At the end of 1912, Edge left the company, which gradually took to the construction of aero engines, although it retained its motoring division until 1924.

Turning again to the history of motoring in Germany, the entire period from 1904 to 1919 was dominated by the two big companies, Daimler and Benz. However, the protagonists had changed as Gottlieb Daimler had died in 1900 and Karl Benz had retired in 1904 because of differences in opinion about the choice of production. Of the old guard, only Wilhelm Maybach remained to manage the fortunes of Daimler, but even his life with the Cannstatt company was not to last for long and he left it in 1907. He was replaced by Paul Daimler, Gottlieb's son who from 1902 to 1905 had run Austro-Daimler. He guided production towards cars of low cubic capacity, like the 8/18, the 10/20 and the 14/30 with four cylinders and cardan shaft transmission, although he kept the big luxurious six-cylinder cars which Maybach had designed in 1906.

Daimler's commitment to racing remained unchanged and with its Mercédès models the company continued to win important events like the French Grand Prix of 1908. The victorious car, designed specially for the occasion, was a four-cylinder of 135 hp with inlet valves on the cylinder head and the exhaust valves mounted vertically at the side.

In 1909 Daimler bought Charles J. Knight's patents for his sleeve-valve engine and, after a series of long and difficult experiments, he solved the problem of the exhaust manifolding which had been under high pressure. At last, the Knight engine could be used in several Mercédès models and was from 1910 to 1924. The four-cylinder 16/45 and the 16/50 were excellent examples of the type.

When production of the large six-cylinder cars of 1911 was discontinued, Paul Daimler presented a new high-performance tourer. It was a 9500 cc, four-cylinder called Model 37/90 which was sold in various versions (the chassis alone cost 26,000 marks in 1913), all with racing overtones, and were characterized by their V-shaped radiators and by the external exhaust pipes. Technically, the car was unusual in that it had three valves per cylinder (one inlet and two exhaust), lubrication by piston pumps of adjustable capacity (the Friedman system), wet liners and double ignition by magneto and battery. Transmission was by twin chains enclosed in special housings, while the brakes, due to the colossal weight of the car, were cooled by water.

Like other companies in Germany, Daimler was interested in the design and construction of aero engines in the period immediately preceding World War I, and these were later used on racing cars with the necessary modifications. For instance, the six-cylinder 120 hp engine with overhead camshafts was used in three Mercédès which took part in the French Grand Prix of 1913 and 1914 and which won the first three places in 1914. This achievement, however, represented the end of the *belle époque* of motor racing for Daimler, as for all the other European companies, and coincided with the outbreak of the war.

In the meantime, Karl Benz's retirement had given Benz a free reign to develop its racing production which until then had been vetoed by Benz. The young engineer Hans Nibel, who joined the company in 1905 and later became the technical director, was a great racing enthusiast. He steered production towards seeking increasingly higher performances and eventually produced the famous 200 hp Blitzen Benz and the sports models Prinz Heinrich and the Grand Prix. From 1906 onwards, Benz became the keenest rivals of Mercédès. Drivers of note like Victor Héméry, Fritz Erle and René Hanriot made up *the* team to be beaten on international circuits.

In 1906 a large car was launched by Benz in competition with the Daimler 60PS and

had the same power; this represented the only occasion that Benz produced large cars. More popular was the smaller 40 hp model, built in a variety of forms and used in the Herkomer races, a classic competition similar to the Prinz Heinrich Fahrt. Both these races had a considerable influence on the development of German technology in the first decade of the century. For example, the 1908 Prinz Heinrich Fahrt limited the cylinder bore while the stroke was unrestricted. This led to the development of long-stroke engines which were then used for more than thirty years.

Among the greatest sporting successes of those years were the Herkomer victories of 1907, the Prinz Heinrich Fahrt and the Petersburg–Moscow of 1908, the Gaillon uphill race and the 1910 American Grand Prix. The list of records broken by Benz is also long. In 1909 at Daytona, Bruce Brown set the mile record and the ten-mile records with a standing-start at 109 mph (175 kph) and 114 mph (184 kph) respectively. The car was a Blitzen Benz 150PS, the same as that used by Robertson who, in the course of the same record-breaking session, set the record for five miles at 109 mph (174·5 kph). Still in 1909, Barney Oldfield improved on the record of the fixed

mile, while Héméry, in a Benz 200, broke the half mile and kilometre records. The following year the list grew when Oldfield broke the record at 131·724 mph (211·4 kph) in a Blitzen Benz 200 at Daytona and retained the record until Burman broke it in 1911 at 141–73 mph (228·1 kph).

With so many successes, Benz entered the second decade of the century in a prominent position in the European motoring industry. Even from the technical point of view, there were innovations of merit and reliability appearing alongside their traditional quality of precision, which consolidated the fame of the Mannheim company.

Meanwhile, the company's technical staff had become strengthened by the arrival of a man called Karl Ketterer who had come from SAF in Gaggenau which was taken over by Benz in 1910. In 1911 Karl Ketterer won a competition promoted by Benz among his own engineers for the design of an economy car. He designed a four-cylinder car in which the design departed from the technology of the day in that the cylinder block detached from the cylinders which in turn were built in units of one or two. Ketterer's design can be considered as a precursor of the modern

The Stutz Bearcat speedster with a four-cylinder, 6·5-litre engine of over 60 hp (Harrah collection). Launched in 1912 this model with its distinctively sporting appearance, was the Mercer Raceabout's greatest rival

single block. The model, marketed as the 8/20PS model, entered production at the end of 1911.

In 1912, adapting to the needs of the moment, Benz began building aero engines which found widespread application in the course of World War I. At the end of the war even the Mannheim company was faced with the post-war crisis which was difficult to overcome. For several years it succeeded in remaining solvent by its own strength, but then had to follow the example of other motoring companies which had merged in order to survive, giving birth to large industrial groups. Benz found its ideal partner in what had always been its greatest rival, Daimler. Thus Daimler-Benz was created in 1926. This was a particularly sensible merger as they had both been outstanding innovators during the early age of motoring and had designed and built some of the most beautiful cars of all time.

Not only nationally, but throughout Europe, the Mercédès represented the last word in cars with sophisticated engineering

A two-seater version of the 1912 Renault AX (J. J. Belet collection). It had the usual twin-cylinder engine with which all the Billancourt company's economy models were fitted

Left *the Itala torpedo model 25/35 hp of 1912–13 (Museo dell'Automobile, Turin). It was third in terms of cubic capacity in the range of touring models offered by the Turin company, and had a twin-block engine (illustrated above) of 5401 cc*

Above *two 1913 Panhard & Levassor models, the X19 from the Quattroruote collection, and a 2600 cc touring model*

as the wide use of nickelchromium steel and the generous application of ball-bearings which reveal Horch's tendency towards technical perfection. However, it was to be the fourth model, the 1904 16/20 of 2613 cc, which was destined to personify Horch's technology. It had several features, such as the system of superimposed valves, inlet in the head and side exhaust, which remained in production for many years. At that time, Horch could not produce more than two cars a week but these were expensive and therefore not very competitive in a market which was inflated by the excessive variety of cars offered.

What brought Horch fame was the victory in the second Herkomer Trophy, a great speed test in which Rudolf Stöss, driving one of the smallest Horch cars, the 18/20, beat a 40 hp Benz and a 70 hp Mercédès.

The key to the success of the small Horch lay in the modernity of the design which sought to reconcile the requirements of light town cars, which were fragile and unsuited to touring, and those monsters of huge cubic capacity which appeared necessary to attain a certain degree of power and comfort. In spite of the apparent contradiction, the commercial success following the Herkomer victory, although strengthening the company's position, weakened the personal power of August Horch who was opposed to the policies of the board of directors. Every decision he made, particularly regarding production, was treated with suspicion by the board whose members were more interested in profitability than refined engineering for its own sake. The atmosphere of mutual distrust was not even cleared with commercial success and in June 1909 August Horch resigned and left the company after yet another argument. The validity of his ideas was later recognized by the fact that all the models produced by the Zwickau company until after the war were built along the general lines of his earlier designs.

However, August Horch's exit from the world of motoring was only temporary. After a month in fact, on 16 July 1909, he founded a new motoring company, the August Horch Automobil Werke, still in Zwickau, very near the one he had just left, the A. Horch & Cie Motorwagen Werke. The similar names of the two companies make it clear that Horch's resignation was in effect expulsion and shows how he immediately started a second company out of pique more than any real interest. The matter finally degenerated into a court case

design and extremely high performance. Few European companies had the courage to compete with it by trying to find a foothold in a market which was almost its untouchable niche. Yet someone did try, a German manufacturer, August Horch, who was bold enough to challenge the sacred monster of motoring on its own ground.

Horch began business modestly in an abandoned stable in Cologne–Ehrenfeld in 1899. Then, after a short spell in a plant at Reichenbach in Saxony, the company finally moved to Zwickau in 1903. Until then, Horch had only produced three cars of which the most interesting was an in-line, four-cylinder model with side valves controlled by two camshafts in the cylinder block. In this car there were already examples of quality engineering, such

and at the end an injunction by the court of Lipsia obliged Horch to change the name of his new company. It was renamed Audi (the Latin for his surname) Automobilwerke GmbH.

In the meantime, Horch had begun production of the 10/28 model, a medium-sized car which was well made and the first examples of which appeared at the beginning of 1910. No longer subject to external pressures, the German engineer could produce a more modern and efficient car with a light, simple chassis with a four-cylinder engine.

In 1912 Audi had a range of four models, the 10/28, the 14/35, the 18/45 and the 22/50, all similar in construction if not in size. The two biggest models were produced until 1920 almost without any modifications, while the 14/35 was more popular because of its good power/weight ratio. In the Alpensieger this version had many sporting successes and was still in production in 1921.

In addition to the acceptance of his cars on a technical level, Horch had the publicity from his assiduous participation in races, as not only was he a serious manufacturer and excellent designer, but he was also a passionate driver and leader of a team of drivers which even included his engineers Graumuller and Lange. The victories in the Tour des Alpes (a race of endurance of 1500 miles (2400 km) which was becoming increasingly important) and the technical significance of the famous Prinz Heinrich Fahrt of 1912, 1913 and 1914 were decisive both in creating Audi's image and in outdoing Horch, which participated in races using the designs provided by August Horch himself before he left the company.

However, relaunch of the marques after the war proved difficult. The standstill in design, common in some measure to all motoring companies, affected Audi more than most. This was due not only to the war and the problem of changing back to civilian production, but also because Horch's limited funds had been absorbed by war production and political engagements, and he left the company (officially in 1920 but earlier in fact), retaining only his seat on the board of directors. In practice, Audi was not to succeed again until 1932 when it was taken over by DKW and gradually lost its original autonomy.

Mercédès, Horch and Audi were fairly expensive cars, but the German motorist could choose economy models from three other companies, NSU, Opel and Wanderer, the most

*The 1913 Stutz
Touring model had a
four-cylinder engine
(Harrah collection)*

important in that sector of the market. At NSU in Neckarsulm, where they occupied a former knitwear factory, car production began in 1905 with several models built under licence from the Belgian company Pipe. They soon realized, however, that Pipe cars were expensive, heavy on fuel and had a delicate mechanism, and thus had a restricted and unprofitable market. For this reason NSU decided to build original models which marked a complete break with Pipe designs. In 1907 three new cars appeared, the 6/12, the 8/15 and the 10/20, all fitted with four-cylinder, opposed side-valve engines which formed the basis of the company's production and enabled them to become well established both nationally and internationally.

In 1909, NSU presented its first popular cars and in particular a two and a four-cylinder of 1100 cc, structurally identical except for the number of cylinders; both had engines with side valves, all placed on one side, pressure-fed oil, convection cooling, an original NSU carburetor and three-speed gearboxes. Because of their reliability and durability, the two models enjoyed considerable popularity. After a few years, the two-cylinder car was discontinued while the four-cylinder model

underwent constant improvements and was counted among the most popular of German economy cars. There is no doubt that these two models enabled the Neckarsulm company to reach an annual output of over 4000 units in the first decade of the century.

Opel cars were equally successful, and they survive today as part of General Motors, although initial production was not based exclusively on economy models. In the very early years of its business, which began in 1898, Opel built Lutzmann cars (which were very similar to the Benz Victoria) and Darracqs under licence. In 1906, when the agreement with Darracq was terminated, their designs gradually became more individual, although still based on those of the French company. The excellent quality of its cars and its numerous successes in the field of racing soon put Opel among the great names of German motoring.

Following the practice of the time, the company in Russelsheim had a large and varied range of models from small, cheap cars to large de luxe cars of 40, 50 and 60 hp. Until 1910, one of the most popular models was the so-called 'doctor's car' (the name implied a cheap, robust and reliable car, particularly

suited to doctors who frequently had to make long journeys), which had a small water-cooled, twin-cylinder engine in the 6/12 and 8/14 models, and which rightly became famous for its reliability and long life. Also very popular were the later small car range with four cylinders which were produced in large numbers from 1910 to the outbreak of World War I; one of these was the famous 1·4-liter Puppchen (Doll).

A Puppchen was also listed in the Wanderer catalogue, the third German company to

Above *the 1913 SCAT torpedo*

Below *the 1913 25/35 hp Isotta-Fraschini with Castagna bodywork*

specialize in economy. Presented in 1911, it was Wanderer's first car as until that time they had built bicycles and motor cycles. The Puppchen was fitted with a four-cylinder engine of 1140 cc with overhead inlet valves and side exhaust valves and had a power of 12 hp at 1800 rpm. Of particular interest was the bodywork with its two seats arranged in tandem. The car's width was only 3 ft 6½ ins (1080 mm) with a wheelbase of 7 ft 1 in (2200 mm). It had a maximum speed of 48 mph (70 kph) and was so successful that within a short time production could not meet demand.

During the first decade of the century motoring had become so common that it was an integral part of life both in Europe and beyond, even extending to countries with a minimum of industry. This does not take into consideration the future great industrial powers like Russia and Japan which have developed much more recently. In czarist Russia there were some timid attempts at car production, but their vehicles were built from imported parts which were assembled locally and sold under local names. In Japan, production was almost non existent.

Of far more importance were the great Belgian car manufacturers with Imperia being added to Métallurgique, Minerva, FN and Excelsior in 1906. In the early years, FN was regarded as one of the most progressive companies of European motoring because of its advanced methods of work and the presence of specialized personnel, both of which led to production of the highest quality. The cars built by the other four companies were also of an extremely high level, and all specialized in the construction of powerful, high-performance cars with a luxurious finish and sophisticated engineering. To this, Métallurgique added an intense and profitable sports division. In neighboring Holland, the Spyker continued to astound with its technical originality. After building the first car with an integral clutch in 1903, the Dutch company presented another novelty in 1909, the cylinder head designed by Valentin Laviolette, which had as many camshafts as cylinders. This unusual design was used for the entire Spyker range until 1917.

In Austria there were two prosperous motoring companies which had been operating since the end of the previous century. These were Gräf & Stift and Austro-Daimler, both engaged in limited-production cars of very

high quality. Gräf & Stift, manufacturers of elite cars and suppliers to the Austro–Hungarian imperial family, began its history with a tragic event of which it was involuntarily a part. It was in one of their cars that the Archduke Ferdinand and his wife lost their lives at Sarajevo, the event which sparked off World War I.

There was no tragedy, though, in the case of Austro-Daimler, the Austrian subsidiary of the German Daimler company, which had gradually become independent since 1905. It was in that year that Paul Daimler who, since 1902 had been both the company's director and its chief designer, was recalled to Cannstatt and the position of technical director was taken by Ferdinand Porsche. It was not so much by his initiative as much as by a series of share transfers and the progressive debilitation of central directives that Austro-Daimler was able to act more freely and even became involved in a transaction which was to make it almost a rival of its parent company.

The person responsible for all this was Emil Jellinek, the Austrian businessman who had established a curious relationship with Daimler of Cannstatt as far back as 1897, at first ordering cars for his personal use and then undertaking to sell an entire series. As he had a say in the company's production, he persuaded them to produce the Mercédès (for which he also chose the name), and Mercédès-Simplex series, that is, what can be regarded as the first modern motor cars. This contribution, which was decisive in Daimler's history, culminated in a conflict of interests around 1905, following which Jellinek sus-

pended his collaboration with the company.

To fulfil his own programme by other means, he founded the Osterreichische Automobil Gesellschaft in 1906, omitting however to provide new premises and subcontracting the construction of vehicles to Austro-Daimler which was also employed to do the design. It is not quite clear if this was a clause imposed by Austro-Daimler or was a specific request by Jellinek. However, the presence of Porsche was the only happy circumstance of the whole affair. The car at the centre of the disagreement, the Maja, was a four-cylinder of 4520 cc which followed the Mercédès design (as all European production did by that time), of good, if not excellent, quality with engineering features which were perhaps advanced at the time of being designed but which were outdated in 1908 when the car could finally be distributed. And so the whole enterprise failed and the Osterreichische Automobil Gesellschaft went into liquidation, while Austro-Daimler continued to produce and sell the Maja and was partially indemnified for the losses it had suffered.

Fortunately, Austro-Daimler had continued to build its smaller models, and in 1908 was ready to place its first modern car of its own design alongside the unfortunate Maja. This was the 8/16 with a monobloc four-cylinder engine. However, the real individualism of the Austrian company as a name equal to any in Europe began with its participation in the races sponsored by Prince Heinrich of Prussia, the Prinz Heinrich Fahrten. The 1909 race was disappointing and the three 60 hp cars specially built by Porsche

Abadal, a small Barcelona company which manufactured cars (or bodywork) from 1912 to 1930, was one of the few Spanish car producers. The model illustrated above dates from 1914 and is now in the Portuguese museum of Caramulo

Opposite page
The 2-litre Renault model EF (Du Pasquier collection). The chassis was sold by the Renault agent in New York in 1915 and was then fitted with a Brewster body, product of one of the oldest and most renowned American coachbuilders

were too slow and did not even succeed in qualifying for entry. Upset by this misfortune, Porsche prepared a completely new vehicle for the next race. This car had a high-performance engine and was built according to standards which were defined as aeronautical at the time, that is with poppet valves at an angle of 45°, separated cylinders of very light structure, and double ignition. With its 96 hp at 2100 rpm and top speed of over 90 mph (140 kph) the car won the next event by a long way and routed the other competitors. But the importance of this model goes further than its sporting successes. It in fact represented one of the first examples of a sports car which was designed in such a way that it could be mass-produced without substantial modifications. It was a new type of touring car which only became widespread in the 1920s with Alfa Romeo, Ballot, Bentley and Bugatti.

The international success of Porsche's extraordinary achievement was aided by the new bodywork designed by Ernst Neumann-Neander, who was considered the creator of the German line of sports cars which consisted primarily of the use of V radiators and concave sides, ending in a tail shaped like the prow of a boat. In 1911 the German stylist designed the new Austro-Daimler emblem which was used when the company finally broke away from Daimler of Cannstatt. From that moment the Austrian company could use its own symbol of the two-headed black eagle, copied with the emperor's permission from the heraldic signs of the royal house.

The touch of nobility and elegance of Austro-Daimler recalls the country where motoring elegance had become a way of life, namely France. France, in fact, had first place among the car-producing countries of the world, although its place was later taken by the United States as the greatest world producer in terms of the number of cars built. However, France remained firmly in the lead for quality, advanced engineering techniques and originality of bodywork. In brief, the French school was most followed and imitated. Its great masters were De Dion, Peugeot and Panhard to which were added the rising stars of Delage, Delaunay-Belleville, Hotchkiss and Bugatti. These companies were only a few of the great number which were operating in France, many of which are worthy of mention. Obviously, all of them cannot be discussed here and a selection has been made to give an idea of the French car industry at that time.

After the great success of the Populaire which, as its name suggests, was a small popular car, there was a radical change in production policy at De Dion-Bouton which led to the construction of large, de luxe models. With this in mind, a series of V8 engines was produced in 1908, the jump in design is surprising considering that De Dion was one of the most enthusiastic supporters of the single-cylinder engine. In the course of the following two years, the company in Puteaux established a complete range of models with two, four and eight cylinders and power varying from 6 to 35 hp. The biggest model was a luxurious V8 limousine with enough power to enable it to reach a speed of 50 mph (80 kph). The eight-

cylinder series was completed by a coupé and a streamlined 20 hp model; one of these took part in the Targa Florio of 1913 and came fourth.

However, despite its sporting achievements, the large number of models in the catalogue and good distribution of the V8, De Dion Bouton's popularity had been in decline since 1912. The innovative and pioneering spirit which had created the company's fame in its early years of business had waned with the introduction of luxury models, an area in which Delaunay-Belleville of Saint-Denis had in the meantime become increasingly dominant. This new name was officially presented at the Salon de Paris in 1904 at which event three touring cars were exhibited, each with four cylinders, the 16/20, the 24/28 and the 40/45 hp. They were designed by the engineer Marius Barbarou, who had come from Benz where he had led the team of French engineers engaged by the directors of the German company to rival Karl Benz.

From the first models it was clear that the Saint-Denis company had a high standard of cars with good finish and precision engineering. Technically, the most interesting detail was in the system of forced-feed lubrication, patented by the company as early as 1897 and tested on the French navy's motor boats (before building cars, Delaunay-Belleville had manufactured steam boilers for the Navy). From the point of view of style, however, the

Above *two Benz models of 1914. The 8/20PS four-seater, a 2090 cc torpedo, and the Touring, with the same cubic capacity* **Left** *1914 40/50 hp Rolls-Royce (Museo dell'Automobile, Turin). This model was also part of the famous Silver Ghost series which was launched at the London Motor Show in 1906 and remained in production until 1925*

round radiator was very distinctive and was to typify the entire future production of the company.

In 1908 six-cylinder engines appeared, which were an inevitable step in building luxury cars for a refined clientele which was especially demanding. Among the French company's famous buyers were Czar Nicholas of Russia and the king of Greece, together with the most prominent politicians of the day.

Until the outbreak of World War I, Delaunay-Belleville was very successful. Its famous twin-block, six-cylinder vehicles with side valves, shaft transmission, and bodywork designed by the master coachbuilders of the time were considered the apex of French car production. From the first six-cylinder models of 1908, the 10/12, the 15 and the 40 hp, were derived the six 1914 models with a power ranging from 12 to 50 hp.

It was in this year that Marius Barbarou left the company in Saint-Denis which, because of the war had turned to assembling aero engines of Hispano-Suiza manufacture. At the end of the war, the motoring business was resumed in full, but Delaunay-Belleville found itself faced with rivals like Hispano-Suiza, Rolls-Royce and Isotta-Fraschini, and was forced to give up its position at the top of European luxury-car manufacturers.

A contemporary of Delaunay-Belleville was another French company, Hotchkiss, distinguished by the construction of large, powerful cars with six cylinders. Indeed, this company, which also had its premises in Saint-Denis, was one of the first in France to use the six-cylinder engine which was installed in the

40/50 hp model of 1906 with a cubic capacity of 7090 cc. In 1908 a new six-cylinder car appeared with a cubic capacity of 9500 cc, and it was considered one of the first and most successful examples of a large, comfortable travelling saloon.

In 1912 the first monobloc four-cylinder engine appeared in the guise of the 12/60 hp of 3700 cc, in addition to which there were larger twin-block versions and the smaller six-cylinder vehicles of smaller size. Unlike Delaunay-Belleville, the fame of Hotchkiss continued, and indeed increased, after the war due to a fortunate series of great touring cars which won numerous international competitions.

After their great successes at the beginning of the century, Panhard & Levassor had abandoned its participation in sporting events and since 1906 had pursued a commercial policy, based on the car as a means of travel and not sport. In this context, the first six-cylinder engine, of over eleven liters cubic capacity – for use in a series of large, heavy cars – was announced in 1909. Still in 1905, the coil radiator was finally abandoned in favour of the honeycomb radiator while the leather conical clutch was replaced by one of multiplate design in 1907. Technical innovations were made cautiously as the Parisian company was conservative in all respects, although this did not alter the strength of its position on the domestic and foreign markets.

In the meantime, there had been some changes within the company. Following the death of Emil Levassor, Panhard employed Adolphe Clément, whose name was connected with a number of different motoring enterprises in France and abroad. His official position was that of commercial director, but in effect his position at the heart of the company was much more important in that he held the majority of shares. The small Panhard-Clément single-cylinder cars were fitted with a propulsion unit designed by Krebs (head of the engineering department of Panhard & Levassor since 1897), and sold directly by Clément & Co of Pré-Saint-Gervais, one of the many companies controlled by Adolphe Clément. This was the only case when the Panhard name was associated with that of another motoring company and was purely for commercial reasons. When Adolphe Clément left and René Panhard died in 1908, the directorship of the company was assumed by Hippolyte Panhard, René's son. He, in

The four-cylinder De Dion torpedo of 1914 For two years the company's popularity had been declining after the marque had occupied a very important position in world motoring for more than twenty years. De Dion-Bouton ceased production in 1933

The 1914 Pilain torpedo *with a four-cylinder, 2-litre engine. From the early years of the century, the company in Lyons was distinguished for its production of a very wide range of high quality cars*

turn, was succeeded by his brother Paul in 1915 who was chairman of the company until 1965 when it merged with Citroën.

Continuing the slow but constant technical improvement of his cars, Panhard introduced a chassis made of stamped plate and shaft transmission which he replaced in all models with chain transmission in 1910. Alongside these innovations another novelty was being introduced which was to influence Panhard production for a long time. This was the adoption of a sleeve-valve engine, proposed by the American, Knight, who had already found firm supporters of the idea in other European companies, like the English Daimler and the Belgian Minerva. The engineer Krebs had studied it and in 1908 had begun his first practical experiments with it. The introduction of the propulsion unit without valves also enabled Panhard to break off all relations with Daimler of Cannstatt which, by the terms of an agreement between Gottlieb Daimler and Sarazin in 1886 and later continued by Panhard & Levassor, stipulated a payment to Daimler of 10 per cent of the value of each engine that was manufactured.

Production of the last series of conventional engines ceased in 1913 while the first generation of Panhard sleeve-valve engines, presented in different versions with four and six cylinders, was to influence the development of other French manufacturers, like Voisin and Peugeot. For Voisin, another important French company operating from 1919 to 1939, and famous for the originality of its models, the use of an engine without valves remained constant in all its car production, whereas for Peugeot it was only a comparatively brief

The small Le Zèbre Model C of 1914. The Le Zèbre marque was noted for its economy models, built from 1909 to 1932 by the engineer, Jules Salomon

A Lancia Theta of 1914, now preserved in the Museo dell'Automobile, Turin. The Theta model was launched in the preceding year and remained in production until 1919 with a total of 1696 examples being manufactured

episode, although an outstanding one, in its varied output.

In the early years of the century the Audincourt company of Peugeot manufactured a very wide range of vehicles to cater for every need, from the small Bébé to three ton lorries. Its success inevitably stimulated competition and Armand Peugeot found himself with rivals in his own family in the shape of his cousins who had initially been his partners in the bicycle factory in Beaulieu. When he moved on to cars, they opted for a separation, as they lacked faith in the future of the motoring industry, and in 1896 the separation came about. Armand Peugeot had founded the Société des Automobiles Peugeot in Audincourt with a plant at Lille, while his cousins had stayed on to run the Société Fils de Peugeot Frères, undertaking to build only bicycles and motor cycles marketed under the name of Lion-Peugeot, but this agreement terminated on 30 June 1912. In 1905, however, seeing that cars had become big business, the Société Fils de Peugeot Frères persuaded Armand Peugeot to draw up a new agreement whereby they, too, could build cars with a clause stipulating that their unladen weight would not exceed 345 kg. Armand Peugeot himself, to avoid competition with his cousins, withdrew his Bébé 6 hp model, which had appeared in 1906, from the market.

The first car using the Lion-Peugeot name was introduced on 1 January 1906. Other models soon followed. These used either single-cylinder engines or V2 or V4 engines,

all designed by the engineer Michaeux. The popularity of the new name exceeded the most optimistic expectations and was largely due to success in the field of racing. Three drivers were to make their names with these cars with their characteristic high hood. These were Jules Goux, Georges Boillot and Guippone who helped to make the new generation of Peugeot cars unbeatable in their class. The success of Lion-Peugeot (more than 4000 examples were built between 1906 and 1910), coincided with a difficult financial period for Armand Peugeot and his company. In 1908 this led to a reconciliation between the two branches of the family with a view to a possible reunification of business. Negotiations were concluded in 1910 with a merger and the creation of the Société Anonyme des Automobiles et Cycles Peugeot, even though the Lion-Peugeot cars continued to be sold under that name until 1915. Indeed, one of these, called Bébé, like the earlier model of 1904, became particularly famous in that it was designed by the young engineer, Ettore Bugatti, who will be discussed in more depth later. From 1913 to 1916, the Bébé was produced in more than 3000 examples, thus constituting the principal model in the Peugeot range. Its tiny engine with four cylinders (55 × 90 mm), had a speed of 40 mph (60 kph) which was equal to that of far more powerful cars.

In the meantime, Peugeot had also increased its sports range and even introduced new designs which were to mark the beginning of the end of large capacity in motor racing engines. Drivers Boillot, Goux, Zuccarelli, and the Swiss engineer Ernest Henry, were involved in this new project and in little more than three years produced three examples of the L76 model of 7·6 liters, for the French Grand Prix of 1912, which at that time was an open formula race, and three examples of the 3-liter L3 model for the Coupe de l'Auto of the same year. This race was exclusively for cars with a cubic capacity of not more than three liters. Their engines were technically advanced and features included the hemispherical head, four valves per cylinder, twin camshafts, desmodromic valvegear and a crankshaft which ran on ball-bearings. The victories gained by these machines and those earned by the 5·6-liter and 4·5-liter cars which won later Grands Prix, made the French company one of the few to rival the extremely powerful Mercédès cars which dominated the racing scene of the time.

Inevitably, Peugeot took part in the war effort of its country and, like all industries engaged in supplying military equipment, developed its own technology and work methods to satisfy large-scale production requirements. These were then also applied to civil production after the war. As a result, Peugeot faced the difficult years of the post-war period with a different entrepreneurial spirit. It drastically reduced the number of models in its list concentrating on low-cost cars for a wide range of motorists. Very wisely it avoided falling into the enticing trap of prestige cars, opting instead for the manufacture of economy cars of excellent quality. So, in 1921, the Quadrilette, or model 161, was created. In spite of a tiny engine which produced only 4 hp it was built in a number of versions until 1931, selling almost 100,000 examples.

The last of the great French manufacturers is Renault which, by the first decade of the century, had broadened its range to include buses, trucks and aero engines. The Billancourt company also made a decisive contribution to the motor car as a means of public transport. In 1905–06, following an order from the Compagnie des Fiacres Parisienne, 1500 Renault taxis took to the streets of the French capital. Larger, more modern versions were to become famous during World War I when they were used to transport troops to the Marne front.

The production of cars revolved around a total of five models using the popular twin-cylinder and middle market four-cylinder engines. To the first category belongs the 10CV, while the 14CV of 3770 cc is part of the second category. This was the most luxurious of the range with an engine based on the winning car in the Paris–Vienna race. The 35CV and the 20CV, the first Renaults to be fitted with four gears in 1906, are also part of the second category. By this time Renault had already acquired its characteristic shape with the radiator set behind the engine and a bonnet shape which slightly resembled the feet of the sphinx. The gearbox was separate from the engine because the circulation of air to the radiator depended on a flywheel which incorporated a fan.

1906 saw Renault's return to the sporting scene after three years' absence (the death of Louis Renault's brother, Marcel, in the Paris–Madrid race made him abandon racing) at the first French Grand Prix. Once again the Renault proved competitive and the powerful

90CV, driven by the engineer Szisz, won the race at an average speed of 62·74 mph.

Two years later only Louis Renault remained to run the company following the retirement of his other brother, Fernand, for health reasons. The company then became known as the Société Louis Renault and its progress seemed never-ending. Its workforce rose to 2600 and the annual output increased from 4600 in 1908 to 10,000 cars by 1913.

1908 marked the appearance of the first six-cylinder Renault, the model AR with a cubic capacity of 9·5 liters. The range increased still further in 1910 when, besides a new four-cylinder car of 20 hp, three other six-cylinder cars with power outputs of 18, 35 and 40 hp were introduced.

At the outbreak of World War I, Renault production was concentrated on military supplies. The famous light armed truck, the model FT, which appeared towards the end of the war, was produced in the greatest volume (3177). Also important was the large aero engine with twelve cylinders which produced 300 hp. The post-war period presented no problems for the Billancourt company which quite simply resumed normal production where it had left off four years earlier.

A common characteristic of the major motoring companies of the time, both in Europe and America, was their regular par-

This coupé was one of the body styles introduced on the Ford T in 1915 and, as with all other versions of that year, the car was fitted with electric lighting

The Dodge Touring of 1915. In July 1916 General Pershing used 150 of these cars for his Mexican expedition against Pancho Villa

The Royal Mail H2 of 1915 was Chevrolet's first great commercial success, enabling the American company to rival Ford in the popular motoring market sector

ticipation in motor racing. These events were considered an excellent means of testing new technical ideas which could then be applied to production cars and were also a means of attracting publicity. In many countries, therefore, there were manufacturers who, in building sports cars, knew how to transfer the knowledge gained in competition into designs. The latter group included Louis Delage and Ettore Bugatti, two of the most talented designers of French racing cars. In fact, Ettore Bugatti was only French by adoption as he never abandoned his Italian nationality, but his personality made him a character of world stature beyond all geographical boundaries.

The first car to bear the Bugatti name was in 1909, but it was certainly not the first to be designed by the Milanese engineer. He had, in fact, already produced cars for other companies (Prinetti & Stucchi, Gulinelli, De Dietrich, Mathis and Deutz) which had earned him European fame. Indeed, at the time of launching his first car he was still connected to Deutz of Cologne and, given that a Bugatti name did not exist, that model was christened *Le Pur Sang* ('the thoroughbred'), a fantasy name but strangely prophetic.

Le Pur Sang was a very simple, light car but it had an important innovation. Differing from other models of its class, which used single or twin-cylinder engines, it was fitted with a four-cylinder engine with overhead valves. This car proved to be efficient from the first race in which it took part. It was put into production in 1910 and became known as the Bugatti Type 13. In the meantime, Bugatti had found a site for his company, an old factory near a disused dye-works in Molsheim near Strasbourg. In 1910 only five cars were produced, but the following year this figure rose to 75. In 1911, moreover, Ettore Bugatti undertook his final job for an outside company, designing and building the prototype of a popular car which was to become the famous 855 cc Peugeot Bébé.

With the Type 13 the company in Molsheim

began series production, a term which when applied to Bugatti, meant that at most a few hundred examples of the same model were built. In fact, Ettore Bugatti's methods of work involved as little mechanization as possible. His cars were literally made by hand with that attention to detail, and precision of workmanship, that are to be found in a watchmaker's workshop, but certainly not in a car factory.

Despite high production costs and the structural complexity of the small four-cylinder engines, Bugatti succeeded, at least initially, in containing the price of his cars. The question of price ceased to be of primary importance later, when the name became established in the elite of world motoring, which was largely due to a series of victories beginning with the Grand Prix of Le Mans in 1911 in which a Type 13, driven by Friedrich, won its class and was classified second overall. Whoever bought a Bugatti was able to pay whatever figure was required for the privilege of owning one. By 1914 the Molsheim cars were considerably more expensive than their most direct competitors, without this having the least effect on sales.

For several years Bugatti concentrated on building fast, light cars with four cylinders. In 1911–12 there was an exception, however, with a small series of large five-cylinder racing

cars with chain transmission. In 1914 these led to the building of a special car for the American Indianapolis race in which shaft transmission was used.

During World War I Ettore Bugatti had to abandon the factory in Molsheim which was in a military zone but, although deprived of the possibility of production, he did not cease to plan new designs, resulting in numerous achievements especially in aeronautics.

The 1920s, with the resumption of business and big international races, were to see the small, irrepressible Bugattis, then fitted mostly with eight-cylinder engines, win everything possible and, given that they were cars which were adaptable for road use, they were sold as quickly as the factory could produce them.

Second only to Bugatti in sporting fame was Delage whose reputation was acquired by a series of powerful and reliable cars of essentially orthodox design.

Louis Delage began business as a car manufacturer in 1905, in a small plant in Levallois-Perret, near Paris, with the help of only two collaborators. Production was based on cars fitted with single-cylinder De Dion-Bouton engines, ranging in power output from 9 to 14·5 hp. The incident that eventually brought the name of Delage into the public eye was an extraordinary sporting event – the Grand Prix

Left *the 1918–20 8/10 hp Temperino. These small, economy cars had only one type of engine while the body styles were varied and were either two or three seaters. Temperinos were also used for transporting goods*

Above *The Packard Twin Six Imperial, second series, of 1916. The main feature of this model was its engine which had twelve cylinders in a V formation and is considered to be the Packard designer Jesse G. Vincent's masterpiece*

The company's main activity, however, still centered around competitions. In 1911 a special car with a four-cylinder, 3-liter engine was built for the Coupe de l'Auto. The car had horizontal valves and a drive shaft built in units which were mounted in separate bearings. Its power was about 50 hp at 3000 rpm which was by no means extraordinary, but once again the general balance of the vehicle was outstanding, enabling the driver, Bablot, to beat the Lion-Peugeot of Boillot, and Thomas to come third.

A new car was also built for the 1912 French Grand Prix, still with four cylinders and 6234 cc. The new car, which was enormous with its long wheelbase, was equipped with double ignition and produced 118 hp at 2250 rpm. Although proving to be the fastest, the car was not placed because of a puncture. Delage cars, however, came first and second in the Circuit de la Sarthe and, with minor adjustments, the same cars took part in the 1914 Indianapolis 500 Miles where René Thomas had an astonishing victory, in spite of a long stop in the pits to repair an exhaust manifold. That was a day of real triumph for the French motoring industry: the victory by Thomas was completed by Duray in second place in a Peugeot, third place by Guyot in a Delage and fourth place by Goux also in a Peugeot.

Delage had an unlucky final race before the war in the 1914 French Grand Prix for which it had prepared two cars for the 4·5-liter formula, both of which were beaten by three Mercédès which took the first three places. Immediately after the war, the company in Courbevoie resumed its production of sports cars with several single-seaters designed exslusively for hill-climb and record-breaking events. The 1920s saw a return to the construction of Grand Prix cars which frequently lost to Alfa Romeos.

The story of Delage obviously does not end here nor does the history of motoring in general, but this outline of the most important cars produced in the world until 1919 is now concluded. Up to this point the car did not have an easy life and was not even spared the trauma of a war which turned the world upside down. Today the car is often the symbol of peace and international unity, but unfortunately history has taught us that this will only be partially successful.

des Voiturettes at Dieppe in 1908, run in conjunction with the French Grand Prix. The winning car, driven by Albert Guyot, was a single-cylinder Delage with four sparking-plugs, double flywheel and induction via poppet valves. The small Delage completed the course without stopping, which explains why its average speed was little different from that of Lautenschlager's Mercédès (the winner in the largest category) although the latter's lap times were greater by as much as twenty minutes. It was clear proof of how economy and reliability could compensate for less power.

The success at Dieppe boosted sales considerably, which exceeded 400 in 1908 with good profits for the company. As a result, it moved to new premises in Courbevoie the following year. After the move the range of models was updated with the introduction of a series fitted with four-cylinder in-line engines built by Ballot but designed in conjunction with Delage. Once on the way to multi-cylinders, an obligatory stage was the six-cylinder engine which appeared in 1911 with a cubic capacity of 2500 cc and a four-speed gearbox. In 1912 Delage was well into production with an annual output of approximately 1000 cars.

From a Craft to an Industry

After the industry had undergone its initial 'trial' period of construction, 'motoring technology' could be considered to have come to car production from the beginning of the twentieth century.

The earliest cars were almost exclusively fruits of the inventiveness and ingenuity of the most enterprising engineers of the day, but the later veteran and Edwardian cars became a much more practical and efficient industrial product than the first strange motor vehicles. In the early stages of motoring history most manufacturers' sole preoccupation was to produce a means of 'auto motion'; later there was an increasing concern with how well a vehicle performed, stemming from the growing availability of different types of engines as well as from the natural and rapid development of technology. The production, and consequently the sale, of cars built to consistent standards meant that, soon, cars could be driven quite easily and safely by a wider section of the public, and the automobile gradually ceased to be the prerogative of motoring enthusiasts.

Having once attained a satisfactory level of performance, a manufacturer's main considerations were development of comfort and reliability in the fullest sense of the words; it was important for a car to be well finished, silent and easy to drive. There was little demand for high performance or speed as these were quite inappropriate on the roads of the time. Nor were they much appreciated by the majority of drivers, for whom it was already quite an undertaking to drive at normal (very slow) speeds.

A certain standardization in the type and arrangement of the principal controls was reached, not so much by any explicit agreement between manufacturers as by the need for simple, practical operation. The brake and clutch were normally operated by pedals. Sometimes a single pedal sufficed for both, declutching during the first part of its travel and operating the brake during the second. Gear selection was by a lever (practically the same as the modern system), except that some simpler models were fitted with an epicyclic gearbox.

A photograph of the CTAV workshop, founded in 1905 in Milan. As can be seen, cars were built entirely by hand and workers frequently hand finished components

This type of gearbox, nowadays used in nearly all automatic transmissions, had the advantage of not requiring a conventional clutch to disengage drive from the engine. Changing from one gear to another was achieved simply by locking together (by means of brake bands) different groups of gears comprising the gear train. For this reason, instead of the usual clutch, some cars fitted with this type of gearbox featured pedal control. The most famous car with this type of drive was the Ford Model T.

Initially, all vehicles were controlled exclusively by levers and controls on the steering wheel as this seemed the most comfortable and practical arrangement. The transition to pedal controls arose quite rapidly from the need to operate more controls simultaneously, maneuvers which required a certain dexterity that is today taken for granted but was not natural to people used to handling reins and stirrups.

Improvements in performance, comfort and ease of driving were made possible not only by developments in design and automotive engineering but also by the development of the engineering industry and technology as a whole.

As production volumes grew, the major companies applied technical developments to construction, and car building became industrialized. Ford's introduction of assembly line construction in 1913 was merely the final act in the general rationalization of production methods. It was only a few years earlier that it had become possible to interchange the parts of identical cars, thanks to the precision of mass-production workmanship, instead of parts being hand finished each time they were required. During this period motoring technology received a considerable boost from the new aviation industry, which demanded lighter, more powerful and more reliable engines than those available for cars. As cars themselves became faster and more dependable, they were fitted with engines of greater cubic capacity and more cylinders.

The more conservative manufacturers resorted to separate blocks for multiple cylinders, largely to obviate the difficulties involved in casting large, complex parts. Twin block engines, with four cylinders, and three block engines with six cylinders became common. Combining pairs of cylinders permitted the use of the same castings for different engines, for example, to give four or six cylinders, with

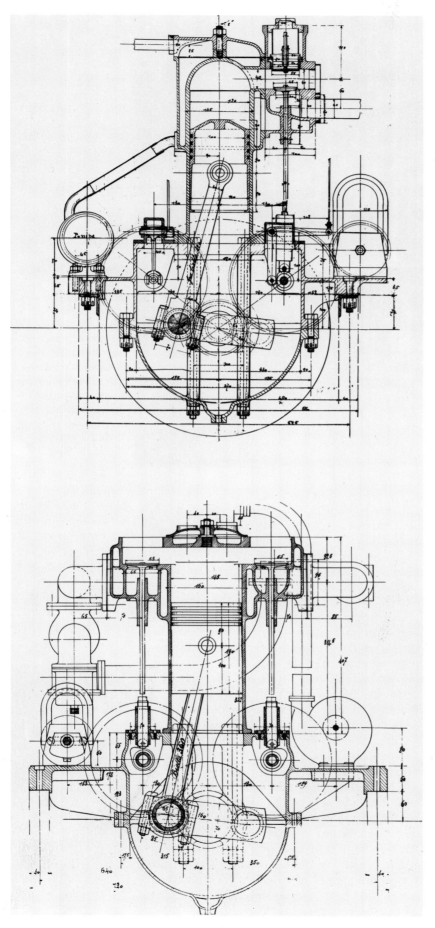

the obvious advantages of structural sim
plicity.

For a long time the 'monobloc' system, wit
all the cylinders bored from one casting, wa
limited to the smaller four-cylinder engines
while a simple development was V8 engine
where two four-cylinder blocks were fixe
onto a common crankcase.

The most important changes concerne
the cylinder head where the design and dis
position of components most affected a car'
performance. With the increase in rotationa
speeds it had become impractical to retain th
old automatic inlet valves and the valves
position, too, had to be changed. The mos
common systems had the valves alongsid
their cylinder, sometimes on the same side an
controlled by a single lateral camshaft, some
times arranged one on either side of the cylind
er and controlled by two lateral camshafts
The latter arrangement, in spite of the greate
complexity of two camshafts, was preferabl
because the manifolds were separated, wit
induction one side and exhaust the other.

The valves were commonly controlled b
roller cam-followers with a clearance adjust
ment system. Usually, there was a screw with
lock nut, though sometimes more sophisti
cated devices were used. Amédée Bollé
(junior) made an interesting innovation b
using a system of automatic adjustment i
1910. Structurally the system was very simila
to the so-called 'hydraulic lifters' patented b
General Motors many years later, whereby oi
under pressure from the lubrication system
kept the rocker arms in continuous contac
with the cam. This had two advantages
namely the elimination of too frequent adjust
ments and a notable reduction of engine noise
Silence was much sought after by both engi
neers and the public, who looked for maximum
comfort and lack of vibration, especially i
the large saloons. In the case of the valve gea
alternatives to the usual poppet valves wer
introduced because poppet valves were noisy
mechanically complex and subject to break
downs and wear.

In 1905 the Hevitt engine appeared in whic
the opening and closing of the ports wer
controlled by an auxiliary piston which acte
as a sliding valve. This system was too compli
cated and expensive to justify its advantage
and was not very successful. The following yea
the Knight system, better known as the sleev
valve system, was patented, and was tested an
used for a long time in car and aero engines.

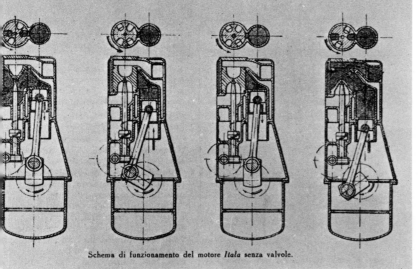

Schema di funzionamento del motore *Itala* senza valvole.

Opposite page and above *two examples of engines from the turn of the century. At the top the 24 hp Fiat of 1902, with automatic inlet valves, and below, the 60 hp Fiat of 1905, with two side valves controlled by two camshafts in the crankcase*
For ten years Itala made engines with rotary valves, which worked as shown in the above plan

In the Knight engine the openings for the inlet and exhaust ports were in two moving sleeves, the inner one of which constituted the cylinder bore. The reciprocating movement of the two sleeves, synchronized to the movement of the piston, caused the ports to open and close, like a gate valve system. The advantages were numerous and extended beyond the simple reduction of noise. The breathing was much more efficient, since, with the port open, all the available area was free, unlike with the poppet valve system. Furthermore, the port apertures faced directly into the cylinder and were not in a relatively remote position, as in the case of side valves. Finally, the absence of moving parts inside the combustion chamber permitted a very compact cylinder head and allowed freedom of design for optimum combustion.

On the other hand, engines with sleeve valves had some major mechanical shortcomings which limited their use and eventually caused them to be abandoned.

The main problem lay in the extremely high rate of wear, both between the sleeves themselves and between these and the piston, a problem which was aggravated by different rates of thermal expansion. To solve the problems, the engine speed had to be limited and it was necessary to have large clearances and copious lubrication of all moving parts, resulting in very high oil consumption and characteristic blue exhaust fumes.

Among 'valveless' engines, one of the best systems was that introduced by Itala in 1912 and kept in production for a good ten years. This system featured a rotating cylinder via which the combustion chamber was alternately opened to the inlet and exhaust manifolds. It was not complicated from the structural point of view, but required an elaborate cylinder head and very precise engineering work to ensure reasonable sealing.

As 'traditional' valve gear developed, improvements in performance led to investigation of new types of combustion chamber which were much more efficient than those with side valves. In fact, the 'L' heads, typical of engines with valves on the same side, and 'T' heads for engines with a valve either side of the cylinder, had a very large surface area in relation to the volume, making combustion rather slow as the fuel had to spread from the sparking plug, which was usually in front of the inlet valve, through the entire chamber and into the cylinder. To overcome this, multiple ignition was used in larger engines with extra sparking plugs distributed at various points in the head, but the results were unsatisfactory.

However, in racing cars more modern (though more sophisticated and more costly) methods were tested. In 1908 Fiat built a very powerful engine (producing some 200 bhp) with valves in the head which were controlled directly by a camshaft. In 1912 Peugeot built a Grand Prix car fitted for the first time with twin overhead camshafts, operating valves in vee-formation in the head in hemispherical combustion chambers.

As a result of improvements in design, other fundamental components, such as ignition and fuel systems, were naturally affected. Battery ignition having been abandoned, magneto ignition became universal, providing a powerful and reliable spark at any engine speed.

The entire structure of cars had to be adapted to cope with the maximum engine power and also had to satisfy the demands for comfort. Ladder-type construction was introduced on the chassis, comprising two strong

Right *the 1906 Berliet engine is a typical example of power units around the beginning of the century, with four cylinders in a dual block, two side valves and sparking-plugs in front of the inlet valves*

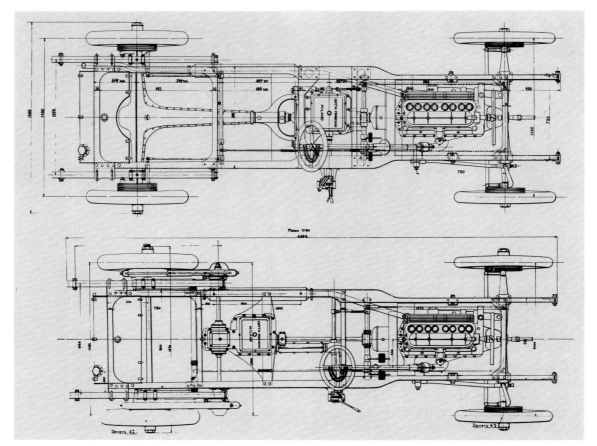

Two diagrams showing two different transmission systems on the same chassis, a 25/35 hp Isotta-Fraschini model OM of 1919-11 Above is the fixed axle system and below the traditional double chain drive with rear gearbox

metal longitudinal members connected by a series of cross-bars and with leaf spring suspension at the ends. The most usual suspension system continued to be that based around the solid axle, as it was very robust and simple. In fact, on corners or on rough ground, solid axles were not affected by the sensitive movements of the chassis, which was generally very flexible, and in this way they ensured consistent and satisfactory road performance.

Front suspension systems, however, were gradually modified to improve handling; more sophisticated steering systems were introduced to make steering lighter and more precise. At the rear, chain transmission was gradually replaced by shaft transmission; the differential was incorporated in the back axle and the propellor shaft was made to pass inside a long tube to the back axle with a universal joint at the gearbox.

Greater performance, of course, also demanded improvements to braking systems. The old transmission brakes proved inadequate and therefore brakes on the wheels had to be used, initially only on the back wheels

and later also on the front. The most difficult problem was to make them work reliably and as independently as possible of the movement of the wheels in relation to the chassis; the result was usually a complex system of brake rods or cams, requiring very frequent adjustments.

For a long time tyres remained the weak point of fast cars because of their tendency to explode as soon as stress was increased. This was due to the fact that the rubber industry was unable to produce heat resistant compounds, quite apart from the condition of the roads and the length of journey which some drivers embarked on. The problem was solved by using tyres which could stand very high inflation pressure, thus limiting (as far as possible) deformation during running and therefore reducing overheating. The tread also had to withstand rough road surfaces and for this reason tyres were often reinforced with a robust leather 'sole' fitted with metal studs, which had the dual purpose of reducing wear on the tread and creating better grip between the tyre and the wheel rim.

The Fascination of Speed

Racing came into being more or less simultaneously with the first cars, or rather horseless carriages, powered by the rudimentary engines of before the turn of the century. The only way that the early manufacturers could inform the public of the new means of locomotion was to display their creations in the streets, to prove their capabilities and to overcome hostility and diffidence. It was also the only way that defects could be brought to light and new techniques could be tested. For these reasons, from the outset, sporting cars gave an invaluable boost to the development of the more mundane machines. Naturally, in the beginning production and 'racing' cars followed much the same paths but their development divided as the phenomenon of motoring became accepted. The link between the two, however, remained insoluble and there were constant transfers of ideas between race track and road – as remains the case to this day.

The earliest motoring milestones were long distance journeys such as those made by Amédée Bollée, with his steam-driven *L'Obéissante*, from Le Mans to Paris in 1875, or by Hippolyte Panhard from Paris to Nice in 1892, and they were plagued by treacherous road conditions and fragile machinery. Even the first authentic 'race', the Paris–Rouen Trial of 1894, was not really meant to be a test of speed. The rules for the Trial, which was organized by the newspaper *Le Petit Journal*, stated only that the competitors should cover the 79 mile (126 km) journey in not more than twelve hours. Participating cars, therefore, needed to be reliable, efficient and safe but not necessarily fast. Comte Albert de Dion entered his steam tricycle and succeeded in covering the distance in 6 hours and 48 minutes. He was far ahead of all the other drivers but was not awarded the prize because his vehicle was judged too fast and dangerous. It had travelled the 79 miles (126 km) at an average speed of 13·6 mph (22 kph)! Victory went to Lemaitre in a Peugeot, who reached Rouen much later than De Dion but was judged to have performed more safely.

However absurd it may seem to separate speed from the field of racing, it would have been against the very concept of the event, though there was a progressive increase in the

The first Daimler to be called a Mercédès was this 35PS of 1901, designed by Maybach as a racing car

average speed in all subsequent races. The fever of speed had by now got the upper hand and by the turn of the century there had already been impressive achievements. For example, in 1902 Marcel Renault went from Paris to Vienna at an average speed of 45 mph (72 kph); the following year Gabriel's Mors reached Bordeaux en route from Paris to Madrid at an average speed of 65·3 mph (105·8 kph), while in 1905 Vincenzo Lancia's 110 hp Fiat Sport reached a maximum of 100 mph (160 kph). Considering the weight on the front axle, the lack of braking power and all the other shortcomings, it is terrifying to think of the speeds attained by those early racing cars. It is possible that timing equipment and distances were somewhat inaccurate, as observed by Count Biscaretti di Ruffia, an Italian motoring pioneer and enthusiast, although, even allowing for some errors, the results which have been recorded are nevertheless astounding.

In the meantime, however, races had already begun to pass on useful information. In the 1895 Paris–Bordeaux–Paris event the Michelin brothers tested pneumatic tyres on their Peugeot, which is considered the first practical application on motor vehicles of the Scot, John Boyd Dunlop's invention, patented by him in 1888. In 1896 the ingenious Comte de Dion introduced the first internal combustion engine with electric ignition and the same year saw the tiller-rod replaced by a steering wheel, though this development was regarded as the cause of the accident in which Emile Levassor, the driver and manufacturer, lost his life.

One characteristic of the early racing events was that cars were often driven by their manufacturers, like De Dion, Renault, Panhard, Levassor and many others, although this practice soon disappeared and the driving was taken over by specialized racing drivers, such as Szisz, Baras, Héméry, Duray, Salzer, Thomas, Goux, Nazzaro, Lancia and Cagno. Above all, these champions were fully acquainted with the mechanics of engines and for the most part were engineers themselves,

Right the Renault in which Marcel Renault won the 1902 Paris–Vienna (Renault collection)
Below right the 999 (left) racing against the Mercédès-Simplex of Henry Harkness
Bottom right the 999 built by Henry Ford in 1903

Three photographs of early motor races
Above René de Knyff in a Panhard & Levassor, pictured after his victory in the Paris–Bordeaux of 1898
Bottom left a Renault in the 1901 Paris–Berlin race
Top left Louis Renault setting off in the Paris–Madrid in 1903, the tragic race which was stopped at Bordeaux because of the many accidents which occurred; in one such accident Marcel Renault, brother of Louis, lost his life

and secondly, they were men of exceptional stamina with great endurance. In particular, they were mature, as young drivers were not considered eligible for such a highly responsible position, requiring many years of experience. Of course, as drivers they were unsophisticated, which was in keeping with the cars of the time, but they were fast and courageous judging by performances based on reports of the difference between average and maximum speeds. Felice Nazzaro lavishly praised the driving abilities of Varzi and Nuvolari, with particular emphasis on their judgement, which is now taken for granted in young racing drivers. It was, however, the development of the car itself which contributed to higher standards of driving from generation to generation.

The adoption of different racing formulae gave rise to much research and to development of cars and drivers alike, although it was a long time before engineering reached a stage where an exciting race could be guaranteed.

The first serious attempt at standardization of racing rules came with the famous Gordon Bennett Cup series (1900–1905), the first of which was also regarded as the first international race. It was instigated by the American James Gordon Bennett, proprietor of the *New York Herald*, when he moved to Paris to set up a French edition of the paper. Extremely rich and a lover of all sport, Gordon Bennett was among the first adherents to the new means of transport, so much so that he decided to aid its progress and popularity by organizing races of great renown in which the major European and American manufacturers would take part.

Thus, in November 1899, the American journalist sent a letter to motoring organizations (which either were or were to become the national automobile clubs) in France, Germany, England, Italy, Belgium, Switzerland, Austria and the United States in which he invited them to take part in a 'Prix International' to take place the following year in France. The rules of the competition, comprising twenty-four articles and composed by Gordon Bennett himself, were attached to each letter. Each nation could enter a maximum of three cars, powered by an internal combustion engine, steam or electricity. The only restrictions were a minimum weight of 400 kg, an insistence on two seats and a minimum weight of 70 kg for the occupants.

Gordon Bennett commissioned a Parisian goldsmith to design a trophy which was to go to the nation which entered the winning car. The competition was described simply as an International Prize or an International Cup, as he disliked all forms of personal publicity; the Gordon Bennett Cup was the name later given by others in homage to him.

The first event took place on 14 June 1900 on the 354-mile (569 km) route from Paris to Lyons. The number of entries was rather disappointing, with only five cars, three Panhards for France, a Snoeck-Bolide for Belgium and a Winton for the United States, on the list. The two Panhards of Charron and Girardot were the only cars to pass the winning post in Lyons. The race was won (at an average speed of 38·6 mph or 62 kph) by the former, who arrived one and a half hours before his team driver, in spite of coming off the road after running over a dog.

In view of the competition's limited success, the organizers decided to hold the 1901 event in conjunction with the Paris–Bordeaux race, on the oldest and most popular of French racing routes of the time. The decision was a wise one as only three cars, all French, were entered for the second Gordon Bennett race, which took place on 29 May 1901; these were the two Panhards of Charron and Girardot and Levegh's Mors. In fact, a fourth car was entered, S. F. Edge's Napier, but that was disqualified because it had Michelin pneumatic tyres – the rules of the Cup demanded that all cars and their components and accessories were exclusively manufactured in their country of origin, and Edge was obliged to withdraw from the Paris–Bordeaux. For the 1901 race the minimum weight had been raised to 650 kg. Of the three cars which took part, only Girardot's Panhard passed the winning post. Its average speed of 37 mph (59·533 kph) was much lower than that of Fournier's Mors which won the actual Paris–Bordeaux race at 53·12 mph (85 kph).

The third Gordon Bennett Cup was also held in conjunction with another race, the Paris–Vienna, for fear of poor participation, but the finishing line was at Innsbruck. Four cars were entered, Girardot's 60 hp CGV, Fournier's 60 hp Mors, De Knyff's 70 hp Panhard for France and Edge's Napier for England. The last named won, thus transferring organization of the 1903 race to England.

This fact was important for the survival and future of the race as, with the French monopoly

Above *the three 90 hp Renaults prepared for the 1906 French Grand Prix with drivers Szisz, who won the race, Edmon and Richet*
Right *Georges Boillot in the Peugeot L76 with which he won the 1912 French Grand Prix*
Below *Albert Guyot being congratulated for his victory in the Grand Prix des Voiturettes in 1908, run in Dieppe in conjunction with the French Grand Prix; the car was a single-cylinder Delage*

**Opposite page
top to bottom**
*the 80 hp Napier driven by Edge in the 1903 Gordon Bennett Cup which took place in Ireland
Felice Nazzaro in a 110 hp Fiat in the 1905 Gordon Bennett, where he came second to Théry in a Richard-Brasier
The racing Locomobile which won the 1908 Vanderbilt Cup*

broken, the Cup finally achieved the fame and prestige that it deserved. The fourth event in the series took place in Ireland, because races on public roads were banned in England, on 2 July 1903. There were twelve competitors, representing France, Germany, the United States and, naturally, England and the race aroused the enthusiasm of the large crowd along the route. Jenatzy's 60 hp Mercédès won, the Cup passed to Germany and interest in the race grew. In 1903 a maximum weight limit of 1000 kg was introduced.

The fifth race took place on 20 May 1904 on a difficult route chosen personally by the Kaiser in the mountainous region of Taunus. Nineteen cars were entered, a total of seven countries – Germany, England, Austria, Belgium, France, Italy and Luxembourg. The prestige of the race among car manufacturers was now such that France and England had to organize heats to choose the three official cars to be entered for the Cup. On the twisting Taunus roads, Théry won, with an 80 hp Richard-Brasier, an achievement which he

Above *a 1903 racing De Dietrich, designed by Ettore Bugatti*
Below *the 1907, eight-cylinder Dufaux had a capacity of almost 13,000 cc (Transport Museum, Lucerne)*
Opposite page *the 1907, 120 hp Itala Grand Prix*

repeated the following year in the sixth and final Gordon Bennett Cup.

In 1904 the American equivalent of the Gordon Bennett Cup came into being. This was the Vanderbilt Cup, named after its sponsor William Vanderbilt, a rich financier and famous motoring enthusiast. From 1906 onwards the race should have taken place in the winning country of the previous year but, to the great disappointment of its creator, it never crossed the Atlantic and was contested only on American circuits. Until 1908 the best European cars and drivers took part in it, but thereafter it lost much of its prestige when it was limited to touring cars and was run in conjunction with the American Grand Prix.

The most worthy successor to the Gordon Bennett Cup was the French Grand Prix, initiated by the Automobile Club in France in 1906. At the time it was called the Grand Prix of the ACF (Automobile Club de France) and only acquired its present name with the first post-war race in 1921. The French Grand Prix also kept Gordon Bennett's maximum weight for cars of 1000 kg; it introduced the first official Grand Prix formula, launched in 1906 by the International Association of Recognized Automobile Clubs (eventually to become the present International Automobile Federation – the FIA).

As has already been seen, engineering standardization is one of the most important facets of motor racing. The search for effective norms was not easy. After weight restrictions, there followed a limitation on fuel consumption (30 liters per 100 km, or around 9.4 mpg in 1907), and a maximum piston area (755 sq cm in 1908), which led to the construction of engines with a very long stroke, often more than double the cylinder bore. It was only in 1914 that cubic capacity was accepted as the principal limitation.

The French Grand Prix, the most long-standing race, is considered a milestone in the history of Grand Prix racing. Thirty-seven cars took part in the first event, twenty-five from France and twelve from Italy and Germany.

The race took place over two days and was an endurance test for both drivers and cars. The Italas driven by Cagno, Fabry and De Caters were forced to retire and the Fiats driven by Lancia and Weillschott were far behind. Nazarro driving a Fiat managed to come second after Szisz in a Renault.

A number of Mercédès cars of the same period: the 60PS in which Jenatzy won the 1903 Gordon Bennett Cup; the 1904 60PS Simplex Rennwagen and the 1914 French Grand Prix 115PS

158

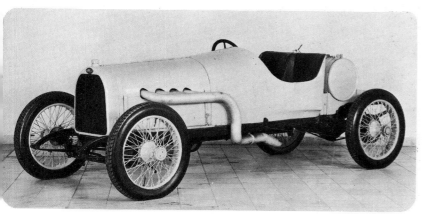

Three Opel racing models from the pre-war period: the 1908 Grand Prix model, the 1910 Prinz Heinrich Fahrt model and the 4500 cc, 110PS Rennwagen of 1913

In 1907 the organizers allowed three cars per manufacturer. For the first time cars were painted with their national colours (Fiat changed from black to red) and the competition numbers were preceded by the manufacturer's initial. Vincenzo Lancia's Fiat started first, followed at one minute intervals by all the other cars. When Lancia withdrew, Nazzaro went into the lead, also in a Fiat, and won the race. For the first time the name of the Turin company was inscribed in the Grand Prix record books.

The 1908 race ended with a clear win for Germany, with two cars in the first two places, these being Lautenschlager's Mercédès followed by Héméry in a Benz.

Racing presented a heavy financial burden for manufacturers, who began to lose interest in it with the result that the French Grand Prix was suspended for three years during which time a new concept of the racing car was developed. The construction of powerful 11- and 16-liter monsters demanded substantial capital and the results did not justify the expense. Less cumbersome cars were needed, with a reduced cubic capacity, but at the same time sufficiently powerful to attain the speeds which were now taken for granted.

Peugeot pointed the way with his prototype of a modern racing car which he entered for the Le Mans Grand Prix of 1911, a less important version of the French Grand Prix which was still not back in the calendar. The 7·6-liter engine had twin overhead camshafts and four inclined valves per cylinder; its power output was declared to be 175 bhp, but in truth it was only around 130 bhp, making it equal to the large earlier cars, but obtained with a thirty per cent cut in the cubic capacity. In the end Peugeot did not take part in the Le Mans race, but entered the Grand Prix when it was resumed the following year, in 1912. The Peugeot, driven by Georges Boillot, won easily. The same driver in the same car, but with its cubic capacity reduced to 5650 cc, won the race again the following year.

Peugeot's innovations were not wasted; nearly all the big manufacturers began making racing cars based on the French company's revolutionary model. The rules for the 1914 race were changed and finally the maximum cubic capacity was fixed at 4500 cc for that year.

The 1914 French Grand Prix took place in a particularly tense atmosphere, on 4 July 1914 on the eve of World War I, and the rivalry between France and Germany seemed to foreshadow the tragic events which erupted on 2 August. The German team scored a sweeping victory, with Mercédès in the first three places. Peugeot came fourth and Delage eighth.

In addition to the French Grand Prix, there was another exciting race on the international scene. That was the Italian Targa Florio, for which cars arrived in Sicily by sea from all over Europe and which was also very important for its generous prize money of 40,000 lire. It was the clever Don Vincenzo Florio, son of a very rich family, who conceived an entirely Sicilian race. With his blend of enthusiasm, intelligence and money it was not difficult to make his dream come true. In truth, the idea of a car race on Sicilian roads seemed madness, but it was gradually accepted. In spite of inevitable opposition, the Targa Florio – or more simply the Targa – became an exciting and fascinating reality. For this achievement Vincenzo Florio can be regarded as one of the great patrons of motor racing, along with the Americans, Gordon Bennett and William Vanderbilt.

The first Targa was on Sunday, 6 May 1906, over three laps of the 92·5 mile (148·9 km) 'Great' Madonie circuit – or almost 300 miles (500 km). Twenty-two cars were entered, ten started. There was Vincenzo Lancia in a Fiat, Henry Fournier, winner of the 1901 Paris–Berlin, the bearded Le Blon in a Hotchkiss, who had his wife with him as his mechanic, the Englishman, Pope, who set off smoking a cigar, and Alessandro Cagno in an Itala, who beat everyone.

There were fifty entries for the 1907 race which was a straight fight between Italy and France. In that year the Targa was one of three European races which formed part of a world championship of sorts. As in the Emperor's Cup in Germany and the Grand Prix in France (the two preceding races), Felice Nazzaro's Fiat was unrivalled. The French manufacturer Darracq entered two cars which both retired because of breakdowns. Darracq blamed his drivers, and his team leader, Louis Wagner, left for Fiat.

In 1908 there were only thirteen participants for the Targa. After Nazzaro and Lancia retired, an outsider won Trucco, in an Isotta Fraschini. The following race was just as disappointing after several local enthusiasts were asked to enter so that there would be a reasonable number of participants. Florio himself

competed in a privately owned Fiat and just missed winning, beaten by Ciuppa in a SPA by one minute.

The car and motoring were at the height of a crisis and it seemed as if racing enthusiasts would turn their attention to the recent development in aviation. The Targa, however, survived in hope of better times. It was won by Cariolato in 1910 and by Ceirano in 1911, and then changed its formula for races preceding World War I to arouse keener interest. In 1912 it became the Tour of Sicily, one thousand kilometers (621 miles) without stopping. Victory went to a young English driver, Cyril Snipe, who had emigrated to drive for SCAT in Turin. Finding himself in the lead by over two hours, Snipe stopped his car, lay down on the ground and fell asleep and had to be woken by his mechanic, Pedrini, with a bucket of water. He set off again and still

This bronze plaque, presented to the winner of the first Targa Florio in 1906, was specially commissioned by Vincenzo Florio, instigator of the great Sicilian event, who is seen below standing beside Alessandro Cagno's Itala, which won the race

passed the winning post with half an hour to spare over his closest rivals.

In 1913 the Targa Florio-Tour of Sicily was divided into two stages, (Palermo-Agrigento, Agrigento-Palermo) as the organizers had obviously realized that the drivers could not be subjected to superhuman demands. In the first car of his own construction, Felice Nazzaro came in first by an hour from the Italian Aquila of Marsaglia. On 24 and 25 May 1914 the ninth Targa took place with a tour of the island in two stages (Palermo-Siracusa, Siracusa-Palermo). Ceirano won in a SCAT. A great number of drivers had to retire, including Nazzaro, Snipe and a young driver destined to have a great future, Giuseppe Campari, who drove one of the first A.L.F.A. cars, later to become Alfa Romeo, in that race.

After the war the Targa was one of the first sporting events to be resumed on a regular basis and the tenth race took place in November 1919. Wind and snow made the route more hazardous than ever and the first to suffer was Antonio Ascari in a Grand Prix Fiat which overturned. The race was won by the young André Boillot in a Peugeot which, in spite of leaving the road six times, beat the Ballot driven by the veteran René Thomas. One of the competitors was the young Enzo Ferrari at the wheel of a CMN, but he retired after being delayed in one of the remote inland villages.

A brief look at the various races in the first part of the twentieth century reveals the

difficulties, hazards and unforeseen problems which faced drivers in terms of both the length and dangers of the route, the unreliability of engineering and the complete lack of outside assistance. Yet all the races so far described are as nothing compared to the marathons in which cars and drivers ventured across entire continents for thousands of miles. The 10,000-mile (16,000 km) Peking–Paris race in 1907 and the 21,000-mile (34,000 km) New York–Paris marathon in 1908, are two events which, seventy years later, still arouse the same admiration and the same wonder.

The 28/40 hp Fiat of Felice Nazzaro, the winner of the second Targa (1907), rounding a corner in the village of Petralia

A competitor, Porporato, in a Berliet in the 1908 Targa, which was won by Trucco in an Isotta-Fraschini

Predictably, the number of teams that eventually set out was considerably less than the number of entries; of the twenty-five cars entered, only five appeared in Peking, after travelling to China by sea. There was Prince Scipione Borghese's 35/45 hp Itala, who was accompanied by Luigi Barzini of the *Corriere della Sera* and the driver-engineer Ettore Guizzardi. There were two De Dion-Bouton 10 hp cars (entered officially by the French company), driven by Cormier and Collignon, a 15 hp Dutch Spyker, driven by Godard, and Pons in a French 6 hp Contal tricycle.

The favorites were the two, light, De Dion cars and also the Contal tricycle which, despite its fragile structure, was held to be capable of victory. Experts, or self-styled experts, maintained that the lightest possible cars, which were easy to handle, were needed to overcome the hazards of such a long and dangerous journey. The large Itala was decidedly unpopular and, according to most people, would sink in the first swamp or come to a halt at the first hill because of its massive structure.

As often happens, all predictions were wrong and the Italian car, fully exploiting the power of its four large cylinders with a capacity of 7433 cc, went into the lead immediately, and continued to increase the gap between it and its rivals. The small Contal, the lightest car of all, was the first to run into difficulties on the treacherous Chinese roads, which were more suitable for carriages drawn by animals. The Spyker and the two De Dions did very well but were much slower than the Itala on account of their lower engine power.

The route crossed the Gobi desert, Mongolia, the whole of Siberia, Russia, Poland and Germany, to the very distant finishing line in Paris.

The first problems for all the competitors were encountered in the Gobi desert and became gradually worse as the days went by and the unstable wheels of the cars covered mile after mile. Prince Borghese, who had planned the journey in the minutest detail, had fitted his car with all the equipment for such an unpredictable undertaking. Although the bodywork was made as light as possible, the car was weighed down by the equipment and there were numerous occasions when natives had to extract it from difficult situations – for which service they were generously rewarded by the Italian prince. Borghese's most serious problem occurred in the heart of

'Will anyone be willing to drive from Peking to Paris next summer?' ran the advertisement which appeared in the Paris newspaper *Le Matin* in March 1907. It was an obvious invitation to a negative response; surely no sensible person would agree to such a mad idea at that time? Yet, incredible as it may seem, by the following April twenty-five teams had already agreed to participate. What had at first seemed an impossible idea was becoming a real race with so many entries that rules had to be drawn up. The organizers fixed the starting date for 10 June from the Voyron French barracks in Peking.

The famous driver Felice Nazzaro changed to car
manufacturing in 1911. His first car was the Model 2,
available in three versions with different wheelbases
(standard, long and racing). Nazzaro himself won the
1913 Targa Florio-Tour of Sicily in one of these cars

Prince Scipione Borghese's 35/45 hp Itala, which won the Peking–Paris race in 1907 in 61 days and is now in the Museo dell'Automobile, Turin

During the journey the Italian team was faced with all kinds of difficulties. The picture shows the Itala stuck in mud near the river Hun in China

When the 'horsepower' of the car was insufficient, Prince Borghese frequently used local peasants to pull the car out of difficulty, for which they were generously rewarded

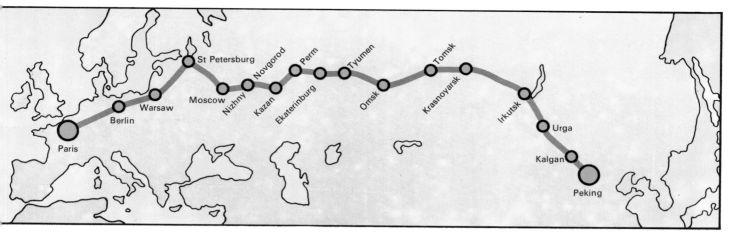

The map above shows the 10,000-mile route from Peking to Paris. In China, the Gobi desert, Mongolia and Siberia, roads hardly existed; animals were used to pull the Itala across rivers as the few bridges there were could not support the heavy Italian car

Siberia when a wheel was irreparably broken. The race seemed lost and even the able engineer, Guizzardi, could do nothing with the wheel. Fortunately, a local carpenter made a new wooden wheel which was sufficiently strong to enable the Itala to finish the journey. The wheel and the car are now in the Museo dell'Automobile in Turin.

On 20 July the Itala reached the border between Asia and Europe and seven days later the Italian team was given a triumphal welcome in Moscow. The two De Dions and the Spyker, which were seventeen days behind, were still struggling in the mud of Siberia.

From Moscow to Petersburg, Warsaw and Berlin, Scipione Borghese, Luigi Barzini and Ettore Guizzardi were enthusiastically hailed by the public, and Berlin was festively adorned for their arrival.

At ten o'clock on 10 August 1907, the three courageous Italians entered Paris. In front of the *Le Matin* office the winners of the incredible adventure, overcome with emotion and fatigue, were literally snatched from the seats of their car and carried in triumph by a delighted crowd. The remaining three cars in the race (the Contal tricycle had been eliminated in Asia), reached the French capital 21 days later.

The day after the Peking–Paris race ended and to celebrate its success, *Le Matin* announced another similar race, the New York–Paris event, a marathon of over 21,000 miles (34,000 km) in which the competitors would set out from New York and travel westwards to Paris. The starting date was fixed for 12 February 1908 and six cars appeared at the starting point, in Times Square in New York. They set off together, cheered by a crowd of over 200,000.

The six cars were a 30 hp De Dion–Bouton, a 24/30 hp Motobloc, a 900 cc, single-cylinder Sizaire-Naudin, a 24/40 hp Züst, a 35/70 hp Protos and a 60 hp Thomas model 36. With the exception of the small Sizaire-Naudin, all had four-cylinder engines.

Opposite page, from top to bottom
Three of the six cars which took part in the 1908 New York–Paris marathon
The winning car, the American Thomas; the Italian Züst and the German Protos
From top to bottom *a Richard-Brasier at the Ardenne race in 1906; the CGV racing model of 1905; Georges Boillot's Peugeot, winner of the hill-climb event at Mont Ventoux in 1912*

166

The favorites were the American Thomas and the German Protos, either for their greater power or for their careful preparation. The Protos in particular was extremely well equipped. The Germans, who had not taken part in the Peking–Paris race, saw an opportunity of reviving their national prestige and asserting the supremacy of their motoring industry. It was Kaiser Wilhelm II who wanted Protos to enter for the race and the team was led by Hans Koeppen, a lieutenant in the Prussian Infantry, together with the military engineer, Hans Knape and an officer, Ernst Maas. Thomas's team was made up of George Schuster, an engineer in the company, the driver, Montague Roberts, and Harold Brankes. Although the car was still an impressive size, it appeared more fragile than the Protos.

The other four cars aroused less interest, even though the French did not conceal their confidence of winning, either with the Motobloc – with its team comprising the baron Godard, the photographer Livier and the engineer Huc – or with the equally solid De Dion, driven by Bourcier Saint–Chaffray, with the Norwegian Hansen and the Austrian engineer. However, there were no hopes for the little Sizaire-Naudin which looked like a toy car compared to its powerful rivals and merely inspired pity.

Finally, there were many people who were convinced that the Italian Züst would win, especially in view of the Italian team's victory in the Peking–Paris race the year before. On this occasion the car was driven by Sirtori and the team included the engineer Haag and Antonio Scarfoglio, a journalist with the Neapolitan newspaper *Il Mattino*.

The race was extremely difficult. The problems started soon after the competitors set off to cross the United States. Rain, mud, snow and ice immediately tested both cars and drivers. The first to reach the Pacific coast was the Thomas which took forty-one days to do so. All the others were caught by difficulties of various kinds.

The Protos, too, ran into trouble and, by Seattle, was already three weeks behind the Thomas. It was at this point that lieutenant Koeppen made a decision which was to cost him dearly. In his effort to gain on Schuster, he loaded his car onto a train and in this way covered more than 1000 miles (1600 km). At first he was disqualified, but was later readmitted with fifteen days' penalty. The other cars were by now out of the race.

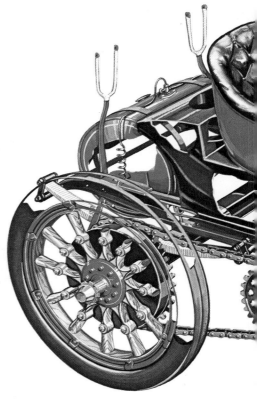

These two pages give an overall view of Fiat racing cars from 1904–1912
Above *a 1904 24 hp sports model*
Right *from top to bottom: Felice Nazzaro in the 100 hp of 1905; Vincenzo Lancia in the 28/40 hp at the 1907 Targa Florio; Nazzaro in the Taunus model which won the 1907 Emperor's Cup*
Below *the 75 hp, the first real racing Fiat, on the eve of the 1904 Gordon Bennett Cup*

Above *a cutaway drawing of the classic 1907 Grand Prix Fiat, showing the novel solution to valve control by means of hinged pushrods*
Below *the 1908 130 hp car at the Circuit of Bologna, won by Nazzaro*
Bottom *the SB4, built for the famous contest between Nazzaro and the Napier driven by Edge, which took place at Brooklands in 1908*

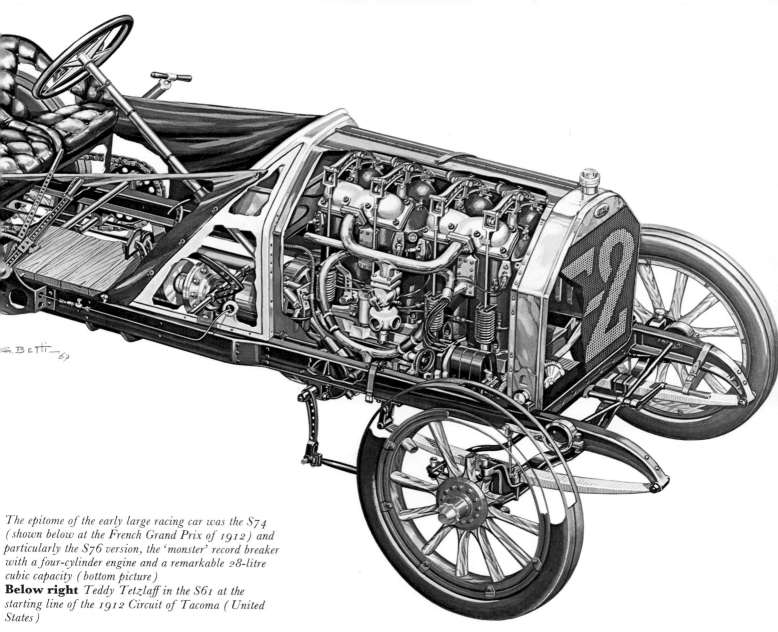

G. BETTI 67

The epitome of the early large racing car was the S74
(shown below at the French Grand Prix of 1912) and
particularly the S76 version, the 'monster' record breaker
with a four-cylinder engine and a remarkable 28-litre
cubic capacity (bottom picture)
Below right Teddy Tetzlaff in the S61 at the
starting line of the 1912 Circuit of Tacoma (United
States)

The German team's tactics again proved unethical when it came to leaving the American continent for Asia. Whereas Schuster, in the Thomas, had followed the rules to the letter and, upon arrival in Alaska had crossed the Bering strait on a steamer, then driven across Japan, again boarding a ship and disembarking at Vladivostock, lieutenant Koeppen put his Protos onto a ship and, crossing the Pacific, reached Vladivostock directly. From here he set out almost at the same time as his rival, Schuster, to cross Siberia.

For several hundred miles the two cars were almost level and followed the Trans Siberian railway, but at one point the Thomas suffered a complete breakdown which the American team had to repair, costing them a few days' work. Koeppen, of course, did not help his rival (which Schuster had in fact done for Koeppen a short while before, when he stopped his car to drag the Protos out of the mud, in which it was completely immobilized) and so gained over two weeks on the American.

Later, however, the German car also ran into trouble and Schuster succeeded in narrowing the gap considerably. Koeppen, however, reached Paris first, on 27 July, amid general apathy. All the celebrations were reserved for the Thomas, which arrived three

Above *the 1914 Mercédès Grand Prix, which had a top speed of over 110 mph* **Below** *the Fiat S57/14B of 1916* **Opposite page, from top to bottom** *the 3000 cc Delage made for the Coupe de l' Auto in 1911; the 3-litre Peugeot of 1913; the 4·5-litre Peugeot driven by Boillot in the 1914 French GP*

days later and was immediately hailed as the real winner of the race. In fact, according to the rules, the Protos was penalized a whole month – another two weeks' penalty being added to the original fifteen days, for crossing the Pacific by sea.

Since the beginning of the century, motor racing had become increasingly varied and sophisticated. Cars and drivers were now faced with a choice between numerous competitions, encompassing the extremely fast Grands Prix, the marathons, traditional road races or hill-climbs and record-breaking events. In practice, the only types of racing which still did not exist were circuit racing on closed circuits, with facilities designed exclusively for motor racing, and rallies. Neither of these were to be long in making their appearance, the former in 1907 with the inauguration of Brooklands consolidated in 1911 with the opening of the famous Indianapolis 'speedway' and the latter with the first Monte Carlo Rally in 1911.

Brooklands was built as the only alternative to the absurdly strict laws then governing British motoring. As racing on public roads was banned, British motorists had no choice but to travel abroad for races, incurring considerable expense. It was Mr H. F. Locke King, backed by his wife and a substantial personal fortune, who solved the problem. In 1906 he bought a large piece of land some 20 miles (32 km) from London and in just over a year (at a cost of £250,000) Brooklands became reality. The first track was a sort of ellipse which was very wide on one side. It was 2·75 miles (4·42 km) long and 100 ft (30 m) wide, boasted two very elevated bends, and could hold 35,000 spectators.

The success of the Brooklands track (Indianapolis came four years later and Monza in 1922) immediately exceeded all expectations. It was not only spectacular but was also technically superb. It was officially opened on 17 June 1907 and about ten days later Brooklands held a record-breaking event. The proposal was sensational and the

Principal Isotta-Fraschini racing cars
Top *the 100 hp model D, built in 1905 from a Giuseppe Stefanini design. It had a 17-litre, four-cylinder engine with camshafts in the head*
Above *the 50/80 hp model 'I Corsa', winner of the 1907 Targa Florio, driven by Nando Minoia, and of the Briarcliff Trophy of the same year, driven by Lewis Strang*

Above right *the small model FE, Stefanini's masterpiece, built for the 1908 Grand Prix des Voiturettes in Dieppe where it won the four-cylinder formula race*
Below right *the imposing chassis of the 120 hp model KM, built in 1910–1913 from a Giustino Cattaneo design. As in all the more powerful Isotta-Fraschini cars, it had chain transmission*

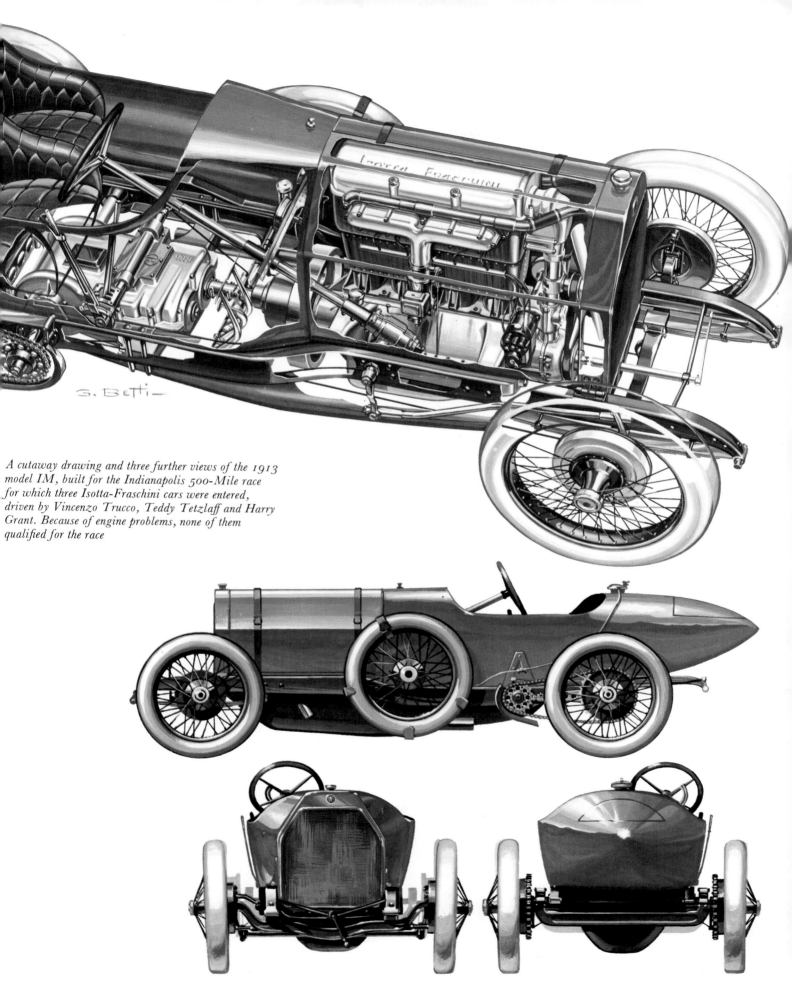

A cutaway drawing and three further views of the 1913 model IM, built for the Indianapolis 500-Mile race for which three Isotta-Fraschini cars were entered, driven by Vincenzo Trucco, Teddy Tetzlaff and Harry Grant. Because of engine problems, none of them qualified for the race

driver Edge in a Napier announced his intention to drive for 24 hours at a speed of between 45 (73) and 60 mph (96 kph) without stopping. It was a complete success; indeed, instead of the estimated 60 mph (96 kph) it proved possible to average almost 66 mph (106 kph) on the track. It defined a role for Brooklands as the ideal ground for attempting records for all distances.

Equally suitable for speed tests was the American equivalent of Brooklands, the Indianapolis track, where the Memorial Day 500, one of the fastest, richest, most spectacular and most dangerous races in the world is now run. Indy represents the keenest spirit of American motor racing and has become part of the country's folklore, enhanced by the excitement, accidents and money which surround it. The most difficult part of the race lies in being accepted for entry. The qualification runs – only 33 cars are allowed to take part – are frequently more interesting than the race itself. Drivers and engineers spend a whole year 'preparing for Indianapolis' and everything can be made or broken on just a few qualifying laps. If all goes well, the car makes the race, and perhaps a good deal of money; if qualifying goes badly, the team has little option but to start preparing for the following year.

The long, exciting story of the Indy 500 began in 1911 with the opening of the race track. A solid gold brick is traditionally concealed within the track on race day (it is removed at the end of each race and kept in a safer place until the following year, either by tradition or as a precaution!). The first winner of the American race was Ray Harroun in a Marmon at an average speed of 74.6 mph (120 kph). A Fiat came third, driven by the American champion, David Bruce Brown. In 1912 the Italian company again entered a car, this time driven by Ted Tetzlaff, which came second, behind Joe Dawson in a National.

In 1913 and 1914 the 500 was won by France, first by Jules Goux in a Peugeot and then by René Thomas in a Delage. In 1915 Ralph De Palma came first in a Mercédès, followed by Dario Resta in a Peugeot. The same Peugeot won the 1916 and 1919 races. At this point European cars had reached the peak of their success at Indianapolis, which they maintained for only a few more years before giving way to American cars.

If racing drivers could vent their desire for speed at Brooklands and Indianapolis, it was

not so for the participants in the first Monte Carlo Rally who, in 1911, were required to average just 15 mph (25 kph). The name of the event came from the French word *rallie* and the English word rally, both meaning a gathering. Its purpose and formula were completely new and it was launched more to promote winter tourism than for any interest in the sport itself. Moreover, it was organized along decidedly original lines. It was agreed that competitors should set out from the capital of their own country and drive to Monte Carlo. Upon their arrival in the Principality, marks would be awarded on the following basis: one point for adherence to the average speed; two points for each person in the car; a point for each hundred kilometers of the journey; up to ten points for the degree of comfort extended to passengers, the condition of the chassis and body of the car upon arrival, and for the elegance of the bodywork.

There were only twenty-three entrants in the first rally. They set out from Geneva, Paris, Berlin, Boulogne-sur-Mer (classified as a capital instead of London), Vienna and

Above *the Marmon Wasp of Ray Harroun, the car which won the first Indianapolis 500, in 1911*

Below *the 1903 Winton Bullet in which the manufacturer Alexander Winton covered the mile in 52.2 seconds at Daytona Beach in March 1903*

	Year	Car	Driver	Speed kmh	Notes
Jeantaud	1898	Jeantaud	Chasseloup	63·150	Electric-engined cars. All the runs were in the Achères park in Paris.
	1899	Jenatzy	Jenatzy	66·658	
	1899	Jeantaud	Chasseloup	70·312	
	1899	Jenatzy	Jenatzy	80·338	
Jenatzy	1899	Jeantaud	Chasseloup	92·697	
	1899	Jenatzy	Jenatzy	105·878	
Serpollet	1902	Serpollet	Serpollet	120·797	Steam car. Record established on the Promenade des Anglais in Nice.
Mors	1902	Mors	Vanderbilt	122·438	First record set by an internal combustion engined car. Record runs made in Ablis and Dourdan.
	1902	Mors	Fournier	123·275	
	1902	Mors	Augières	124,128	
Ford	1903	Gobron-Brillié	Duray	134·331	The records set by Duray, Rigolly and De Caters were set in Ostend and Nice. Those set by Ford and Vanderbilt were achieved on the frozen Lake St Clair and on Daytona Beach and were only recognized in the USA.
	1903	Gobron-Brillié	Duray	136·359	
	1904	Ford	Henry Ford	*147·045	
Mercedes	1904	Mercedes	Vanderbilt	*148,542	
	1904	Gobron-Brillié	Rigolly	152·533	
	1904	Mercedes	De Caters	156·508	
Gobron-Brillié	1904	Gobron-Brillié	Rigolly	166·647	
Darracq	1904	Darracq	Barras	168·208	Macdonald's record at Daytona was not approved because it was timed manually instead of automatically.
	1905	Napier	Macdonald	*168·48	
Napier	1905	Darracq	Hémery	176·464	
Stanley	1906	Stanley	Marriott	195·647	The Stanley was a steam car. Hémery's record at Brooklands was the last record set in Europe for a run in only one direction.
	1909	Benz	Hémery	202·696	
	1910	Benz	Oldfield	*211·266	
	1911	Benz	Burman	*227·512	
Benz	1914	Benz	Hornsted	199·719	
Sunbeam	1919	Packard	De Palma	*241·199	The record runs by De Palma and Milton were only recognized in the USA. The Sunbeam's achievement marked the beginning of a series of records set by cars with piston aero-engines.
	1920	Duesenberg	Milton	*251·105	
	1922	Sunbeam	Guinness	215·249	

* Records marked by an asterisk were not officially recognized.

first in Monte Carlo after travelling almost 2000 miles (32,000 km). Other factors also aroused interest and curiosity, such as the increase in average speeds recorded by several drivers, tragicomic adventures on the way, nights spent in the open, inaccurate navigation, and collisions with other competitors who had come from very distant cities and arrived at a half-hidden crossroads at the same time.

All this led to an initial atmosphere of euphoria and enthusiasm which soon waned when the results became known. The majority of participants were dissatisfied, if not indignant (victory did not go to the driver from St Petersburg, who was classified ninth, but to Beutler, in a Berliet, from Berlin). The organizers were accused of prejudice and incompetence and the event ended in universal condemnation. The Monte Carlo Rally was not resumed until 1924 and attained great popularity only after World War II.

There is just one field left to discuss in the fascinating history of motor sport, but it is a very important one throughout the world, namely world speed records. In motoring there are records of every kind covering the type of car, cubic capacity and performance, to name but a few, but the most prestigious record is undoubtedly that for outright speed.

The idea of speed records originated with the Frenchman Count Chasseloup-Laubat and the manufacturer Charles Jeantaud who,

Above *Jenatzy's Jamais Contente which won the contest with Chasseloup-Laubat's Jeantaud on 1 May 1899, reaching a speed of 65·79 mph*

Brussels between 21 and 25 January and eighteen arrived at their destination. After a careful examination of the cars and a whole day of precise calculations, H. Rougier was finally proclaimed as the winner. Rougier had come from Paris in a Turcat-Mery of 25 hp. In spite of the complicated method of choosing the winner, which gave rise to a number of objections (of which the loudest came from a German competitor from Berlin who was the first to reach Monte Carlo but was awarded only sixth place on account of the condition of his car), the rally was considered to be a success and aroused considerable interest in European motoring circles.

There were eighty-eight entrants in the second rally, one of whom was one André Nogel who left from St Petersburg and arrived

Below *the 1904 Darracq with a 200 hp V8 engine*

Below *four views of the Blitzen Benz, including, below left, Barney Oldfield's after it broke the world speed record in 1910. In 1911 Burman did the mile in a Benz at 141·37 mph*

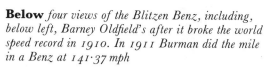

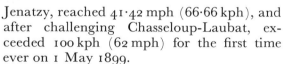

Above *the Packard record breaker which raised the mile record to 149·87 mph*

on 18 December 1898, in conjunction with the journal *La France Automobile*, organized the first speed event in the park at Achères, north of Paris. It was Chasseloup-Laubat himself, in a Jeantaud electric car, who reached a speed of 39·24 mph (63·15 kph), thus becoming the first land speed record holder in motoring history. His supremacy, however, was short-lived and a month later the Belgian,

Jenatzy, reached 41·42 mph (66·66 kph), and after challenging Chasseloup-Laubat, exceeded 100 kph (62 mph) for the first time ever on 1 May 1899.

The Automobile Club of France had in the meantime drawn up rules to govern such events and based them on covering one kilometre in just one direction.

The first petrol car to set a world speed record was Vanderbilt's Mors, which, in 1902, exceeded 75·8 mph (122 kph), breaking the mark set by Serpollet's steam car which had recorded a speed of 75·06 mph (120·797 kph) the same year. Approximately ten years were to pass before the record of 200 kph (124 mph) was attained. In 1909 Victor Hémery broke the record in a Benz and made the speedometer stop at the incredible figure of 125·95 mph (202·696 kph) at Brooklands. Over the years, speed records have continued to be broken, but on purely human grounds Jenatzy's achievement in 1899 when he exceeded the barrier of 100 kph (62 mph) is just as impressive as, if not more impressive than, that of Gabelich who, in 1970, became the first man to exceed 1000 kph (621 mph) in a vehicle on land.

A photograph of a recent London–Brighton run. Since 1927 the run has taken place in November every year to commemorate the first London–Brighton run of 14 November 1896 which celebrated the repeal of the 'Locomotives on Highways Act'

Motoring Curiosities

The term automobile is now so common that it is hard to believe that it could have been the subject of so much heated controversy, and even parliamentary debate, at the end of the last century. The word is of French origin and appeared for the first time in September 1875, used as an adjective in the expression *voiture automobile*, and an adjective it remained until about 1890 when it came to be used as a noun.

Today, a car is usually referred to as 'she'; the distinguished linguist Michel Bréal, (1832–1915) said that as it had originally been used as an adjective for a feminine noun, the word was feminine.

The purely academic controversy about the

Below *the writer Giosuè Carducci during a trip by car near Madesimo in 1902*

gender of the car was indicative of the great interest which the new means of locomotion aroused. Interest, however, does not necessarily go hand in hand with approval and, in fact, in its early days, the car had more enemies than supporters. Although the majority of public opinion condemned the car as demoniac, dangerous, noisy and smelly, there were few people who went as far as the excesses advocated in the famous editorial in the *Journal de Genève* which declared that every motorist was a potential murderer and that in the absence of appropriate legislation, citizens should defend themselves by shooting at the tyres of every car they came across.

A photograph of the Via del Corso, Rome, around 1915. Traffic is very light and consists mostly of horse-drawn carriages and carts. The rule of the road still insisted on driving on the left

' On the one hand, opposition was kindled by those who had a vested interest in animal traction and who therefore saw the car as a rival to their lucrative business, and on the other hand left-wing political parties considered it an elitist product – which indeed it was – and maintained it was an insult to the proletariat. It was to be the proletariat, however, who laid the foundation of its success and it was the proletariat who acclaimed the very first motor races and the first champion drivers.

It soon became essential that motor vehicles should be subject to some form of traffic law. As often happens with something so completely without precedent, the early traffic laws were counterproductive to the development of motoring and almost killed it at birth. The problem is well illustrated by the 'Locomotives on Highways Act', introduced by the British government in 1861 and stating that all automotive vehicles should be preceded by a pedestrian waving a red flag, as a danger warning. In 1893 the prefect of Paris formulated a more sensible ruling which contained the principles of modern traffic laws, namely some rules on safety, and speed limits. The former, which included requirements for double braking systems, a horn and headlamps were readily accepted by manufacturers, but the latter (including a maximum speed of 12 kph or 7½ mph in residential areas) provoked contempt on the part of motorists. The time had come for them to organize themselves to oppose, on legal grounds, the stupidity of the authorities in governing motoring matters. Consequently, the first Automobile Clubs were formed throughout Europe before the end of the last century. Clubs appeared in Austria and Belgium in 1896, in Great Britain

in 1897, in Italy, the Netherlands and Switzerland in 1898, and these were gradually followed by clubs in all the other 'motorized' countries of the world. The work of these organizations, the real champions of motoring, immediately proved very useful in promoting good propaganda for the car, by organizing the first international competitions and by intervening at the right level in all questions of motoring.

Traffic laws everywhere were as ill-defined as ever and were generally based on old laws dating back to the late nineteenth century. These defined broad general regulations for vehicles, but of course made no mention of cars as they did not yet exist. With the advent of motoring, and in the absence of any international legislation, each country enacted its own traffic regulations and in some countries the regulations varied even from district to district. This was the case in Italy, for example, where in Milan, with the heaviest motor traffic in the country, the district council demanded a traffic tax and further required that all owners of motor vehicles should apply in writing to the local authorities each time they intended to travel in their vehicle, stating the time and proposed route. This gem of bureaucracy on the part of the Milanese district councillors came into force in May 1897, and naturally aroused the indignation of members of the Italian Automobile Club, which had been founded in March of the same year. The Club appealed directly to the government and accused the Milanese council of abusing its power. The Club contended that the council had no right to legislate on a matter which was for the state alone to decide. The government sided with the motorists and the absurd law was repealed, although the

Opposite in stark contrast to the picture above is this photograph taken a few years later in the United States. If it was not for the cars, which clearly belong to an earlier period, the scene could show present day road conditions

traffic tax remained, albeit paid thereafter to the government and not to the local council.

In Britain it was Harry J. Lawson, father of the Daimler Motor Company, who by his continuous lobbying persuaded Parliament to take the sting out of the appallingly restrictive Locomotives Act. The new Act abolished the need for a 'flag-man' and raised the 4 mph (6·5 kph) speed limit to 12 mph (19 kph). The motorist's new-found freedom was celebrated by a motor run from London to Brighton on 14 November 1896 – 'Emancipation Day'. The event has been commemorated regularly ever since by the annual London to Brighton Run for pre-1905 vehicles.

Drivers, vehicles and roads all became the subject of legislation. Around the world, from the end of the last century, drivers had to have a licence. On the occasion of the Paris–Amsterdam–Paris race in 1898, an Italian newspaper said: '. . . among other things, the Paris police have insisted that each competitor is in possession of a permit for the race and a driving licence'. A year later the English paper *Truth* said: '. . . indeed, it is impossible to understand why a motorist should be tested before being allowed to drive a car, which can be easily controlled and does not have any speed of its own, while any scoundrel is at liberty to drive, without any test whatsoever, a strange animal with its own will and no brakes'.

In Italy, for example, the first legislation was introduced in October 1901; it consisted of fifty-one articles, with a lengthy section on the vehicle – stating that it was undoubtedly dangerous. Of the driver, it said: 'Motorists will be subject to appropriate visits and tests . . .' and a little further on: 'Whoever intends to drive a car must be provided with a licence issued by the prefecture after a test by the Civil Engineers, consisting of a test drive . . .' Later, in 1912 and 1914, the law in Italy was made more precise and licences were issued only when drivers had passed a test which in turn was preceded by a medical examination. In Britain, although a licence was obligatory there was no qualification for its granting. In 1902, to condemn the system, *The Autocar* obtained a licence for a blind beggar, who was then photographed, wearing a label saying 'Blind', sitting in a car. Nevertheless, compulsory driving tests did not come to Britain until 1934.

Number-plates also became obligatory for all motor vehicles from the very early days of motoring. The idea of identifying individual cars by number was first introduced for steam-powered vehicles in France in 1865, followed at various intervals by all other countries. Initially, only a rear number-plate was required and the front number-plate became *de rigueur* more recently. In Italy number-plates became law in 1903, and in Great Britain vehicle registration became compulsory in 1904.

From the earliest days, laws came into force to settle the question of which side of the road drivers should use; most European countries opted to drive on the right, although the

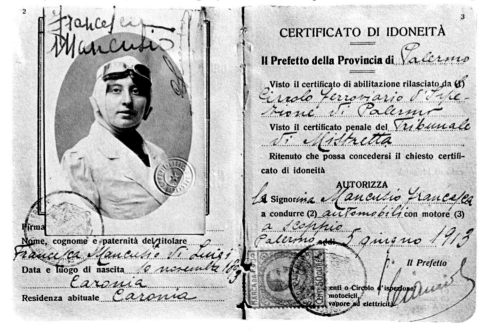

An Italian driving licence of 1913, one of the first issued to a woman. A year earlier a law had been passed requiring drivers of motor vehicles to take a test

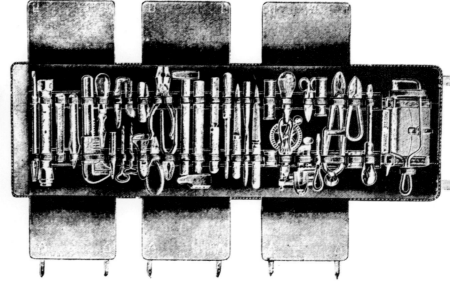

Above right *a very comprehensive tool kit of 1908*
Above *a lady driver coping with a puncture*

A variety of accessories advertised in magazines at the beginning of the century

British rule was 'drive on the left'. A particularly strange system existed in Italy where the general rule was 'drive on the right' but districts with over 25,000 inhabitants could adopt 'drive on the left' if they wished! In 1923 driving on the right was introduced for the whole of Italy. Speed limits varied from country to country, from day to night and from city to open road, and it also took some time in most countries for road tax to be standardized. In most cases the tax payable was based on the power of the engine, and was paid directly to the government.

From the outset the motorist was afflicted with a whole series of certificates, papers, licences and restrictions, as is still the case today. However, the modern motorist at least has the consolation of knowing that his struggles against bureaucracy are not the first and he has one further great advantage over his predecessors in that he can at least use a good road network with proper road signs. For early drivers any journey, however short, was an adventure.

KIRBY-ATLAS

Fig. 1. — Gonfleur KIRBY-ATLAS complet avec tuyau, raccord et manomètre.

LE GONFLEUR KIRBY-ATLAS

actionné par le moteur se monte en 2 minutes à la place d'une bougie.

Fig. 2. — Gonfleur KIRBY-ATLAS monté sur une 4 cylindres et gonflant un gros pneu en 3 minutes.

Notice No 431 envoyée franco sur demande, KIRBY, BEARD, Co. L., 5, rue Auber, Paris.

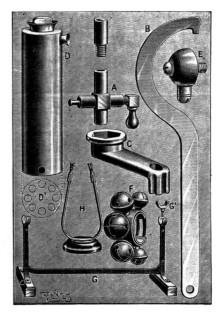

The condition of the roads was pitiful and cars, carriages and carts had to share the narrow, winding tracks of the time, which, in most places, were dry and dusty until the first rains came, when they became impassable swamps. The biggest nightmare for the early motorist was punctures and he could be plagued by several in just a few miles, each of which meant removing, stripping and re-mounting the wheel, which was time-consuming and tedious. Undoubtedly, the number of punctures was largely due to the fragility of the primitive tyres (even the later types with a leather tread were just as vulnerable) but the problem was also aggravated by stones and nails on the roads.

As a result of road conditions of seventy years ago, and not forgetting that cars were usually open and so gave little protection to either drivers or passengers, suitable clothing became an absolute necessity when travelling by car. Innumerable photographs of the time reveal a new type of fauna, the motorist in travelling garb. He was covered from head to foot in a long oilskin coat, wore goggles, and gloves up to the elbow. He was almost a parody of a medieval knight, dressed in armour ready to face the dangerous tourneys on the road which early motoring involved. Such armour, of course, was pure necessity to prevent the motorist being blinded by dust, injured by stones thrown up by other road users or simply to avoid succumbing to pneumonia in the event of rain.

It was not long before fashion came to play an important part in motoring, with the appearance of a whole series of specially designed clothes which were elegant as well as practical. Fur coats became popular, fur, until then, having been used mainly as a lining for collars and cuffs.

At the same time, cars too were becoming more elegant and a flourishing coachbuilding and accessory industry was growing to answer the motorist's desire to improve and embellish.

An accessory is now considered as any part which is not essential to the working of the car. Initially many devices which are now standard, such as horns, indicator lights, windscreen wipers, and so on, were launched as accessories. Other accessories were purely aesthetic or ornamental, the most common embellishment being radiator caps in the form of animals or other shapes. There were also expensive plated radiator covers, vases or elegant headlights to the strangest designs.

Above photographs of curious clothing as exhibited at the International Motoring Exhibition in Milan in 1901
Centre a team, wearing original clothes of the period, taking part in a modern race for veteran cars
Below since the beginning of motoring, fashion designers have been interested in designing motoring clothes for women and children as well as for drivers themselves

Count Roberto Biscaretti di Ruffia, one of the founders of the Italian Automobile Club, photographed in 1900 with his daughter and nieces in one of the first Fiat cars

Even more important were the coach-builders who clothed the chassis, as their work not only had to satisfy aesthetic demands, but was also very technical, particularly in terms of striking a balance between safety and comfort, for the bodywork protected both driver and passengers. Appearance was, naturally, the coachbuilder's first considera-tion as the first reaction to any object depends on whether it is pleasing to the eye. Knowing the weakness of human nature, coachbuilders tried to satisfy motorists' aesthetic demands,

A 1905 picture showing a car and passengers bespattered with dust and mud, bearing witness to the appalling condition of the roads of the time

Above *steering by tiller-rod with two vertical handles. The picture is dated 1896, by which time the steering wheel had already been introduced, as can be seen from the 1897 Daimler (left), with a vertical column topped by a wheel with florid ornamentation* **Below** *two steering wheels of 1897 and 1905. The first has a starting handle under which there are various controls, such as the accelerator and gearchange. The second, on the right, has an inclined column with two central controls for the accerator and ignition advance*

but never forgot the technical aspect of their work, a devotion which was unfortunately appreciated only by a few people within the trade.

In the early days of motoring, most manufacturers only supplied the mechanical components and left the bodywork entirely to the discretion of coachbuilders. The latter, as their name implies, were used to building coaches; when they were suddenly presented with an unfamiliar mechanical carriage they not surprisingly reproduced the line and style of horse-drawn vehicles, complete with whip-holders, umbrella stands and a plywood frame.

At the end of the century, bodywork was often confined to two uncomfortable seats and offered virtually no protection from the wind, dust and rain. The short wheelbase of the typical early car, and the innate fragility of its engineering, demanded restrictions in size, giving rise to strange designs to accommodate four passengers in the narrow *tonneau, vis-à-vis* and *dos-à-dos* styles in which most fashionable carriages of the time were built. In the first type access was from the rear, under the arches of the hood frame. There was not enough room for side doors because of the short wheelbase and the position of the chain transmission. A little progress was made with the advent of access from the side in the *tonneau* style, made

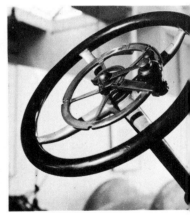

possible by making one of the front seats moveable (usually the left one as in most countries the steering wheel remained on the right until the 1920s). In the *vis-à-vis* the two passenger seats faced each other and the driver's seat was in the centre, although sometimes the driver's seat occupied an extra place in the front. In the *dos-à-dos* configuration passengers in the back seat had their backs to those in front.

After early attempts at building covered cars, perhaps the most famous example being the 1899 Renault made by the great French coachbuilder, Labourdette, this type of bodywork was largely ignored because it was

Accessories were used initially to improve a car's performance, but soon acquired an esthetic function. These photographs show some examples of horns and filter caps. There is also a very sophisticated little speaking tube system through which passengers could talk to the driver in the 1913 De Dion-Bouton (two centre photographs). Finally, the rear lamp, to illuminate the number-plate, and the tool box are not only useful, but elegant, too

Several of the early accessories were directly derived from the furnishings on horse-drawn carriages. For example, the umbrella-holder seen here was none other than the former whipholder of carriages

BERLINA

COUPÉ

SPIDER

CABRIOLET

These two tables show the development of coachbuilding from the beginning of motoring to 1920

1910   1920

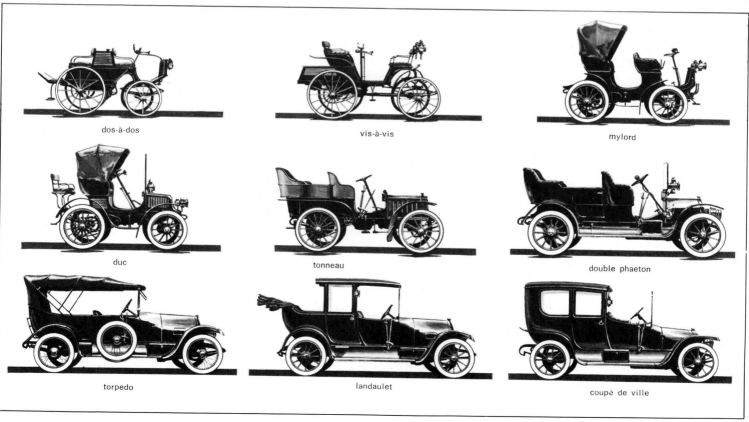

dos-à-dos

vis-à-vis

mylord

duc

tonneau

double phaeton

torpedo

landaulet

coupé de ville

considered too heavy. With the gradual
lengthening of the wheelbase, largely made
possible by the introduction of metal in place
of wood for chassis construction, cars became
more comfortable and, around 1904, covered
bodywork reappeared, although generally
only for the back, while the two front seats
(for the driver and his servant) were open, or
at most protected by a hood.

1908 saw the first example of 'torpedo'
bodywork, designed by the French coachbuilder, Lamplough, with a coherent, integ-
rated shape. The 'torpedo' shape started at
the radiator and continued unbroken to the
end of the car, with lines essentially parallel
to the ground. It was a very satisfactory shape
from the aesthetic viewpoint.

With the introduction of mass-production
in engineering, coachbuilding, too, had to
become industrialized. In Europe, most large-
scale car manufacturers set up their own
coachbuilding departments, whereas, in
America, responsibility for the bodywork

was usually assigned to specialist companies.
The title of Coachbuilder (the capital 'C' is
obligatory) was then used for the great masters
in the field, who specialized in creating
exclusive models with a beautiful finish and
very sophisticated accessories.

As the car became more popular, elegant
and comfortable, it also became faster and
therefore more dangerous. The risk of accidents increased and drivers found it necessary
to take out third party insurance policies,
which had already existed for a long time for
horse-drawn vehicles. However, at the beginning of the century the value of insurance for
private motorists was still largely ignored.
Insurance companies themselves did not
encourage policies with motorists. In a
circular sent by the Societa Anonima Italiana
d'Assicurazione contro gli Infortuni (Italian
Accident Insurance Company) to its agents
in 1901, regarding 'civil responsibility', it
was recommended that 'policies should be
sold for horses, owners of firearms, cyclists and
pharmacists as the widest and most profitable
field of operations, whereas motor insurance
is of much less interest for the scope is narrower
and the risks very high'.

However, one famous motorist of the period,
the Austrian emperor, Franz Josef, had
greater foresight. In 1908 he had to travel
from Vienna to Bad Ischl to meet King Edward
VII. It was an extremely important meeting,
arranged to discuss the 'triple alliance' and
the 'entente cordiale' which preceded World
War I. Having decided to travel by car, Franz
Josef decided to take out insurance before
leaving.

As he was widely known as an excellent
administrator, his historic policy brought
home the validity of motoring insurance to
many less illustrious drivers. Many years were
to pass, however, before this extremely useful
practice became obligatory instead of being
dependent on the motorist's civic responsi-
bilities. The first country to introduce compulsory insurance for cars was Denmark in
1918, followed by Austria in 1921, and subsequently every country followed the example
of the small Scandinavian state as the dangers
of crowded roads became evident.

From the beginning, coachbuilders played an essential role in motoring by improving not only the appearance of cars but also the standard of engineering work
Left the 24/40 hp Fiat Sparviero, 'dressed' by the Milanese coachbuilder, Cesare Sala, in 1906. The car belonged to the Italian Queen Mother

Three views of an elegant and refined Züst torpedo of 1915, with wind shields to protect back-seat passengers

Part 2
The Great Marques

The golden age of the automobile was the 1920s and 1930s. As
engineering advances combined with the lure of still uncluttered
roads, motoring entered an era of comfort and pleasure. Those
years saw the flowering of the huge and ostentatious luxury car –
of true masterpieces powered by extraordinary and often huge
engines and tooled with almost incomparable craftsmanship. The
pages that follow present a gallery of the finest vehicles of the
inter-War years, arranged according to their country of origin,
and describe in brief the histories of the classic marques of that
time, and indeed of all time.

Left *the 1927 4½-litre Bentley*

FRANCE

France, unlike Great Britain for example, was a hotbed of invention and innovation in motor car technology at the turn of the century. Indeed, with companies such as Voisin, and later Citroën, the French have a record of originality stretching up to the present day.

It was as early as 1898 that Emile Levassor devised the archetypal form of the motor car, having a front-mounted engine and rear-wheel drive through a sliding gear transmission, it became known as the Système Panhard. In 1896 Leon Bollée's voiturette became the first car to be sold with pneumatic tyres as standard, and in 1909 De Dion-Bouton built the first production V8.

The success of one of the most inventive companies of all, Citroën, illustrates the point that more than sound design and good engineering was necessary to survive in the car business. A combination of using the most up to date mass production techniques in the crucial years of the 1920s, and an unrivalled emphasis on promotion – it was Citroën's name in hundred foot high lights around the Eiffel Tower from 1925 to 1934 – saw Citroën established as one of the giants of the French car industry by 1933. It must be admitted, however, that in 1934 André Citroën overreached himself in the drive for greater production capacity, and the company was taken over by the Michelin tyre company where it remained until Peugeot took over Citroën in 1974.

Peugeot, one of the pioneers in France, built their first car back in 1885. In the years before 1920 Peugeot produced several notable racing machines, such as the 5.6-litre double-overhead-cam model which won at Indianapolis in 1913, and popular cars such as the diminutive 6hp Bébé of 1913. The company prospered all through this century; by 1939 they were second only to Citroën in France and produced a total of 52,796 cars that year. Although Peugeots were renowned for their strength and reliability, cars such as the 1921 Type 153 3-litre sports tourer and the 1938 Type 402B 2.1-litre saloon and the Darl'Mat 2.1-litre coupe were certainly striking in appearance, even if the last two listed were not exactly beautiful.

What is now the other great giant in France, Renault, achieved its position through the solid foundation laid by its autocratic founder in the 1920s. In that decade Louis Renault built up the well organised modern industrial machine which stood the country which nationalised it in 1945 in such good stead. Although somewhat staid, Renault cars were, like Peugeot's, aimed at the right, mass, market.

As in all the car producing countries, it was the well organised volume manufacturers that survived the Depression into the rather different society post-war. Later these companies were able to branch out in a new attempt to cover both ends of the market; now it does not seem strange to see Citroën produce both the 2CV and the magnificent CX2400.

French industry has always been individualistic, not to say chauvinistic, American involvement, for example, has been limited and not exactly successful. The firm which Chrysler, the only American company to penetrate the French market on a large scale, took over was Simca – a company which did not exist until 1935 when they started to produce Fiats under licence, before building their own machines in 1939. Simca acquired the short-lived (1947–54) Ford France concern in 1954, became part of Chrysler in 1970, and the wheel came full circle in 1978 when the strongest independent French company, Peugeot, took over Chrysler's European organisation to make the French industry once more totally French, and give the company a toehold in the British industry.

While Peugeot, Renault and Citroën are now the important figures, marques such as Bugatti, Hispano-Suiza, Delage, Panhard and Voisin were the focus of interest before World War II, before mergers and financial collapses struck them down. Hispano-Suiza and Bugatti are so renowned as to need little comment here, save to point out the three strange facts that Hispano-Suiza (as the name suggests) were originally Spanish, that the Spanish company outlived its more famous French counterpart by six years, and that Bugatti was founded by an Italian from Milan – Ettore Bugatti!

Delage, Salmson, Talbot-Lago, and to a lesser extent Delahaye, produced cars of rare elegance, but certainly one of the most underrated, and now almost forgotten, marques of the period was Voisin. The company's twenty-year existence covers virtually all the period which could be called 'The Golden Age of Motoring' – from 1919 to 1939 – and their record of engineering innovation and styling eccentricity, which produced some truly bizarre designs, helped to enliven the French scene before World War II in a way that was sadly absent from the more utilitarian post-war motoring era.

Ballot

Thirteen fascinating years

Even though Etablissements Ballot of Paris were only in the car manufacturing business from 1919 to 1932, they did produce some interesting models in their thirteen years history.

Before World War I, the Ballot brothers, Ernest and Maurice, built four-cylinder engines for Mass and Delage. Six weeks after the Armistice, however, Maurice Ballot recruited two well-known figures to help him create a French racing team to compete in the 1919 Indianapolis 500. They were René Thomas, winner of the 1914 Indianapolis race, and Ernest Henry, the renowned Swiss engineer, designer of the prewar, double-overhead-cam, four-valve racing Peugeots of 1912–1914 which Thomas raced.

The Ballot racer duly appeared in 1919 and featured a straight-eight 4917cc engine, with double overhead cams and four valves per cylinder like the Peugeot. The Ballot engine benefitted from the work Henry had put in on the wartime Bugatti aero-engine, which was also a straight-eight, but even so the cars proved unsuccessful at Indianapolis that year.

The first Ballot production car, a tourer, was based on the four-cylinder, 2-litre, racing car which finished third in the 1921 Le Mans, and second and third in the 1922 Targa Florio in a slightly different form. Despite its racing car derived performance,

only about fifty were produced. Its successor, the 2LT, was a more practical version of the tourer, introduced in 1921 with a single-overhead-cam 1986cc engine.

The 2LT grew into the 2LTS in 1924 – this was a tuned version with a very good performance for the time, which sold at a more competitive price than the 2LS. This model remained unchanged until 1927 when it was given a six-cylinder engine of the same capacity.

Also in 1927, a new tourer, the RH model, appeared. This was the first straight-eight car built by Ballot since their Grand Prix racing cars of 1921. Three years later the RH was developed and the engine changed to a 3-litre unit to form the RH3.

By this time, however, Ballot was in a shaky financial position; the Depression had taken its toll and the company was taken over by Hispano-Suiza. Following the take over, a Hispano-Suiza 4.6-litre, six-cylinder engine was fitted to a Ballot chassis to form the HS26 'Junior' model – a rather unfortunate hybrid machine not in the same class as previous Hispanos.

The 'Junior' only lasted until 1935 when it was superseded by the 4.9-litre, six-cylinder, model, but by this time Ballot was no more.

Below: while Ballot were famous mainly for their sporting models, they did build touring machines as well. This is an unusual cabriolet version of 1929 by Henri Labourdette

Bugatti
Masterpieces from Molsheim

After World War I, Alsace and Lorraine were taken from Germany and annexed by France. Thus the Bugatti company, whose factory was in this area, became French, but in fact the foundations of Ettore Arco Isidore Bugatti's career were laid in Milan, where he was born on 15 September 1881, the son of a cabinet maker and silversmith.

During his first job, as test driver, demonstrator *cum* mechanic, with Prinetti and Stucchi (makers of motorised bicycles), Bugatti built his first car. Of completely original design, it was exhibited on the Riccordi stand at the 1901 International Sports Exhibition in Milan, where its compactness and efficiency caused a sensation.

De Dietrich, railway equipment manufacturers wishing to expand into the automobile business, promptly recruited Bugatti on a particularly generous contract, necessary to attract him to Alsace. Bugatti was granted an engagement fee of 50,000 gold lire, and a royalty equal to ten per cent of the product value. He requested that a joint trade mark should be used and reserved exclusive rights on the Italian market, where only he would be able to sell De Dietrich-Bugatti cars. It was this contract, on the basis of which Bugatti designed no fewer than five different models for De Dietrich in the course of two years, that gave him a professional reputation throughout Europe.

The first car to bear Bugatti's name alone was built in his own house in Cologne, following his move to the post of technical manager with the Deutz Gas Motor Werke, for whom he worked from 1906 to 1909. However as the Bugatti trade mark was not yet registered, the car was privately called *Pur Sang*; built between 1908 and 1909 it was the first of a generation of real thoroughbreds. It was a simple and extremely light car, with an overhead-valve, four-cylinder engine (62 × 100mm), revolutionary and truly modern in shape. It was structurally similar to the type FE Isotta Fraschini which had made its debut and won its class at the 1908 Grand Prix des Voiturettes in Dieppe.

The first races in which the small car took part showed it to be very effective and it gave birth to Bugatti's first production model, the Type 13, an estimated 500 of which were made. As far as marketing was concerned, Bugatti, unlike Isotta Fraschini for example, knew how to find the right balance between the constructional complexities of a four-cylinder, overhead-camshaft engine and the simplicity of mediocre finish, and this permitted a reasonable price. Being in Germany, which was the cradle of motoring and the centre of European trade, Bugatti was further helped by the environmental circumstances and by the easier access to the markets in England, which was appreciative of the cars' sporting qualities, and France whose taste influenced the whole continent.

The Bugatti works had a relatively modest beginning. After having experimented with *Pur Sang* –

The Bugatti Type 40 can be considered the touring version of the Type 37; it was powered by a four-cylinder engine of 1.5 litres, with five main bearings and a bore and stroke measuring 69 × 100mm. *Below*: is an example of the Type 40 from the Longoni collection

Left: the eight-cylinder, 2.3-litre, Type 43 Bugatti.
In its day the fastest sports car built, with a top speed of 110mph. This model features an unusual complete hood and pointed tail

Five versions of the Type 44. *Left, from top to bottom:* a boat-tailed four-seater sports, and two cabriolet models. *Below:* a two-tone coupé, and *bottom:* a two door sports saloon

Top: a four-door saloon version of the Bugatti Type 49, from the Artom collection. The Type 49 was a development of the Type 44, and was produced from 1930 to 1934. The engine of the Type 49 is shown *above right.* Developed from the 44's eight-cylinder, 3-litre engine, it had a bore increased from 69 to 72mm to give a displacement of 3257cc. *Below:* a false cabriolet Type 49 by Gangloff

which he used as everyday transport for a long time – Ettore Bugatti decided to resign from Deutz and leave Cologne for Strasbourg, thus returning to Alsace. The reason for his attachment to these places has never really been established; perhaps it was simply habit, perhaps it was the possibility that here, where he was well known, it would be easier to obtain financial help.

Ettore, a friend and shareholder called de Vizcaya, and his long-standing mechanic Friderich, settled in Molsheim, where they inspected an abandoned dyeing plant which they decided to rent in order to set up a factory. Friderich spent Christmas 1909 whitewashing the walls and generally clearing up the place, while Bugatti travelled between Cologne and Paris, buying the necessary equipment, which was despatched during January and February 1910. Friderich had an even more important job, that of

what higher than those of its rivals. It is said that Bugatti made little use of publicity, leaving it to the local agents to produce a few posters; it was a time when the more serious and poorer companies let the racing results speak for themselves. From 1924 to 1927, Bugattis won 1851 races and, since they were cars which a good driver could also use on the road for touring, it is not surprising that the company was able to sell as many cars as the factory could produce. The firm never became enormous; perhaps because the market for some of the very special cars (such as the large Royale, which was to be the 'king of cars') was limited.

For many years, Bugatti concentrated on the production of fast and light cars, with either four- or eight-cylinder engines, whose racing successes were due not so much to superior speed or power as to the general balance of the vehicle, in which the road-

recruiting a labour force. When the plant was in working order, a nucleus of draughtsmen, from the drawing office which Bugatti had directed at Deutz, joined him at Molsheim. Only five cars were produced in 1910 but at the beginning of 1911 the number of employees had risen to 65 and the number of cars produced during 1911 rose to 75.

Also in 1911, working in a studio completely detached from the factory, Bugatti – aided by Friderich and only three workmen – once again started work on behalf of a third party, designing and making the prototype of a utility car which, after having been offered to the Wanderer company in Chemnitz, was to become the famous Peugeot Bébé. The car used a side-valve engine of 855cc and Bugatti adopted reversed quarter-elliptic springs for the first time (with the thick part of the spring anchored to the extreme rear of the chassis and the flexible apex forwards and attached to the axle) which from then until 1939 were to be features of his cars.

As a result of a series of astonishing victories, beginning with the Grand Prix of Le Mans in 1911, when a production Type 13, driven by Friderich, won its class and finished second overall behind a big Fiat driven by Hemery, Bugatti prices were some-

holding played a predominant role. Larger cars were not to be produced in quantities until the 1930s, when the possession of a Bugatti became the fashion in the society world, even for those who did not take part in sporting events. In 1911 and 1912, there was an exception – a small series of 5-litre racing cars (100 × 160mm) with chain drive, one of which was acquired by the famous aviator Garros. From these cars a special model, with a bore and stroke of 100mm × 180mm, was developed for the Indianapolis 500 of 1914. This had experimental cardan-shaft transmission, an unusual feature on very powerful cars in those days. Friderich broke a bearing in the differential during the race, while running third, so he was forced to retire.

During the war years, Bugatti had to leave Molsheim, which was an operational zone. He settled in Paris and, although without the possibility of manufacture, he did not stop working out new mechanical solutions and registered many industrial patents. Wartime events gave impetus to the development of aviation and, during his time in Paris, Bugatti was occupied in the field of aero-engine design.

After World War I European appreciation of the Bugatti Type 23 was shown by the fact that it was

Above: the Bugatti Type 46 of 5350cc, known as the little Royale, built in 1929 by Labourdette – a combination of advanced mechanical components and, even by 1929 standards, somewhat traditional bodywork

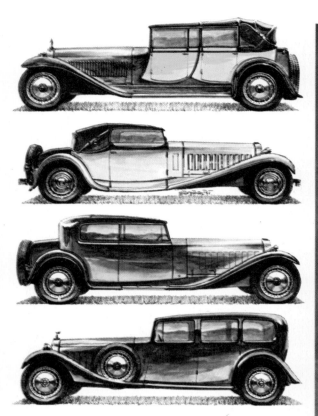

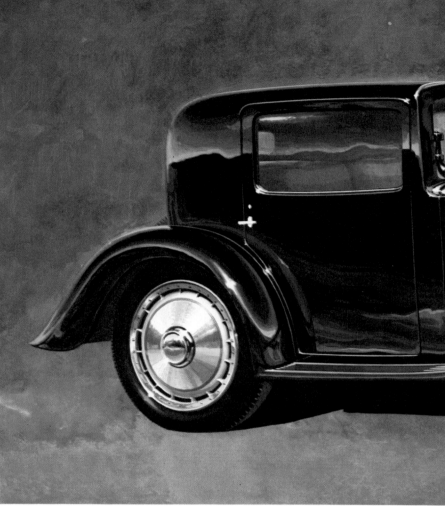

Above: four versions of the most prestigious Bugatti of them all, the Bugatti Royale. *From the top:* a landau from the Harrah collection, a cabriolet from the Ford Museum, and two saloons from private European collections

also produced under licence by RABAG in Germany and by Crossley Motors Ltd in England. These concessions did not have any great financial significance for Bugatti, because each of the licensees produced only a few cars, but they gave the seal of fame to a car which, despite the multiplicity of designations corresponding to detail modifications and different chassis lengths, was conceptually still the little *Pur Sang* of 1910, Bugatti's early 'baby'.

The Bugatti team which won Le Mans in 1920 was actually composed of cars built for the 1914 Coupe de l'Auto; these had never been used, having been stored during World War I. The famous engine, with four valves per cylinder and dual ignition, therefore dates back to this period. These were systems which were then extremely unusual on small, high-performance engines, although they had already been adopted for some specials and 'prehistoric dinosaurs' of enormous capacity, such as the 1911 Fiat record car (which actually had three plugs per cylinder in order to improve ignition in its almost-seven-litre pots). Despite these advanced characteristics, the small racing Bugattis were substantially similar to those put on sale; cars exhibited at the 1919 London Motor Show were the same,

apart from an increase in the amount of room inside the bodywork, as those which were to win at Le Mans the following year.

For the race at Brescia on 8 September 1921, where the Bugattis sensationally routed all opposition and finished in the first four places in their class, the bore was increased to 68mm and the lubrication deficiency, which had been made obvious by the breakdown of several examples used at Le Mans, remedied in typical Bugatti fashion, not by redesigning the oil supply system but by fitting a roller-bearing crankshaft. Bugatti made his first excursion into the realm of luxury cars in 1921, taking the type 28 – a 3-litre straight-eight – as far as the experimental stage. The idea of an eight-cylinder engine had also been explored in 1913, coupling two Type 13 engines one behind the other. Bugatti was not to embark upon the manufacture of de luxe cars (not to mention the legendary, gigantic Royale – an eight-cylinder of about 12 litres capacity) until later on, when the eight-cylinder racing cars had won him fame and industrial respect. In fact the first eight-cylinder car offered for sale was the Type 30 of 1922, which also achieved some racing success. This car saw the introduction of a new valve system which was to

ast ten years in Bugatti production. It consisted of three vertical valves per cylinder, operated by a single overhead camshaft. The originality of this system was in the adoption of two small inlet valves and a single large-diameter exhaust valve – reversing the customary arrangement which had one large inlet valve and two small exhausts.

In Grand Prix races, the increasing aggression of the supercharged Fiats and Sunbeams soon threatened the normally aspirated Type 30. Bugatti spent the winter of 1923–24 carrying out a complete re-examination of the design, adding two more main bearings and revising the lubrication system. Thus he outlined the Type 35, perhaps the most famous and most versatile of his cars which, in its various forms – supercharged for Grand Prix and Formula Libre races, and normally aspirated as for its victory in the Targa Florio – won innumerable races over opposition such as Delage and Alfa Romeo.

It is not possible to describe here all the Bugatti models, nor to write a history of their famous sporting successes. We shall therefore try to explain the truth behind the legend of the supposedly faultless Bugatti cars and of their genial and eccentric designer.

Bugatti's cars were, in fact, anything but faultless, but they had an irresistible appeal, formed by a well balanced mixture of efficiency, individuality and aesthetic qualities, a mixture crowned by that quality which can only be defined as class. The virile beauty of the chassis, a typical example of the good workmanship which often provokes the phrase 'they don't make them like that any more', was soon matched by the elegance of the bodywork. This was after the initial functional roughness of the Type 13 and after several disconcerting aerodynamic designs which were interesting theoretical exercises (the Type 30 was produced with cigar-shaped bodywork and also with an all-enveloping flat-sided body shell – the so-called Tank type). The Type 35, with its economy of line, was certainly the most beautiful Grand Prix car of the 1930s, while the elegance of the coachwork designed for the Gran Turismo cars by Jean Bugatti (Ettore Bugatti's eldest son) rivalled that of the leading French and Italian coachbuilders. This was probably the most famous racing Bugatti of all.

Ettore Bugatti had an extraordinary ability to secure the right drivers – both able mechanics (Friderich, Pietro Marco, Baccoli) and gentlemen who passed on some of their own prestige to the

Above: one of the most superb examples of the coupé de ville, the Type 41 Royale with coachwork by Henry Binder. Originally intended for King Carol of Rumania, this example now rests in the Harrah collection in the USA

marque (men like Tchaikowsky, the younger de Vizcaya, the Marquis de Casa Maury, Prince Cystria, Varsi and Dreyfus – not to mention that likeable self-made man Louis Chiron). This ability resulted not only in the opening of a small hotel at Molsheim, with a table prepared for friends, drivers and the most loyal customers, but also in the achievement of securing the services of Meo Costantini – already an excellent driver – as unpaid team manager.

Long before the technique of public relations was developed, Bugatti was unsurpassed in the creation of a glamorous image for the marque and in his ability to develop a select clientele. His everyday life – full of stylish little eccentricities, such as constantly having himself photographed in riding clothes and wearing a bowler hat – played a not unimportant part in the formation of the legend, as did the continuous flow of improbable or completely useless inventions. Luigi Castelbarco, who knew him well,

easy way. For example, in order to pay Dreyfus's salary (he received a very modest amount for his services as test-driver), Bugatti was obliged to devise a means of giving Dreyfus several chassis to sell for himself. However, Bugatti's extraordinary realism and enormous organisational ability made amends for his bizarre pleasures. When he presented the new Grand Prix Type 35 at Lyon in 1924, he not only organised a display of the cars, which attracted the attention of the world's press to a new system of fitting the tyres to the rims, but he arranged accommodation for 45 people in a field of tents equipped with running water, electricity, refrigerators and individual showers, for the convenience of the guests.

When sales of the Royale declined, leaving a large number of engines lying idle, Bugatti contrived to install them in railcars, thus placing France in the forefront of the locomotive field. This contribution makes it easier to forgive him for the fact that his

Above: an unusual sports version built by the Swiss coachbuilders Worblaufen on a Bugatti Type 57 chassis, and exhibited at the 1935 Geneva Salon

once related a somewhat bizarre anecdote: it seems that Bugatti in order to be more comfortable had several pairs of shoes made with toes, as if they were gloves. This was perhaps only one of the results of his passion for leather-work and for small cabinet-work and the minor arts in general – evidently inherited from his father's professional *milieu*; he even possessed an enormous collection of saddles – both for dogs and horses – but he demanded that the saddle makers were lodged in the factory so that he could supervise their work while looking after the all-important motor business.

Like most Latins, Bugatti adored his children and surrounded them with solicitude. He trained Jean to be an excellent successor, only to lose him in an accident. He lived in a princely fashion, as the part demanded, but he was not a rich man, nor was the business wealthy, as all available money was invested and sometimes wasted in research or development of new inventions. He overcame his financial difficulties by the most unusual methods and in a free-and-

aero-engines were not able to fly and that he spent sleepless nights trying to design a superfast torpedo-boat.

The years of the Depression were difficult for Bugatti, as they were for many other firms, and they changed irreparably the significance of his creative presence in the factory. His paternalistic management was no longer acceptable to a work force made aware of the first stirrings of organised trades unions, and this induced him to spend long periods in Paris, leaving the management of the business to Jean and the excellent Pietro Narco.

Jean Bugatti, who had been forbidden to compete in races, died when testing a car in August 1939. The business more or less died with him, although the outbreak of World War II also influenced its fate: the occupying forces transformed the Molsheim works into a torpedo-factory. After the liberation of France, the factory was occupied by the Canadians and Americans. The former accidentally caused a fire and the latter removed most of the surviving

The Type 57 (1934–1940) can be considered the last real Bugatti. *Above:* an Electron Atlantic coupé Type 57 C with a double-overhead-cam, supercharged engine

Right: a two-door convertible Type 57 by Gangloff from the Quattroruote collection. *Below:* a Type 57 S coupé of 1936 from the Volonterio collection. Around 800 Type 57s were built in a six-year production run

machine tools and dispersed drawings and documents. In a fit of stupidity, the new French government confiscated what remained as the property of an enemy: Bugatti had, for sentimental reasons, always retained his Italian citizenship. He was obliged to take the case to court, where his rights were restored after an exhausting debate. Nevertheless, weary from exertion and weakened by adversity, he did not live to see car production resumed: he died in 1947.

The company attempted to re-enter the car market under Pietro Narco's management, producing a luxury car – the Type 101 (1951) – based largely on the pre-war Type 57. The principal differences were the chain-driven camshaft and the electromagnetic preselector Cotal gearbox. Very few 101s were produced and the experimental competition car, type 251, raced only once, at Reims in 1956.

The new reality of the second post-war period did not have room for cars like the Bugatti, nor was it possible to keep the legend alive after Ettore's death.

Citroën

Mass producers with an eye for promotion

1915 was the year that the 37-year-old André Citroën decided to build, on thirty acres of vegetable gardens and waste land at Quai de Javal (now Quai André Citroën) in Paris, what was to become one of the most modern car producing factories in the world.

On 28 May 1919 the first Citroën left the assembly line. With this car, an open tourer called the Type A, André Citroën immediately broke new ground; it was the first car to be mass produced in Europe, and the first to be delivered complete with its hood, spare wheel and other such paraphernalia.

Fate played a helping hand at this time, for in June of that year, as the first Type A was delivered to a customer, the major rival, Renault, suffered a strike. In just four months, the Type A and its builder were the toasts of the Paris Motor Show at the Grand Palais.

However successful his products were in those early days, André Citroën was never slow to spot ingenious ways of gaining further publicity and prestige. At that 1919 Motor Show he had fifty demonstration cars waiting to take prospective customers for a joy ride. In 1920 Citroën renewed the entire fleet of Paris taxis in one sweeping operation, and later he even founded a reduced-rate insurance company for his customers. He was also the first to use aeroplane advertising – with letters written in smoke – and from 1925 to 1934 the company name shone from 250,000 electric light bulbs, forming a 100-foot-high advertisement around the Eiffel Tower.

The first Citroën model, the Type A, was joined in 1921 by a revised four-cylinder design designated the B2, a car which made history by becoming the first to cross the Sahara Desert. The B2, in turn, was followed by a sports version, equipped with light-alloy pistons, called the Caddy. Credited as the first 'sports' car to be derived from a standard production model, the Caddy had a top speed of nearly 56mph.

To demonstrate the reliability of Citroën equipment an ambitious project was undertaken in 1924. Sixteen men in eight half-tracks, based on the 9hp B2, left North Africa on the famous 'Black Cruise'. Starting from Columb-Bechar, in Algeria, they crossed the Sahara, then proceeded through more than 5000 miles of pathless jungle in the Congo – navigating by compass – to Lake Victoria. There the expedition split, one party going via Cape Town, and two others through East Africa, to the final rendezvous in Madagascar.

The 5CV two-seater came out in 1922, followed by a three-seat version – the famous 'Clover Leaf' – a year later. The B2 design was further developed,

the B10 appeared and then, in 1925, the B12, which featured a single-piece all-steel Budd body and four-wheel brakes, was introduced. With this car, Citroën again achieved two 'firsts' in the field of mass produced vehicles.

During this period a considerable expansion of production facilities took place in Paris. New plant was opened at Levallois, Saint-Charles and Saint-Quen. At the Javel works, opened in 1923, a hundred cars a day were soon being produced.

In 1932 the factory launched a new range – the 8, 10, and the 15 – with 'floating power' engines, and it was an 8A fitted with a special body that, in 1933,

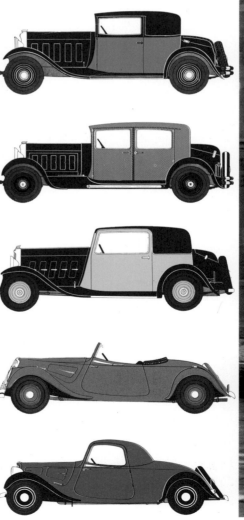

created a record that still stands: 186,400 miles in 134 days at an average speed of 58mph.

Having proved the worth of his existing range, André Citroën once again turned his attention to the future, laying plans that would see his company successfully through the next two decades. Contemplating a daily output of 1000 cars while considering the introduction of his new front-wheel-drive model, he decided, in 1933, to demolish the Javel works entirely and rebuild them, all within a tight schedule of five months. While this work was being carried out, Javel continued producing cars at a steady 360 units a day!

For all his qualities, André Citroën also had his failings. His aggressive marketing policies did not always tally with his accountant's demands, and in 1934 he found himself in serious financial difficulties, so much so that he could not meet his commitments. At the French Government's request, Michelin, one of Citroën's largest creditors, settled the outstanding accounts and took the car manufacturer in hand.

The new 'Traction Avant' model everyone had been waiting for appeared in 1934, taking the country by storm. A 7hp model – subsequently 9hp and 11hp – with a 'floating power' four-cylinder, overhead-valve engine, its front-wheel-drive layout endowed it with roadholding powers which at that time were considered astounding. Other technical innovations adopted in the 7CV for the first time in a mass produced model included an integral underslung steel body with no running boards, flat floorboards, seats inboard of the side chassis members for protection against lateral shocks, and torsion-bar suspension. Weighing under 2000lbs, the car had a top speed of 75mph, and a fuel consumption of 32mpg.

A year after the 7CV's introduction, André Citroën died, but the company – now in the safe hands of France's premier tyre firm – moved into a new era of expansion. Development work on the 2CV began in 1936, a larger six-cylinder version of the 7CV, called the 15-Six, appeared in 1938, and by May 1939 250 prototypes of the 2CV were ready at the Levallois works – for an autumn Paris Motor Show that never took place. Instead war came to Europe, and Citroën production came to a halt.

Opposite page: a series of Citroëns in chronological order, *from top to bottom*: a C6G of 1931; another C6G with coachwork by Million-Guiet, also of 1931; a 15AL false cabriolet (ie one where the roof does not fold down as it should in a cabriolet); and an 11CV cabriolet from 1935
Below: a 15 Six built just prior to World War II, in 1939 (Mocauto collection)

205

Delage

England's favourite French car

Louis Delage, born in Cognac in 1874, was the founder of one of the greatest firms in the French automobile industry. In 1905 he risked borrowing 35,000 francs to set up his own car-manufacturing business in a small workshop, after having worked for a time as manager of the Peugeot experimental and testing division.

The first Delages appeared in 1906, and were voiturettes based on sound conservative lines, thanks in part to Delage having taken Chief Designer Legros with him from Peugeot. There was only one chassis style, which could be powered by either a 4¼hp or 9hp single-cylinder De Dion engine.

In two years, however, business had picked up, and in 1908 over 300 cars were sold. In 1909 Delage went over to four cylinders, and in 1910 the move was made to 138 Boulevard de Verdun where all future Delages were made. By 1912, Delage was employing 350 men and turning out well over a thousand cars a year.

After World War I Delage turned to producing large cars rather than the small medium-powered models on which the company's reputation had been built. The first big post-war Delage was the CO, with a long-stroke, 4.5-litre, side-valve engine of six cylinders. In 1921 the CO became the CO2 with an overhead-valve engine which enabled it to exceed 80mph. The smaller 3-litre DO model was dropped in favour of the DE which, in turn, was developed into the famous 14hp DI series of 1923 onwards.

The DIs had pushrod, overhead-valve, 2.1-litre engines, and continued from 1923 in conjunction with the GL (Grand Luxe), which replaced the CO2. The GL had a six-cylinder, overhead-cam, 5.9-litre engine, featured servoed hydraulic brakes, and was Delage's luxury model designed to compete with cars such as the Hispano-Suiza.

The DI was the most sedate of the 14/40hp series, and had Rolls-Royce-like, RAF hub-locking arrangements, a 10ft 6in wheelbase, and a wide-ratio gearbox; it was the mainstay of the company's tourers from 1924 onwards. The later cars in the series, the DIS and DISS, had single-plate clutches which tended to be a weak point, but in general the DIs were excellent, reliable cars, not very quick off the mark, but with a good 60mph cruising speed, a maximum speed of 75mph, and impeccable handling. All the engines used had five main bearings, four-speed gearboxes and Zenith carburettors.

The Delage Grand Prix cars of 1925, with supercharged 1995cc engines developing 195bhp, enjoyed much success, winning the French and Spanish Grands Prix. These cars were evidently as fast as their main rivals, the P2 Alfa Romeos, although they were seldom in direct competition. The next year saw the advent of the famous and successful Lory-designed straight-eight twin-cam. This car, of 1½ litres and five speeds, was supercharged to give 170bhp at 8000rpm and 130mph; it was destined to be the last GP model from Delage.

The DM series was announced in the summer of 1926; a 3.2-litre six, it had the virtues of the DI together with the refinement and flexibility gained through going to six cylinders. It has been termed the ultimate development of the vintage Delage. The DMS was a high performance version, which differed in quite a number of ways such as having double valve springs and a more sporting cam.

In 1929, the celebrated 85mph D8 Delage was announced as a pushrod straight-eight, initially with a 4050cc engine and a chassis destined to be fitted with some very exotic bodywork. Three chassis lengths were available, ranging from 10ft 10in to 11ft 11in. The 100mph Grand Sport was introduced in 1932, at first with a short wheelbase, but this was lengthened for the 1934 model. Although the later super-sports D8120 was often overbodied, it did gain one International class 12-hour record at 112mph.

In 1934/5 a completely new and smaller D8 was introduced, the D8 15 which featured a 2668cc engine, and transverse leaf and wishbone independent front suspension which was also used under licence by Studebaker in the USA. The D8 15, and some of the 4-litre D8s had valves divorced from their springs, the link being a rocker mechanism, a design eccentricity intended to counteract valve bounce. The D6/11 had similar features and a smaller six-cylinder engine of 2149cc, just as the original D6 of 1932 had been a six-cylinder version of the D8 of that time. There was also a 1½-litre four-cylinder produced from 1934 to 1936.

By 1935 Delage had been taken over by Delahaye, and as that firm's last competition success had been a rather insignificant best time in the touring class of the Paris-Amsterdam-Paris race of 1898, the sudden racing successes of Delahaye from 1935 onwards must have owed more than a little to Delage know-how. Following the take over, Louis Delage was promptly pensioned off, and lived thereafter in comparative penury.

Under the new regime the later D8s were perhaps not quite worthy of the earlier models, but the six-cylinder Delahaye-built Delages commenably carried on the DI and DM traditions. Delage was eventually absorbed along with Delahaye by Hotchkiss in 1954, and no more cars were made.

Right: the last true Delage model before the Delahaye take-over was the Delage D6, a medium sized six-cylinder car introduced in 1933 The version shown here is a 1934 example by Letourner and Marchand (Taminau collection)

Introduced in 1929, the Delage D8 was the grandest of the Delages. It was a favourite with many coachbuilders, as these illustrations indicate. The Delage was a particular favourite in England, and, *top left*, is a sports model built by the English coachbuilders Van den Plas in 1929. *Above middle*: a saloon version on a long-wheelbase chassis of 1936 (Musée de Val de Loire). *Bottom left*: a 1937 cabriolet on a D6, six-cylinder, 2.7-litre chassis of 1937, built in England

Above: a 1929 Delage D8 with elegant open sports bodywork (Musée de Rochetaillée-sur-Saône).
Right: a two-door saloon built on a D6 chassis by Letourner and Marchand

Delahaye

Early innovation gone to seed

Emile Delahaye had been chief engineer of a Franco-Belgian firm that built railway rolling-stock when, around 1890, he took over a machine shop in Tours, specialising in the manufacture of steam, gas and paraffin engines.

Before long, Delahaye was experimenting with a car modelled on Benz principles, and produced belt-driven, four-cylinder, rear-engined cars.

In 1898 the Delahaye works were moved from Tours to what was to become a permanent home in Paris. By this time, Emile Delahaye had joined forces with Leon Desmaris and Georges Morane in the business. The new Paris factory, where hydraulic machinery had previously been made, actually was owned by Morane's father. An important event happened at this time in the appointment of Charles Weiffenbach as works manager. 'Monsieur Charles', as he became known, was destined to be the *eminence grise* behind Delahaye throughout the life of the firm.

Until the turn of the century, three Delahaye models were being produced: two twin-cylinder models, 4½hp and 6hp; and a 1.4-litre single-cylinder called the Type Zero, which appeared towards the end of 1898. All had rear-mounted, water-cooled engines with automatic inlet valves, surface carburettors and trembler coil ignition.

In 1901 Emile Delahaye retired from the company, whose destinies were guided by Desmaris and Morane until 1906, and thereafter by Monsieur Charles. By 1907, Delahayes were being made under licence by Protos in Germany, and they entered the English market in 1909.

After World War I, Delahaye spent fourteen years producing what motoring historian Michael Sedgwick has described as 'stodgy, dependable and uninteresting cars', until in 1935 Delahaye took over the Delage company. They continued to build the successful Delage models, and in 1936 Delahaye entered the big league of sports-car racing with the 135 'Competition', breaking the Ulster TT lap record for all time. In 1937 Delahayes were second and third to a Type 57S Bugatti at Le Mans, won the twelve-hour sports-car race at Donington Park and were third in the Mille Miglia to two 2900A Alfa Romeos.

After concentrating on the production of trucks during World War II, Delahaye were quickly back to car production in 1946, and between 1946 and 1950 the Type 135S won several races such as the GP de Frontières and the Comminges GP.

By 1951 Monsieur Charles was being assisted by his son Raymond, but sales were dropping dramatically, and after production of a Jeep-like vehicle, Delahaye were taken over by Hotchkiss in 1954, when car production ceased and only trucks were made. Not long afterwards, the new company was taken over by the Brandt organisation and renamed Hotchkiss-Brandt, and the honoured name of Delahaye was dropped altogether after 1956.

Left: the mammoth, six-cylinder, 3.5-litre, Delahaye exhibited at the Paris Salon in 1938 where its sweeping aerodynamic lines caused much interest and curiosity

Hispano-Suiza
Cosmopolitan classics with royal approval

For most car fans the name Hispano-Suiza recalls four famous models: the Alfonso, a spartan light-weight introduced in 1912 that was certainly one of the world's first true production sports cars; the 6.3-litre H6 of 1919 that was then beyond doubt the world's most advanced luxury chassis; the most powerful 8-litre version of the same, called the 46CV, dating from 1924; and the great 54-220CV V12 of the 1930s.

The designer of these famous cars was a Swiss, Marc Birkigt, born in Geneva in 1878. His connection with Hispano-Suiza stemmed from 1904 when a creditor, Damien Mateu, took over the firm which Birkigt worked for, and renamed it Fabrica La Hispano-Suiza de Automobiles. This combination of Spanish finance and direction along with Swiss engineering brain prepared two large four-cylinder cars for the Paris Salon of 1906, a 3.8-litre and a 7.4-litre. By this time, the youthful King Alfonso XIII already had his first Hispano in the royal stable, and continued to patronise the marque for the rest of his reign.

Two big sixes were added next and by 1908 there was a choice between five chassis. All these, incidentally, had multiple-disc clutches, four-speed transmissions and live-axle final drive.

Voiturette racing was entered, very succesfully, in 1909 and 1910, and having proved a point Hispano-Suiza withdrew from direct factory participation in racing. Perhaps the decision to do this was not absolute, because Birkigt was rumoured in 1912 to be working on a supercharging device consisting of two extra pumping cylinders. The 1913 regulations nipped this in the bud, so to speak, by banning any form of forced induction.

From the 1910 Coupe des Voiturettes car, however, sprang the famous production Alfonso Type 15T (a car the Queen of Spain once gave her husband for a birthday present). It was similar to the racer, though having a wider bore and shorter stroke. The power output from the 3620cc engine was very healthy for those days – 64bhp at 2300rpm – and as the car was very light, the power/weight ratio was extremely favourable. Indeed the shorter of the alternative chassis weighed only about 13cwt. Birkigt was one of the first to unite the gearbox with the engine, and this was a feature of the Alfonso; early examples had three speeds, later ones four, and there was a change also from a dry multi-plate, metal-to-metal clutch to the leather-faced cone variety. Top speed was around 70–75mph depending on body style and weight, and the Alfonso was soon popular in European markets. An assembly plant was opened in Levallois-Perret, Paris, in 1912 and in 1914 it was shifted to larger premises in the Bois-Colombes. From here emanated the great luxury cars of the 1920s and '30s although the Spanish factory's output, of mostly more mundane models, far exceeded that of Paris.

During World War I, Hispano-Suiza produced a

Below left: the chassis of the most sophisticated car of its time, the 1919 Hispano-Suiza H6. This chassis featured servo-assisted brakes on all four wheels, and a superb, 6.5-litre, engine with double overhead camshafts.
Below: a double-phaeton version of the H6B from 1925
(Winkler collection)

sophisticated, alloy, overhead-cam, V8 aero-engine for the allied forces which was comparable to the air-cooled rotary engines, which were the norm at that time, in power to weight ratio; the Hispano of course had the advantage of a smaller frontal area. From 1918 every Hispano-Suiza radiator cap carried the famous flying stork mascot commemorating the squadron emblem of one of France's most daring air aces, Georges Guynemer – a personal friend of the Hispano designer Marc Birkigt – killed in action in 1917. All Guynemer's SPAD fighters were Hispano driven and armed.

Although several pre-war models were carried forward for a few years, the big news came with the Paris Salon of 1919 and the presentation there of the French-made H6 chassis. At a time when Rolls-Royce had not progressed beyond side valves, cylinder blocks cast in threes, and rear wheel brakes for their cars, and long before they adopted monobloc cylinder castings for their aero-engines, here was a compact, 6.5-litre, overhead-cam engine showing the benefit of the work put in on the wartime aero-engine, and set in a finely engineered chassis equipped with the world's best brakes, complete with mechanical servo, which incidentally, was used by Rolls-Royce until the 1960s.

Anyone lucky enough to have driven an H6 as well as some of its contemporary rivals will have been astounded by its generally modern 'feel' and road manners, and the superb brakes matched by accurate and responsive steering that taxed the driver's biceps far less than most large chassis. Although Birkigt considered that three speeds adequately matched his engine's torque characteristics, some critics saw this as a mean economy in an expensive vehicle, in the sense that four speeds must cost more than three, and it is true that wide ratio spacing can be a disadvantage in some localities. Other luxury-car makers usually provided a very low first speed and suggested that it was used for emergencies only, like restarts on steep hills. In matters of quiet running and general unobtrusiveness, the Rolls-Royce Silver Ghost side-valve engine with its heavy cast-iron cylinder blocks and simple valve gear remote from the bonnet top, tuned for low-speed torque as distinct from high-speed power, was difficult to match, and the standard of Rolls-Royce gear cutting and quality control complemented the engine down the transmission line. Marc Birkigt's cars, however, were based on a very different philosophy, in tune with the French sybarites' way of life. Their motor carriages had to

move gracefully and look magnificent while gliding down the Champs Elysees, yet be equally in their element while dashing down the long *routes national* to the Riviera.

Thus the H6 32CV gave 100bhp at 1600rpm, which was a lot more than the Silver Ghost delivered flat-out, and 135bhp at 3000rpm; the fact that it made something of a commotion was accepted without demur by the clientele. The H6 was as good in action as its specification on paper promised, and merited all the press acclaim it received. It was good enough to remain in production in France without major alterations up to 1934. An ideal platform for the specialist coachbuilder, it was clothed in some of the most magnificent metal finery ever created by the top European houses. The King of Spain was only one among a number of royal customers, and it soon became a prestige symbol for Hollywood film stars and other *nouveaux riches*.

Although not envisaged as a competition car, the big Hispano had its moments of glory in this scene, first in 1921 when the wealthy sportsman with a commercially alcoholic background, André Dubonnet, won a sports-car race at Boulogne: the Coupe Boillot. Two or three years later, he repeated the success, this time with a new 8-litre engine, from

which the production 46CV got its name 'Boulogne'. Also in 1924, Dubonnet ran a 46CV in the famous Targa Florio road race in Sicily. It was fitted with an exotic body of riveted tulip-wood planking made by the Nieuport aviation people; far too cumbersome for such a mountainous and endlessly snaking course, and hampered by tyre failures, it nevertheless finished in sixth position.

In 1928, there was a challenge match for 25,000 dollars, arranged between a 4.9-litre Stutz Black Hawk straight-eight and a Boulogne Hispano, of a 24-hour speed and reliability contest around the Indianopolis 'brickyard'. The Boulogne brought over for C.T. Weymann to drive was extremely suspect, probably being an ultra-short-chassis job built for racing, and one source suggests its engine was tuned to about 170bhp! Having, so to speak, opened its big mouth, the Stutz soon swallowed a valve. By the time the Hispano had trundled round for eighteen hours at just over 70mph, the Stutz was running again, erratically, after over nine hours in the pits, and victory was then ceded: a crushing example of Hispano superiority.

How much power did the 46CV develop? There are quotes between 144 and 200bhp, both at 2600rpm. For the luxury trade, Birkigt would have

Above: an extravagant creation of 1924, a sports body of riveted tulip-wood planking, built by the Nieuport aircraft company on an 8-litre Hispano Boulogne H6C chassis, and originally owned and raced by André Dubonnet

been more concerned with the torque curve than absolute power, and 154 could well be the figure for early examples with low compression ratios. However, some big 46CV saloons could certainly approach 100mph, which would call for more power than that, and the short-chassis sporting Boulogne version could comfortably exceed the magic century and may well have packed 200bhp. To most Hispano addicts, the 46CV is remembered as Birkigt's masterpiece, despite what was to follow.

The huge S4-220CV now makes one amazed that so much had been achieved so long ago, for it first appeared at the Paris Salon of 1931. Together with a number of multi-cylindered exotica hatched around that time in the USA, it arrived in an unfavourable financial climate, yet nevertheless attracted quite a few takers among those who managed

to a throw. Unusual, may be unique, were the deeply-finned connecting-rod caps, dovetailed into the rods and secured by riveted horizontal pins. A big-end bearing failure entailed removing and stripping the engine almost completely.

Unfortunately, the cars had only a three-speed transmission and a sad alliance between a very high first gear and an inadequate multi-plate clutch. Thus the V12 did not crawl willingly in city traffic, nor yet could get that torque through to the road for restarting on steep hills.

Despite its performance – o to 60mph in about 12 seconds, o to 80mph in around 20 seconds with a top speed in excess of 100mph – the Type 68, as it was called, was frankly a bit archaic in concept, apart from its engine and brakes. In the chassis layout there was an almost arrogant disregard of passenger space

Above: a coupé de ville version of the Hispano-Suiza H6B, with body by the French coachbuilders Henry Binder, a stylist of the Bugatti Royale. The H6 chassis was a favourite with Binder; from 1924 to 1937 no less than two hundred bodies were built by this firm

to preserve their balances during the international Depression.

The engine, of 9.4 or 11.3 litres, depending on which stroke option was chosen, although looking extremely like a scaled down aviation unit, broke with Birkigt tradition in having pushrod overhead-valve gear in place of overhead camshafts and was thus almost miraculously quiet and refined. The stove-enamelled black cylinder blocks were still fixed-head aluminium castings with screwed in nitralloy liners; of the two valves per cylinder, the exhausts had sodium-cooled stems and the nine-bearing crankshaft carried tubular rods paired two

in relation to the external dimensions, and one needed an almost bottomless purse to feed the monster.

In 1931 Hispano-Suiza took over the Ballot company, and fitted a small 4.6-litre six-cylinder engine in a Ballot chassis to produce the rather undistinguished Junior model. This was, in turn, superseded by the six-cylinder 4.9-litre K6 model which remained in production up to 1938.

In 1936 the Spanish Civil War started, France was riddled by industrial unrest and the under-currents of war, and in 1938 Birkigt stopped car production to concentrate on aero-engines and armaments.

Left: the very neat and tidy V12 Hispano engine of 1931, which had a displacement of 9420cc and produced 200bhp. This enormous engine, the work of the Swiss designer Marc Birkigt, gave the Hispanos so engined a top speed around 112mph with great ease

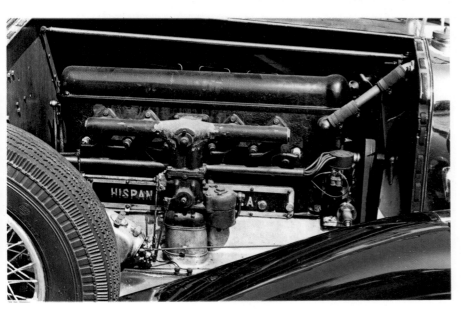

Above: an imposing Hispano-Suiza H6C of 1932, with body by Vanvooren. This model, introduced in 1924, was a more potent version of the H6B. Its motor, shown left, was an in-line, six-cylinder, unit of 7982cc with bore and stroke measuring 100 × 110mm. The increase in size over the H6B engine gave it an output of 135bhp at 3000rpm

215

In 1931 Hispano-Suiza took over the Paris based firm of Ballot,
where they produced the Hispano Junior which was basically a
Ballot chassis with a 4.6-litre Hispano engine. This combination
was not particularly felicitous, and the Junior was dropped, to be
replaced by the model shown here, which is the six-cylinder,
4.9-litre K6, introduced in 1933 and produced up to 1938.
Above: a K6 saloon of 1935 (Museo dell'Automobile di Torino)
and, *left*, a 1936 two-door model by Vanvooren

Panhard et Levassor

A blend of tradition and progress

The firm of Panhard et Levassor dates from 1886 when Louis-René Panhard and Emile Levassor took over the Périn company they were working for, following Périn's death, and became one of the main pioneers of the motor industry.

It was Panhard, for example, who designed engines with forged steel cylinder barrels and integral heads. Each cylinder was bolted separately to the upper deck of the crankcase, with inlet and exhaust ports and sparking plug bosses welded onto the head of each cylinder, and a thin copper water jacket neatly tailored to fit around the cylinder. This form of construction lasted for many years.

In everything else, Panhard remained doggedly conservative, and the touring cars suffered just as much as the racers. However, shortly before he died in 1908, Louis-René Panhard retired from the business and handed over its control to his sons Paul and Hippolyte; and it is surely significant that within a year the old wooden chassis frame began to be replaced by pressed-steel frames, that a new monobloc 2.4-litre engine had high-tension magneto ignition, and that by 1910 the quadrant gearchange had been ousted by a gate type such as Mercédès had introduced nine years earlier. 1911 marked an even more significant departure from the firm's previous practice: not only was it the last year in which the two-cylinder engines were made, it was one in which the first production Panhard with a sleeve-valve engine was introduced, although its performance was not particularly outstanding.

When they resumed normal business in 1919, after the intervention of World War I, Panhard did make some poppet-valved cars, but it was a brief production run, finished in 1922. Their main programme was built around the Knight sleeve-valve engine, and by the middle 1920s they had improved its performance considerably. The larger versions of the Panhard could be impressively fast, even though they trailed an oppressive cloud of oil smoke in their wake when driven hard. By 1924, when all models had front-wheel brakes, dynamotor starters, and four-speed gearboxes, the 4.8-litre, four-cylinder Panhard needed little modification before taking the world hour record at 115.3mph in 1925. Enlarged to 5.3 litres in 1929, the standard car could then exceed 90mph. A six-cylinder series was begun in 1927, followed shortly by a massive and refined straight-eight, with centralised chassis lubrication, coil ignition and an all-helical constant-mesh gearbox. Of course, not all the cars were big and fast, but they were all smooth and impressive, many of them carrying bodywork of considerable charm and sometimes elegance. The best were very expensive, costing more than the most luxurious Renault of the day, which was no mean car itself in any sense.

Modern design features continued to be introduced, but seldom with such startling effect as was achieved in 1937 when a model known as the Dynamic was introduced. As ever, it had a sleeve-valve engine, a six-cylinder affair in sizes ranging from 2.5 to 3.8 litres. However, with its hydraulic brakes, backbone chassis, worm-gear final drive, and all-round independent suspension by torsion bars, it was almost aggressively up to date in its chassis. As far as the body was concerned, it was more than up to date, it was positively futuristic: the driver sat in the centre, the headlamps were faired in, all four wheels were largely enclosed by deep spats or valences on the mudguards, there were wraparound extensions to the windscreen, triple windscreen wipers, and some extremely bizarre styling. It is possible that the car might eventually have been successful, particularly after its constructors relented and put the driver on the left again in 1939, but war came and such questions had to be left open.

Left: a solid and conventional looking Panhard of 1936 with what was termed a Panoramic body (Musée de Rochetaillée-sur-Saône)

Below: the Panhard Dynamic was introduced in 1937 with a choice of side-valve, six-cylinder engines, ranging from 2.5 litres to 3.8 litres. Note the faired-in headlights and the centrally mounted steering wheel; all in all the styling seems positively oriental (Musée de Rochetaillée-sur-Saône)

Renault

Nationalised monument to the brothers from Billancourt

The now state-owned Renault concern started life as a family firm; the three Renault brothers, Louis, Marcel and Fernand formed Renault Frères at Billancourt in 1898, but by late 1908 Louis was virtually on his own, following the deaths of Marcel in 1903 and Fernand early in 1908.

The first production Renault was a two-seater model, with tiller steering, which could travel at 30mph and return 47mpg. Technical innovation and steady development saw the company producing twenty per cent of French car output by 1913.

In the early 1920s came full electrical equipment, four-wheel brakes, factory built bodies, sleeker lines and a welcome relief from the troublesome old quadrant gearchange. Monobloc engines became the rule, with the exception of the two clusters of three cylinders in the FI. This model grew in 1921 to become the most glamorous and powerful of all, the mighty 40CV known in Britain as the Renault 45, a huge, two ton, 9.1-litre car capable of 100mph.

Its appeal, however, was limited and Renault began to compete with the newly created Citroën concern in the increasingly important mass market. The pretty little 6CV was brought out in 1922 to rival Citroën's 5CV: it was the first Renault to have a detachable cylinder head, and its sturdiness was proverbial – demonstrated by a 10,000 mile run around the Miramas circuit at 49mph in 1926, and the first solo crossing of the Sahara in 1927.

However, while André Citroën's fast growing company went on to become a firm famous for technical advancement, Renault lapsed into a turgid phase of reactionary design. On the face of it the cars were improving: by 1931 they all had frontal radiators, steel disc wheels, coil ignition, unitary gearboxes and in some cases servo brakes and pumped cooling, while synchromesh was soon to follow. Unfortunately, throughout the 1930s the cars became more and more soggy in their handling (the transverse springing at the rear was largely to blame) and spavined in their performance, in a misguided attempt to combine American fashions in styling and appointment, with European notions of economy, but even so, by the eve of World War II the Renault factories were turning out 250 cars a day.

Following the liberation of France in 1944 Louis Renault was pilloried, somewhat unjustly, as a collaborator and his company confiscated, starting a new lease of life as a nationalised concern, and flourishing under its new ownership.

Below: a rather severe looking example of Renault's Reinstella. The Reinstella was Renault's first straight-eight car; it appeared in 1929 with a 7.1-litre engine, and servo-assisted brakes (Renault collection)

Salmson

A marriage of speed and comfort

Originally manufacturers of pumps, and then buildings of rotary aero-engines in World War I, the first car produced by the Paris-based Salmson company was the English GN cyclecar, in 1919.

The first real Salmsons were those in the AL range which appeared in 1921 in voiturette, landaulet, and sport versions, with an Emile Petit designed 1086cc, water-cooled, four-cylinder engine.

Twin-overhead-cam examples went into production with the announcement of the 1250cc, 10hp, Salmson at the 1922 Paris Salon. This was a proper light car with a curious patented rear suspension by pairs of quarter-elliptic rear springs, one pair facing rearwards in the conventional manner, the other forward.

Performance capabilities of the AL series had always been quite surprising, and the sports variants came to typify the name Salmson. As performance rose, the chassis became more robust; one of the first steps being the adoption of semi-elliptic front suspension for the new Type VAL3 in 1925.

By 1928 the vogue for the small French sports cars, such as those designed by Petit, was virtually over, and the first non-Petit Salmson car was the S4 of 1929. It featured a double-overhead-cam 1300cc engine and a three-speed gearbox, although its performance was not exceptional.

Salmson continued producing saloons, including the British Salmsons built in England, until the take-over by Renault in 1956 when car production ceased.

From a company famous for its sports cars, this Salmson was proof that comfort and speed could go hand in hand. This is one of the most impressive Salmsons, a 1938 cabriolet built on an S4E chassis and featuring a 2320cc double-overhead-cam, four-cylinder, engine (Musée de Rochetaillée-sur-Saône)

Talbot-Lago
Exotic products of a complicated history

The name Talbot-Lago identifies the cars built by Automobiles Talbot SA from 1934 to 1959, following the demise of the Anglo-French combine of STD (Sunbeam-Talbot-Darracq).

In 1934 the English division of STD was taken over by Rootes Brothers, and the French Talbot branch came under the control of a Major Anthony Lago.

Cars had been manufactured at the Suresnes works since 1896 when the famous Darracq company was formed. Darracq existed as an independent concern up to 1920 when the two English companies, Sunbeam and Talbot (who had themselves joined forces in 1919) absorbed the French company. After the formation of STD very similar cars were marketed under the various marque names in different countries, leading to some confusion. STD's racing cars, for example, were known as Talbot,

Talbot-Darracq, Talbot Special or Sunbeam, depending where the cars were built and raced.

Following the Rootes takeover, the English Sunbeam and Talbots rapidly lost their individuality; in France, however, Talbot flourished under Lago's control. Lago's ideal was the fast luxury car which would be easily identifiable with Talbot's successful racing models.

In an attempt to realise this ideal Lago, in collaboration with his Chief Engineer Walter Becchia, introduced a new line of six-cylinder cars of varying engine capacity: the 2.7-litre 15CV, the 3-litre 17CV, and the top of the line 4-litre 23CV. The engine of the 23CV had a particularly impressive specification; the crankshaft ran on seven main bearings and the cylinder head was an efficient hemispherical design with overhead valves operated by a curious cross-over pushrod system. This 4-litre engine would

The Talbot name came into existence in 1920 when the Darracq works at Suresnes were merged with Sunbeam and Talbot. *Below* is a two-seater sports M75 of 1930 (De Wurstemberger collection)

Top: a Talbot M67C of 1930 with royal coupé
bodywork, once owned by Prince Albert I of Monaco.
Above: a large Talbot saloon of 1935, now in the
Musée des Arts et Métiers in Paris

Left: a Talbot-Lago Record series cabriolet of 1938.
From 1934 onwards the cars from Suresnes were
known as Talbot-Lagos

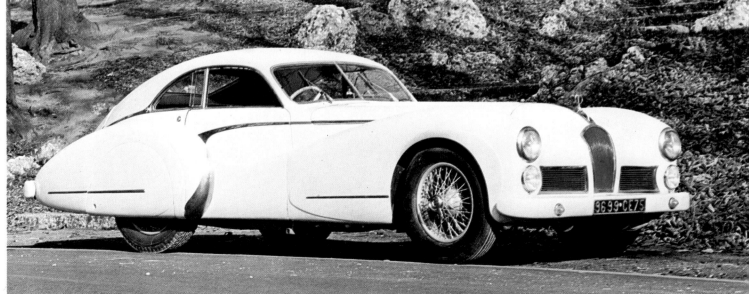

Left: a front three-quarter view of the amazing Talbot-Lago by Saoutchik. The flowing and harmonious lines are particularly noteworthy, although perhaps slightly marred by the radiator and ancillary grilles which seem too shallow and formless for this model

produce 165bhp at 4200rpm, and endowed the Lago Special with a top speed easily over the 100mph mark. Apart from these impressive engines, the cars featured substantial cross-braced chassis, independent front suspension, and synchromesh gearboxes.

Talbot-Lago's performance on the track doubtless helped sales during the 1930s; in 1937 the first three places in the French Sports Car Grand Prix, at Montlhéry, were filled by the Talbots.

The Talbot six-cylinder engine was enlarged to 4.5 litres in 1938, and this helped increase the power output to a maximum 240bhp. There was little further development on the road car side before World War II interrupted car production, but following the end of hostilities, the company was quickly into its stride, and the 4.5-litre racing cars enjoyed several years of success, culminating in a win at Le Mans in 1950.

Whereas World War II marked the end of many exotic designs, the Talbot-Lagos of the 1940s were exceptionally stylish, and the designs by Saoutchik in particular must have seemed very impressive in the period of post-war austerity. The rakish, 4.5-litre, Lago Record sports saloon by Saoutchik was a car of outstanding, if exaggerated, appearance for 1946. As their looks indicated, Talbot-Lagos were rather expensive in the late 1940s, and the company did not manage either to produce or sell very many. Only eighty, in fact, were sold in 1950, the year that a less expensive and less sophisticated model was introduced. This was the four-cylinder Talbot-Lago Baby, with an engine capacity of 2.7 litres, and which again used the cross-over pushrod arrangement. The Baby was well named as it did not live beyond childhood, and the range was restyled for 1952.

By now time was running out, a new 2.5-litre GT appeared in 1955, and in 1957 the company made an unsuccessful attempt at the American market with the Lago America, which was the 1955 chassis with a BMW 2.6-litre V8. In 1959 Simca took over the company, and the marque was dead by 1960. Ironically, like Rootes, Simca came under Chrysler control, and so all the members of Sunbeam, Talbot-Darracq suffered the same ultimate fate.

The inscription on the chapel reads:

CHAPELLE
DÉDIÉE A SAINTE COLETTE
(DE L'ORDRE DE S¹ CLAIRE) QUI FIT
PROFESSION A NICE LE 14 OCTOBRE 1406
ENTRE LES MAINS DU PAPE BENOIT XIII
CE SANCTUAIRE FUT SOLENNELLEMENT BENIT
PAR M⁹ʳ RICARD LE 6 MARS 1929 ET CONSACRÉ
PAR M⁹ʳ RÉMOND LE 30 AVRIL 1933

Voisin

Practicality before elegance

Gabriel-Eugène Voisin, born on 5 February 1880, was one of the most remarkable figures in the history of transportation in France. Having made his name in one element, the air, after World War I he turned to car manufacture, producing some of the most original – and potent – vehicles of the 1920s and '30s, cars designed for function and efficiency which eschewed all the conventional tricks of the stylist.

Throughout World War I it was Voisin's success as an aircraft constructor that dominated his life, and during that period the Issy, Paris, factory turned out some 10,000 aircraft. After the Armistice, however, there was no demand for warplanes, nor was there much call for civil aircraft for some years. An attempt to build prefabricated houses was opposed by the entire French building industry, and so Voisin turned to his old love, the motor car.

After World War I, Voisin acquired the rights to a design which André Citroën had been considering for mass-production before he decided to concentrate on the 1.3-litre Type A. It was a 4-litre car with Knight sleeve-valve engine which went into production as the 18CV Voisin. Four of these were shown at the 1919 Paris Salon, a bare chassis, a skiff, a limousine, and a saloon. Hallmarks of the Voisin were a distinctive vee radiator, and the liberal use which was made of aluminium in the power unit to give a far more spirited performance than was usually associated with sleeve valves. Alloy pistons were standardised from the start, and lubrication was so arranged that the supply of oil to the sleeve valves was proportional to the engine speed. The Voisin was also one of the first cars to have brakes on all four wheels.

The special merits of the Voisin design were amply demonstrated in 1921 when a standard 4-litre won its class at Le Mans in the Fuel Consumption Trials with an average consumption of 43.9mpg. Voisin cars came home in the first three places in the 1922 Touring Grand Prix; the winner, the veteran racing driver Rougier, averaged 66.9mph for 443.7 miles on a fuel allowance of 16.6mpg.

In 1923 Voisin entered Grand Prix racing proper, at the French Grand Prix, in an attempt to prove that having a large-capacity engine was not the only way to ensure a fast car. Unfortunately, the racers, made in a unitary tubular-steel structure of aerofoil section featuring an entirely flat underside (a concept more than fifty years ahead of its time), proved to be reliable but slow. The engine, a 2-litre six which produced 75bhp, was simply too small, and fifth place was the best the Voisin could manage. For 1924 the Voisins appeared in a slab-sided guise, some with 2-litre, some with 4-litre engines, and

took second, third and fourth places at the Grand Prix de Tourisme to mark the end of Voisin's racing involvement, as long-distance record breaking became Voisin's next interest. In 1927 a Voisin with a 7938cc, straight-eight, engine broke the 24-hour record, held by Renault, at an average speed of 113mph.

Away from racing and record breaking, Voisin's pre-war motoring experiences had left him with a healthy respect for steam power, and indeed in 1920 he fitted a steam engine into an 18CV chassis for experimental purposes. He came to the conclusion that what was needed was an internal-combustion engine with the flexibility and silence of steam, which resulted in the construction of a sleeve-valve V12 luxury car which appeared at the 1921 Paris Salon. In prototype form the V12 had only two forward speeds, but development troubles meant that the design never reached production status.

Instead, from 1921, there was a new, small but

Left: a Voisin C4 of 1924, with a sleeve-valve engine of 1250cc, from the Dreya collection.
Below left: the C7 was the last four-cylinder model to leave the Issy-les Moulineaux works. This 1926 example has a 1550cc engine with an output of 44bhp (Pichon collection)

Facing page: the C14 Voisin Chartreuse of 1928 from the Grosgogeat collection. The C14 was one of a series of cars, beginning with the C11, which featured the six-cylinder Knight sleeve-valve engine. Voisin were notable for their long allegiance to the sleeve-valve engine

still luxurious, Voisin, the 1244cc 8CV. With this model Gabriel Voisin's flair for designing coachwork which put practicality before elegance began to assert itself. The early Voisin designs had been very elegant and had attracted the custom of celebrities as diverse as the President of France and Josephine Baker, as Rudolph Valentino and H. G. Wells, but some of the 8CVs had tartan fabric coachwork and an uncompromising, squarecut, appearance.

An enlarged version, the 10CV with a sleeve-valve, 1551cc engine, producing 44bhp at 4000rpm, was introduced in 1925. In 1926 this was available with production-line four-seat, two-door coachwork scaling less than five hundredweight. Built up in sections on jigs, the new coachwork was based on a wood and sheet aluminium tray bolted to the chassis, and stiffened by metal ribbing; footwells for the passengers' feet kept the centre of gravity low. The idea behind the strange coachwork was ease of construction, low cost, and of course, weight saving. It was simply unfortunate that the result was so bizarre and ugly that prospective customers were kept away from the fine machines Voisin built.

Both the 18CV and 10CV remained in production throughout the 1920s; they were joined in 1927 by light sixes based on Voisin's Grand Prix racing experience. The touring development of this model was the 13CV, of 2.3 litres and 66bhp; this became the most successful of the Voisin models, achieving sales of some 8000 (nearly a third of total Voisin production) in a decade. It was the first six-cylinder sleeve-valve, Knight-engined car to be marketed in France, and the sports version, capable of over 75mph and known as the Charmant, remained in production until 1934. There was also a 4.5-litre six in 1927, which gradually supplanted the old 18CV.

In 1929 Voisin built two V12s, one of 3.9 litres, the other of 4.9 litres, but V12 output was always low. There were experiments, too, with the De Lavaud semi-automatic transmission, which almost reached production . . . but was superseded by a Cotal pre-selector gearbox.

In 1936 the legendary straight-twelve was built as a prototype, but never put into production. Its engine was basically two 3-litre in-line sixes joined together, which it was claimed would give the car a top speed of 125mph.

Gabriel Voisin lost control of his company in 1937, and the new incumbents produced a horrid confection with a Graham 3.5-litre engine, a power unit usually supercharged but used by Voisin in its normally aspirated form, and this, one of the last Voisins, was the first to use the more conventional poppet-valved engine. Gabriel Voisin took over again in 1939, but the days of the Voisin were over, and Issy was turned over to the manufacture of aero-engines. Total output of Voisin cars amounted to 27,000 in twenty years.

After World War II, Voisin developed a modern cyclecar, the 125cc Biscuter, also produced under licence in Spain with a 200cc Hispano-Villiers engine – a far cry from the early Voisins and a curious finale for a manufacturer of large V12s.

Left: a Voisin C23 Carène of 1931 with a six-cylinder, sleeve-valve, 3-litre engine. The six-cylinder layout was adopted for nearly all Voisins from 1927 onwards. The sole exceptions were the 1930 C18 Diane which featured a 4.8-litre V12 producing a maximum power output of 115bhp, and the low-chassis Sirocco of 1930 which used the same V12 engine. The Sirocco was short-lived, but the Diane was still available in 1938

Opposite page: a C24 Caravelle of 1932, and, *left,* a C28 Ambassade of 1936, derived from the C23 with an enlarged engine displacement of 3300cc. All the cars shown on this page are from the De Wurstemberger collection

GERMANY

Germany can rightly be regarded as the cradle of the motor industry. Not only was Karl Benz's Benz three-wheeler of 1885 the first motor car driven by the internal combustion engine – a water-cooled $\frac{3}{4}$hp single cylinder unit – Daimler built the world's first motor cycle the same year. In 1889 Daimler's car, a four-wheel two-seater with a rear mounted vee engine, was the one to inspire Panhard et Levassor and Peugeot into producing cars, and founding the French car industry. 1900 saw Alexander Horch design the first car with a shaft driven rear axle, and 1901 was the first year pressed steel chassis members, rather than the customary wood, were used in a car's construction – on the four-cylinder Daimler of that year. Pioneering work and an emphasis on very precise and original engineering have been constant features of the German industry ever since.

Despite the problems facing Germany after World War I, the reparations and the later runaway inflation of the Weimar Republic, surprisingly there was considerable scope for the volume producers such as Opel, Ford, BMW and later, of course, Volkswagen.

The Adam Opel company of Russelsheim was founded in the nineteenth century and at first, like many other companies, produced bicycles before going into the car business: a copy of the 1902 Darracq being their first successful model.

It was Opel who were the first to follow the American pattern of mass production (ironically as it transpired) with an assembly line method being set up in 1923/4, and Opel's was the first popular volume German car. This was the four-cylinder 951cc 4/12PS 'Laubfrash' – basically a copy of the contemporary Citroën 5CV. The 4/12PS sold well, helped by the institution of a country-wide service network, again following the lead of the Americans. By 1937 some 39,000 had been sold, and by the next year Opel were the biggest car manufacturers in Germany with a 38 per cent market share.

That same year, General Motors took control of Opel to become the second US company with a stake in the German market. In 1925 Ford had started to assemble the Model T in Berlin, and in 1931 Ford Werke was founded in Cologne where cars such as the Köln (akin to the English Ford 8) and the popular 1157cc Eifel model were produced.

BMW entered the mass car market as late as 1928, with the Dixi model. This was in fact the Austin Seven built under licence; it proved so successful that by 1932 32,000 had been sold. However, the popular car for which Germany is best remembered before the war is, of course, the Volkswagen.

In 1934 the Nazi régime had directed Ferdinand Porsche to build a car for the masses, and this duly appeared as the famous 'Beetle', with either a 704 or 984cc flat-four, air-cooled, engine; it was the car destined to sell more than the legendary Ford Model T.

The Volkswagen story highlights one of the major differences between the German industry and those of the other major car producing countries before World War II. Germany was the first country where state involvement, so much a feature of post-war Europe, played a significant part in the car industry.

The mighty Mercedes, and the Auto Union combine (Horch, Audi, Wanderer and DKW), were both heavily subsidised by the Nazi government in a two-fold bid to gain success and badly needed prestige on the race track (and of course Mercedes were immensely successful during the 1930s) and to ensure a healthy manufacturing industry in preparation for the coming conflict. This, and the fact that Germany tended to escape the worst of the Depression thanks to a policy of very heavy public expenditure, helps to explain why, when marques such as Bugatti or Duesenberg were doomed, the luxury car makers of Germany were able to enjoy some success at least up to World War II. That Karl Maybach, for example, was able to continue building his fabulous V12 Zeppelins throughout the 1930s is explained partly by their being a side-line to the main concern of producing heavy diesel engines – a very sound business as Germany geared up for the war. Maybach's example is certainly proof that one successful way to carry on the production of really exclusive vehicles was to be part of a larger industrial concern.

Thus, compared with other countries, Germany enjoyed a long and slightly unreal 'Golden Age'. In a way it was indicative of the great strength of the German industry. The aftermath of World War II hampered it of course, but we are now seeing the resurgence of the German luxury car in the form of the large BMWs, Mercedes and Audis. It was surely symbolic that, in 1978, the Audi company was seriously considering reviving the famous old name of Horch for their top of the range models.

Adler

The Adler eagle once graced cars, now it adorns typewriters

The first Adler car emerged in 1900, inspired by, and very similar to, the Renault voiturette of 1899. It was a new departure for Adler, hitherto a bicycle manufacturer.

By 1914, Adler had succeeded to the extent of producing over thirty models, ranging from 9hp twins to 65hp four-cylinder cars.

In 1925 Adler built the company's first six-cylinder cars in 2.6 and 4.7-litre form, and 1929 saw the first Adler eight-cylinder car, the Standard 8, a solid American-style 3.9-litre which was hydraulically braked and resembled the contemporary Chrysler.

It was, in fact, around that time of shaky German economics that talks were held with Chrysler of America about a possible take-over. Then came news of General Motors' acquisition of Opel and the controlling Deutsche Bank halted the Chrysler-Adler negotiations.

1930 brought Adler into its last and most adventurous decade. New designer Rohr produced a daring new small car with front-wheel drive, all-independent suspension, a punt-type chassis with welded-on bodywork, and rack and pinion steering. It was called the Trumpf (meaning trump) and despite its modest 1.5-litre, side-valve, four-cylinder engine, its agility and cornering power were remarkable for the time. In production by 1933, it preceded Citroën's famous front-wheel-drive car by a year.

In an effort to offset modest engine performance by aerodynamic efficiency, Adler produced the famous *Rennlimousin* in 1935. The normal chassis was clothed in a beautiful streamlined body which aided in the breaking of many long distance records.

The company applied the lessons learnt from the *Rennlimousin* in producing a range of improved and very shapely cars – the new Trumpf and Trumpf Junior, the Diplomat, and new 2-litre and 2.5-litre models, with wind tunnel-developed saloon bodies.

Car production ended with the start of World War II, and Adler turned to typewriters after the war.

Below: a sensation when it was introduced in 1929 was the rather American-styled Adler 3.9-litre, side-valve, straight-eight, Standard 8. It was designed by Walter Gropius, with a nine-main-bearing engine with centralised lubrication, and featured hydraulic braking on all four wheels

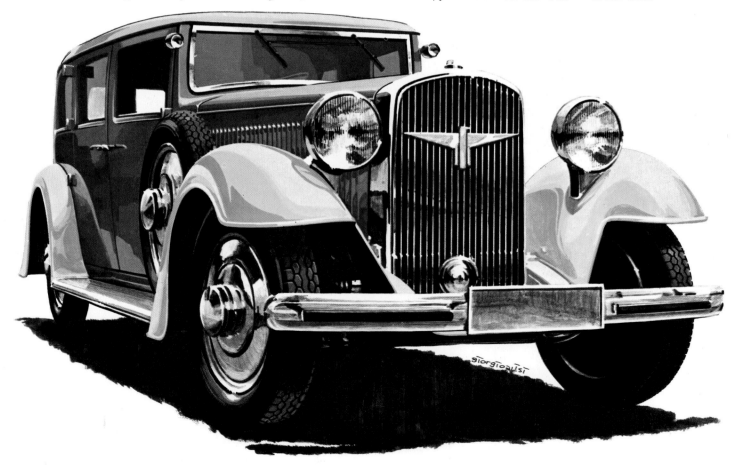

Audi

Advanced engineering with a Latin name

After being forced to sell his own company, August Horch started up again in 1909, calling the new firm Audi (the Latin for Horch). His first car under the new name was the B10/28 of 2.6 litres. This was followed by the C14/35 'Alpensieger' which had a four-cylinder, 3.5-litre engine giving 35bhp at 1700rpm.

The M18/70 which appeared in 1923 was probably the best Audi built up to that time. Its 4.6-litre, overhead-cam six had a silicon-aluminium block, duralumin connecting rods, steel cylinder liners and a seven-bearing crankshaft. It was a smooth unit, producing 70bhp at a modest 3000rpm and was capable of shifting the big car along at 75mph.

The fortunes of Audi, however, gradually declined when Horch himself no longer had anything to do with design, and the firm went deeper into trouble when they introduced the straight-eight R type or Imperator in 1928. The 4.8-litre engine gave 100bhp, and made use of several light metals, but it was still a rather prosaic side-valve unit. Even the chassis layout was ordinary, with two rigid axles and leaf springs front and rear. It was produced up to 1932 but never sold well.

The parlous state of Audi led to the takeover by DKW in 1932. Audi's individuality gradually disappeared following the merger, until the factory was really an assembly area for parts supplied by others in the Auto Union group. In 1932 Audi introduced the 225 which featured an enlarged DKW front-wheel-drive chassis with a Wanderer 2.3-litre, six-cylinder engine, the chassis being clothed in a body designed at Audi. The engine, designed before the merger by Ferdinand Porsche, was a light, overhead-valve six using an alloy block, cast-iron head, wet liners and a seven-bearing crankshaft. However it produced only a relatively feeble 40bhp at 3500rpm. The car suffered various teething troubles, and it never sold in any quantity.

In 1938 Audi introduced the 920, an ambitious design which used a box-section chassis with independent front suspension by wishbones and transverse leaf springs; the car was powered by a six-cylinder engine which was evolved simply by removing two cylinders from the Horch straight-eight. With a capacity of 3281cc, the single-overhead-cam engine produced 82bhp at 3600rpm, which was enough to propel the big saloon and cabriolet bodies at 85mph with ease. Having a good syncromesh four-speed gearbox with overdrive, and sumptuous bodies, the Audi once more challenged the prestige makes – but sadly production was curtailed by the onset of World War II.

Audi

Top: an Audi Type 225 Front coupé of 1937. This car had front-wheel drive from a six-cylinder Wanderer engine. *Right*: a Type 920 cabriolet with a Horch six-cylinder engine of 3200cc, this time driving the rear wheels. From 1932 onwards, when Audi became part of the Auto Union group with Wanderer, Horch, and DKW, a good choice of engines was available to Audi

Below right: a sports version of the Type 225, produced from 1936 to the beginning of World War II in 1939

Opposite page: a sequence of Audi models. *Top*: a six-cylinder, 3838cc Dresden model, circa 1928. *Middle*: a Zwickau model with an eight-cylinder Rickenbacker engine. *Bottom*: an Audi Front-litre of 1934

$\mathcal{BMW}$

Foundations of a sporting tradition

The story of the Bayerische Motoren Werke began when Gustav Otto founded an aeroplane factory on the outskirts of Munich in 1911. In 1913, Karl Rapp opened another factory nearby to build marine and aviation engines. The two companies moved close together in 1916 when Otto formed the Bayerische Flugzeug Werke, building military aircraft powered by Rapp engines, and by the next summer Rapp had turned his operation into the Bayerische Motoren Werke – BMW.

The two companies, BFW and BMW, remained separate but co-operative entities until 1922 when a Viennese banker called Castiglioni bought them both.

The new company's first venture into road transport came with the production of a motor cycle by BFW called the Helios. It utilised a 500cc, flat-twin unit, designed by Max Friz of BMW who had worked on the Daimler Grand Prix engine of 1917. Following BMW's merger with BFW, Friz was instructed to improve the Helios – the new design was called the BMW R32 and was introduced to the public at the 1923 Paris Salon. The main technical features employed, such as a transverse twin-cylinder engine in unit with the gearbox, combined with shaft drive, were not original, but the Friz combination of them in a 265lb, side-valve, 500cc touring motor cycle was, and this basic layout is still used for current BMW production motor cycles.

In 1926, the company introduced the overhead-valve R37 and, all told, eight versions of this machine were built in the first five years of production; nearly 28,000 were sold and 573 events won.

Eventually, in 1928, BMW went into the car business, albeit by the acquisition of the Dixi company and a licence to manufacture that company's model. The Dixi was the vehicle with which BMW embarked on its four-wheel career. Available as a roadster or as open tourer, it was actually the British Austin Seven manufactured under licence, and BMW had the first of their many competition successes with this model, winning the team prize in the 1929 Alpine Trial, with a team of three cars from 200 starters. In 1930 a BMW Dixi won its class in the Monte Carlo Rally.

The Dixi would do 55mph and there was a 65mph Sport model available as well. Over 32,000 of these BMW miniature cars had been sold by 1932, the year in which BMW customers were offered a new model. This was the 3/20PS model of 20hp, which featured a tubular backbone chassis and independent suspension. A year later came the first of the company's famous six-cylinder cars, the 1175cc, 30bhp, 303 model. This was soon enlarged to a 1.5-litre 315 model fitted with twin carburettors and a four-speed gearbox.

The first really famous BMW motor car was the 315 roadster, a car capable of reaching 75mph, which

Below: the BMW 315/1 in the guise of the 315 sports model of 1936. With this car BMW laid the foundation of their dominance in the 1500cc sports car class

Examples of two of the very successful BMW sports cars of the
1930s. *Below*: a 328 version of 1937, with a 1971cc engine with a
maximum output of 80bhp. *Above*: the last pre-war BMW
model, the 335. This possessed a larger, 3485cc, 90bhp engine,
and was intended primarily for the British market, where the
cars were known as Frazer Nash BMWs

won the Alpine Trial as well as enjoying success in many other sporting events of the time. Basically a simple car, the BMW 315 had a 1490cc, six-cylinder engine producing 34bhp. Drum brakes were fitted all round. The tax laws prevailing in Germany at the time dictated that a 900cc engine should also be available, but the star of the company's expanding range was the 319, which was introduced in 1936. When fitted with two carburettors, the 1875cc engine produced 45bhp, while a three carburettor version was capable of producing 55bhp.

The next important stage in the company's development was later in 1936, when a 2-litre engine was offered in the 326 model, complete with a sports-touring body. A simpler 320/321 version had only two doors and a single carburettor, but this range was the first from BMW to feature the marque's distinctive 'vertical ovals' radiator grille.

As such cars edged towards sporting prominence, BMW motor cycles were also winning international laurels. In 1929 Henne, already a circuit champion and 1928 motor cycle Targa Florio winner, became the first German to claim the absolute two-wheel speed record, on a BMW 750 twin, and by 1937 he had taken it to 174mph on a supercharged 500cc twin.

Henne moved from two wheels to four in 1936, making his debut at the Nürburgring in a 328. He won the two-litre class first time out, driving against pure racing cars, and by 1939 the starting grid for the Nürburgring race found BMW 328s occupying the first four rows.

Recognizing their potential, BMW decided to develop the cars, beginning with the 326/327 coupé and cabriolet models which produced 55bhp. By fitting light-alloy cylinder heads, with overhead valves opened by cross-over pushrods, larger ports and three Solex carburettors, the engines were improved enough to produce 80bhp at 4700rpm. This gave the cars a top speed of 95mph, in normal customer trim, and the ability to cruise all day at 4000rpm and 80mph on the Autobahn. Customers could choose which set of gear ratios they wanted by specifying either a ZF or Hirth gearbox.

Four of these cars started the 1938 Mille Miglia, finishing seventh, ninth, tenth and eleventh overall to sweep their class. The same model won the Spa-Francorchamps 24-hour race and went to Le Mans in 1939 with the first streamlined coupé body seen at the circuit, taking fifth place overall. With 130bhp engines these cars could reach 125mph, and it was just such a 328 that scored the marque's crowning prewar victory, coming first overall in the Brescia Mille Miglia driven by Baumer and Baron von Hanstein, at an average speed of 103.5mph.

So ended the prewar story of BMW, except for the introduction of the 335 model. Announced in 1939 and fitted with a 3.5-litre, engine developing 90bhp, it was the largest BMW up to that point.

In the aftermath of World War II, sheer survival took precedence over new-car production. The Eisenach plant of BMW was nationalised by the new East German government, and it was not until 1952 that production was resumed in Munich.

Right: a roadster version of the Horch 850. This example is by Driesden and once belonged to Hermann Goering

BMW originally entered the car business intending to aim for the mass market with their Dixi model. All this changed, however, with the introduction of their six-cylinder models. *Below:* an example of the BMW 327, 2-litre coupés which were built between 1937 and 1939

Horch
Luxury in the Mercédès idiom

From 1896 to 1899, Dr August Horch was an engineer at the Benz company works in Mannheim, however in 1899 he resigned, to found his own company in 1900.

His first car, which has a very good claim to being the first German vehicle with a shaft-driven rear axle, had a twin-cylinder engine mounted at the front of the chassis, driving a constant-mesh gearbox by belts, and was built in a factory in Cologne. Limited production took place there and, after a couple of years, at Reichenbach. The company, however, did not really get under way until 1904, when they moved into a new works at Zwickau in Saxony. There, the 2.7-litre 18/22 model, with four cylinders and overhead inlet valves, was built, followed a year later by the similar 35/40; both cars made extensive use of ball-bearings in engine, gearbox, rear-axle and hubs, and had the mechanicals well encased so that dust and dirt could not creep in.

Late in 1906 came the 31/60 six, virtually a 35/40 with two extra cylinders giving a swept volume of 8.7 litres. Clutch troubles eliminated an attempt to run a team of three 8-litre sixes in the 1907 Kaiserpreis race before the cars had even reached the eliminating trails. 'I must have been drunk to send them', Horch frankly admitted afterwards.

In 1909 Dr Horch resigned after a quarrel with his fellow directors, and immediately founded a new Horch company. After his old company took legal action to stop him using his own name, Horch called his new vehicles 'Audi', the Latin version of his name, which means 'listen'. The first cars from the second Horch company were designed by Chief Engineer Paulmann. Not only did he design the new range of four-cylinder cars, ranging from 1588cc to 6395cc, Paulmann also drove them with some success in 1913, in events such as the Austrian Alpine Trials and the Swedish Winter Trials.

A 1914 design, the 8.4-litre 33/80PS, headed the postwar line-up. Then in 1921 Arnold Zoller planned two new Horch models, a four and a six, with light-alloy engines and overhead camshafts, but he resigned before they were fully developed. This task was left to Paul Daimler, who had just joined Horch from his family company. He turned the 2.6-litre four into the sporting 65mph 10/50, with four-wheel servo braking and an all-up weight of over two tons; he also further developed the six-cylinder car.

Paul Daimler, however, really wanted to produce a luxury car in the Mercédès idiom; and this duly appeared a couple of years later in the guise of the 3120cc 300 straight-eight, with twin overhead camshafts, supplanted at the end of 1927 by the 305/306 range, with the swept volume increased to 3375cc, joined in 1928 by the 3974cc 375. With such advanced features as four-wheel air brakes, the Daimler-designed Horchs were moderately priced luxury vehicles, but reputedly suffered from chronic overheating. Daimler left the company in 1930, but his designs were further developed into the 400 and 405 ranges.

A new model, the 450, appeared in 1930, available with 4, 4.5 and 5-litre engines, still straight-

Right: an elegant cabriolet version of the Horch Type 853 of 1938, with a straight-eight engine of 4944cc. Horch specialised in the production of fast and expensive cars, and this policy was continued even after Horch's inclusion in the Auto Union group in 1932

Right the Horch stand in the 1936 Paris Salon. After World War II, Horch found itself in the German Democratic Republic (East Germany), and was promptly nationalised. In 1956 the company produced a new car known as the Sachsenring – the name Horch being the property of Auto Union

eights, but now with only a single overhead cam. The designer was Fritz Fiedler, and the cars featured a chassis of rigid construction with an X-shaped crossmember of the approved latest style. This chassis was also used on the most luxurious Horch, introduced in 1931, which had a 5990cc V12 power unit and 90mph performance. It was, however, too much car for those depressed days, and its wings were well and truly clipped in 1933 when it reappeared as a 3517cc V8. By this time, Horch had become part of the Auto Union combine, and the Porsche-designed Auto Union racing cars of 1934-on were, in fact, built in the Horch works at Zwickau, into which Audi had also moved by that time.

After the end of 1933, the two smaller versions of the straight-eight Horch were dropped, and the 5-litre became the company's prestige model, often clad in typically Teutonic sporting coachwork, and favoured by those whose position in the Nazi hierarchy did not quite qualify them for a Mercedes.

Chassis layout changed with bewildering frequency: the solid rear axle was replaced by a unit along de Dion lines plus, on the 951 model of the mid 1930s, independent front suspension by transverse leaves and radius arms. Eventually, on the 951B, the solid rear axle appeared once again.

By the outbreak of World War II, the range was made up of two versions of the V8, now uprated to 3823cc, and three straight-eights. That, at the peak of its fame, was the true end of the Horch story for, in 1945, Zwickau found itself in the People's Republic of East Germany, where luxury cars were redundant.

239

Maybach
Motoring in the grand manner

The Maybach Motoren Werke appeared, almost by default, in 1921 and lasted a mere twenty years, and yet it produced some of the most majestic and enormous cars of the age.

The founder, Karl Maybach, had become an automobile designer of note following the ban on the German aviation industry after World War I: before and during the war, Karl and his father Wilhelm had worked as aero-engine designers for Count von Zeppelin at Friedrichshafen. Prior to this, Wilhelm had played an important part in the development of the early Daimlers and Mercédès, again as an engine designer.

Maybach brought a completely fresh approach to the concept of the luxury car in producing the original Maybach of 1921, the W3. He was convinced that the driver should never need to take his hands from the wheel. The pedal that operated the throttle also activated the electric starter, and gearchanging was equally easy, for a pedal gave low 'mountain' drive when it was pushed down, and 'normal' gearing when it was released. Yet another pedal gave reverse, and other refinements included a chassis boxed for strength, and an engine cooling fan which was automatically disconnected in cold weather. The W3 was also the first German production car to have brakes on all four wheels. In all it was a magnificent motor car, but hardly the ideal car for a Weimar Germany undergoing runaway inflation.

The year 1929 saw the first manifestation of Maybach's most fabulous model – the V12. This had a 7-litre engine producing 150bhp at 2800rpm, and had six forward gears; the driver simply selected the gear required which was then automatically engaged as soon as the throttle foot was lifted. Before long this model had gained an arrogant second name – Zeppelin – recalling its designer's associations with airships.

For 1932 there was a bigger version of the Maybach Zeppelin, this time of 8 litres and 200bhp, the DS8. With a chassis weight of two tons, it was hardly surprising that the average DS8 Zeppelin scaled over three tons ready for the road. Designed to go from a standstill to 100mph in top gear, it nevertheless had a five-speed, later seven-speed, transmission, of some complexity, with vacuum selection from a steering column lever.

At least two of these 8-litre Maybach Zeppelins were made with aerodynamic Spohn coachwork, based on the Jaray patent 'teardrop' design which added 30mph to the top speed.

In the mid 1930s Maybach introduced two smaller models, both straight-sixes, the DSH (1934–37) and the SW series which ran from 1934 to 1939. The DSH was relatively conventional, but the SW demonstrated Karl Maybach's love of experiment to the full. It had independent suspension all round by transverse leaf springs aided by coil springs acting on thrust rods, and the rear swing axle was in unit with the five-speed gearbox. The six-cylinder engine had an overhead camshaft, and valves closed by triangular leaf springs. The original SW 35 had a 3.5-litre engine which was enlarged to 3.8 litres for the 1936 SW 38 and to 4.2 litres for the SW 42 in 1939.

Although Karl Maybach attempted to emulate Rolls-Royce in the quality of his fabulous cars, they were always something of a sideline for the firm, and no more than 2000 were built before production ceased in 1941. The company thereafter concentrated on the design and manufacture of the heavy diesel engines, which had been Maybach's principal business through the 1930s.

Right: a styling exercise done by the Maybach designer Jaray for the 1935 Berlin Salon with the idea of producing an aerodynamically efficient shape. The SW35 Maybach was one result of this work, and featured a smooth bodyshell by Spohn of Ravensburg

Below: a cutaway of the fabulous Maybach DS8 of 1932; the 7-litre V12 engine is clearly visible. This type was given the name Zeppelin, partly as an echo of the work Wilhelm Maybach had done on the Zeppelin airships and aero-engines, and partly to convey an impression of size and grandeur

Mercedes

German prestige personified

The name Mercédès was first used in 1901 on the four-cylinder Daimler of 35hp. This car, designed by Wilhelm Maybach, broke new ground in automobile design, having pressed steel chassis members rather than the customary wooden chassis, and other innovations such as a honeycomb radiator in place of the usual grotesque lengths of finned tube.

Mercédès was actually the name of the elder daughter of Emil Jellinek who handled the Daimler concession in several European countries. Legal difficulties with Panhard et Levassor, who claimed sole right to sell Daimlers in France, prompted the idea that the new model should be called simply the Mercédès, and its success established the name.

In 1907, Maybach left Daimler to found his own aero-engine company, and his place as Chief Engineer and designer was taken by Paul Daimler. After his accession most Mercédès cars acquired shaft drive instead of chain, and in 1909 Daimler acquired a licence to build the sleeve-valve Knight engines, and versions of these engines powered cars such as the 4.1-litre 16/45 which was produced up to 1923.

In 1922 Ferdinand Porsche moved from Austro-Daimler, like Paul Daimler before him, to become the new chief engineer and designer, and he inherited the revolutionary work that had begun on supercharged aero-engines in 1915. The first production Mercédès to be fitted with superchargers appeared at the Berlin Motor Show of 1921 in the form of a 1½-litre and 2.6-litre car.

The supercharged Mercédès preceeded by two years Grand Prix cars with forced induction. In addition to being first on the scene, the Mercédès system was very sophisticated, the supercharger could be cut in or disconnected at will by the driver pressing down or releasing the accelerator pedal accordingly – following which a clutch would operate in the drive to the Roots blower.

In 1922 another pair of blown Mercédès was marketed, this time they were six-cylinder machines of four and six litres. Inevitably the competition cars had to follow suit, and a brace of two-litre designs – the first with four cylinders, the second with eight – were raced wherever possible. The straight-eight was very fast and difficult to manage but the four was a very effective machine and scored victories in the Targa and Coppa Florio races of 1924.

That was a year in which Mercédès and Benz cars between them scored no less than 293 victories in assorted competition events, but the victories were Pyrrhic. Times were very hard, especially for motor manufacturers in Germany. In view of the poverty spreading throughout Germany as a result of the war, and the consequent reparations and inflation, one single factory would have sufficed to supply the whole of the German market. Accordingly Benz & Cie and the Daimler Motoren Gesellschaft amalgamated to form Daimler-Benz at the end of June 1926. Already other manufacturers had sought to survive by cutting prices and cheapening their products, but they failed and their failure confirmed Daimler-Benz in their determination to maintain their high standards. To serve as a reminder of those traditions, the new Mercedes-Benz badge (the accents being dropped from the name) embodied the Mercédès three-pointed star encircled by the Benz laurel wreath.

Apart from the commercial vehicles and diesels, which proved an important company asset, production was concentrated on the heavy but flexible

Top right: a Mercedes Sportwagen, this one a supercharged S26 120/180hp model of 1927
Bottom right: a superb example of the Daimler-Benz 770 'Grosser Mercedes'; it featured the classic 'U' sectioned chassis, rigid axles and semi-elliptic springs (Daimler-Benz Museum)

Below: an unusual Mercedes cabriolet, unusual in that it was the work of the, then, Belgian coachbuilders Van den Plas

16/50 Benz and the supercharged Mercedes. New 1926 models were a pair of heavy, side-valve, six-cylinder tourers. They were of very conventional design, and still featured wooden wheels. The 2-litre was known as the Stuttgart and the 3.1-litre model as the Mannheim, so named after their respective places of manufacture. The Stuttgart was later developed into the 2.6-litre Stuttgart 260 and the Mannheim into the 3.5-litre Mannheim 350. The Nürburg 460 with a 4.6-litre straight-eight was added in 1928, and developed into the Nürburg 500. The existing six-litre Mercedes design, dating from 1922, was developed into the sports model K with shortened wheelbase, and engine enlarged to $6\frac{1}{4}$ litres to give 110 horsepower without the blower engaged, or 160 when supercharged. This was the fastest touring car of its kind on the world market, and sired a line of immensely successful large high-performance cars that kept the firm's racing reputation alive through the difficult years of the late 1920s and early 1930s. The 6.8-litre S type was a long and relatively low four-seater with rakish lines and corresponding performance. It was, in fact, nowhere near as heavy as it looked because the huge cylinder block was a light-alloy casting. Allied to the high performance, the S type had exceptional handling thanks to the superb steering geometry. From the S came the SS, the short chassis SSK, and finally the ultra-sporting and drastically lightened SSKL – all of 7.1-litre capacity.

These were not racing cars, but there were many occasions when stripped versions of the big tourers and sports cars not only provided a useful leavening of the field but also provided good opposition for the thoroughbred racing cars. With them Mercedes managed to win events such as the Ulster TT in 1929, the Irish Grand Prix in 1930, and even the Mille Miglia in 1931. The pinnacle of Mercedes early '30s racing programme was Caracciola's 1931 German Grand Prix victory in a lightened sports SSKL 7-litre over the Bugattis of Chiron and Nuvolari. By this time the SSKLs produced nearly 300bhp and dominated the Avus races in Germany.

Nevertheless, despite these successes, the directors judged it prudent to withdraw from racing for a while when they entered the economy market with the six-cylinder, 1.7-litre, model 170. This was the first Mercedes–Benz to have independent suspension, by double transverse leaf springs at the front and by

helically sprung swinging half-axles at the rear. This car was a landmark in the company's history, being full of technical niceties. The chassis was built up from box-section members instead of the traditional channels, the gearbox had an overdrive top speed, all four brakes were hydraulically operated, there was centralised chassis lubrication, thermostatically controlled engine cooling, and great attention paid to structural stiffness, from the short-spoked wheels to the extensive bracing of the chassis. For the model 380, which appeared in 1933, wishbones and helical springs replaced the transverse leaf springs.

The 130H model which followed was something of a departure from Mercedes practice in some ways. Its chassis consisted of a large-diameter tube as a backbone with cross members front and rear, carrying independent suspension and the steering and propulsive units. The engine provided the major departure in that it was a rear-mounted, side-valve four, in unit with a transmission that had an overdrive fourth gear that was semi-automatic as it could be engaged without using the clutch. The whole car was simple, soundly made and sensibly proportioned – an outstandingly practical predecessor of Ferdinand Porsche's later Volkswagen. Even

Below: a cutaway of the 540K, showing clearly the in-line engine of 5.4 litres. Normally aspirated, this engine developed 115bhp; with a supercharger, output could be raised to 180bhp at 3300rpm. The advanced, all-independent, coil spring suspension can also be seen

Left: a Mercedes 290 saloon of 1934; this was derived from the 270 model and featured a six-cylinder engine of 2867cc, which produced 68bhp at 3200rpm

Below: a Mannheim Sport 370S cabriolet of 1932. The 3663cc, six-cylinder engine of the Sport gave it a top speed of 75mph

though Mercedes added a two-seater version with an overhead-camshaft engine giving 55bhp in 1934, the 130H was overshadowed by the conventional front engined 170V which was so successful that the rear engined machine was soon superseded.

Coming on the market in 1936, the 170V was a lightweight all-purpose design with a 38hp engine. The chassis would take a two or four-seat saloon body, ambulance or delivery van bodywork, and was a cruciform type composed of oval-section tube. A mechanically refined model, it could reach 62mph and return 28 miles to the gallon. It was held in high esteem in Europe, as its sales of over 90,000 by 1942 indicate.

The first of the Grosser Mercedes was produced in 1930. Its 7.7-litre, straight-eight unit would develop 150bhp, 200 if supercharged, and the car was

built in this form up to 1937. 1938 saw its replacement by the 770 model, which was of a much more modern configuration with independent suspension on an oval tubular chassis frame. The 155bhp, 230 when blown, which the 770 produced, transmitted through the new five-speed synchromesh gearbox, could propel the car at over 100mph.

The rest of the Mercedes range in the middle and late '30s consisted of the 170V, a similar model in the six-cylinder 290, and the glamorous 500 and 540K supercharged coupés.

In 1934 Mercedes returned to Grand Prix racing to take part in the unlimited capacity formula introduced at the end of 1932. Their overwhelming success brought great prestige to the company up to World War II – during which the destruction of their plant marked the end of an era.

Above: the imposing front of the Mercedes 540K; this particular GT was built by Stoccardi in 1936 (Quattroruote collection). More a prestige motor car than a true sports model, it was none the less capable of a top speed of over 90mph

Left: a 540K with a rather futuristic looking cabriolet body on a 540K chassis, note the exaggerated length of both front and rear wings, and the way in which the radiator grille is set well back to give a purposeful overall aspect (Strinati collection)

Below: a truly elegant two-door coupé, built on yet another 540K chassis. The particularly harmonious lines tend to disguise the fact that this example is a little in excess of sixteen feet in length

GREAT BRITAIN

The story of the British car industry really revolves around topics as mundane as volumes of production, and economies of scale.

In the early years of the twentieth century there was a proliferation of car manufacturers, indeed by 1914 there were over 200 makes of car on the British market. Many marques, like Morris, Triumph, SS and Riley, started life in the bicycle business, diversified into car manufacture, flourished for varying lengths of time, and were eventually forced to merge with similar, or larger, concerns to survive.

The two British high-volume manufacturers, Austin and Morris, were notable exceptions to this pattern. They survived to combine into the British Motor Corporation in 1952, and later formed the basis of British Leyland in which marques such as Daimler, Jaguar, MG, Riley, Alvis and Rover found their final resting place.

Morris Motors was a success due to William Morris's willingness to assimilate the lessons of the pioneering work on mass-production and marketing done by Henry Ford in the first decade of the twentieth century. Morris spent some time in the USA, both in 1913 and 1914, studying American techniques, and in fact at one stage used American engines and components on the 1915 Morris Cowley.

Following World War I, Morris was in a good position to be able to undercut his rivals in a price war which saw several of his competitors go to the wall. The Cowley two-seater, which cost £465 in late 1920, was a mere £225 at the end of 1922. With steps like this, Morris were able to compete with Ford's Model T, which in 1920 had forty per cent of the British market with the output of the Trafford Park, Manchester, Ford factory.

Ford, in fact, was the first foreign car company to establish a sound base in Britain; the first factory appeared as early as 1911, and for a while Ford was the largest car builder in the UK. General Motors were the next American firm to appear on the scene; in 1925 they bought themselves into the British market by acquiring a domestic manufacturer, Vauxhall.

In 1922 Herbert Austin's Austin Motor Company produced its most famous popular car – the Austin Seven. With a 747cc side-valve engine producing 13bhp, the Seven had a top speed of 52mph. It was an example of volume production on a more limited European scale; 29,000 were built up to 1939 at the end of a sixteen year production run. Nevertheless, the Austin Seven did for Austin, albeit on a smaller scale, what the Model T had done for Ford, in establishing the company as one of Britain's major car manufacturers.

A mention of what was to become the Rootes Group, later Chrysler UK, and form the third largest vehicle producers in the country in the latter half of the twentieth century, will serve to cover the mass market in Britain.

After World War I, the Rootes brothers' company had become the largest car distribution company in Britain, if not in Europe. It was this organisation which, like BMC/Leyland in the 1950s and 1960s, took over several ailing manufacturers who found themselves too small to cope as independent concerns. The Hillman Car Company was taken over in 1927 (the year Wolseley became the first company to be swallowed up by Morris), Humber was acquired the next year, the Sunbeam-Talbot-Darracq combine in 1935, and Singer last of all in 1956.

Perhaps it says something of the business sense and marketing acumen of many of the British car companies that a distribution company should find itself controlling such a large section of the industry.

In the 'golden years' of the 1920s and 1930s Britain was known chiefly for the two prestigious marques, Rolls-Royce and Bentley, and for the development of the sports car as a type.

The Bentleys, of course, are famous for racing with such success at Le Mans; indeed in 1929 a Speed Six was followed home by three 4½-litre models to give Bentley an overwhelming 1-2-3-4. Even so, Bentley was another company struck down by poor business sense, and in 1931 the company was taken over by Rolls-Royce. Rolls-Royce themselves did not vacillate and their single-minded pursuit of the very highest standards ensured their survival.

Many other companies helped in making sports cars the country's main contribution at this time. Aston Martin was never a very large concern; its best sales year prewar was 1933 when a mere 105 cars were sold. Even so, this company built fine 1½ and 2-litre sports and touring models with a great reputation. Sports cars from Lea-Francis and Frazer Nash were a common sight on British roads. MG was famous for its Midgets and T series, Riley for its Nines, and SS, later Jaguar, produced one of the most impressive examples of the genre in the classic SS 100.

Alvis

Creators of some of Britain's most beautiful touring cars

In 1919 Thomas George John left the Siddeley-Deasy Company and founded his own concern of T.G. John which was to become the Alvis Car and Engineering Company in 1921.

The first cars produced were the 10/30hp 1460cc side-valve machines; designed by G.P.H. de Freville with sporting pretensions, in fact they had little competition success. After G. Smith-Clark and W. Dunn joined the company in 1922, however, as Chief Engineer and Chief Designer respectively, Alvis began to produce sophisticated cars such as the 12/50 overhead-valve 1496cc machine which took the 200 Mile Race at Brooklands in 1923 at 93.3mph.

1925 saw Alvis produce a real innovation in their front-wheel-drive sprint car. The new Alvis had a 12/50 engine turned back to front, with the drive through a reversed de Dion-type front axle. The chassis was of duralumin and the rear tube axle was supported on reversed quarter-elliptic springs. Super-charged, the car was capable of lapping Brooklands at 104mph, and in 1926 Alvis decided to produce a similar design for the 1.5-litre formula, utilising a supercharged straight-eight engine. For an under-capitalised company the GP venture was a mistake, and the decision to go into production with a complex front-wheel-drive, four-cylinder, car in 1928 possibly unwise, although the machines were very quick as a class win at Le Mans demonstrated.

Until 1931 the 12/50 was the mainstay of Alvis sales, but a pushrod six-cylinder model was produced in 1927 using the 12/50 chassis which had lost its original sub-frame in 1926. In 1929 the capacity of the 12/50 'six' went up from 1879cc to 2148cc to form the Silver Eagle. This was the forerunner of all the successful Alvis sixes of the 1930s, notably the 2.5 and 2.7-litre Speed 20, the 3.5-litre Speed 25 and the 4.3-litre.

The elegant sports models were known for good performance at a reasonable price, and in fact the 4.3 was at one time the fastest production saloon on the British market; an all-synchromesh gearbox and independent front suspension were added in 1933.

The four-cylinder line continued through the 12/60 of 1931/2, similar to the 12/50, to the handsome 1.5-litre Firefly, then the 1842cc Firebird, and culminated in the more powerful 12/70 in 1937.

After World War II Alvis returned to car production with a 14hp model based on the 12/70. After an abortive attempt at an Issigonis designed front-wheel-drive V8, one of the most attractive models appeared in 1956, with the Graber bodywork which was produced up to the 1967 Rover takeover.

Alvis are perhaps best remembered for their sports and touring models. Below: a Speed 25 of 1938. The Speed 25 was one of the best Alvis creations; its six-cylinder, overhead-valve engine of 3571cc produced a maximum of 106bhp, to give the car a top speed in the region of 95mph.

Left: the Sphinx mascot of the Armstrong-Siddeley which appeared mounted on all Armstrong-Siddeley radiator grilles, to signify that the cars were 'silent and enigmatic like a Sphinx'

Armstrong-Siddeley

The accent on quality

In 1919 Armstrong-Whitworth merged with the Siddeley-Deasy company, and Armstrong-Siddeley was born. The new company produced solid and reliable family saloons with the accent on quality, like the six-cylinder, 5-litre, 30hp car and the 18hp which followed it.

In 1923 a new, small Armstrong-Siddeley appeared —this was the 14hp, a 2-litre, four-cylinder model which was a refined and silent car if somewhat slow. In 1924 four-wheel braking on the larger cars was adopted, and the range continued virtually unaltered until 1927. The Wilson pre-selector gearbox became an option on all models in 1929, and in 1933 the magnificent Siddeley Special was produced.

The Special was notable for its 5-litre engine, built largely of hiduminium light-alloy, which gave the car a very flexible top-gear performance.

The 2.4-litre Seventeen and Seventeen Sports appeared in 1934, followed by the 1670cc 20/25hp, which in fact produced 85bhp for a 'greater reserve of power for arduous conditions'. After another 20/25 model, this time with a 3663cc six, was introduced in 1937 the range remained virtually unchanged up to 1939.

The early post-war models, named after famous Hawker-Siddeley warplanes such as the Typhoon and Hurricane, proved popular, but following the merger with BAC in 1960 car production ceased.

The solidity, accurate engineering, and attention to detail of the Armstrong-Siddeley was well known and respected right up until the time the company ceased car production in 1960. *Above*: a Siddeley Special of 1933. Produced up to 1939, it was a prestige sports model with a hiduminium, 5-litre, overhead-valve, six-cylinder engine which produced 124bhp at 3200rpm to give the Special a top speed of over 90mph

Bentley

'The silent sports car'

The Bentley story really becomes interesting with the birth of the most famous of Walter Owen Bentley's creations; the 3-litre was completed in prototype form for the 1919 Motor Show at Olympia, but was not on sale until 1921, as the design took some time to be perfected. By the time this model was ready to be marketed, its technical advances, such as four-wheel braking, had been largely eroded as competing marques improved their specification, and the 1922 sales figure of 145 was hardly remarkable.

From the start, Bentley pursued an active racing programme in order to publicise their products: 'We were in racing not for the glory and heroics, but strictly for business', recalled W.O. in his autobiography.

Following this policy, sales picked up slowly: in 1923, 204 Bentleys were produced, but in 1924 3-litre output peaked at 403, the largest annual production of any Bentley model. Much of the 3-litre's popularity was due to word-of-mouth recommendation and competition successes by customers, most accomplished of whom was John Duff, son of a missionary and born in China.

In 1924 Duff came first at Le Mans, a victory which set the pattern for Bentley's competition motoring, although the 1925 and 1926 Le Mans events brought the company no honours.

In 1925 Bentley introduced the 6½-litre, to cater for the luxury saloon market. The power unit was basically a six-cylinder version of the 3-litre, except for the camshaft drive. Sales of the 6½-litre were never over 129 in a year; in the model's first twelve months only 58 were produced.

Though the 3-litre had been Bentley's most successful model, and was available in several forms including a short-chassis 100mph version, W.O. now decided it was played out. As the 6½-litre had been intended as a town car, a new four needed to be developed, to give enthusiasts the 'bloody thump' that the six lacked. In 1926 work started on the 4½-litre four – the Big Six less two cylinders – and was completed early enough in the following year for one of the first models to compete at Le Mans. There it was eliminated 5½ hours after the start in a multiple pileup, at White House corner, which also involved the other two works cars – both 3-litres – in addition to two French cars.

The Bentley swansong came in 1929 – for the first time the company was showing a profit, mostly due to the modest sales of the 6½-litre, now available in sporting Speed Six guise – and the works team had

Left: a 1928 Bentley which has been rebuilt; the chassis is, in fact, that of a 3-litre model, and the radiator is from a 4½-litre

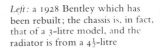

Right: a Bentley Speed Six with bodywork by Gurney Nutting. This is the car in which Woolf Barnato raced, and beat, a famous French express, the 'Blue Train', in 1931

254

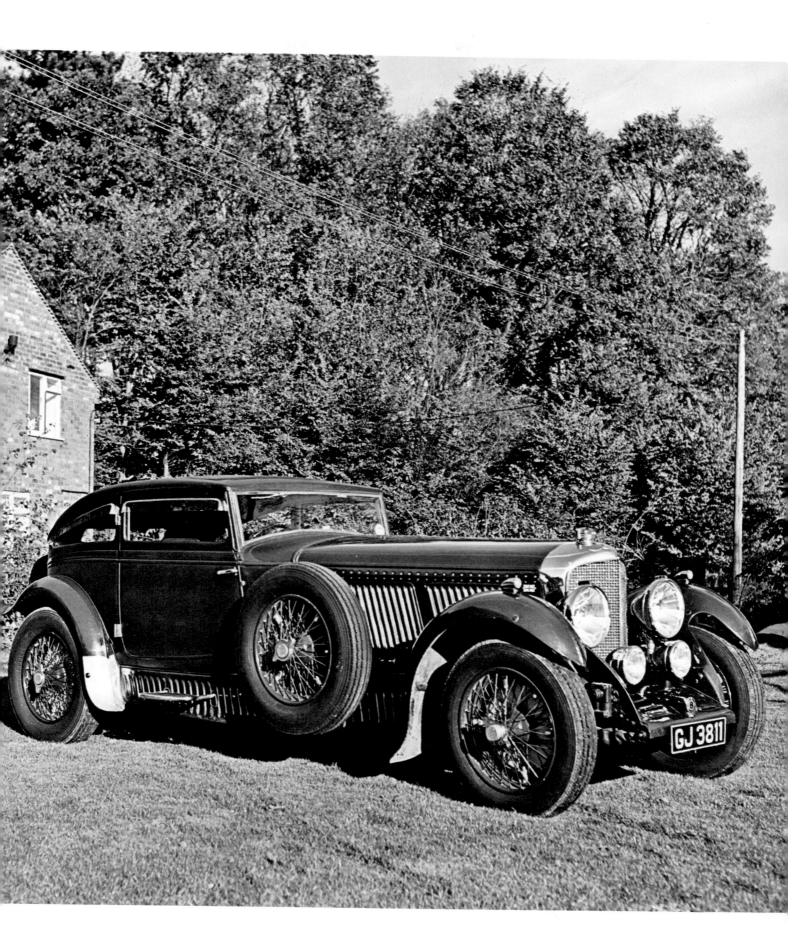

Above: a cutaway of the Bentley 4½-litre. This 4398cc, four-cylinder machine was built at the insistance of one of W.O. Bentley's most important customers, Sir Henry Birkin. Supercharged, this car produced 182bhp from its 4.4 litres. Birkin used this car in the 1930 Le Mans 24-hour race

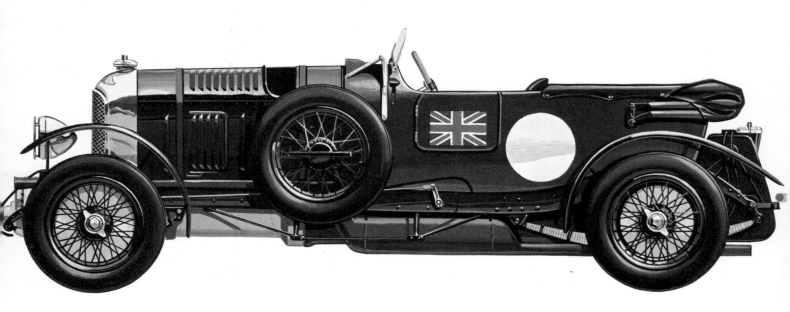

Right: front and rear views of the supercharged Bentley 4½-litre, in which Sir Henry Birkin had one of his best results by coming second in the *formula libre* French Grand Prix in 1930

Left: a Bentley 4½-litre with coachwork by Maythorne; around five hundred of these cars were built, for an exclusive clientele, between 1927 and 1930

Right: somewhat unusual, in having a body by the French coachbuilders Franay, this is a 3.5-litre Bentley of 1934 (Museo dell'Automobile di Torino)

Right: a typical example of the work of the English coachbuilders H.J. Mulliner, on a 1939 Bentley. Mulliners continued to be one of the most popular stylists for Bentleys after World War II

Left: a Hooper-bodied Bentley of 1935. Hooper bodywork appeared regularly on Bentleys after the Rolls-Royce take-over in 1933. This model was the first Bentley produced after the take-over, and featured a Rolls-Royce-based 3699cc, six-cylinder engine, giving it a top speed around 95mph, and the title 'the silent sports car'

their best-ever season, culminating in an impressive 1–2–3–4 victory at Le Mans, with Barnato's Speed Six leading three 4½-litres home. But the seeds of disaster, sown by Bentley's undisciplined marketing tactics – yet another model, the 8-litre six, was already on the stocks – were beginning to sprout. Although production of 3-litres had ended in 1929, the 4½-litre failed to come anywhere near its sales figures and output of this model tailed away from the start.

The need to build fifty supercharged 4½-litres – a 'go-faster' version devised by Sir Henry Birkin – was, according to W.O., a perversion of the model's *raison d'etre*; but he built the Blower Bentleys all the same, when the company's delicate finances should have persuaded him to refuse to have anything to do with it.

The worldwide slump had, judging by the sales figures, less effect on the company than is often claimed, for 1929 and 1930 were outstanding years for the 6½-litre, with sales of 129 and 126, while 4½-litre output in the period was 260 and 138, but despite the good sales figures the firm was rapidly running out of money.

The new 8-litre, which replaced the 6½-litre at the end of 1930, was probably Bentley's most successful model, but it arrived too late. The stop-gap 4-litre, introduced at the demand of the Bentley Motors Board to combat the Rolls-Royce 20/25, was a flop which absorbed much-needed capital.

The blow fell on 11 July 1931, when it was announced that the London Life Assurance Company had applied for a receiver for Bentley Motors, as Woolf Barnato, the principal investor and Chairman, had refused to meet mortgages totalling £65,000. Total output of Bentleys was 3051 – ten more were to be built after 1931 from spares.

Rolls-Royce pre-empted Napier Motors in acquiring Bentley, and from then on the marque inexorably moved towards being merely a Rolls with a different badge and radiator grill.

Daimler

Pioneers of the British car industry

In 1896 Harry J. Lawson floated the Daimler Motor Syndicate, acquired a disused cotton mill in Coventry, and began to produce cars along the lines of the contemporary Panhard. The name Daimler was adopted as the cyndicate had bought the Daimler engine patents for the United Kingdom and colonies, and the company remained Daimler long after Daimler-based engines were discarded.

Once the marque got under way, a bewildering variety of different models was turned out; the multitudinous types built in the first five years included 4½, 6, 7, 8, 9 and 11hp, twin-cylinder models

and 12, 14, 18, 22 and 24hp fours. Then, in mid 1902, Daimler ditched this complicated line-up in favour of a three-model range designed by Edmund Lewis. One of the first customers for the new 22hp model was Edward VII, whose enthusiasm for the marque dated back to 1900, when he had bought a 6hp Hooper-bodied phaeton, marking the start of a long period of Royal patronage.

In 1904 the company was reformed as the Daimler Motor Company following the collapse of Lawson's business empire. Around this time too, the distinctive fluted radiator made its appearance.

Below: one of the most successful Daimlers was the Double-Six of 1927, powered by a 7.1-litre, V12 engine; shown here is a rare open sports version, built in 1931

Early Daimlers were noted for their high performance, and works entered cars competed in hill-climbs and the Herkomer Trophy – without conspicuous success. A team of three cars ran in the 1907 Targa Florio, but the team could achieve no better than thirteenth, twentieth, and twenty-sixth places. Four-cylinder and six-cylinder models of 3.3 litres to 10.4 litres were produced during this period, but in 1908 the company began to switch the emphasis from performance to refinement.

The change coincided with the acquistion of the manufacturing rights to the Knight sleeve-valve engine, designed by Charles Knight of Wisconsin. Development of the new power unit was carried out under the supervision of Dr Frederick Lanchester. The use of the sleeve-valve unit created the prestige image of Daimlers – tall stately cars with a dated appearance going about their business in silence and a faint haze of oil smoke.

In 1910 came a merger with the Birmingham Small Arms Company, which resulted in some rationalisation of the Daimler and BSA car ranges;

Daimlers did not have to be fitted with ugly bodies was proved by the activities of various enthusiasts in the early 1930s. Reid Railton collaborated in the production of two lowered-chassis Double-Sixes by Thomson and Taylor of Brooklands for two discerning customers; the first was an open sports four-seater, the second a Weymann coupé. Joseph Mackle, of the London Daimler agents, Stratton-Instone, won many coachwork competitions with his specially-bodied Daimlers, like the 1929 Magic Carpet with aerofoil-section running boards.

In 1930 Pomeroy developed a fluid-flywheel transmission, which used the Föttinger coupling (originally used for driving the propellers of warships) in conjunction with a conventional cone clutch and crash gearbox to simplify gear changing. The combination of the fluid flywheel with the Wilson pre-selector gearbox, which followed, became the standard transmission on all Daimler, BSA and Lanchester (acquired by Daimler in 1931) cars, eliminating the clutch and giving an ease of control which was unrivalled.

an early benefit of the amalgamation was the development of all-metal body construction.

After World War I, car production was centred on three models, launched at the November 1919 Olympia Motor Show – two 30hp types and a 'special' 45hp model. All had engine lubrication interconnected with the throttle: the oil troughs supplying the big-end bearings were raised by the throttle, so that the faster the unit ran the more lubrication there was. Behind the somewhat dated facade of the fluted radiator, Daimler hid more advanced engineering developments: four-wheel-brakes became standard in 1924, as did thinner, lighter, steel valves for the engine, which resulted in greater power output, rated at 57hp.

In fact, these 57hp engines only lasted a couple of years, for in 1926 they were replaced by the company's sensational and complex new Double-Six power unit – a 7136cc, sleeve-valve V12 designed by the Chief Engineer Laurence Pomeroy.

In 1931 George V acquired a new fleet of notably mal-proportioned Double-Six 50hp cars. That

As the fluid flywheel came in, the Knight engine was on its way out. Technological developments had overcome the sleeve-valve unit's former superiority in terms of silence, and its extra complexity was no longer economically justifiable.

It did, however, have a worthy successor in the shape of Pomeroy's second great engine design for the company, the 4.6-litre, overhead-valve straight-eight of 1935, based on the 1934 sleeve-valve engine. The 3.4-litre 'Light Straight-Eight' of 1936 was a sign of the changing social climate, for it was designed 'especially for the owner-driver'. The large car range of the mid-1930s was completed by three sizes of straight-six, although a few overhead-valve Double-Six cars were built for prestige purposes. Towards the end of the decade, coil-spring independent front suspension was introduced on both Daimler and Lanchester cars.

After World War II, Daimler continued building their luxury cars up to the take-over by Jaguar in 1960, following which Daimlers were, apart from the Limousines, Jaguars with different radiator grills.

Above: a four-door DB18 of 1935 with typical English saloon type bodywork. *Above left:* the 2.5-litre, six-cylinder, in-line engine, showing clearly the SU carburettor which has changed shape so little over the years

Jaguar
A tradition of speed and value

'Jaguar' was the name that was given to several models produced by the SS Car Company in the late 1930s, and chosen as the new company name for SS in 1945, following World War II; since then it has become synonymous with the idea of the fast luxury car.

The SS story, as it was up to World War II, began in Blackpool in 1922, when William Lyons and William Walmsley formed the Swallow Sidecar Company to produce sidecars, octagonal in cross section and fabricated in polished aluminium. Their success enabled them, in 1926, to fulfil an ambition of branching out into car bodywork. The model they chose to endow with specialist coachwork was, interestingly enough, the car which most threatened their livelihood as sidecar manufacturers – the Austin Seven.

The Swallow coachwork had an exaggerated voluptuousness which made it stand out from other attempts to coachbuild on the Seven, and was a resounding success. Three months after the appearance of the Austin Swallow, the Morris Cowley Swallow two-seater was announced, but only a few examples were built. In any case the Austin Swallow was prospering, and in 1928 a four-seater saloon was added to the range.

At the London Motor Show at Olympia in 1919 it could be seen that Swallow had extended the range, producing enlarged versions of the Austin coachwork on the Swift Ten, Fiat 509A, and most significantly, Standard Big Nine chassis. In 1931 William Lyons took a step nearer to becoming a car manufacturer in his own right when he announced a new conversion, on the six-cylinder Standard Ensign chassis.

As the 1931 Motor Show grew near, tantalising advertisements began to appear: 'SS is the name of a new car that's going to thrill the hearts of the motoring public and the trade alike. Its something utterly new... different... better. Long, low and very FAST!', and so on in a similar vein.

The SS duly appeared that October. It was a matter of some conjecture what the SS stood for, perhaps 'Standard Swallow' or 'Swallow Special', but whatever the truth of the matter, the cars had engines and chassis built by Standard to Lyons' specifications, and were fitted with bodywork of exaggerated lowness. While the Standard Sixteen, from which it was derived, stood 5ft 8in high, the SS was only 4ft 7in off the ground, thanks to a double-dropped chassis frame and a minimum of headroom.

The Autocar magazine considered the SS to have: '... modern lines, long low and rakishly sporting, the general effect being that of a powerful sports coupé costing £1000, although the actual price is less than a third of that figure... performance in keeping with its looks... steering which is light and positive.' The 48bhp from the side-valve 2054cc engine gave the SS a 0–50 time of 20 seconds, a maximum speed in the region of 65mph and a fuel consumption around the 22mpg mark – hardly startling performance, but the styling tended to disguise the fact. Overdone the styling may have been, but it created the desired effect, and public response was good.

Below: the SS 90 of 1935, with its 2.7-litre engine, was the start of what was to be a long line of sporting Jaguars. This short chassis model had a twin-carburettor Standard engine, and was capable of around 90mph. (Renault-Isidori collection)

Above: a 1938 example of the most famous car of the SS range, the SS 100. The SS 100 gave the public a genuine 100mph sports car for only £445. It was powered by a 3.5-litre engine producing a maximum power of 125bhp (Renault-Isidori collection)

Left: what could be termed the first Jaguar, although strictly speaking it is an SS, was the SS I introduced in 1931. This example is a 1934 model with the Standard 2054cc, six-cylinder engine and Standard mechanical components (Renault-Isidori collection)

Below: a fine example of the first car to bear the name of Jaguar, the SS Jaguar of 1936. This was a four-door sports saloon, which used the Standard 2.7-litre, overhead-valve engine, suitably modified by Harry Weslake and W.M. Heynes. The SS company changed its name to Jaguar in 1945 following World War II

Such styling excesses were toned down for 1933 with the SS I 20hp 2.5-litre saloon, a four-seater with sliding roof. The SS II was first produced in 1932, based on the Standard Little Nine. The SS II coupé was propelled by the Standard 1005cc side-valve engine, which managed to develop 28bhp at 4000rpm, and gave the small machine a maximum speed of 60mph: all for a mere £198.

Late in 1934, the SS Car Company Limited was floated to take over car manufacture, and the increasingly neglected sidecar building side of the business was carried on by the Swallow Coachbuilding Company. By this time SS were already expanding their thirteen-acre factory in Coventry to which they had moved, from Blackpool, only six years previously.

The SS I and SS II were continued until 1936, the SS II being developed into the SS II 10, and later 12, being given a 1343cc, side-valve unit, bored out to 1608cc for the 12. The line was augmented in 1934 by the SS I Airline saloon, a two-door model with rounded lines at the rear – the roof line sweeping in a simple curve down to the rear bumper.

In 1935 the 2.6-litre side-valve six, the SS 90 sports model, appeared, and in the same year, William Walmsley resigned, leaving William Lyons to become the autocratic ruler of SS and, later, Jaguar.

In the autumn of 1935, the first SS Jaguar appeared – the name Jaguar was chosen by William Lyons because it denoted power, speed and courage. The first Jaguar was a four-door sports saloon, its 2.6-litre engine an overhead-valve version of the Standard engine, developed by Harry Weslake and W.M. Heynes to give 102bhp, enabling the Jaguar to reach nearly 90mph.

The high point of the SS history, however, was of course the SS 100, one of the classic sports cars of the 1930s. The SS 100 appeared first with the same 2663cc engine as the Jaguar; this gave it a top speed of just under 100mph, a 0–50 time of 8.8 seconds, and the standing quarter-mile could be covered in under nineteen seconds.

In 1938 the 100 was given a 3.5-litre engine, and the extra litre pushed it over the 100mph mark, and improved its acceleration appreciably. At that time the SS 100 offered unrivalled performance for the price – only £445.

The first saloon Jaguar made its appearance in 1.6-litre form in 1936 and, like the SS 100, was given the more powerful 3.5-litre engine, in 1937, and continued in similar form after World War II.

The SS Car Company was a resounding commercial success in that a low price was made possible by the mechanical realities, under the fashionably glamorous bodies, being essentially humdrum. A simple girder chassis carried beam axles on semi-elliptic leaf springs, and it was not until 1948 that the first engine designed and built by Jaguar appeared – the famous 3.4-litre, double-overhead-cam six, in the equally famous XK 120 which was a worthy successor to the much loved SS 100, and the forerunner of a long line of sporting cars and performance saloons in the SS tradition of striking appearance and value for money.

$\mathscr{MG}$

'Safety Fast' from the Morris Garages

The MG, for Morris Garages, Car Company was founded by Cecil Kimber in 1928, and from its early days of building special bodies onto Morris chassis it soon came to epitomise the classic English open sports car.

The first 'real' MG was the Sports Six 18/80 of 1928 featuring an overhead-cam 2468cc engine which produced 75bhp. With a top speed in the region of 80mph, and with steering, braking and handling to match, the 18/80 was more than competitive. It was in fact faster off the mark than other, larger, cars of the time, such as the Lagonda Six 3-litre, or Alvis Silver Eagle.

The 18/80 went through three versions until it was dropped in 1932, following which more emphasis was placed on the smaller Midget. The Midget, initially a combination of a Morris Minor chassis and a Wolseley 847cc engine, made its debut at

the 1928 London Motor Show and went from strength to strength both in sales and on the track.

The J2 Midget, incorporating twin carburettors and a cross-flow cylinder head, was recognised as a classic from the moment of its introduction in 1932. Its low rakish lines were carried on in MG sports cars until the mid '50s when the monocoque MGA heralded a new generation of MGs.

The famous T series started in 1935 with the TA, a Midget development with a 50bhp, 1292cc, overhead-valve engine and hydraulic brakes. The T series lasted until 1955 and the TF 1500, the last of the traditionally styled MGs.

Tourers, and later saloons, were also produced. Perhaps the most stylish of the former was the SA 2-litre of 1936, a car which was unfortunately overshadowed by the 2½-litre Jaguar SS which was introduced at the same Motor Show.

Below: an MG Midget PA of 1934, with Aerline body by Carbodies of Coventry

Bottom: an MG WA of 1938. This was a handsome and popular four-door saloon, with a 2.6-litre, six-cylinder engine, built between 1936 and 1940

Above: a magnificent MG TA. The T range was one of the most famous and popular built by MG. The TA model appeared in 1936 with an overhead-valve, four-cylinder engine of 1290cc (whereas the Midget had utilised an overhead-cam engine) and hydraulic brakes (Pasquale collection) *Left:* an MG PB of 1936, a smaller car than the TA, it featured a 939cc, four-cylinder engine, with overhead cam, which gave a maximum power output of 43bhp at 5500rpm (Medici collection)

Riley

'As old as the industry – as modern as the hour'

The first production Riley, known as the Royal Riley, appeared in 1900 and was an almost exact copy of the De Dion motor tricycle with rear-mounted single-cylinder engine, and Riley continued building tricycles up to 1907.

After World War I, production resumed in 1919 with the Riley Eleven of 1.5 litres and 35bhp. The famous Redwing version of the Eleven, which appeared in 1927, was so called due to its red-painted chassis and wings which contrasted with the polished aluminium body. The Redwing was capable of around 70mph from its 42bhp.

It was the Riley Nine, however, that was the most well known pre-war Riley, achieving many competition successes; it captured eight international records at Brooklands in 1928, from the five kilometres at 97.5mph, to the six hours in which it covered 511 miles – a wonderful performance from an unsupercharged engine. This twin-cam engine of 1087cc developed 32bhp and did, in fact, form the basis of Riley engine design right up to 1957.

A major improvement to the Riley Nine was made in mid 1929 with the introduction of the Mark IV chassis, which featured strengthened side-members, 'more supple but no less stable' springs, larger brake drums and stronger wire wheels.

Throughout the 1930s, Riley continued to produce popular variations on the Nine, such as the Brooklands, Monaco, Imp and Kestrel, in addition to six-cylinder cars like the 1726cc Falcon, but it was in part the very proliferation of models built by the Abingdon-based firm that caused the financial trouble leading to the Nuffield take-over in 1938.

The stylish post-war Riley 1½ and 2½-litre tourers are well remembered, but the company gradually lost its identity within British Leyland.

Left: a Riley Sprite, Riley's elegant sports model of 1936, which was later developed into larger and faster models like the Kestrel and Lynx. A four-cylinder 1496cc engine provided the power for these models

Rolls-Royce
Ghosts, Phantoms and Wraiths

Rolls-Royce Limited grew out of the unlikely alliance of Frederick Henry Royce, a dour perfectionist engineer who built his first car in 1904, and the Hon Charles Stewart Rolls, an entrepreneur with several motor agencies, including Panhard, in London.

Rolls became interested in marketing a quality English car, and hearing of Royce's ability he reached an agreement with Royce to take all the cars he could manufacture, and in due course Rolls-Royce was formed in 1906.

Already Royce had advanced his plans for new versions of his original two-cylinder car, with three, four and even six cylinders, and in addition designed the famous and distinctive radiator grille. The car which really first caught the attention of the market was the four-cylinder, 20hp Rolls-Royce, demand for which exceeded production in 1905 and 1906, although production did only amount to forty cars.

In 1906 Royce's masterpiece was created – the 40/50, later known as the Silver Ghost. There was nothing superficially outstanding about the design for Royce was not a deliberately innovative engineer; but there was an abundance of detailed perfection. Its chassis was broadly similar to that of the early 30 horsepower car, but the engine was completely new, being a 7-litre, side-valve unit, with two

blocks of three cast-iron cylinders with integral heads and side-by-side valves. These blocks were perched on a long aluminium alloy crankcase carrying seven main bearings for a crankshaft distinguished by pressure feed of oil to its bearings through the hollow journals. The engine excelled in matters of detail; the timing drive to camshaft and ignition, for example, was by gears, and all the electrical apparatus was of outstanding quality.

The 40/50 was a car that forgave bad drivers, but it was also one that stimulated good ones, and was soon being driven quite successfully in motoring competitions of all kinds, ranging from the Alpine Trials to long distance record breaking runs.

The Silver Ghost was put into full production at the rate of four cars a week. A total of 6173 was built in the course of eighteen years – an average of better than seven a week. In 1913 a normal direct-top four-speed gearbox replaced the three-speed, first in the Continental models and later in the standard chassis, but in matters of design Royce was deliberately cautious and conservative. Thus it was not until 1919 that the Silver Ghost acquired electric lighting and starting apparatus, and not until November 1923 that it was given four-wheel brakes, augmented by a servo adapted from the Hispano-Suiza. Royce had been aware of the need for four-wheel braking for a

Above: the famous Rolls-Royce badge in its original, red, form, in which it appeared from 1906 until 1933, just before Royce's death. The change was made to the familiar black lettering, as red could clash with some bodywork

Left: a Rolls-Royce 40/50 of 1914 (Museo dell'Automobile di Torino), one of the line known as Silver Ghosts, built between 1906 and 1925

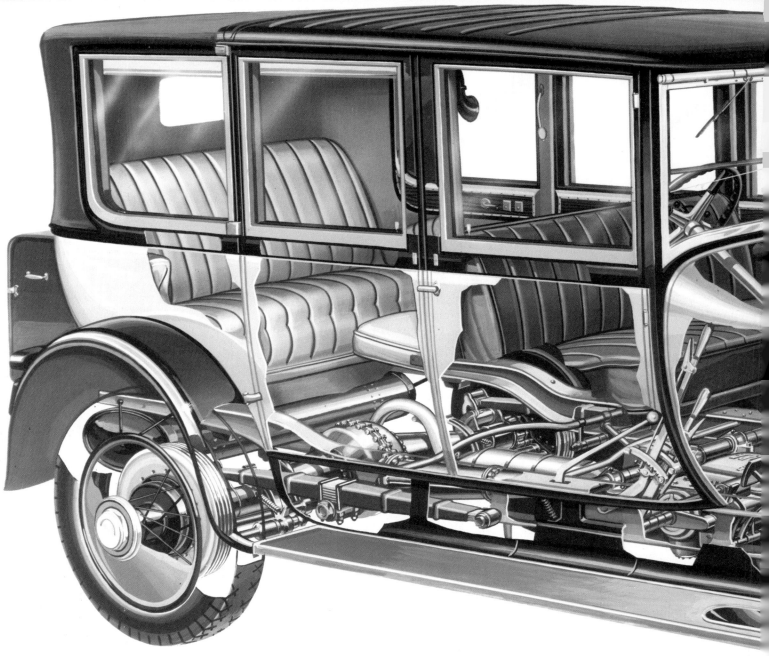

Right: a Phantom I of 1926, the model which replaced the Silver Ghost. The Phantom I was powered by a 7.7-litre, overhead-valve, six-cylinder engine (Quattroruote collection)

Above: a cutaway of the 1926 Phantom I with landaulet body by Hooper, showing the six-cylinder, 7668cc engine. Production of the Phantom I lasted from 1925 to 1929, during which time 2212 examples were built, excluding the 1241 made by the short-lived Rolls-Royce America Inc of Springfield, Massachusetts

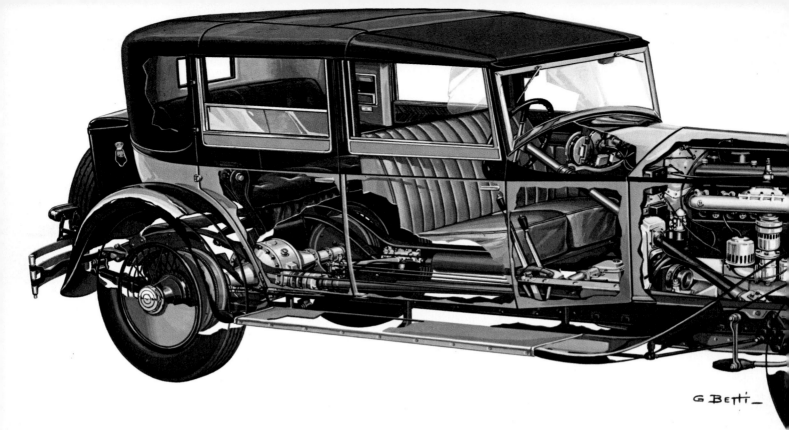

G BETTI

Below: a Rolls-Royce Phantom II of 1930 with body by Hooper, from the Quattroruote collection. *Bottom*: a 20/25 model of 1932 with convertible sedan body by Barker

long time, but the improvement was late in coming as time was needed to make the system as good as possible. The Rolls-Royce was in fact made with an expensive disregard for any consideration which might prejudice its quality; the quality would still be appreciated, as Royce was so fond of remarking long after the price had been forgotten.

The new, smaller, 20hp Rolls-Royce arrived in 1922 with a 3.1-litre, overhead-valve, six-cylinder engine. The three-speed gearbox and Hotchkiss drive, rather than the torque tube axle location of the Silver Ghost, were adopted, presumably on cost grounds, the chassis selling at £1100 originally.

The introduction of the 'baby' Rolls made it clear that the future for Rolls-Royce was to be different. The Silver Ghost, suffering from increasing weight and diminishing performance was given a new 7.7 litre engine which restored its performance. With the new engine, along with other detail changes, it was time to change the name to New Phantom. The New Phantom was short lived and went out of production in 1929, although it was a success in the USA, where it was built by the American branch of Rolls-Royce.

The Phantom II, which came out in 1929, was judged too complex to be put into production at Springfield, and by 1934 Rolls-Royce of America Inc died of bankruptcy.

The changes made to the Phantom II and the smaller 20/25 in 1929 gave the two a great deal in common. The heavy rear axles were left to the mercies of simple semi-elliptic springs and Hotchkiss drive; the gearboxes were given synchromesh on third and top gears, and centralised chassis lubrication was introduced. An extra version of the Phantom II, the Continental, with a short wheelbase of 12ft, carried some of the most handsome bodies to grace

the marque. When it was suitably bodied, the Phantom II Continental was easily capable of more than 90mph. Its performance came from a developed version of the original Phantom engine, with a one-piece detachable light-alloy cylinder head with cross-flow porting and greatly improved manifolding. Perhaps it lacked the smoothness of earlier Royce big sixes, but the car was still perfectly capable of dawdling along at 5mph in top.

Although the company insisted that the death of Royce in 1933 made no difference to the product, the next big car, the Phantom III, which appeared in 1936, was significantly different from anything that had gone before, including the first Rolls-Bentley, produced following the take-over of Bentley by Rolls-Royce in 1931. Under the bonnet, now reaching higher and further forward than ever before, was a V12 engine of 7.34 litres with an output of 165bhp at 3000rpm, which later grew to 180bhp. As ever, torque was extremely high at very low engine speeds, so that the Phantom III's top gear flexibility was excellent. The overhead valves were operated by a single camshaft mounted in the vee of the crankcase via pushrods, rockers and zero-lash hydraulic tappets.

The space liberated by the independent front suspension, after the fashion of General Motors, and

Above: a cutaway of the Phantom II of 1930 showing the very traditional chassis layout of this model. Suspension is by semi-elliptic springs all-round, with solid axles. Rolls-Royce relied on very high standards of craftsmanship, allied to well proven methods, rather than the greater sophistication of Bugatti or Hispano-Suiza, to achieve a similar effect. The Phantom II was a definite improvement on the Phantom I with features like a hypoid back axle and redesigned combustion chambers in the engine

Above right: a Rolls-Royce Phantom III, with sedan de ville bodywork and 7340cc, twelve-cylinder engine, belonging to the Harrah collection. *Right:* a typical Rolls-Royce of the period, this is a 20/25 of 1934 (Achille Motors collection)

the relatively short vee engine made it possible for the wheelbase of the Phantom III to be eight inches less than its predecessor, yet allowing more space for the passengers. The proportions of the car undoubtedly made it imposing, but the established coachbuilders found it difficult to adapt their equally established, not to say hidebound, styles to this change in proportion, and many of the bodies on the Phantom III looked ungainly.

Even discounting the sycophantic flattery that any Rolls-Royce was guaranteed, the Phantom III was one of the most outstanding luxury cars of its time and a very impressive performer. When not impossibly bodied, it would do 95mph; later cars would do a genuine 100mph, and the last thirty or so, with their overdrive gearing, were even faster. More to the point was the acceleration: from standstill to 60mph in 16 seconds was truly formidable by contemporary standards.

For those who were not afraid to use what was really a very smooth gearbox, there was now synchromesh on all except bottom gear and the right-hand lever was in just the right place, alongside the drivers's seat, instead of being up ahead of his knee, as in earlier cars. This was because the gearbox was again separate from the engine not only to improve weight distribution a little, but also to allow a particularly massive cruciform cross-member to be set well forward on the chassis, so that its crux came between the gearbox and the engine.

Scarcely had the Phantom III been introduced than there was fresh news from Rolls-Royce of yet another new model, the latest descendant of the original 'baby' 20. The engine had been bored out yet again to give it a capacity of $4\frac{1}{2}$ litres, and thus the 20/25 became the 25/30 – an exquisite car that was beautifully balanced, sensibly dimensioned and adequately fast. The small car in the range had always been slower than any Roll-Royce should be, a want of power being aggravated by an excess of body-work; the 25/30 certainly had no excess of power, but was fast enough not to be a source of embarrass-ment and would do a genuine 80mph.

Unfortunately, however, the 25/30, one of the nicest Rolls-Royces of all, endured for only two years before giving way to modernism in the shape of the Wraith which was tantamount to a 25/30 engine in a scaled-down Phantom III chassis. The Wraith chassis was another departure from the Rolls-Royce norm in that it was welded, rather than held together with fitted tapered bolts in reamed holes in the traditional Derby manner. The Wraith looked ungainly and remained in production for only one year during which 491 were made, before World War II intervened to give Rolls-Royce other things to do, such as supplying the RAF with the famous Merlin aero-engine.

Car production was resumed in 1946, with the 4.25-litre Silver Wraith as the first post-war model.

Right: an elegant coupé de ville, the Rolls-Royce Wraith, derived from the 25/30 model, which was destined to last but one year. Only 491 were built. The use of wire wheels does perhaps detract from this example's overall appearance (Musée de Rochetaillée-sur-Saône)

Triumph
Traditionally sporting

Even though the first Triumph car did not go into production until 1923, the company traced its origins back to Siegfried Bettmann's Triumph cycle, later motor cycle, firm dating from the turn of the century.

The first car was a 1393cc, side-valve, four-cylinder Weymann-bodied saloon, but it was the 1927 Super Seven of 823cc that really made Triumph's name, enjoying considerable success in trials and hill climbs. A supercharged Seven was introduced as standard in 1929, with a Cozette blower mounted on the left of the engine, which developed 32bhp at 4500rpm, and gave a 65mph maximum speed – all for £250.

A Gnat sports two-seater version was introduced in 1930, and Triumph chased the success of the rival Wolseley Hornet with a small six of their own, the side-valve, 1202cc Scorpion. The Super Nine was introduced in 1932 with a Coventry-Climax four-cylinder, 1018cc, 32bhp engine with overhead inlet, but side exhaust, valves.

Donald Healey joined the company as chief experimental engineer in 1933, and a new car, the Gloria, was introduced in 1934, supposedly named after a famous London mannequin of the day, and offered in 1087cc, four-cylinder and 1476cc, six-cylinder form.

A Gloria Speed Model soon followed, with a triple carburettor engine and open four-seater bodywork, and 1934 saw the introduction of yet another sporting Triumph, a two-litre supercharged straight-eight Dolomite with body style and engine design 'borrowed' from Alfa Romeo.

Frequent successes in southern European competitions led to the renaming of the Gloria Speed Model as the Monte Carlo Tourer, while in 1935 the special equipment version of the same car was called the Vitesse – but by this time Triumph were concentrating on production cars. The Gloria range was continued and developed until 1937 when the Dolomite name was revived for a new range powered by Triumph's own overhead-valve engines – a 1767cc, four-cylinder unit in the Dolomite 14/60 and Roadster coupé, and a six-cylinder, 1991cc engine in the Dolomite Two-litre.

Wood framed and steel covered, as there was insufficient capital to go over to steel pressings, the Dolomites nevertheless sold well and had a good reputation, but the motor industry went into the doldrums prior to World War II and Triumph failed, but of course they emerged after the war as an important part of the Standard Motor Company, and later the Leyland group, wherein they concentrated on sports car production.

Below: a Triumph Dolomite coupé of 1938 with bodywork by Walter Belgrove. The Dolomite came in two versions, a 1.8-litre four, and a 2-litre six. The unusual radiator grille was inspired by an American Hudson, design. In the 1960s and '70s, the Dolomite name was revived by Triumph, with the 2-litre Dolomite Sprint the most famous example

Wolseley
Utility with a touch of class

By 1914 Wolseley was one of the largest car manufacturers in Britain, producing nearly 3000 vehicles that year. The company's early history was very involved: Wolseley Motors stemmed, in fact, from the Wolseley Sheep-Shearing Company which Frederick Wolseley moved to England from Australia in 1899. In the early days Herbert Austin was associated with the company as car designer and competition driver until he left in 1905 to found the Austin Motor company, and become a pillar of the British industry.

After World War I the company was in a very sound financial position, thanks to the profitable wartime production of equipment ranging from shells and armoured cars, to aero-engines and even complete aircraft. Nevertheless Wolseley Motors went to the wall in 1926, owing £2 million, partly due to the price war of the time started by William Morris, and in fact was taken over by Morris.

The famous 16/45 Silent-Six was kept in production after the take over, a four-cylinder 12/32 version appeared, and later an eight-cylinder 21/60: all were similar overhead-camshaft designs with a vertical cam drive. The six-cylinder Messenger arrived in 1928, seven being sold to the Prince of Wales for use on an African Safari, but 1930 brought the model by which Wolseley is best known – the Hornet.

The Hornet was basically a Morris Minor chassis, lengthened by 12½ inches, with a 1271cc overhead-cam six-cylinder engine. With a maximum speed of 75mph it had a 0–60 time of thirty seconds. The car had an appalling turning circle of forty feet, and took 69 feet to stop from 40mph, but despite the drawbacks it sold well.

Even though it was not regarded as a 'real' sports car, Hornets were raced and rallied in competition with the MGs and Rileys of the day. The Hornet ran from 1930 to 1933 and spawned the Hornet Special of 1935 with a bigger, 1378cc, engine. A year after the introduction of the Hornet, the 16hp 2-litre Viper made a brief, year-long, appearance. As the '30s wore on, however, Wolseley began to move into the luxury class with free-wheels, automatic clutches, sun roofs and lots of leather and polished wood, producing an air of luxury which even extended down to small cars like the Nine, a 1-litre, four-cylinder saloon.

Fourteens, Sixteens and Eighteens, which were indistinguishable except by their size, then became the staple diet. Large, heavy well built saloons, they set the scene for later Wolseley production as the Morris Nuffield organisation increasingly rationalised the company, until even the name itself was dropped by Leyland in 1975.

Below: a Wolseley Hornet sports of 1932 from the Ponchia collection. The Hornet was powered by a small, six-cylinder, engine of only 1271cc, with twin SU carburettors. It was good value at only £185, even if it did look more of a sports car than its performance warranted

ITALY

The Italian motor industry is perhaps mainly associated in the public mind with the great industrial giant that is Fiat, Ferrari racing cars, 'super cars' such as the Maseratis, Lamborghinis, and Ferraris themselves, and finally the great car stylists such as Bertone, Pininfarina, Zagato and Giugiaro, who have had such a profound influence on car design all over the world, building on the sound reputation built up by stylists like Touring and Castagna.

If this is an accurate picture of how the Italian contribution is commonly seen, it is wholly appropriate as it illustrates what have been the strengths of the Italian industry over the years. Nowhere else, with the possible exception of Great Britain, has there been the same concentration on racing, and racing car design, as in Italy, and this has duly rubbed off onto the contemporary saloons and touring models. The fruits of this policy have perhaps best ripened in cars like Alfa Romeo's GTVs and Alfettas of the 1960s and '70s.

Alfa Romeo produced its first sporting model as early as 1911, in the 6.1-litre 40/60. Itala did not even make a closed model of any description in the first seventeen years of its existence up to 1920, so great was the concentration on sports and racing cars. OM's first successful car was the 1.5-litre 469 of 1922 — an attractive and competitive sports car. The list could be extended; even Fiat and Isotta Fraschini, makes now associated with the mass market and cars of enormous opulence, respectively, were actively involved in racing in their early years. Isotta Fraschini built their first racing car, the Tipo D, a huge overhead-cam 17-litre model, in 1905, and followed this with two smaller and more successful 7.9-litre racers before going over to the production of their huge luxury cars. Fiat, too, produced monster racing cars in the first decades of this century, like the S76 of 1911 with its enormous 28.3-litre, four-cylinder engine. Now the wheel has come full circle for Fiat; a fifty per cent holding in Ferrari was acquired in 1970, and the company pursues an active and very successful involvement in rallying to the extent of being World Rally Champions in 1978.

For a country with such a passion for racing it is not surprising to find Italy the home of two of the most famous road races of all, the Targa Florio and the Mille Miglia. The Targa Florio was first run in 1906, was won by an Itala machine the first year and has been won by an Italian machine on over thirty occasions since then. The first Mille Miglia was won by an OM, in 1927, and Alfa Romeo and Ferrari both enjoyed great success in this race until its demise on safety grounds in 1957.

While the various Italian manufacturers were busy building thoroughbred cars of great distinction, the industry as a whole suffered somewhat in the periods of economic depression. Despite the opportunities which seemed to present themselves, Italy escaped the attentions of the giant American Car firms; partly due to the regime in power in Italy all through the Depression and into World War II which was not, of course, kindly disposed to the USA, and unlikely to look with favour on GM, Ford or Chrysler taking over any domestic manufacturer. It was Fiat, rather than General Motors or Ford, who took over the ailing companies such as SPA in 1925, Ansaldo in 1929, OM in 1933, and, later, Bianchi in 1955 and Lancia in 1969.

As Fiat were building themselves into the dominant force in the Italian car industry the Italian State was doing its part in helping preserve the domestic manufacturers, through the IRI, the Reconstruction Finance Corporation, in addition to taking over Alfa Romeo in 1933.

Government intervention was necessary in a country like Italy which had lagged behind the rest of the European car producing countries, and the USA, in terms of social and economic development. Up to World War I, Italy's was largely a rural, agricultural economy and, even following the war, the domestic market was too small to allow more than one successful volume producer. It was, of course, Fiat who filled that position, first with the 501, 1.5-litre model, 45,000 of which were sold up to 1926, and then with the 990cc Tipo 509, 90,000 of which were produced in a four-year production run between 1925 and 1929.

It was, however, the Depression, and an increasing stolidity of design, rather than a limited market which killed of the exotic Isotta Fraschini company, which in its heyday had provided the chassis for great coachbuilders like Sala, Castagna, Stabilimenti, Farina and Touring. In a way, the demise of Isotta Fraschini suggested that the Italians liked exotic machinery that worked well, rather than simply looking the part, and nowadays ostentatious prestige is manifested in cars like the Ferrari 400 saloons, or the Lamborghini Countach.

Alfa Romeo
The essence of Grand Touring

For such a distinguished sporting marque, Alfa Romeo had a rather humble and unusual origin, owing its existence directly to the failure of the French manufacturer, Alexandre Darracq, to manufacture and market his taxicabs successfully in Italy.

By 1909 Darracq was ready to close down his Italian factory, but it was rescued from this fate by a group of Milanese industrialists. In 1910 they reformed the company as the Societa Anonima Lombarda Fabbrica Automobili, or ALFA for short, with the intention of making an all-Italian car.

The former Marchand, Fiat and Bianchi designer, Giuseppe Merosi, was hired and he produced a series of monobloc, four-cylinder, side-valve cars in both 2.6 and 4.1-litre form in 1911; sturdy but lively machines, they quickly established the marque on a sound footing.

The next design from Merosi's drawing board indicated Alfa's sporting intentions. The car was the powerful 40/60 of 6.1 litres, distinguished by having overhead valves operated by rockers and pushrods from twin camshafts high in the crankcase. This unit would produce 73bhp at only 2000rpm, and propel the car at over 75mph – very respectable performance for a 1913 car.

In 1914, two of the 40/60s Alfas, driven by chief works tester Franchini, and Campari, managed third and fourth places in the Coppa Florio to foreshadow Alfa's sporting prowess.

After World War I, Alfa, now SA Italiana Ing Nicola Romeo – after the new owner Nicola Romeo who had taken over the company in 1915 – concentrated on producing sporting cars to bear the new name of Alfa Romeo.

Below: an example of the RL Sports series, produced between 1922 and 1927 by Castagna. Basically similar to the RL, the RL Sport differed in having a more powerful, six-cylinder 2994cc engine (Zanotelli collection)

The 4.2-litre, four-cylinder, 20/30 went into production in 1920, followed by the more sporting 20/30ES in 1921, and a large uninspiring six-cylinder, side-valve luxury car, the 6.3-litre G1.

In late 1921 a new Alfa-Romeo, the 3-litre, six-cylinder, pushrod overhead-valve RL, was introduced, both in touring and sports forms. From the latter a very handsome racing machine was evolved for the 1923 season, and the company's racing fortunes climbed, when, after six attempts, victory came at last in the Targa Florio for Ugo Sivocci's RL.

'30s. The first of these was the 1927 single-overhead-cam, 1.5-litre, six-cylinder tourer, followed in swift succession by a 1750cc single-cam, and 1500cc and 1750cc twin-cam models, with and without superchargers. The workmanship and finish of these Jano sixes was sheer artistry, and their performance confirmed them as among the world's classic designs, accentuated by superb Italian coachwork executed by such masters as Castagna, Touring and Zagato.

Inevitably the twin-cam sixes were raced, and equally inevitably, in a period when Grands Prix

Left: a superb Alfa Romeo RLSS of 1927. Note the four-seater torpedo body by the French coachbuilder Weymann with the four vestigial doors. Later, of course, Alfa Romeo relied on Italian coachbuilders like Alessio, Touring, and Montescano

Alfa's first attempt at a Grand Prix car, the PI, was a shortlived failure, yet its replacement was a sensational success. Enzo Ferrari, at that time one of the works drivers, had persuaded Vittorio Jano, designer of the Grand Prix Fiats, to join Alfa Romeo. The result was the 2-litre, straight-eight, supercharged P2 Alfa Romeo of 1924. This classic design won its very first race, the Circuit of Cremona, and its very first Grand Prix, the French. In 1925 P2s took the first two places in the European Grand Prix at Spa, with ease, and would almost certainly have won the French GP again but for the fatal accident which Antonio Ascari suffered while leading the race.

While Alfa Romeo was becoming a world-famous name in racing, the lessons of the track were being applied by Jano to an outstanding series of road cars extending from the mid 1920s to the mid

were eclipsed by sports car races, they won; their score included three Mille Miglias, two Belgian 24-Hours, Grands Prix in Ireland and Boulogne, and the Ulster TT.

The sixes were succeeded by Jano's 2.3-litre supercharged straight-eights, having the same bore and stroke as the 1750, but distinguished by central gear drive to the twin overhead camshafts. The '2.3' carried the Alfa torch to even greater success, their many triumphs including four Le Mans 24-Hours in a row from 1931 to 1934, and three Mille Miglias.

Meanwhile Alfa Romeo's production road cars, six and eight-cylinder models ranging from sober saloons to intoxicating supercharged 'spyders', were enhancing the reputation of the Portello factory still further, while the company was now also engaged in the production of aero-engines, buses and trucks. Nicola Romeo retired in 1930 – he died in

Right: a 6SC 1750 sports of 1930 from the Quattroruote collection. The 6C model (the 6 represents the number of cylinders) was one of Vittorio Jano's first designs for the company, and can be regarded as Italy's first GT model, entering production in 1500cc form. The supercharged versions of the 6SC enjoyed great racing success between 1928 and 1930

38 – and the company was refloated as the SA Alfa Romeo, with a government grant to assist it. With many commitments, however, it found itself short of working capital, and in 1933 came under government control, where it remains to the present day.

None of these behind-the-scenes activities affected Alfa's racing success. In 1932 Jano produced a worthy successor to the P2 Grand Prix car in the Tipo B 'Monoposto', commonly called the P3. This superb racing machine had a supercharged 2.6-litre straight-eight engine based on the 'Monza', but with twin superchargers, a single-seater body and a classical purposeful appearance. With master drivers such as Nuvolari, Caracciola, Chiron and Fagioli, it swept all opposition before it.

The engine was enlarged to 2.9 litres in 1934, when the P3 won fifteen races, and to 3.2 litres for 1935, when it won thirteen. By then, however, the German challenge by Mercedes–Benz and Auto Union had taken full effect, and the Monoposto's later successes were in lesser races, apart from Nuvolari's most

Opposite page top to bottom: a cabriolet version by Stabilimenti Farina on a 1750 chassis (Centenari collection): a 1750 Gran Sport series 6 of 1933, and another 1750 cabriolet, from the Accorsi collection. The two lower models are examples of the work of Touring of Milan

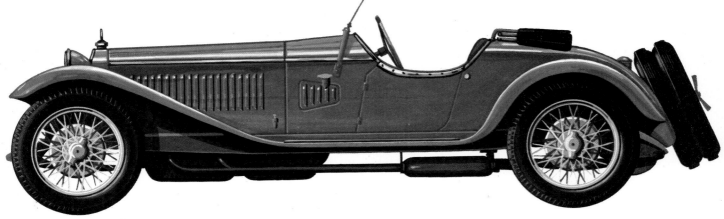

Three variations on the ubiquitous 6C 1750 chassis. *Top:* a 1929 model by the English coachbuilders Young. *Middle:* a profile of a Gran Sport series 4 and 5 of 1929–30, and, *Below:* another Gran Sport, series 4 of 1930 by 'La Sportive' of Milan (Quattroruote collection)

282

283

famous victory of all. the 1935 German Grand Prix.

A more modern, all-independently-sprung GP car appeared late that year, at first with a 3.8-litre eight-cylinder engine, but in 1936 with a 4.4-litre V12 unit. By 1937, however, the German cars had gained total domination. For the 1938, 3-litre, GP Formula Portello half-heartedly built eight, twelve and sixteen-cylinder cars with small hope of success, but they also adapted one bank of the sixteen-cylinder design to produce a 1.5-litre straight-eight supercharged voiturette racer.

Designed by Gioacchino Colombo, the car was called the Tipo 158 and nicknamed the Alfetta. It won two races in 1938, its first year, and four more in 1939–40 before war interrupted a great career.

Many features used by Alfa in racing, such as the very effective independent suspension, were inherited by the sports and touring cars produced by the company. A 2.3-litre six called the 6C 2300 was the basic production model in the last years before the war, while the 8C 2900 supercharged eights set standards for performance and appearance hard to equal; the 1938 Mille Miglia-winning car with light alloy 'Superleggera' open two-seater bodywork by Touring remains a classic shape today.

World War II intruded dramatically on Alfa Romeo car development, and the company returned to peace with the famous Portello factory three-quarters destroyed, but despite this the company has survived and flourished.

Above: two examples of the work of Pininfarina on the Alfa Romeo 8C 2300 chassis, *top* is a four door saloon, and *below* a false cabriolet. It only takes a moment's glance to see the influence of the sports car design on these two models. The lines are distinctly rakish for this type of vehicle

Top right: an Alfa Romeo coupé of 1939 on the 6C 250 SS chassis. The very elegant lines of this body, fabricated in aluminium, were a taste of things to come. *Right:* a 'Superleggera' 2300B saloon of 1927 from the Bonfanti collection, built by Touring of Milan. Both these cars featured double-overhead-cam engines, now almost a trademark of Alfa Romeo

Bianchi

A conservative strain in Italian design

Like many other car manufacturers, Edoardo Bianchi started his career with bicycle production; in his case in Milan in 1885. Motor cycle manufacture was begun in 1897, and in 1898 Bianchi produced his first car.

It was based on bicycle techniques, with a steel-tube frame and a single-cylinder, air-cooled De Dion engine driving the rear wheels. The next year a similar vehicle appeared, again using the 942cc De Dion with chain drive to the rear wheels, and Giuseppe Merosi joined the company as engineer in charge of motor car development.

A range of increasingly powerful and fast touring cars was evolved: by 1907 a new factory was producing three chassis types of different wheelbase lengths, all using interchangeable components. The engines were of the four-cylinder, side-valve type, driving the rear wheels through a four-speed gearbox and a chain. The scale of production was stepped up still more and an ultra modern factory built in Milan, helping to give the marque a reputation for quality, sound construction, and good performance at a reasonable price.

New for 1908 was the type G, which featured a modern, L-head, monobloc, four-cylinder engine and, initially, a three-speed gearbox (by 1910 it had acquired a further ratio). An interesting development, for an Italian manufacturer, was the type S of 1914, an inexpensive 1244cc three-speed car, available in only one body style and one colour. Electrics were an optional extra, but were standard on Bianchi's wartime newcomer, the 3.3-litre B-type of 1915. The S was enlarged to 1460cc in 1916, but disappeared shortly after World War I in favour of the type 12.

Vintage Bianchis typified the more conservative strain in Italian design, with little sporting flavour, although they did build a contender for 2-litre Grand Prix honours in 1922. The car had a twin-overhead-cam four-cylinder engine producing over 90bhp. Unfortunately the project was shelved. In 1923, a new model, the type 16, was produced to replace the 12, and it featured a detachable cylinder head. The firm also brought out, at the same time, the 2-litre, pushrod type 18, which was very popular with English coach-builders of the period.

It was not until 1924, with the arrival of Antonio Santoni to the company as Chief Engineer, that the company turned to the small car sector of the market, with the S4. Like the larger, 2300cc type 20 which was produced at the same time, the S4 retained one distinguishing feature, that of a separate gearbox driven by a short shaft from the clutch and driving the rear wheels via another short shaft.

Santoni's S4, which was Bianchi's answer to the Fiat 509, developed year by year via the S5 of 1927, until it was replaced, in 1935, by the 1452cc S9, which remained in production until 1939. It featured a five-bearing crankshaft and, by 1936, had acquired hydraulic brakes and a synchromesh gearbox, although, unusually for a cheap Italian car, it rode on beam axles all round and wore Rudge-type wire wheels. Also made was a long-wheelbase six/seven-seater version of the S9 which was used as a taxicab.

During World War II, the Bianchi works were turned over to the production of heavy commercial vehicles, most of which utilised diesel engines. Towards the end of 1943 the Milan factory was almost completely destroyed by bombing, but production continued in other premises. In 1946 Edoardo Bianchi died, aged 81, his principal collaborator Gian Fernando Tommaselli having died a few years earlier. After this, car production ceased, lorries being responsible for the company's survival until 1955 when, with Fiat and Pirelli backing, the company was given a fresh lease of life under the new name of Autobianchi.

Right: a Bianchi berlina S5 of 1932. This model was powered by a 1452cc, side-valve, four-cylinder engine, which by 1932 produced 40bhp. The S5 entered production in 1928, replacing the S4 from which it was derived

Below: a Bianchi S8 false cabriolet by Touring. The S8, introduced in 1928, represented a none-too-successful attempt by Bianchi to move up-market. The S8 featured a straight-eight engine of 2.7 litres, with overhead valves and dry sump lubrication

Fiat

Fabbrica Italiana Automobili Torino

Fiat is now, by a huge margin, the largest car manufacturer in Italy, and the fifth largest in the world in terms of vehicle production. The seeds of this success were sown long ago, in the first decade of this century.

The Fabbrica Italiana Automobili Torino was founded in 1899 by various members of the patrician families of Turin, including Giovanni Agnelli, and the company is unusual in that the Agnelli family was still in control during the 1970s. It was realised by the management from the earliest days that one key to a successful future lay in being part of a large and diverse industrial group. To that end commercial vehicle production was undertaken in 1903, ball bearings and ship building started in 1905, aero-engine, aircraft, marine engine, and even railway rolling stock production followed in the next ten years. This broad industrial base stood Fiat in good stead in depressed times in the car business, such as the early 1970s. It must, however, be admitted that Fiat's numerous other interests did rather contribute to their neglecting to modernise their car range at that time.

The first FIAT car was built in the Ceirano works which FIAT had taken over to start their car production. The car was a 679cc horizontally-opposed twin-cylinder, rear-engined machine which was chain driven, and this was followed by a front-engined model of 1.2 litres in 1901.

Up to World War I, Fiat (the company's title was changed from FIAT at the end of 1906) models grew larger and more refined; pressed steel chassis were introduced in 1904, and the first shaft-driven Fiat appeared in 1911. The company also pursued an active racing programme, as did most Italian car makers at this time; a Fiat driven by Felice Nazzaro won the French Grand Prix, the Kaiserpreis and the Targa Florio in 1907. The Fiat racers before World War I were, in general, quite huge – the 1913 28.3-litre four being the largest, but by 1914 Fiat had managed to get a respectable 135bhp out of the much smaller 4.5-litre machines.

Even though Italy was on the winning side during World War I, the end of hostilities saw the Fiat works briefly taken over by a workers' soviet before car production resumed with the 1919 Tipo 501. The 501 was a small 1.5-litre, side-valve-engined car, built for a wider public than hitherto. It enjoyed a long production run (45,000 were made up to 1926) and steady development; front-wheel brakes soon became an option, and companion models with larger, 2.3-litre and 3.4-litre, engines were introduced.

The Tipo 519, which appeared in 1922, catered for the more traditional up-market clientele than the 501. Its six-cylinder, overhead-valve engine of 4764cc had an output of 77bhp, and the 519 featured the novelty of a hydro-mechanical servo on the braking system. While the 519 was initially overshadowed by the 'Superfiat', it was certainly longer-lived. The Superfiat, with a large, overhead-valve V12 of 6.8-litres and front-wheel brakes, had been

Below: a Fiat 519 S from the Fiat collection. The six-cylinder 519s were built between 1922 and 1927 and formed the top of the Fiat range at that time; the Superfiat of 1921, intended for that role, had been a failure. A six-cylinder, 4.8-litre engine powered the 519

Top: a D'Orsay convertible coupé on a 525 chassis by Stabilimenti Farina, from the Caproni-Lazzaroni collection. The 525, which appeared in 1927, was a large six-cylinder, side-valve machine designed to replace the 519. *Below left:* a 525 SS built by Viotti (Cupane collection). *Below right:* a 525 N sports from the Quattroruote collection. Also in 1927, Fiat introduced the 520; *left* is a touring version, and *above,* a coupé

intended as the Fiat flagship, but it proved unpopular, and less than a dozen were made in 1922 before it was discontinued in favour of the 519.

At the time of the Superfiat and the 519, Fiat began to revise their styling; the rounded radiator shell was discarded, and a new, sharper and straighter line given to the bodywork, which, incidentally, became cheaper to produce. After revising the styling, the range itself was revised in 1927. Two new side-valve, six-cylinder models were introduced within two months of each other: the Tipo 520 and the 525. The engines of both were long-stroke units designed to produce a lot of torque at low revs; that of the 520 was 2234cc in capacity with dimensions of 68 × 103mm, and that of the 525 was 3739cc and measured 82 × 118mm. The combination of the American-influenced styling and a major increase in body size helped the 520 sell in large numbers. 21,000 in all were produced, compared with sales figures of 4000 for the 525, although the latter was about an average production run for a luxury car at that time.

The 525 was a versatile machine which appeared in several versions, ranging from a berlina (one of which was given to the Pope) to the spyders which ran in the Coppa Venezia, and in fact a series of spyder replicas was made after the race. This series used the six-cylinder engine of the 525 but with modifications to the cylinder head and carburation which raised its output to 88bhp. Its torpedo-style bodywork made it the most elegant Italian sports car of the time, and the 525 spyder was produced up to the onset of the Depression.

By the end of the 1920s Fiat had begun to pay more attention to the more utilitarian mass-market; the Tipo 509 of 1925 had been an early indication of this trend. An overhead-cam, 990cc model, it sold in large numbers and by 1929 90,000 had been sold. In 1932 the 508 Balilla appeared, it was compact, light, economical to run and lively – in fact the ideal popular car. This 995cc saloon was equipped with hydraulic brakes, and by 1934 had acquired synchromesh and a four-speed gearbox. Better still the

Balilla had within it the makings of something more convincing: this became apparent in 1937 when a new 508C was introduced, with independent front suspension, and a larger, 1098cc, engine.

On a larger scale, 1933 saw the arrival of the 518 Ardita, which was essentially a large Balilla. The Ardita was built in both 1750 and 2000cc four-cylinder versions and intended to replace the 522 and 524 models. Between 1934 and 1936 the last of the old long-stroke six-cylinder-engined cars, the 527, was produced, in a bewildering variety of styles, ranging from the traditional torpedo to a compact sport berlina with bodywork by Bertone. All in all no less than 260 different versions were available in the 527's brief, two-year, life.

In 1936 Fiat started production on a cleanly, and aerodynamically, styled family saloon known as the 1500. The engine was new, a short stroke, overhead-valve, six-cylinder unit with the same dimensions as the 508 Balilla's engine (65 × 75mm), and the car featured independent front suspension of the Dubonnet type (known in America as 'knee-action springing'). Much as the Balilla was a turning point in small car design, the 1500 was a great advance in the progress of the family saloon.

At this time Fiat interests had veered away from the large prestige car; it was not until 1938 that a new vehicle in this class appeared. The 2800 was, as its name suggests, a 2.8-litre model. The six-cylinder engine had dimensions of 89 × 90mm, and the body was well proportioned for a seven-seater car. Few 2800s were made, and most that were seen were run by various government departments.

Fiat recovered well from World War II, but the postwar environment of Italy was only really conducive to the production of small cars such as the famous 570cc Topolino, which had first appeared in 1936 and proved popular after the war. It paved the way for a succession of Fiat 500s and 600s before the company was able to consolidate its position and become the huge concern it was in the late 1970s, when Fiat produced cars ranging from the tiny 126 DeVille to the stylish double-overhead-cam 132s.

In 1939 Fiat put a large, 2.8-litre six-cylinder car, called the 2800 into production. Few, however, were built before World War II interrupted production. *Left:* one of the first 2800 models, from the Lana collection

Isotta Fraschini
A symbol of aristocratic dignity

In 1899, Cesare Isotta and Vincenzo Fraschini got together to import single-cylinder Renault voiturettes, Mors cars and Aster engines from France. After a while they brought in parts to assemble in their Milan factory, and gradually more and more locally made components were incorporated until there was a finished product which could be called an Isotta Fraschini.

Accordingly, the Societe Milanese d'Automobili Isotta Fraschini & Cia was formed in 1900, and the respective brothers, Stefano Isotta, and Oreste and Antonio Fraschini taken on board. Up to 1902, the Isotta Fraschini was basically a Renault derivative, a twin-cylinder 12hp model. In 1903, however, the brothers forsook the Renault formula with its neat transmission through cardan shaft and live axle, and went in for bigger things with the cruder but more versatile chain drive.

The first true Isotta Fraschini was a 24hp four, with separate T-head cylinders, and by 1904 the range had expanded to three models of 12, 16, and 24hp. Strong financial backing paid for the erection of a new factory in Milan's via Monterosa, and the company reformed as Fabbrica Automobili Isotta Fraschini. It was around this time that the able young design engineer, Giustino Cattaneo joined the company with which he was destined to remain until 1933.

Cattaneo's first design, in 1905, was a vast racing car, the 120hp Tipo D, with a 17-litre, overhead-cam, four-cylinder engine, and although this made little impression on the opposition, the later 7.9-litre Isottas were successful racers.

For 1909 the range consisted of five models, including an overhead-cam 10hp model with four-speed gearbox. Multi-plate clutches, four-speed transmissions and fixed wooden wheels were common to all, but only the two smallest had shaft drive as standard. Shaft or chain drive was optional on the 20/30hp and 30/40hp, chains being used on the huge 10½-litre 50/65hp. Late that year, Isotta Fraschini introduced four-wheel braking, designed by Oreste Fraschini, but these were not fitted to all models for some years to come.

1910 was notable for another overhead-cam design, this time a huge 100hp car, with enclosed chain drive, front wheel brakes and water-cooled transmission brakes for the rear wheels. The Tipo KM engine was a long-stroke four of 10.6 litres, said to deliver about 124bhp at 1800rpm. The cylinders were cast in pairs, with four valves per cylinder, and a shaft-driven camshaft. Already Cattaneo was involved with aero-engines, and the cross-breeding between the two elements was clear in the KM.

Surprisingly, these were the last Cattaneo cars to have overhead camshafts, and the rest of the story centres round one design that promised great things when introduced shortly after World War I, but became progressively more stolid by comparison with its competitors. The nigger in the woodpile, so far as Cattaneo's Tipo 8 was concerned, was the Swiss Marc Birkigt's 32CV Hispano-Suiza, made in Paris and first shown at the 1919 Paris Salon. This had a 6¼-litre, overhead-camshaft engine much more compact, and daintier, than Cattaneo's eight-cylinder 5.9-litre, in a chassis that combined excellent road-

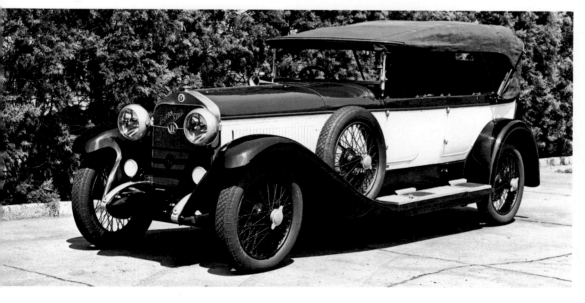

Left: an Isotta Fraschini Type 8. This model featured a 5880cc, straight-eight engine of sophisticated configuration, having overhead valves and an alloy cylinder head, which produced 80bhp at only 2200rpm. The Type 8 was the car with which Isotta Fraschini resumed production after World War I. Shown here is an example by Castagna of 1920 (Museo dell'Automobile di Torino)

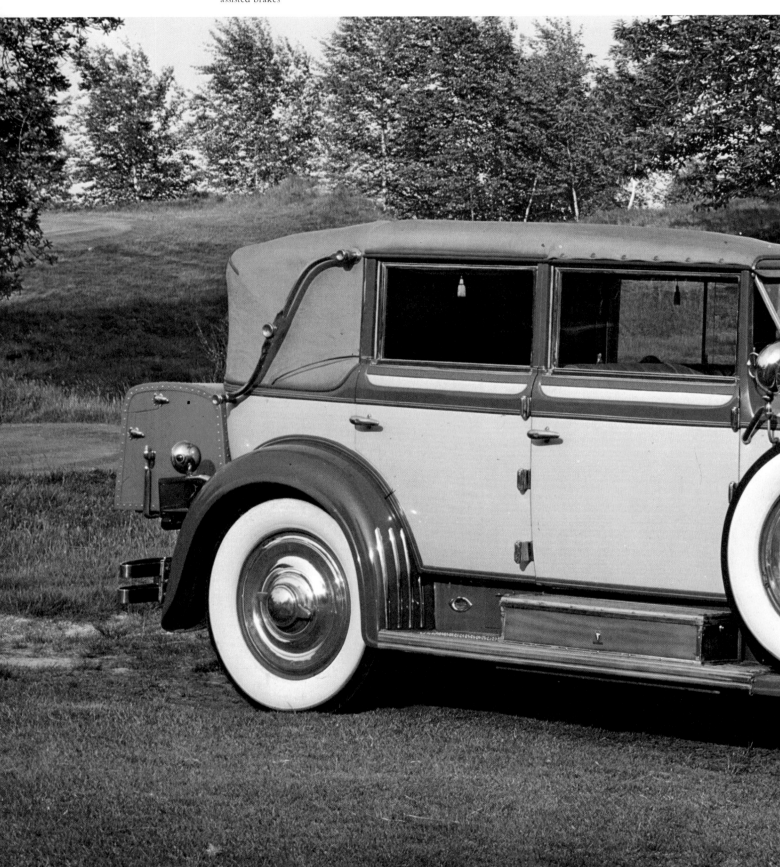

Below: an enormous and stately Isotta Fraschini 8 A, in convertible form by Stabilimenti Farina, from the Quattroruote collection. The 8 A was introduced as a replacement for the Type 8 in 1925, and featured a 7.4-litre engine, and servo-assisted brakes

Left: an open landaulet by Castagna on an Isotta Fraschini Type 8 A chassis (Museo dell'Automobile di Torino)

Left: a cabriolet version, attributed to Figoni and Falaschi, on a Type 8 AS chassis of 1928 (Vignale collection), and, *below,* a D'Orsay landaulet on a Type 8 A by Sala, (Isotta Fraschini collection)

holding with easy steering and matchless brakes assisted by a mechanical servo. There was also the threat of two rival Italian super-cars from the Lancia and Fiat factories, both with large V12 engines but, fortunately for Isotta Fraschini, neither of these two were ever to be put into production.

Although announced in August 1919, the Tipo 8 took a year or two to get off the line, due to labour problems affecting all Italian industry. Even so, it has a strong claim to being the world's first true production straight-eight. The monobloc aluminium cylinder casting was topped by two four-cylinder heads, and the overhead valves were opened by pushrods and rockers. Nine main bearings supported the vibration-damped crankshaft, which was arranged like two fours in series, in the Bugatti manner. This layout was claimed by Cattaneo to provide better mixture distribution, although it was inherently less well-balanced than the 2–4–2 disposition later adopted by Bugatti, in line with US designs. Cylinder proportions were strictly small bore/long stroke and the original output was a modest 75–80bhp at 2200rpm. Transmission was through a multi-plate clutch and a wide-ratio, three-speed gearbox, with centre ball-change, in unit with the engine.

With neither the power and manoeuvrability of the Hispano, nor anything approaching Rolls-Royce unobtrusiveness, it is difficult to understand how the Tipo 8 was such a success. It was not even a pleasant car to drive. The answer probably lay in the huge chassis, with its 12ft-plus wheelbase, which formed a wonderful platform for the specialist coachbuilders of Italy and the USA in particular. Some of their creations behind that noble radiator were amongst the most magnificent ever conceived, and the majority were expressly for paid drivers to handle (who would not complain) while the owners sat in the mobile drawing-room behind a winding glass division. Italian houses, like Sala and Castagna, and the better known Farina and Touring, were at their peak in both style and execution, and in America, England and France, the IF become a symbol of aristocratic dignity.

Just as the Tipo 8 was coming to fruition, in 1920–1, Oreste Fraschini died, and his brother Vincenzo, with Cesare Isotta, left when new management, with much-needed capital backing, took over; but the faithful Cattaneo stuck to his post. Towards the end of 1924, after about 400 Tipo 8s had been sold, he released the 7.4-litre Tipo 8A which gave 110–120 bhp at 2400rpm, much of the extra power no doubt being absorbed by heavier coachwork. It had a stouter chassis frame and larger brake drums with vacuum-servo assistance, and rode on larger-section tyres. The 8A was soon supplemented by Spinto and then Super Spinto versions with higher compression ratios and other tuning devices. These still failed to match Birkigt's new 46CV 8-litre Hispano, although a short-chassis 8ASS with sporting bodywork could allegedly exceed 100mph.

Although the world slump around 1928–30 nearly put paid to the company, in April 1931 it launched the 8B, a great improvement, on paper at least. A lot of development had gone into its engine, which now gave up to 145–160bhp at 3000rpm; the chassis was deeper again and with added cross-bracing; hydraulic

Below: further proof that Isotta Fraschini received appropriate treatment from the great Italian coachbuilders, here is a sports saloon by Castagna (Tschudi collection)

Above: a good example of the skill of Cesare Sala is this saloon body on a Type 8 A chassis, built in 1929 and belonging to the Pozzoli collection

Left: a somewhat unusual Isotta Fraschini, in fact a 1931 Flying Star sports model by Touring, on the Type 8 ASS chassis. This model had a straight-eight engine producing a maximum of 135bhp, and giving the car a top speed around 105mph

dampers replaced the friction Hartfords and a four-speed Wilson pre-selector gearbox was optional. There were very few takers, however, and only about thirty were sold before the close-down in 1935. That was when aeroplane manufacturer Gianni Caproni took over, with enthusiastic encouragement from the belligerent Fascist government; there was great prosperity then from aviation and marine engines, and from trucks of German design built under licence.

After the war, Caproni initiated two parallel projects to get back into the private-car market. One was to be a small car for the common man, for which Ing Fessia chose a platform frame with all-independent suspension, the front wheels driven by a 1250cc, overhead-valve, flat-four engine. Called the CEMSA-Caproni, it appeared at shows in the late 1940s, but never got off the ground.

The other more ambitious venture was a luxury model called the Isotta Fraschini Monterosa, dreamed up by Ing Rapi. The only things in common with the 8B were its eight cylinders, arranged in a 90-degree vee and placed behind the rear wheels in a platform frame, with all-independent suspension employing rubber in compression. The overhead-camshaft engine progressed from 2.5 to 3.4 litres, and it appeared in bodies of varying aesthetic merit before Monterosa was closed down in 1950.

Itala

Grand Tourers with a sporting heritage

Founded in 1903 in Turin, by Matteo Ceirano, Itala spent the years up to World War I concentrating on the manufacture of racing cars. A policy followed with some success, it saw Itala win the Coppa Florio in 1905 with the 14-litre 100hp racer, and take the first Targa Florio in 1906 at an average speed of 29.07mph.

Encouraged by their early racing successes, the company went on making competition machines, but after 1907 seemed to have shot their bolt, although they produced a variety of sporting models before the first closed model appeared in 1920, although the coachbuilders Locatti and Torreta had fitted a landaulette body to a 1909 model 20/30, and there was also an Alession-bodied tourer built on the 50/65 chassis in 1911. The 1920 model was the Type 50 coupé de ville, a four-cylinder 2.8-litre car.

In 1910 Itala made 350 cars, and they doubled this in 1911, concentrating on the four and six-cylinder touring models with the customary Itala shaft drive. At the 1912 Turin Show the Itala designer Alberto Balocco presented the abortive novelty of a variable-stroke engine, which was supposed to be able to run without a gearbox.

During World War I, in 1915, the Itala works were completely redesigned to produce the V8 Hispano-Suiza aero-engine. This was a fateful step for the company; by the time the factory had re-tooled from the unsuccessful 200 to the 300hp engine the war was nearly at an end. The government cut orders by half and the group was in financial trouble from which it never really recovered, and by 1920 the workforce had fallen to a fifth of the 1911 mark of 1000 employees.

After the war, Itala continued with cars designed by Baloco which were basically a continuation of the 1914 range, with the addition of full electrics and spiral-bevel back axles. The Tipo 50 was a good example of the postwar offering, being a 2.8-litre side-valve four, produced from 1919 to 1926.

A derivative of the 50, the Tipo 51 Sport, was a class winner in both the 1921 and 1922 Targa Florios. The Sport's engine, featuring aluminium pistons, developed 55bhp and could propel the car at 80mph. By 1925, however, the hand-to-mouth existence of Itala became too difficult and a receiver was called in under a government scheme organised through the IRI, the Reconstruction Finance Corporation.

The ex-Aquila and Fiat engineer, Cesare Cappa, was appointed technical consultant, and produced the last-but-one Itala, the Tipo 61 of 1924. The 61 was a light-six of handsome appearance with a radiator grill suggestive of a Rolls-Royce. The 1991cc engine, an overhead-valve design, used aluminium for the pistons and block, and the crankshaft ran on seven main bearings. Despite its attractive specification the 61 was not a success.

Cappa also produced a prototype Grand Prix voiturette with wooden chassis, front-wheel drive, and supercharged 1100 or 1500cc V12 engine, but the model remained experimental. The Tipo 65, similar to the 61, but with a double-overhead-cam, 2-litre engine, did not sell, and in 1929 Itala was reorganised with a capital of 35 million lire, but the company was still liquidated in 1931.

The following year the firm was reformed as Itala SACA, produced the short-lived 2.3-litre Tipo 57, but gave up the struggle at last in 1934.

Left: the Turin-based coachbuilders Garavini built many interesting variations on the Itala 61 chassis. The 61 was a large, 2-litre, six-cylinder car, produced between 1925 and 1932, which never seemed to enjoy the success its advanced specification merited

A spread of Itala 61s in various guises. *Top:* an early coupé de ville by Garavini. *Middle left:* another Garavini creation, a six-seater saloon (Rinaldi–Cuttini collection). *Above:* a false cabriolet by Lavocat and Marsaud (Museo dell'Automobile di Torino). *Left:* a saloon from the Quattroruote collection, note the different radiator grille treatment

Lancia

Alpha, Beta, Gamma, Delta…

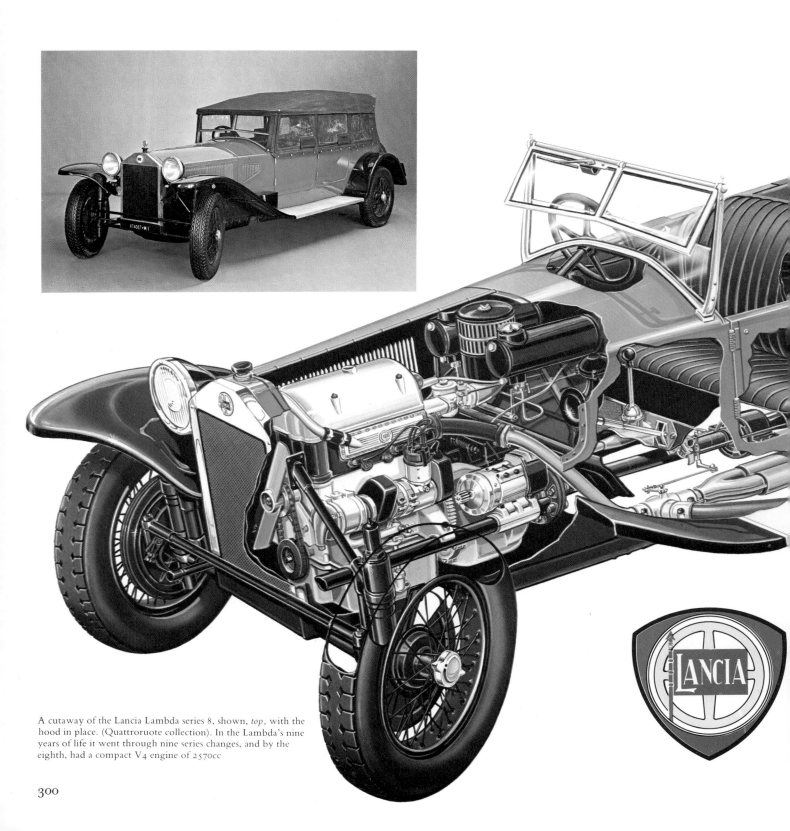

A cutaway of the Lancia Lambda series 8, shown, *top*, with the
hood in place. (Quattroruote collection). In the Lambda's nine
years of life it went through nine series changes, and by the
eighth, had a compact V4 engine of 2570cc

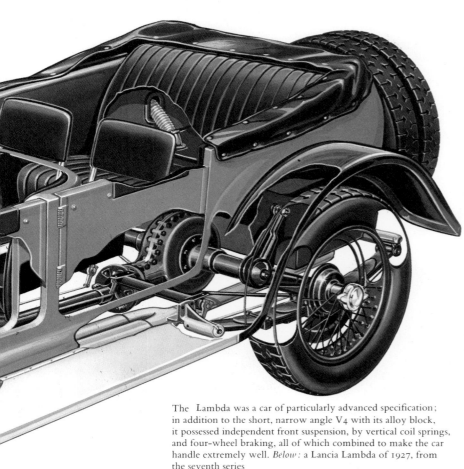

The Lambda was a car of particularly advanced specification; in addition to the short, narrow angle V4 with its alloy block, it possessed independent front suspension, by vertical coil springs, and four-wheel braking, all of which combined to make the car handle extremely well. *Below:* a Lancia Lambda of 1927, from the seventh series

It was in November 1906 that the Fabbrica Automobili Lancia was officially incorporated, the two partners, Vincenzo Lancia and Claudio Fogolini, having met in the Fiat works where Lancia was Chief Inspector and Fogolini a test driver. They rented premises in Turin that had formerly been occupied by Itala, only for the factory to be ravaged by a fire in 1907, which destroyed many parts and drawings.

Despite this setback, however, Lancia managed to put a car on the market for the first time in 1908. Known first as the model 51, later as the 18–24 horsepower, and eventually as the Alpha, 108 examples were sold in the first year and a half. The car had a double-block, four-cylinder engine of 2.5 litres displacement, producing 28hp at 1800rpm and was reputed to be capable of 56mph.

Lancia then embarked on a six-cylinder car, the model 53, with a displacement of 3.8 litres, but in 1909 Lancia reverted to the in-line four with the 2-litre Beta. In 1913 came the first Lancia to be a really big success, a car that made its own contribution to progress in the standard embodiment of a complete electrical installation at a time when most cars were given their electrics after construction on a piecemeal 'customer-option' basis. Almost two thousand customers testified to the attractiveness of the Theta, as it was known, and put the company on a sound basis, with production increased fifteenfold in the five years since the introduction of the Alpha.

The four-cylinder Kappa, Lancia's first car after World War I, derived from the pre-war Theta, was predictably successful, none of its innovations – an adjustable steering wheel and a central gear lever for example, being hard to accept. The 1921 Dikappa was a sports version with overhead valves and an extraordinarily light body made of aluminium sheet on a walnut and acacia frame. The 1922 Trikappa was the long-postponed V8, a 4.6-litre machine for which 98hp was claimed.

It hardly mattered, for in October of the same year the Lancia Lambda first saw the light of day at the London and Paris shows. This was Lancia's materpiece, the car which best expressed all his engineering and artistic ideals. It was the car that confirmed the company's status for years to come and ratified a new line of reasoning in structural design and, furthermore, it marked Lancia himself as a designer and engineer who had achieved true maturity.

The torpedo-bodied touring Lambda was based on a deep-sided sheet metal frame that was itself strong and stiff enough to carry all the mechanical parts and support all suspension and other loads, while imparting to the body most of its structural strength. Its

engine was a structurally stiff, narrow-angle V4 with overhead camshaft, the whole being so short that the gearbox had to be located under the bonnet with it, prompting the strange device of a tunnel along the centre of the uncommonly low floor to accommodate the drive shaft and gearlever. The front suspension was by helical springs as the hub carriers slid up and down on pillars that also acted as steering kingposts, and were supported by widely splayed tubular connections to the chassis. It was a system that was retained in principle by Lancia until 1963 and, apart from giving the independent movement of the wheels that Lancia sought, it also made possible an extremely good steering lock, and steering almost beyond compare in its feel and precision.

The virtues of this superb design were confirmed by the sale of 13,000 Lambdas in nine series between 1923 and 1931. As with practically all later Lancias the engine of the Lambda was increased in size as time went on, the capacity going up to 2.4 litres in 1926 with the seventh series and to 2.6 litres with the eighth, two years later. Four-speed gearboxes were standardised on the fifth series, and a separate chassis became an option with the seventh, and standard on the eighth and ninth series. While the speed kept going up (the ninth series could reach 78mph), the roadworthiness of the chassis remained more than adequate for its performance. In 1928 this touring car came within sight of winning the Mille Miglia before a trivial accident eliminated it, and although in Italy it was always accepted as a touring car, the Lambda was welcomed as a sporting machine in other countries on account of its excellent roadholding, prodigious brakes and unrivalled steering.

The first of the Lancias with Roman names (after the ancient roads of the Roman Empire) was the Artena, a four-cylinder, 2-litre, car which, with the lightweight 2.6-litre V8 Astura, superseded the Lambda series in 1931. The Astura was a favourite with body builders until 1937, but even before that the Augusta of 1933 appeared as a straw in a new wind. It was perhaps the first really successful embodiment of an ideal which several manufacturers had long sought: an elegant, attractive and completely

Above: a particularly handsome V8 Lancia Astura coupé from Stabilimenti Farina; the two tone paintwork enhances the car's already handsome lines

Below: a rather plainer berlina, on a 1930 Dilambda chassis (Quattroruote collection). *Bottom:* A Dilambda royal coupé which belonged to the famous German writer, Eric Maria Remarque, author of *All Quiet on the Western Front*

Left: a 1934 Lancia Augusta cabriolet from Pininfarina, belonging to the Leprati collection. For the period, this model has a rather more modern aspect, it was in fact a V4 of unit construction. *Middle:* a 1.9-litre Lancia Artena of 1935 in cabriolet form. *Bottom:* the profile of a beautiful four-door sports model of the Le Mans type from 1933. The body is by Viotti on a Lancia Astura chassis

convincing good small car. With it, Lancia reverted to unitary body construction, for the first time in saloon form. In it, he perpetuated the idea of the compact narrow V4 engine, and continued the tradition of steering precision, roadholding and braking ability. Nevertheless it was essentially a transitional design, but one which enjoyed deserved popularity while the factory readied their next car.

Its replacement was another Lancia masterpiece, the Aprilia which appeared in 1937. It carried the Augusta formula several steps further, with independent rear suspension by torsion bars, a well-streamlined stressed-skin saloon body of pillarless construction, so that when all four doors were open each flank was completely unimpeded, and with a 1352cc engine of 47bhp in a car that weighed only 1800lb. With a top speed of 80mph allied to a fuel consumption around 30mpg, and with handling qualities that qualified it to rank with the better sports cars of the time, the Aprilia laid down an entirely new set of standards by which all other small cars might be judged for years to come.

A great success, the Aprilia remained in production after World War II until 1950. Despite the death of Vincenzo Lancia in 1937, the company prospered after the war under Gianni Lancia as Chairman and maintained its independence up to, and a definite identity beyond, the Fiat take-over in 1969.

OM

From trains, to cars, to trucks

The OM company was formed in Milan in 1899, representing the merger of two firms in the railway business, one of them making locomotives and the other rolling stock. OM's first departure from this field was to make Italy's first tramcars, and car manufacture was encompassed in 1918 by their acquisition of the Züst company which had been making big touring cars since 1905.

Up to 1923 OM relied on the 4.7-litre S305, inherited from Züst. The first OM proper was designed by an Austrian, Barratouche, and featured a 1327cc, side-valve, four-cylinder engine. Although the 465, as it was called, was basically very ordinary it was well constructed, with light weight and good handling characteristics as cornerstones of the design, making it a delight to drive even though not blessed with a very high performance. The performance problems were remedied by 1922 with the 469 model, a full 1.5-litre affair that was to be a success in Italian sports car competition.

By 1923 OM had added two more cylinders to the side-valve four and produced the 665 2-litre, sporting versions of which accelerated and handled well, and could reach 75mph. This was the car which really made OM famous in competition and popular in the market place. In 1925 it won the Tripoli Grand Prix, took a class victory in the 12-hour race for touring cars at San Sebastian, and fifth place in the Targa Florio, behind four Bugattis.

The great year for the 2-litre OM, however, was 1927, for that was the year that saw the birth of the Mille Miglia – the first was almost an OM procession with the OMs first, second and third; the winning car averaging 40.27mph. The following year OM would take the first eight places in the two-litre class of the Mille Miglia, the best of them finishing second overall.

From 1926 onwards the British OM concession aires, L. C. Rawlence, offered numerous modifications to the OM: special axle ratios, overhead-valve conversions, and cylinder heads with three carburettors and twelve sparking plugs, and so on, which could make it a respectable high-performance car.

Eventually OM themselves cottoned onto the possibilities still inherent in the 665 and started making their own high-performance versions. In 1929 they built some low-chassis cars with finned cylinder heads and Roots superchargers. These cars developed 80bhp at 4000rpm. The following year the capacity was increased to 2.2 litres, though the type number 665 was retained; and if the designation in the Rawlence catalogue was anything to go by, these blown sports versions developed 95bhp.

The factory went one better for its own team of sports racers, with three cars of 2.35-litre capacity. but although the OMs were still a force to be reckoned with inside Italy, elsewhere they seemed consistently unlucky.

In any case the company was losing interest in car manufacture by this time, and preferred to concentrate on the more certain truck market; it may be that they could foresee the coming of the slump that was to spell the end to the hopes of so many other manufacturers.

In 1930 the entire stock of cars at the Brescia factory was sold off, and finally the takeover of OM by Fiat in 1933 precluded any prospect of a return to car manufacture. OM's involvement in car production had been brief, a mere twelve years, although truck production did continue unabated.

The OM 665 was a 2-litre, six-cylinder, side-valve, development of the earlier 400 series OMs. The 2-litre engine produced only 40bhp in its original form, but as the 665 was a light car performance did not suffer unduly. *Left:* a 665 by Garavini

Above: the OM 665 SS MM Superba, a 2-litre, six-cylinder, machine. This model, in supercharged form, was capable of a top speed approaching 100mph (Pozzoli collection)

Left: a 665 N5 Superba of 1931. The OM Superbas had many sporting victories to their name, including the first ever Mille Miglia in 1927 (Museo dell'Automobile di Torino)

USA

In the last decade of the nineteenth century the automobile took its first tentative steps towards the New World. The automobile industry's development in the USA, however, was such that the meagre 1900 production total of 5000 had been increased to 180,000 by 1910. America's entry to World War I in 1917 gave a great boost to the rapidly growing industry, so much so that by the end of the war one million vehicles a year were being produced. The fact that England was only able to match this figure in 1954, Germany in 1957, and Italy as late as 1963, gives a good indication of the sheer size of even the early American industry.

It is hardly surprising that the industry was able to take off in this way; all the factors were favourable The industrial base was sound and modern, the country large and the population numerous. US society was more mobile and egalitarian than any in Europe, with a large enough middle class to provide a good market for mass-produced cars. Ford's Model T, which appeared in 1908, pioneered mass production and answered the needs of millions; in fact over fifteen million Model Ts were sold in the car's eighteen-year production run.

The giants of the American industry took shape early in the twentieth century. It was in 1909 that a wealthy industrialist from Flint, Michigan, William Crapo Durant, formed what was to become the biggest company in the world, General Motors. The consortium was formed out of Durant's Buick company, Cadillac, Olds and Oakland (later Pontiac), and very nearly included Ford. Henry Ford had thought seriously about selling out (for eight million dollars, a figure which Durant could not raise) before developing the Model T, the car which ensured that the Ford Motor Company became the largest car manufacturer of the 1920s. The mass production of the Model T was so successful that Ford had over fifty per cent of the US market by 1921, a figure which Ford was never to reach again.

With manufacturers such as Ford, Chevrolet, Chrysler and Plymouth taking care of the mass market, the booming affluence of the United States, both before and after World War I up to 1929 led to a proliferation of luxury car manufacturers. With over twenty million petrol driven vehicles on the road by 1925 there was great scope for even the most expensive specialist manufacturers such as Packard, Cord, Duesenberg, Stutz and Pierce Arrow. Consid-

ering the market size it was not difficult for Packard to sell nearly 46,000 vehicles in 1925, or for Auburn to reach sales figures of 28,000 in 1931, and in this context the total output of Cord (under 7000 in sixteen years) seems almost trivial.

Cars such as the great Duesenberg Model J of 1928, or the Pierce-Arrow V12s of 1933, were superb examples of the luxury car. With its twin overhead cam, four valves per cylinder, straight-eight producing 265bhp, the Model J had a top speed of around 116mph. The chassis alone would sell for $8500, and with some examples of the impressive coachwork available, the Model J could cost as much as twenty thousand dollars. Lincoln, Cadillac, Pierce-Arrow, Auburn and Franklin all offered V12s – the epitome of the smooth fast luxury car, while Marmon and Cadillac at one stage even marketed cars with V16 engines.

Not only did American makes encompass both the mass produced popular car, and the flamboyant luxury models, America was responsible for many 'firsts' in the industry. Cadillac developed their Synchro-Mesh as early as 1928, five years after introducing the process of chroming over nickel plate both innovations are now fundamental features of all modern cars. The Cord L-29 of 1929 introduced front-wheel drive in a production car, but this was a lead virtually ignored in North America for nearly fifty years.

The Wall Street Crash of 1929 and the subsequent Depression dealt the prestige car makers a grave blow. The story of the Cord empire mirrors the changes which took place. Errett Lobban Cord at one stage owned Auburn, Cord, Duesenberg and American Airlines in addition to Lycoming engines. While General Motors prospered, the exotic equivalent, so Cord hoped, was killed off by a combination of the changed circumstances of the Depression years plus some mismanagement. Following the Depression, it was marques like Cadillac and Lincoln, with the volume producers GM and Ford behind them, which flourished and catered for the luxury market after World War II.

The age of the Pierce-Arrows and Duesenbergs had passed as, to a great extent, Americans turned away from their own industry for the exotic or prestige car after the war. It became more fashionable to own a Rolls-Royce, Mercedes or Ferrari than simply to own a Lincoln or a Cadillac.

Auburn

Speed and elegance from Indiana

The name of Auburn is now remembered chiefly for the golden years that occupied less than a third of the company's lifespan, although in fact Auburn was a true pioneer make, dating back to 1900.

Frank and Morris Eckhart, of the Eckhart Carriage Company, formed the Auburn Automobile Company in 1900, and by 1903 their first car was ready. It was a small centre-engined, chain-driven one-cylinder runabout with nothing but the basic essentials, although it did ride on pneumatic tyres. The company grew gradually, going from two to four, and eventually to six cylinders in 1912, and by 1918 Auburn offered four body styles – Chummy Roadster, five-seat Tourer, Sport Roadster, and Touring Car with detachable top; all were sixes.

Auburns, however, were inexpensive but rather ordinary cars with nothing more to offer than many other rather dull but sound makes. The Eckharts needed a financial boost and the Auburn a face-lift – in 1919 they sold out to a group of Chicago businessmen in the hope of reviving their fortunes.

With the takeover came the face-lift in the shape of the 1919 Beauty-Six, and for a time it seemed that this would pull Auburn out of the doldrums. The Beauty-Six had a 25.6hp engine, a somewhat flashy exterior and a wealth of attractive equipment, but it was no dynamic marvel. The sponsors great expectations were briefly encouraged but never fulfilled, and by 1924 daily output was down to a meagre six cars or so when Erret Lobban Cord appeared on the scene, as General Manager.

Following Cord's arrival, the unsaleable Auburn stock was jazzed up and backed by a vigorous sales campaign, and sold off. A new chief engineer, James Crawford, was put to work designing a new car to carry a straight-eight, L-head, Lycoming engine. In next to no time Cord was Vice-President, and in 1926 at the age of 32 he became President of the company.

The 'Eight in Line' appeared in early 1925, but by the time of the New York Motor Show that winter the engine had been enlarged to 4.5 litres, and the car named the 8-88: the first of a famous line. Behind a deeply cowled nickel radiator shell were some of the handsomest bodies on the market, and customers began to line up. Particularly intriguing was the rumble-seat roadster by McFarlan, with a small side door to let a passenger enter and leave gracefully without having to clamber up and down steps on the rear fender.

New for 1928 was a power increase for the 8-88 motor, already enlarged since the original and now equipped with a twin-barrel updraught Stromberg carburettor; it was designated the 8-115. To

Below: an example of the Auburn Type 8–115, derived from the 8–88 of 1926, and featuring a Lycoming straight-eight engine, fitted with a double-barrel Stromberg carburettor. The model illustrated is a convertible 8–115 limousine photographed during a *concours d'elegance* in Rome

supplement it, a new and smaller eight was added, the 8–77, with a smaller 24hp engine. Apart from these, the range still included a six, the 6–66, but the four had been dropped earlier. New engineering features included a redesigned chassis frame with deeper side members and extra cross members, a change from mechanical to hydraulic brakes, and centralised chassis lubrication, operated from the driver's seat by a pedal under the dash.

There were also two new bodies available, a convertible sedan-phaeton, and the first of the classic boat-tailed Speedsters (styled by Count Alexis de Sakhnoffsky) which from that time were never absent from the Auburn family although the style evolved through several phases.

On one of the most extrovert cars of the time, the two-tone finish emphasised the Auburn feature of sweeping the belt lines up and over the hood to meet at the radiator filler cap; other notable styling features were the steeply-raked split windshield, and the long pointed tail. Speedster bodies were available

on both eight-cylinder models produced, and in both cases at a lower price than the competition.

At the 1928 motor shows Auburn exhibited a three-model range as before – all uprated once more – the 20hp 6–80, 26hp 8–90 and 34hp 120. Prices ranged from $995 for the six-cylinder Sport Sedan to $2095 for the five-seat Phaeton Sedan on the 120 chassis. One of the cars offered that year turned out to be Auburn's most glorious failure. This was the Cabin Speedster on the 120 chassis – the most rakish machine imaginable from an American factory. Its distinctly European look was accentuated by the close fitting cycle wings which moved with the front wheels. The dropped frame used was special, rising over the front axle and under-slung at the rear to provide a lower line and centre of gravity; the chassis was covered by a streamlined panelled aluminium body. With 125bhp under the bonnet it was guaranteed to exceed the magic 100mph, and all for $2195. The public, however, just looked, marvelled and walked away: the US market was

Above: the imposing Auburn 6.4-litre Speedster, produced from 1932 to 1934, which won the American Stock Car Speed Championship in 1932 and 1933. Note the unusual steeply raked split windscreen

proving strongly resistant to *avant-garde* concepts stemming from its own side of the Atlantic.

Despite the Cabin Speedster fiasco, the next year, 1929, was the peak pre-Depression year for Auburn sales, with over 22,000 sold. 1930, however, saw the effect of the Depression and sales dropped to under 14,000. Cord closed the Auburn ranks by dropping all existing models and bringing out a new medium-sized eight in a short-term one-model policy. This was the 8–98, fitted with a bored-out derivative of the old 1927 engine, which gave 98bhp at 3400rpm.

By this time Auburn were recognised style-setters and were producing a body range every bit as handsome as the specialist coachbuilder could create for the individual customer. They were bold designs and the engineering beneath was simple and very sound. Auburns always had exceptionally stiff frames, but the 9–98 was given a brand new one with cruciform bracing, and a free-wheel, to permit clutchless gear shifts, was added to the three-speed transmission. Overnight the Auburn fortunes rose,

and sales for 1931 were the highest ever, at over 28,000.

In a time of terrific rivalry between the class manufacturers producing super-cars using V12 and V16 engines, Auburn lept in with a V12 priced from under a thousand dollars. Designed by George Kublin of Auburn, the new Lycoming engine had a capacity of 6407cc. The cylinder banks were set at a 45 degree angle, and a strange feature was Kublin's unique valvegear and combustion chamber arrangement. The valve stems were horizontal, actuated through rockers from a central camshaft, the chambers forming deep pockets above the cylinders which had individual removable water jackets that gave access to the valves with the heads still *in situ*. A two-speed axle by Columbia, with vacuum-controlled selection and giving six forward speeds overall, was optional for both the eight and the V12, typical alternative final-drive ratios being 4.55 and 3.04 to 1.

There was little to distinguish the V12 from the 8–100 (successor to the 8–98) except for a few extra inches in the wheelbase; as many parts as possible, including the bodies, were kept identical to help keep the price down. Later there was a Speedster V12, which captured so many records that it won the American Stock Car Speed Championship in the first two years of its production, 1932–3. These records included distances of up to 2000 kilometres and speeds up to 117mph.

The fickle public, however, took little notice, and the V12 was little better than a flop. Moreover the eight, too, fell from grace, so much so that 1932

ended with Auburn suffering a loss of nearly a million dollars. 1933 was even worse, with only a wretched 6000 or so customers, and in 1934 Cord left to live in England.

Next, Gordon Buehrig, later to earn international repute with his futuristic 810 front-wheel-drive Cord, was asked completely to restyle the boat-tailed Speedster, and duly produced the Model 851 Speedster. This was a very impressive machine, particularly the supercharged version with four enormous flexible exhaust pipes sweeping from its bonnet side panel. A tiny cockpit, behind the usual raked split-screen, emphasised the length of the bonnet and downswept tail, and exhibitionist tear-shaped wings enclosed the wheels. A hinged metal panel concealed the top when lowered. It was extremely dashing and equally impractical, seating only two and having no external access to the baggage compartment in the tail.

With its Schwitzer-Cummins centrifugal blower driven at six times the engine speed through an ingenious frictional planetary gear, the Lycoming gave about 150bhp at 4000rpm, compared with the 115bhp at 3600rpm of the unblown car. Each 851, and the 852 of the next year, carried a plaque to confirm that it had been tested at over 100mph.

The writing was now clearly on the wall, however, for the Buehrig Speedsters were sold at a loss and orders for the rest of the cars, despite a face-lift with new skirted wings and a vee-shaped grille with painted surround, were nowhere near sufficient to sustain the plant, and production ended in 1936.

Above: perhaps the ultimate in Auburns, the Type 851 Speedster of 1935, designed by Gordon Buehrig. With a Schwitzer-Cummins supercharger, the Speedster's Lycoming engine put out 150bhp at 4000rpm, enabling the car to exceed 100mph with ease

Buick
A pillar of General Motors

To David Dunbar Buick, the creation of the first Buick car was only a short phase in a long life of experimenting and inventing that ended with the Scots-born machinist virtually destitute.

After building and testing a prototype, Buick and his engineer, Walther Marr, sold the first production Buick automobile in August of 1904. Called the Model B, it used an opposed-twin engine placed under the seat, developing about 20hp from 2.6 litres. The drive line was a two-speed planetary transmission and a chain to the rear axle. It was a good little car, but it had taken so long (by the standards of those days) to get it ready for production that the investors had run out of time and money. So they appealed for help to one of Michigan's millionaire carriage-builders, 43-year-old William Crapo Durant. That November, Durant took over financial control of Buick. During these several changes of ownership David Buick found his share of the company amounting to less and less; finally he was only an employee, and in 1908 he left the company.

By then, the Buick car had become nationally famous, with 8800 cars built and sold, twice as many as in 1907. In addition to the two-cylinder model there were four other basic Buick types, powered by three different four-cylinder, in-line engines of 2.7, 4.2 and 5.5 litres. The smallest was used in the Model 10, new in 1908 and the most popular Buick, priced right in line with the new Model T Ford at $850. From that point onward, however, Fords became cheaper and Buicks more expensive. The small four-cylinder car remained an important part of the Buick line until 1924, the last year it was produced. None of the larger fours lasted through World War I.

Buick had grown so rapidly under super-salesman Durant that by 1908 it was one of the 'big four' of the US auto industry that also included Ford, Reo and Maxwell-Briscoe. Durant began thinking about merging his Buick with another firm to build an even larger combine, and, with that end in view, incorporated a new firm which he named 'General Motors' on 16 September 1908.

Below: an elegant coupé de ville body by the French coachbuilders Fernandez and Darrin on a Buick 90 chassis

Three views of the 1936 Buick straight-eight 66-SR sports coupé, designed by General Motors' stylist Harley Earl, in a typically American style of the mid 30s. Note the curious dicky seat separate from the enclosed body

From 1919 to 1926, Buick's sales were the highest in the auto industry, in terms of dollar volume. This was helped by the fine reputation the durable and good-looking Buicks had earned early in the export market. The first coast-to-coast crossing of South America by automobile was accomplished by a Buick in 1914, and Buick dealers shepherded a single car on a round-the-world tour in 1925. In most countries overseas, the smaller, handy Buick was the most desirable prestige car from America.

During the 1920s, the Buick was fitted into its now-traditional upper-medium-price bracket under Alfred P. Sloan's careful organization of the GM marketing structure. In 1924, it gained added stature with the addition of four-wheel brakes and the replacement of a rather bland radiator shape with a new one that some people—especially Packard—thought looked quite a lot like a Packard.

Through the 1930s and 1940s, Buick gained fame as one of the strongest apostles of the smooth, powerful and quiet straight-eight engine. The Buick conversion to in-line eights took place in 1931 with engines of 3.6, 4.5 and 5.7 litres. The 5.7-litre was the first production Buick engine producing more than 100hp; 104 at 2800rpm to be exact. GM men hoped the new model would spark Buick sales, which had

been falling steadily due to the Depression and also to the conservatism that had sapped the vigour of once-eager Buick, but, by 1933, Buick sales had plummeted to only 40,620.

The 1934 Buick line brought independent front suspension, new but hardly exciting styling, a lower-priced model, and a new general manager, Harlow H. Curtice, one of the most dynamic and dominating personalities in the company's history. Curtice headed Buick until 1948 and kept a watchful eye on it through another ten years as GM's president.

Curtice really went after his engineers, getting them to adopt aluminium pistons and hydraulic brakes. He hired a new advertising agency, and took the then-controversial step of giving names instead of numbers to each line of cars: Special, Century (for a car that could do a claimed 100mph), Roadmaster and Limited. Another line, the Super, was added in 1940. Buick's new 1936 models received a good reception, and in the same year a great car enthusiast, Charles A. Chayne, became the division's chief engineer. Sales kept on climbing until they reached 377,428 in 1941, the last full year before the USA entered World War II.

After the war Buick continued as one of the main pillars of the GM group.

Cadillac

'Craftmanship a creed, accuracy a law'

Founded in 1902 as the Cadillac Automobile Company, and renamed the Cadillac Motor Car Company two years later with Henry Leland as President, the firm produced its first car in October 1902.

A single-cylinder lightweight vehicle, it was primitive by European standards but very well suited to American road conditions at that time, and consequently was a great success in selling over 16,000 units in various forms between 1903 and 1908. The 1610cc engine had a power output of 10hp in its final form, and was fitted under the front seat, driving the rear wheels through a two-speed planetary transmission.

By 1908 Cadillac's growing reputation had attracted the attention of the legendary William Durant and he chose Cadillac along with Buick, Olds, and Oakland, as the components of his General Motors Company in July 1909. Cadillac became a division of GM when the company was reorganised as a corporation in 1916. This, however, did not mean that the high standards of Cadillac set by Henry Leland and son Wilfred were lowered in any way, and it remained an independent operation, perhaps the most independent of all the GM divisions, building what it called 'the most moder-

ately priced strictly highgrade motor car in the world'.

Cadillac began producing four-cylinder cars in 1905 with the 5-litre Model D, and the smaller Model G was introduced in 1907 and continued until 1912. Around 75,000 fours were produced in total up to 1914, the year that the company took the major step of deciding to bypass the six-cylinder engine and adopt the V8 configuration for future cars.

Announced in September 1914 as the standard Cadillac engine for 1915, the 5150cc V8, developing 70hp, came as an unpleasant surprise to the company's competitors and was both a technical and commercial success. In fact since 1915 Cadillac have had a V8 engined car in the range every year.

Following World War I, Cadillac entered the auto market of the 1920s with a product of unsurpassed reputation but rather undistinguished appearance: advanced and stylish bodywork was a rarity on all American cars of that period. The basic car was then built on a 132-inch wheelbase, weighed about 4200lb, and sold for around $3200, and by 1924 the V8 had been given a new dynamically balanced counterweighted crankshaft. This made the engine smoother, and fought off, as far as Cadillac

Below: a Cadillac 355 of 1932 with limousine body and V8 engine. Cadillac, later part of General Motors, was in fact the first US company to adopt a V8 engine for its range – it was in 1915 that the 70bhp, 5150cc, V8 unit first appeared

313

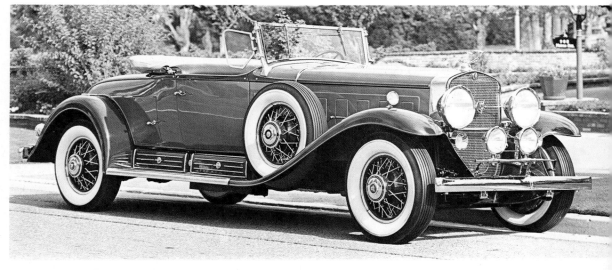

In 1930 Cadillac surpassed themselves with one of the greatest engines of the age, the overhead-valve, 7.4-litre, V16, which produced 165bhp. All the bodywork for the V16 range was by the American coachbuilders, Fleetwood, who have continued to be Cadillac stylists up to the present day. *Above*: a V16 model 452 B of 1932. *Right*: two more of Fleetwood's V16 creations; *top* is an impressive 1932 roadster, and, *bottom*, a 1933 phaeton. Both are from the Harrah collection

Left: a curious, slightly hunchbacked, Fleetwood V16 Cadillac sedan model; the styling was a foretaste of what was to follow World War II

was concerned, the attack of the straight-eights that enjoyed such a vogue in the 1920s and 1930s.

In 1928, a new 5.6-litre V8 was introduced, having side-by-side connecting rods instead of the earlier fork-and-blade type, although it retained an aluminium crankcase with a separate cast-iron cylinder block for each row of four L-head cylinders. The new V8 was first produced in a small-bore 5-litre size in 1927 to power the La Salle model, introduced as a smaller companion car to the Cadillac, and which survived until 1940.

Other Cadillac changes during the 1920s included the adoption of four-wheel brakes in 1923, and the pioneering use of chrome plating over nickel trim surfaces to prevent tarnishing, in 1928. Also in 1928 Cadillac became the first manufacturer to offer a synchronised-shifting transmission; called Synchro-Mesh the term has since become part of the English language. Vacuum-servo assisted brakes were provided on the larger cars in 1932, and the change over to hydraulic brakes was made in 1937.

Many of these changes were the work of Ernest Seaholm, Cadillac's brilliant chief engineer from 1923 to 1943. In January 1930 the world learned of the finest achievement of Seaholm and Cadillac: the model 452, the world's first V16 production car. If there had ever been any doubt about Cadillac's position as the premier luxury car maker in the USA, the fabulous V16 erased it. Silent overhead valves with automatic hydraulic adjustment were used in the 45 degree, 7.4-litre, engine that developed 165bhp at 3400rpm, and was carried in a special chassis on a 148-inch wheelbase. All coachwork was by Fleetwood, exclusive suppliers to Cadillac since 1926.

In August 1930 Cadillac introduced a V12 model which utilised the same chassis and bodywork as the V8 cars. Both the V12 and the V16 were superb engines and remained in production up to 1937 when the twelve was dropped and the sixteen, 3863 of which were built, was replaced by a radical new Seaholm designed V16 with only half the number of parts. It was an L-head engine with the cylinder banks at the unusually wide angle of 135 degrees, however only 511 were made up to 1940.

Since 1940 Cadillac has been faithful to the V8 in producing the USA's best known luxury cars.

Chrysler
Smallest of America's Big Three

Walter P. Chrysler, born in Kansas in 1875, started his career on the mid-west railroads, but by 1905, when he bought his first car, the automobile had supplanted steam in his affections.

By 1912 Chrysler was a General Motors employee, becoming President and General Manager of Buick division four years later. Following clashes with GM's famous William Durant, however, Chrysler resigned, and after assisting the ailing Willys-Overland company he came to the aid of the Maxwell company.

In 1920 Maxwell cars had a dubious reputation, due to their insubstantial rear axles which broke with crippling regularity. The result, not surprisingly, was a vast stock of unsold cars.

Walter Chrysler cleared the stocks by redesigning the rear axles, and the 'Good Maxwells' quickly regained the marque's lost reputation; by 1923 the losses had been converted into a profit of $2,678,000, and by 1924 the figure had risen to $4 million plus.

The revived company was an ideal basis for Chrysler's ultimate ambition—a firm bearing his own name. He had brought three gifted young engineers from Willys-Overland and the trio, Carl Breer, Fred

M. Zeder and Owen R. Skelton, began work on a new car that would take advantage of wartime developments in high-compression engine design. Zeder had already made preliminary studies for a six-cylinder unit with a high-compression cylinder head that seemed to owe more than a little to the work of the British engineer Harry Ricardo; this 70 horsepower unit was used in a new model, the Chrysler Six, marketed under the Maxwell banner. To match its 70mph performance, unique for a car in its price and capacity bracket, the new model was fitted with four-wheel hydraulic brakes—an innovation of some magnitude for the ultra-conservative American market. The brakes were, however, of the slippery-when-wet external contracting type, which had long been obsolete in Europe. At a basic price of $1565, the car sold rapidly, for its power and styling gave the owner the feeling that he was driving a far costlier vehicle. In the first twelve months nearly 32,000 Chryslers were sold, creating an industry sales record of $50 million worth of cars. It was the result Walter Chrysler had been waiting for.

In 1925 he bought Maxwell outright, killed off the

1928 was an important year for Chrysler; it was the year that Dodge was taken over, and the successful Plymouth and De Soto ranges introduced to compete with Oldsmobile and Pontiac of General Motors. *Below:* a Chrysler 72 roadster of 1928, complete with dicky, or rumble, seat, and 4-litre, six-cylinder engine

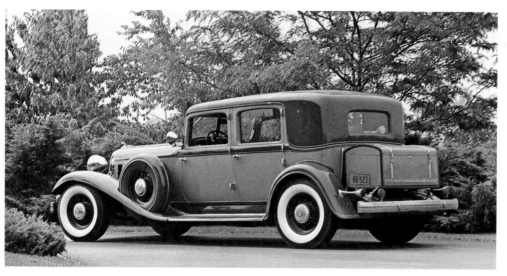

Left: a Chrysler Imperial Eight of 1933, with a 6.3-litre, straight-eight engine, and bodywork by LeBaron

Below left: a Chrysler 77 of 1930, the first American car to have a radio as an option. *Below right,* and *bottom:* two views of a Custom Imperial roadster of 1931, again by LeBaron

Left: a Custom Imperial in a convertible phaeton form of 1932, by LeBaron. The Imperial range was brought out by Chrysler as competition for the contemporary Cadillacs and Lincolns

Below: the famous Chrysler Airflow of 1934 was an eight-cylinder car with unitary welded construction, and aerodynamic styling, which proved to be a commercial mistake, although it continued in production until 1937

Maxwell and Chalmers marques and formed the Chrysler Corporation; sales continued to rise, to the extent that, starting from 32nd place in the American industry in 1924, Chrysler had zoomed to fifth place by 1926, moving into fourth slot the following year, when sales reached nearly 200,000. Profits over the three-year period were around $46 million, which enabled Chrysler to finance an ambitious plan of factory modernisation and expansion.

In 1926 the range consisted of the 58, a four-cylinder model, and two six-cylinder models, the 70 and the luxury Imperial Six. By 1928, however, Walter Chrysler felt it necessary to take over the Dodge concern in order to gain greater capacity in the popular car market. The 1928 Plymouth, basic price $670, was the first fruit of this marriage – by May of 1929 output of the Plymouth ran at one thousand a day.

In 1928 Chrysler emphasised the performance and

reliability of the six-cylinder models by entering a brace of tourers at Le Mans; and although the battle for first place, between Bentley and Stutz, stole all the headlines, the achievement of the Chryslers in coming third and forth was none the less remarkable.

By now the marque had acquired a reputation for innovation, and the narrow-shell 'ribbon' radiators of the 1929 models were widely copied by European makers, and by then internal-expanding hydraulic brakes were a standard feature of the range.

For 1931, however, there was a new look: styling was obviously inspired by the long low look of the L-29 Cord, as was the gently vee'd radiator shell. Two new straight-eights, the 40–125hp Imperial 6.3-litre and the 29–80hp 3.9-litre, were introduced in conjunction with the established 4.4-litre Model 70 and the economy 2.6-litre Light Six model. The three larger cars had four-speed 'silent-third' gear-boxes.

Chrysler's emphasis on research was responsible for features such as the flexible 'Floating Power' engine mountings of the 1932 models, which also had automatic clutches and freewheels, while the announcement of synchromesh in 1933 was followed by automatic overdrive for 1934. Research also led to the introduction of the controversial Airflow range in 1934. Carl Breer was supposed to have found, through wind tunnel tests, that the average car of the early 1930s was more efficient aerodynamically when going backwards. The resultant 'back-to-front' design was a technical success but a commercial disaster.

The Airflow had a wide, fully streamlined body whose steel-tube frame was welded to the chassis members, while forward mounting of the engine reversed the traditional concept of weight distribution by placing 55 per cent of the car's weight on the front axle; long springs were intended to give a 'floating' ride.

The front-end styling, however, proved to be too radical a step for the customers to take, although the Corporation's more conventional models, which shared the Airflow's full-width styling with spatted rear wheels from the scuttle back, apparently sold well! To mask the front end, a dummy vee-bonnet was fitted to the Airflow range for 1936. The range was shelved after 1937, but technical progress continued under the skin of the other models with the adoption of independent front suspension in 1937, and steering-column gear-change and optional fluid drive in 1939.

While the Airflow fiasco is so well remembered, it was no more than a mild ripple in the smooth progress of Chrysler's corporate success. Indeed, in 1933 the Chrysler group overtook Ford to move into second place, behind Chevrolet, in total sales – a position it was to hold until 1950.

With the company he had founded ten years before firmly established, and with the outstanding debts, incurred at the time of the Dodge takeover, fully paid, Walter P. Chrysler retired; he died in 1940 and his death seemed to mark the end of innovative Chrysler styling, if not engineering development, for many years.

Cord

A reality less than the legend

Despite the fact that by the late 1920's Erret Lobban Cord's empire included ownership of Auburn, Duesenberg, American Airlines and Lycoming engines, it was not until 1921 that a model line bearing Cord's own name appeared.

This, the Cord L-29, was the first American car with front-wheel drive to reach serious production status. Designed by Carl Van Ranst who had worked with Harry Miller on the front-wheel-drive racing cars which had dominated Indianapolis since 1926, the Cord followed the general layout of the Miller, with a de Dion-type front axle and inboard front brakes. There the resemblance ended, for the Cord was built to carry the finest luxury coachwork, and custom-built versions were produced by such coachbuilders as Murphy and Hayes.

The car used a similar straight-eight power unit to that of the Auburn 120 with a swept volume of 4934cc. Instead of being turned around for the front-wheel drive application, the engine had its flywheel extended at the front; as an unfortunate consequence the timing chain was rendered inaccessible.

The suggestiveness of the Cord L-29's styling, however, was not followed through in the performance: an all-up weight of over two tons, allied to inappropriate ratios in the three-speed gearbox and final drive, limited the maximum speed to a little over 80mph, which the cheaper and less sophisticated Auburn could exceed easily. Acceleration figures, apparently, were ten years behind the time.

Other features hardly likely to endear the L-29 to the press-on motorists of 1929 were the low-geared steering – four turns lock to lock – and the gear-lever, which protuded horizontally from the fascia. The inboard front brakes, however, did keep unsprung weight to a minimum, and the handling was said to have been 'incredible', despite the restriction of a $137\frac{1}{2}$-inch wheelbase.

The price was a little high, at around $3000, but it was not completely unrealistic and quite a few other specialist models like Stutz, Marmon, Franklin Lincoln and Packard cost a great deal more. The Wall Street Crash, a few months after the L-29's launch, ruined the car's chances – the purchase of a new and untried luxury car of unorthodox specification was a venture that few well-off Americans were willing to make.

In three years, only 4400 L-29s were sold, and production ended in 1932. It cannot have been the styling that let the Cord down, for the new 1930 Chrysler straight-eight copied several of its features, especially the design of the slightly vee'd radiator shell.

The second car to bear the Cord name, the 810, designed by Gordon Buehrig, was certainly unorthodox in appearance, having headlamps which could be cranked down flush with the pontoon-style front wings, and in fact its shape earned the car the unflattering nickname of 'Coffin-nose Cord'.

On the 810 the de Dion front axle was discarded, and replaced with independent front suspension making it the first front-wheel-drive car with this feature in America. In addition it had rheostat-controlled instrument lighting, variable speed windscreen wipers, complete sound insulation and a radio as standard. The box-section chassis formed a rigid unit with the all-metal body, and the engine was once again a 125bhp Lycoming, a 4730cc V8.

All Buehrig's design skills were nullified by annoying mechanical setbacks, and although one hundred cars appeared ready for the 1935 New York Show, they lacked the complex front-wheel-drive unit, which was still undergoing development. Ironically, the car was an immediate success, and the many prospective customers were doomed to disappointment.

Although the advanced specification of the transmission – pre-selected gears controlled electrically by a tiny gearlever moving in a miniature gate on the steering column, plus an overdrive fourth – promised great things, the unit turned out to be a disaster. Even when the system was set up properly there was an annoying time lag between depressing the clutch pedal and the automatic engagement of the selected ratio by a complex arrangement of electromagnets and vacuum-operated diaphragms. Moreover, early production models suffered from obscure transmission maladies and they were also prone to boiling up, for the water passages in the cylinder heads were too small, and the aluminium heads tended to crack under stress.

In the first year of production, only 1174 Cord 810s were sold – about a twelfth of the anticipated figure. It was the car's mechanical shortcomings that had caused the situation, rather than its unorthodox styling which was widely admired. In 1936 sales continued to slide, and even the introduction of the 100mph-plus Cord 812 in 1937 failed to remedy the situation, although the new Cord had a supercharger-boosted power output of 170bhp and boasted huge external chrome plated exhaust pipes of which any enthusiast would have been proud. By the end of 1937 the Cord saga was over, and Cord himself retired to Nevada. Over the next thirty years several attempts were made to revive the marque, the latest in 1968; none, however, was very successful.

Right: a Cord L-29 cabriolet shows a strong similarity with some of the cars built by the other two companies in the Erret Lobban Cord empire, Auburn and Duesenberg

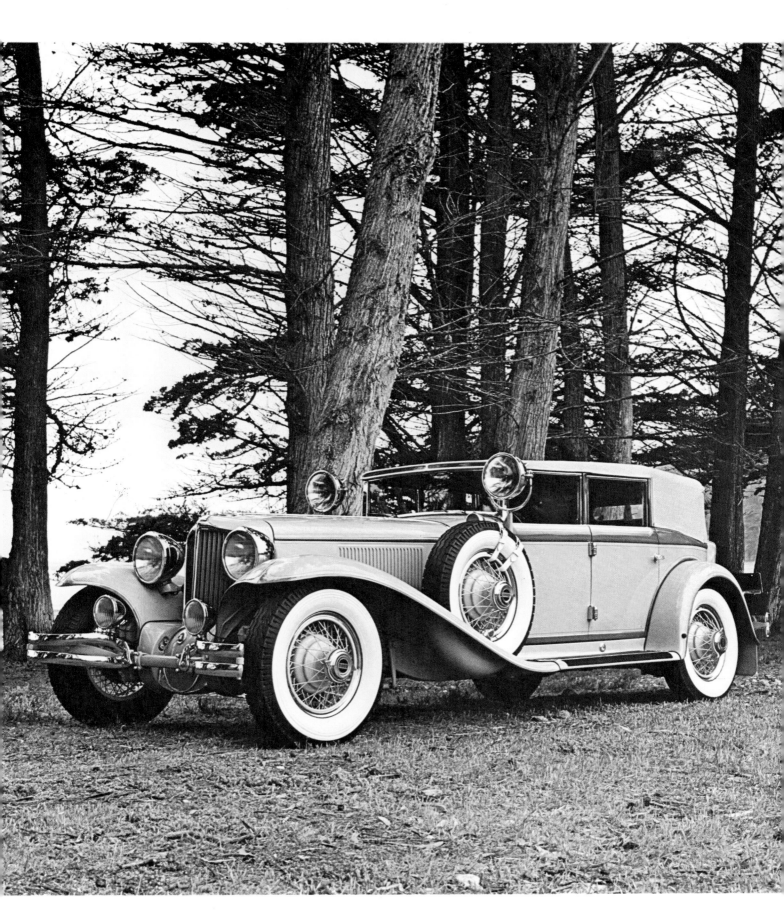

Top left: a Cord L-29 in original 1929 form, powered by a Lycoming straight-eight engine of 4934cc.
Left: a supercharged Cord 812 of 1936 (Harrah collection); the 812 replaced the 810 'coffin-nose' Cord, shown *below*

Above: the Cord L-29 of 1932, this time with a 5270cc engine.
Below: a conventional looking example of the Cord 935 of 1936,
this has a limousine body by LeBaron. Cord ceased car
production in 1937

Duesenberg
The ultimate in American cars

Duesenberg – the very name has an arrogant ring to it, totally befitting what was, arguably, the finest motor car to have been built in the United States.

The Duesenberg family originated in Lippe in Germany, and emigrated to America in the mid 1880s. By 1906 the two young Duesenberg brothers were in business at Des Moines, Iowa, building a 24hp, flat-twin car with an epicyclic gearbox and chain final drive. Finance was provided by a lawyer named Mason, from whom the car took its name.

In 1914, however, the brothers cut loose from their sponsors, and set up business in St Paul, Minneapolis, building racing cars which were largely similar to the Mason-Duesenbergs, except for a high exhaust pipe curling out of the top of the bonnet. Breathing was improved on some of the 1916 engines by fitting four valves per cylinder instead of two. Many leading drivers raced Duesenbergs during this period – Eddie Rickenbacker, Ralph Mulford, Willie Haupt and Tommy Milton – and by 1916 the marque's reputation was such that the brothers' firm was chosen to produce Bugatti aero-engines for the US Government during World War I.

After the war, the Duesenbergs went back to building cars. Inspired by their work on the Bugatti U16 engine, which was basically two straight-eights side by side, they developed their own 4.26-litre straight-eight. This engine was fitted into a series of racing cars for the 1920 season, and then work was begun on two new and exciting projects. The first was a sixteen-cylinder car with two 4.9-litre straight-eights mounted side-by-side; Tommy Milton set up an unofficial world land speed record of 156.05mph with this car at Daytona in April 1920. More important, though, was the company's first passenger car, which had a 4.26-litre engine similar to the racing units (but with two valves per cylinder instead of three). This was completed in time to be displayed at the 1920 New York Salon.

This was the first production straight-eight on the American market, and also the first to feature four-wheel hydraulic braking. In the former respect, it was three years ahead of the rest of the market, while the brake layout was even more advanced. Valves were operated by a single overhead camshaft, and the engine design made extensive use of aluminium; it also pioneered alloy pistons in America, though cast-iron units were available for conservative buyers.

Only a handful of prototypes were built before Duesenberg moved into an impressive new factory, in Indianapolis, which could cope with all aspects of car production. Contrary to contemporary American practice, the Duesenberg brothers built their own

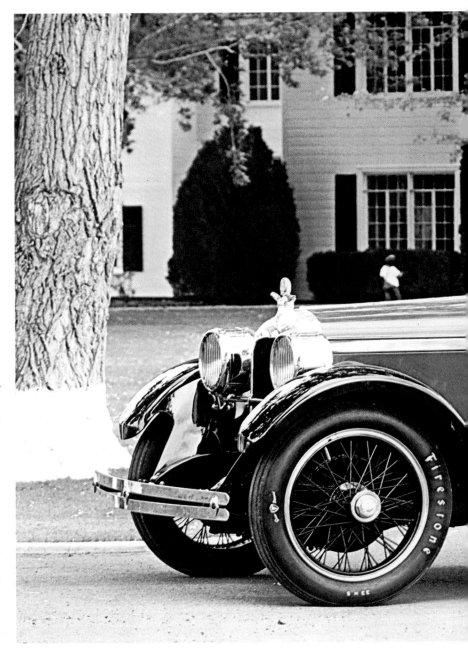

Above: a Duesenberg Model A roadster of 1925 with a straight-
eight engine of 4.2 litres, and 90bhp. (Harrah collection).
Introduced in 1922, the Model A was an important milestone
in American automobile history, being the first car to have
hydraulic brakes on the front wheels

engines and most other mechanical components; the three-bearing crankshaft was notably rigid, and carefully balanced to eliminate vibration.

At the time of the Straight-Eight's introduction, the racing models had already established 66 American records on the Sheepshead Bay Board Speedway, and the passenger version of the racer was naturally billed as 'The World's Champion Automobile—built to outclass, outrun and outlast any car on the road'.

However, victory at the French Grand Prix in 1921, and other track achievements such as the Duesenberg's first place at Indiapolis in 1924 (plus the marque's many other successes, which culminated in a second Indiapolis win and the AAA Championship in 1926), failed to have any great effect on passenger car sales. For one thing, the marque's Teutonic-sounding name counted against it in the years immediately following the Armistice. More importantly, while to European motorists a racing pedigree was indicative of high engineering standards and a good road performance, to the Americans rich enough to afford a Duesenberg, racing cars meant noise, smell and smoke, and though the Duesenberg Straight-Eight was guilty of none of these vices, it was credited with them by association.

Sales, therefore, were not as good as they should have been; although poor body styling is a criticism sometimes levelled against the 1921–26 Duesenbergs, they were as good in this respect as most of their contemporaries, the plain fact of the matter being that American coachbuilders of the 1920s lacked the flair of their European counterparts, both in overall conception and in the treatment of details and accessories.

Also, Fred Duesenberg was an engineer first and a financier a long way after. He could, it is said, work out the dimensions of key components, like con-necting rods, by eye, and arrive within one or two thousandths of an inch of the carefully stress-calculated computations of engineers with more formal training. What is more, he fully expected every member of his staff to work the same long hours as himself.

Small wonder, then, that the marque's *succès d'estime* was not reflected in its bank balance, and that Straight-Eight production totalled no more than 500–650 units in the model's six-year life. In 1926, the company was taken over by that up-and-coming entrepreneur, Erret Lobban Cord, who immediately instituted a programme of styling changes. Wisely, however, he left Fred and August in charge of engineering, and all he insisted on was that the brothers should produce a new car which, in terms of style, engineering and sheer panache, should rival the best the world had to offer. In December 1928, they revealed the result of their labours to the public —it was, they claimed, 'The World's Finest Car', the Model J Duesenberg. Its 6.9-litre power unit was built by another Cord subsidiary, Lycoming, well known as suppliers of proprietary engines; however, this was no off-the-shelf side-valve six, but a race-bred straight-eight with twin overhead camshafts operating four valves per cylinder. Claimed output was 265bhp, twice that of any other American passenger car. The model J had a top speed in the region of 116mph and its chassis price was $8500.

The engine was rubber-mounted in a chassis of exceptional rigidity; frame side-members were $8\frac{1}{2}$ inches deep, and there were six cross-members plus diagonal bracing. Of course, much use was made of aluminium, and the car had hydraulic brakes all round (with variable servo assistance from 1929 on). Hardly in line with the best European practice were the long, willowy, central gear lever and handbrake, but the standard instrumentation was obviously

The model J Duesenberg, introduced in 1929, was the most sophisticated car seen in America up to that time, as the engine specification suggests. The Model J was powered by a 6.9-litre Lycoming straight-eight engine, with two chain-driven overhead camshafts, and four valves per cylinder, giving an output of over 265bhp

Right: a Duesenberg Model J Dual Cowl Phaeton of 1929 by Murphy. Such a car would cost in the region of $14,000 in 1929

designed to impress the most gadget-conscious of owners. Across the somewhat spartan fascia were scattered 150mph speedometer, altimeter, barometer, brake-pressure gauge, tachometer, ammeter, oil-pressure gauge, combination clock and stop-clock, and a complex set of lights operated by a train of timing wheels which drove a device known as the 'timing box' under the bonnet. Every 75 miles, the box automatically lubricated all the chassis greasing points; a red light glowed when it was working, a green one when its lubricant reservoir needed refilling. Every 700 miles, a third light exhorted the

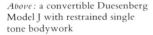

Above: a convertible Duesenberg Model J with restrained single tone bodywork

owner to have the engine oil changed while, at 1400 mile intervals, the fourth light acted as an *aide memoire* to have the battery water level checked at the nearest service station.

On this chassis, the finest coachbuilders of America and Europe—Murphy, Derham, Bohmann & Schwartz, Hibbard & Darrin, Barker, Letourneur & Marchand, Graber, D'Ieteren Frères. Gurney Nutting and Weymann – constructed their finest bodies, bringing the total cost of the car, as the model name of one convertible phaeton version reminded the world, to 'Twenty Grand', give or take a few thousand dollars.

The rise of the Model J Duesenberg is all the more remarkable when one considers that, at the time the model was on the market, there was a world depression, but the Duesenberg clientele was made up of those who were above mere details like the collapse of the stock market; so it is perhaps not so curious that the company introduced an even more flamboyant model in 1932, when the American car market was virtually on its knees.

This was the SJ, which added a centrifugal supercharger, spinning at five times crankshaft speed, to boost the power output to a claimed 320bhp and the top speed to almost 130mph.

The bulk of the blower installation made it impossible to accommodate the standard exhaust system under the bonnet, so Duesenberg brought the exhausts out through the bonnet sides in four chromed flexible downpipes. Outside exhausts were

Above: a roadster version of the Model J from the Harrah collection. Around 470 Model Js were built between 1929 and 1935

Left: the Model J improved. This is the Model SJ of 1932, which had a claimed output of 320bhp! To help cope with this extra power, various engine components were strengthened, and the short version of the Model J chassis used, with up-rated brakes and a higher axle ratio

Below: a Duesenberg Model SJ roadster of 1933, with coachwork by the French house of Weymann, rather than the customary American styling by Murphy or Le Baron. The SJ had a top speed in the region of 130mph, and 0–100mph was said to come up in a mere seventeen seconds!

Above: a Duesenberg Model SJ of 1936 built by the coachbuilders Rollston, and sold for $17,500. The SJs were the last models built by Duesenberg, and the company suspended production in 1937

Left: the great eight-cylinder, double-overhead-cam engine of the Duesenberg SJ, probably the most sophisticated and powerful engine fitted in any American prewar car

a relatively common styling trick in Europe (where the Duesenberg cost more than either Rolls-Royce or Hispano-Suiza), but came as a novelty on the American market. There were even owners of the 'unblown' J who had the external plumbing fitted to make their cars look more exotic. Rarest of all the Duesenbergs was the SSJ, built on the 'ultra-short' (10ft 5in) wheelbase; only two were made, one for Clark Gable and one for Gary Cooper.

Greta Garbo owned a Duesenberg, too; so did Marion Davies, Mae West, Joe E. Brown and William Randolph Hearst. Royal customers included King Alfonso XIII of Spain, King Victor Emmanuel of Italy, Queen Marie of Yugoslavia and Prince Nicholas of Romania, who raced one of his three Model Js at Le Mans, in 1933, 1934 and 1935, with an outstanding lack of success.

However, even all the top customers in the world could not save Duesenberg. Fate had already claimed Fred Duesenberg, killed in 1932 at the wheel of an early SJ, and now the break-up of the Cord empire would destroy the company he had headed.

The company showed its 1937 models at New York and Chicago as though all was well, but then the Cord bubble burst, and the purchasers of the group's assets decided to curtail car production. The Duesenberg factory was bought by local truck builders Marmon-Herrington, one last chassis was assembled to the order of a rich German client by August Duesenberg and his devoted workmen in Chicago, and a new spares and service company was specially created in Auburn, Indiana, during 1938, for owners of Auburn Cord and Duesenberg cars.

Despite its ultimate failure, the Duesenberg name still carries the old magic – quite an achievement when it is realised that total output of Straight-Eights, Js, and SJs amounted to little more than one thousand cars in eighteen years.

Du Pont

Expensive cars for an exclusive market

In 1920, Du Pont Motors Incorporated, of Wilmington in Delaware, was founded by E. Paul Du Pont, a member of the wealthy Du Pont family famous for the chemical company which bears their name. In 1923 the company was moved to Moore, Pennsylvania, where it remained for the rest of its brief, twelve-year, existence, during which time only 537 vehicles were porduced – all for the expensive luxury market as competition for Stutz, Packard and Duesenberg.

The first Du Pont was unveiled at the New York Salon in 1920. The Model A used a 4.1-litre, four-cylinder, side-valve engine, built by Du Pont themselves, and sold for $2600. It was this model, slightly changed, which appeared the next year as the Model B and remained in production until 1923. 1923 saw the arrival of the Model C, the first Du Pont to have a Herschell-Spillman six-cylinder engine. Its successor, the Model D of 1925, was powered by a 4395cc six-cylinder Wisconsin engine developing around 75bhp, and introduced four-wheel hydraulic braking to the Du Pont line.

What was commonly considered the best Du Pont built, the Model G, first appeared at the 1928 Salon in New York. The Model G's engine, a Continental straight-eight of 5275cc, produced 115bhp at 3600rpm, and was capable of propelling the speedster versions at a guaranteed 100mph. One Model G did in fact race at Le Mans in 1929, driven by Charles Moran, only to retire on the twentieth lap with a broken propeller shaft. While the Model G speedster was fast, its styling was disappointing; faired-in headlights and sweeping wings did not seem to suit the car. This was in stark contrast to the roadster version, a very attractive machine.

The Model H with the long, 12ft 2in, wheelbase was the last Du Pont car, and although the quality of the cars was beyond question, the cost of producing luxury cars in such small numbers made the Du Ponts prohibitively expensive, and in 1932 production ceased.

Below: a Du Pont Model G, in Royal Town Car form of 1933, with bodywork by Merrimac, from the Harrah collection. A Model G sports, with a more powerful 140bhp engine and four-seater sports body, took part in the 1929 Le Mans 24-hours, but was forced to retire

Ford

The founders of mass production

Strangely, one of Henry Ford's first cars was a two-cylinder racing machine, built in 1901, which won, with Ford driving, on its first outing. After building two more racing cars, the famous *999* and *Arrow*, Ford attracted enough good publicity to be able to raise $28,000 and founded the Ford Motor Company in June 1903.

The first Ford production model was the Model A, a simple design in line with most contemporary cars. It had two water-cooled cylinders, producing 8hp. Maximum speed was just short of 30mph, and, at a time before thermostats had been developed, the original Model As were said to boil when nearing their maximum speed. This was, perhaps, just as well as the car never had a great reputation for brakes.

The Model B which followed proved to be relatively unimaginative, and to a publicity conscious Henry Ford something had to be done to lift it a little in the public mind. He resurrected the old *Arrow* and attempted the world land speed record on a frozen Lake St Clair where he managed an average speed of 91mph – unfortunately without official timekeepers being present, and so the record stayed in the hands of the French.

The six-cylinder Model K was never a Henry Ford favourite, and Ford debated selling the company to William Durant's General Motors to form a company that could produce Ford's dream, a popular car for the masses. Durant was unable to raise the necessary $8,000,000, and in 1908 Ford brought out the car which really made his name. The Model T was an advanced 2.9-litre car with a top speed near 45mph, so popular it sold 15,007,033 in a production run of eighteen years, by the end of which, of course, it was regarded as basic and crude. Demand for the Model T was such that Ford could get away with offering black as the only colour from 1914 to 1925, and in fact even the brass radiator was replaced by a black painted one in 1917.

In 1919 Ford bought out all the shareholders at a cost of $100 million to give himself sole control of the company, and this move was so successful that the Ford Motor Company doubled in value in the next ten years.

By the end of World War I, Ford were in a good position, producing 750,000 cars in 1919 to give the company a third of the US market. By 1921 they had over fifty per cent of car sales in America, and

Below: a sensation when introduced in 1932, this is the Ford V8 of 3.6 litres. In 1935 V8 production was up to one million per year, and the next year a smaller, 2.2-litre, V8 appeared, but was not the same success as its bigger brother

Below: a phaeton V8 of 1938 from the Artom collection. Like all Ford models at that time it was available in both standard and de luxe versions, the former with either the 60 or the 85bhp engine, the latter with the 85bhp option only. The 1938 Ford V8 was notable for its more rounded bodywork, introduced that year. Production of the V8 continued throughout World War II

by that time Edsel Ford, Henry Ford's son, was company President. It was Edsel who made the bold step of suggesting that the Model T be replaced by something more modern – and he was snubbed for his pains. In 1922, however, Ford was thinking of the next step; an air-cooled engine was being considered and although development work continued through 1925 it was a conventional water-cooled, four-cylinder car which eventually supplanted the Model T – this was the new Model A.

The car had a high body with a flat vertical windscreen, and it was attractive in its own way. It had taken some convincing to make Henry Ford drop his beloved Model T, but the Model A was something different. It looked robust, strong and stylish, and was just what the market wanted. Its engine produced enough power to make the A faster than its rivals and it was a success from the start.

Among the items which created interest in the Model A was the use of a laminated safety-glass windscreen – the first to be produced as standard equipment in the motor industry. Where the Model T had established mass production, the Model A introduced proper assembly-line methods, with the careful weighing of pistons and connecting rod assemblies typical of attention to detail.

The Model A had a four-cylinder engine with a three bearing crankshaft made of carbon manganese steel. The pistons were of aluminium, and chrome-

silicon alloy heavy-duty valves were used. There was a three-speed gearbox, worm and peg steering, Houdaille double-acting hydraulic dampers, cable-operated four-wheel brakes, welded wire wheels, and thief proof Electrolock ignition.

Enthusiasm for the Model A, while considerable, was not as long-lived as for the Model T, and by 1932 the first Ford V8 was added to the range. The car used a 3.6-litre V8 engine which produced around 70bhp at 3400rpm and gave it a very respectable performance. Suspension was by the all-round transverse leaf spring system used on the new Model B, introduced alongside the V8 as an insurance policy in case the bigger car was a commercial flop. The V8, however, was a resounding success, and by 1935 two million had been sold. In 1939 the V8 was given hydraulic brakes, and a column gear change came in 1940.

In 1941 Henry Ford overcame his well known dislike of six-cylinder cars in producing the 3.7-litre six as a companion car to the V8.

From the 1930s onwards the Lincoln division of Ford dealt with the luxury market, with cars such as the V12 of 1932, and Ford concentrated more and more on the mass market following World War II. The survival of the Lincoln company was, in fact, due to Edsel Ford; it was he who urged the takeover by Ford in 1921, and Lincoln was Edsel's special interest up to his death in 1943.

Franklin

Air-cooled unorthodoxy from the USA

The Franklin was perhaps the most unorthodox car to be marketed successfully in the United States; every Franklin built was air-cooled, most had full-elliptic suspension, and most had wooden chassis frames.

The Syracuse, New York, company's first car appeared in 1902 with a four-cylinder transverse engine with overhead valves. Subsequent Franklins displayed similar technical innovation; the 1915 model, for example, had aluminium pistons and a reputation for reliability that instilled great brand loyalty among Franklin owners.

By 1925, the marque was breaking new ground with the J. Frank De Causse-styled Series II, with a handsome square-cut 'radiator' with vertical chrome strips across the grille. Especially successful was the 1925 Coupé, often referred to as the Doctor's Coupé, produced until 1927; orders for this car were received in such numbers that production quotas were first doubled, then trebled. Beneath the modern styling, however, a Franklin was still a Franklin, with the laminated ash frame which the company claimed was more durable than steel, and the full-elliptic springs which, aided by Wahl two-way dampers, gave an excellent ride on smooth roads and kept the car down very well over bumps, so that really bad roads could be taken 20mph faster than many contemporary systems allowed.

During the late 1920s custom bodies on Franklin chassis proliferated, almost in inverse proportion to sales which began to sag in the face of the Depression. The new Series 14 appeared in 1930, followed the next year by the essentially similar Series 15, and still sales fell.

By 1931, the Franklin's most distinctive feature, the wooden chassis, had disappeared. Steel frames had made their first appearance at the end of 1927 on long-wheelbase models, and had gradually ousted the older chassis, although partial wooden construction was still evident on 1930 models.

In 1932, Franklin introduced a magnificent air-cooled V12, styled by Dietrich. This car not only had a steel chassis but also dispensed with the full-elliptic springs using conventional semi-elliptics all round. Priced at $4400, the new V12, offering 95mph performance, was the wrong car for the times, and even a forty per cent price cut failed to attract sales.

Franklin's last model was the Olympic, but this was a Franklin in engine only. All the rest was Reo, for cheapness. It was as unsuccessful as its more expensive stablemate and, in 1934, the factory produced its last car, although there was an unsuccessful attempt made to refloat the company in 1936.

Throughout the life of the Franklin company (1901 to 1934) it was renowned for the diversity of the models produced, and their undoubted quality of manufacture. *Above:* one of the last of the Airman models, which were built between 1931 and 1934, from the Harrah collection

Far right: a large Franklin limousine of 1930, and *right* a Franklin six-cylinder engine, characteristic in that it is air-cooled; the cooling fins for each cylinder are just visible below the manifold (Pozzoli collection)

Graham-Paige
A sense of adventure

In 1927 the three Graham brothers, Joseph, Ray and Robert, after having sold Graham Brothers Trucks to Dodge, returned to motor manufacture by acquiring the Paige-Detroit Motor Company.

Under the guidance of the Graham brothers, the Graham-Paige company prospered spectacularly: in 1928 it achieved its highest ever placing in the American sales league, reaching twelfth position, and the following year production peaked at 77,077. European demand was sufficient to warrant the opening of an assembly plant in Berlin in 1928, but all this was swept away in the Depression which followed.

1932 saw the announcement of a new range of the Blue Streak Eights, with pontoon wings, vee-shaped grille and narrow windscreen. The low-slung Blue Streak look was widely copied, but it did Graham-Paige's sales figures no good at all – sales dropped by 7000 that year. Nevertheless, the company continued to be adventurous; the 1934 range was crowned by the 4350cc Custom Eight, which had a centrifugal supercharger driven at five times the engine speed by the waterpump shaft – this gave the car 90mph performance with sparkling acceleration.

The six-cylinder model range was completely restyled for 1936. The low price model was dubbed the Crusader, while the 3.6-litre became the Cavalier, and a new supercharged six appeared in 1937.

The 1938 range – all 3.5-litre sixes – were fast but ugly and did not sell well. They were the last real Graham-Paiges; in 1945 Graham-Paige was taken over by Kaiser-Frazer and the marque died out.

Below: a photograph of what is now a very rare car, a Graham-Paige coupé de ville of 1930

Hudson

A foundation stone of American Motors

The first car from the Hudson Motor Car Company (founded 1909), was the Model 20, a car which conformed in every respect with the established US pattern for a low-to-medium price automobile in technical specification and body style. It featured a 20bhp four-cylinder side-valve engine, and semi-elliptic springs front and rear.

By 1914, however, with the advent of the Model 40, Hudson considered themselves the world's largest manufacturer of six-cylinder cars: total sales that year being 10,261. In 1916 production leapt to over 25,000 through the introduction of an instant winner in the Super-Six, and thereafter there was never to be another four in the Hudson range.

For 1919 Hudson introduced a cheaper line under another name – the Essex. In the years 1919–32 some 1,331,000 Essex cars greatly expanded Hudson business, and in fact their sales in the years 1925–29 easily exceeded those of the parent company.

In 1931 the Super Six was replaced by a straight-eight which became the sole Hudson power plant. Its 1932 capacity of 4168cc remained the same until 1953, a testimony to its power and smoothness.

For Hudson, the 1930s were a turbulent period of fluctuating fortunes, profits and losses, with annual production dropping from around 114,000 in 1930 to only 41,000 in 1933, up again to 123,000 by 1936 but down to 51,000 by 1938 in which year they suffered a trading loss of nearly $4.7 million.

After a postwar revival, Hudson were finally forced to merge with Nash-Kelvinator, to form American Motors in 1954.

Below: a six-cylinder Hudson cabriolet of 1934, with the curious Axleflex independent front suspension, by swinging axles and semi-elliptic springs

Hupmobile

A small manufacturer with big ideas

The Hupp Motor Corporation of Detroit, founded in 1908, produced a 2.8-litre runabout as their first car, and continued to produce this four-cylinder car, with progressive updating, until 1924.

A revolutionary new model, America's first popularly priced straight-eight, was announced in 1925; it made wide use of aluminium in its construction, had external contracting Lockheed hydraulic brakes, and an engine capacity of 4 litres.

Although sales dropped drastically during the Depression, the 1923–33 Hupmobiles were perhaps the most handsome models produced by the company. 1934 saw the announcement of the aerodynamic range, with its ultra-modern form, including special wings, slanting radiator, extended tail and elongated headlight fairings. The new range

was designed for lightness and consequently made wide use of high tensile materials. For increased rigidity, the chassis was mounted in unit with the all-steel bodywork, crossbraced and stiffened by a special truss extending from the scuttle forwards under the bonnet. All the new models featured three-speed all-synchromesh gearboxes, and the eight-cylinder had a 5-litre engine with fully counter-balanced five bearing crankshaft.

A new 4-litre six was announced for the spring of 1935, and this, along with the old 3.6-litre six, and the 5-litre eight, brought the Hupmobile range to its most comprehensive. Nevertheless, falling sales led to Hupmobile suspending production for several months in mid 1936, and in 1940 they ceased to make cars, and diversified into other fields.

Right: one of the last Hupmobiles, a 1939 model with straight-eight engine and automatic overdrive as standard

Below left: an eight-cylinder cabriolet of 1932 and, *right,* a cabriolet version from the Aerodynamic range of 1934. This model was available in 4-litre six-cylinder and 5-litre straight-eight engine forms

La Salle

GM's cut-price Cadillac

In 1927 the management of General Motors thought it necessary to introduce a new division into the company to fill what they felt was a gap in their market coverage between their Buick and Cadillac marques. Thus La Salle was born.

The name of La Salle came originally from a certain René Robert Cavelieur de La Salle, a member of the French aristocracy who had emigrated to the New World in the seventeenth century, This name, it was thought, would give the new marque an association of nobility, and La Salle followed Cadillac in being named after a French emigré.

The particularly good design, and the consequent initial sales success of the La Salle cars on the American market (27,000 were sold in the first year of production) was due, in large part, to the young stylist, Harley Earl. His chassis design was based on the contemporary Hispano-Suiza, and he could hardly have chosen a better or more renowned make on which to model his creation.

Even in that first year, there was a range of eleven body styles, and two chassis, to choose from. The short chassis was 10ft 5in long and the long version measured 11ft 2in. On the mechanical side, the engine was a V8 similar to that of the Cadillac in that the bore dimensions were the same (3.12in) and the crankshaft ran on only three main bearings. There

Two views of a 1931 La Salle coupé. The ill-fated La Salle marque was an intermediate line, introduced by General Motors, which survived only until 1940. There was no room within GM for both Cadillac and La Salle, and La Salle had to go

Below: a La Salle series 50 of 1938, with a 4.2-litre, straight-eight Oldsmobile engine. Note the considerable similarity between this La Salle and its Cadillac stablemate on p 132

the similarity ended, as the La Salle motor utilised a shorter stroke, bringing its displacement down to 4699cc. Engine cooling was helped by the introduction of thermostatically controlled louvres which opened and closed to keep the water temperature at a constant level. Another interesting feature of the model was a fuel feed regulated by the vacuum in the inlet manifold; the idea behind this was to eliminate the chance of mechanical or electrical failure in the fuel system, but of course, as drivers of the many cars which had vacuum powered windscreen wipers could also testify, a long uphill stretch would prove a great problem as the engine laboured!

The fact that La Salle had, like Cadillac, a French name suggests that La Salle was intended to be nearer to Cadillac than Buick in the pricing structure and intended market, and in fact the price of $2600 was high for the time and after a while sales began to drop off. The public was willing to spend heavily to buy a true Cadillac, but loathe to buy what was felt to be rather an expensive, but still down-market, substitute.

No real changes were made to the La Salle for six years, until minor changes were introduced in 1933, and a major revision undertaken in 1934. That year both the styling and the mechanical specification were changed. A new, Harley Earl-designed, slim-line radiator grille appeared which characterised all the new models, and a new engine was selected from another General Motors' car; the Oldsmobile side-

valve, straight-eight of 3920cc produced 90bhp, but the main reason for its inclusion was, not surprisingly, cost. With the cheaper motor, GM were able to slash the price of the La Salle in the hope that it could compete in what had become a depressed market by 1934. This move proved insufficient to revive the fortunes of La Salle, neither did a return to the V8 format in 1937 materially improve matters, and by 1940 General Motors had ceased production of the La Salle.

Lincoln

A little bit of Cadillac, a little bit of Ford...

Henry Leland's Leland and Falconer precision casting and gear cutting company of Detroit began supplying engines to Oldsmobile in 1901. Leland's precision engines attracted such attention that he was chosen to replace Henry Ford as chief engineer with the Detroit Automobile Company in 1903, when it was renamed the Cadillac Automobile Company.

Leland's career at Cadillac came to an end in 1917 when Cadillac's owners, General Motors, refused the company permission to build the Liberty aero-engine. Leland resigned, taking his son Wilfred with him, to form the Lincoln Motor Company in 1917.

After producing the Liberty engine through what remained of World War I, Lincoln built their first car in 1920. It was powered by a side-valve V8 engine of 5.8 litres, developing 81bhp. Pressure-fed lubrication, rather than the splash system then in vogue, and the thermostatically controlled radiator blinds, were notable features of the first Lincoln. The quality of the engine, however, was not matched by the car's styling and low sales meant that the company remained in financial trouble dating from the huge initial loans needed to set up Lincoln Motors, and in 1922 Lincoln was acquired by Henry Ford.

The new Lincoln Motor Company, with Edsel Ford as second Vice-President along with Wilfred Leland, was operated as a separate company, even though all its shares were now held by the Ford Motor Company. With Edsel's influence Lincoln became a viable proposition. The old body designs were phased out and new, more attractive, styles introduced. Prices were cut drastically and orders worth $2 million taken.

The mutual incompatibility of the Fords and Lelands, however, meant that, by June 1922, the short-lived Leland-Ford alliance was all over and the Lelands given their marching orders. Now that Edsel had sole command the quality of the cars improved, certain production processes were rationalised and limited conveyor-belt assembly introduced. The standard bodies were styled by Brunn, while custom coachwork was series-produced by LeBaron, Willoughby, Judkins, Dietrich and Locke.

Below: the Lincoln Coaching Brougham built in 1926 for the film actress Ethel Jackson, by the coachbuilders Judkins

Above: a Lincoln club roadster model 151, built by Locke in 1929. *Below:* two four-door saloons of 1932 on Lincoln KB chassis, the top model is by Rollston, and the lower by Lincoln themselves

The cars were built to such accurate limits that they required, according to the chief engineer, no running-in. Their acceleration made them a favourite with both police and gangsters. Indeed, special police models were available from 1924, with four-wheel brakes (which the general public did not have until 1927), bullet-proof glass, twin spotlights, shotgun racks and, in some cases, special tuning to bring the maximum speed up to more than 80mph.

All Lincolns were subjected to an intensive test programme before leaving the factory, even those carrying coachwork by outside coachbuilders, and the standards of finish were comparable with those of any top quality car in the world. Yet the Lincoln incorporated many Ford ideas, such as the inter-changeability of parts between new and old models, so that the earlier cars could be bought up to date at modest cost.

The year 1928 saw an increase in engine size to 6.3 litres and the crankshaft was fitted with counter-weights to retain the car's traditional smooth running. The next major specification change came in 1931, with a chassis lengthened to give the car a 145-inch wheelbase. In addition, it came equipped with a freewheel. Eulogised N. W. Ayer & Son, Inc, who handled publicity for this model: 'Low-slung and rakish, this new open sport type is expected to be a familiar sight around country clubs and fashionable beach and mountain resorts during the coming summer'.

Typical of the standard equipment of the Lincoln range at this time was a cabinet inlaid with pewter, recessed into the back of the front seat. Access to it was provided by doors fitted on each side of a centre panel in which a cigar lighter, tonneau light and switch were fitted.

Further engineering innovations came in 1932, with a V12 – hitherto the province of low-production high-cost cars. It was one of only seven V12 models on the American market that year, the others being produced by Auburn, Cadillac, Franklin, Packard and Pierce-Arrow. It was, stated *The Autocar*, 'one of those exceptional cars which in both construction and performance rise much above the general practice of contemporaries... detail work is very well done, as would be expected, the whole car is beauti-fully finished, and the workmanship beneath the bonnet is reminiscent of the best European practice, than which there can be no higher praise'. This was the last new Lincoln to be introduced in the lifetime of the company's founder, for Henry M. Leland died a few months later, aged 89. Although the firm had been part of the Ford organisation for the last decade, there had been no let-up in the standards of accuracy to which the car was built. Indeed many of the components of the Lincoln KB were machined to an accuracy of between 1/5000 and 1/10,000in.

Unfortunately, however, sales of the new model, and its slightly smaller stable mate, the KA, were disappointing – only 2112 in 1933 – and for 1934 a new Model K was promoted, replacing both the KA and KB and having a swept volume of 414cu in.

The opportunity to own a Lincoln was soon to be

Right: a four-door Lincoln Zephyr H-73, the most popular of the Zephyrs. 16,663 examples of the type were built, from 1936 onwards. The aerodynamic lines are reminiscent of Chrysler's 1934 Airflow

Below: a cabriolet version of the Lincoln Continental. Entering production in 1939 the Continental was the first of a long line of Lincoln Continentals

placed before a vastly increased sector of the public with the arrival of what Ford Sales Manager, William C. Cowling called a 'sensational, completely new motor car', the Lincoln Zephyr. The Zephyr had a V12, 4.4-litre engine which produced 110bhp, in a 122-inch wheelbase body of semi-unitary construction and ultra streamlined appearance. The Zephyr was amazingly popular, retailing at a mere $1275, but its success stifled the sales of the more expensive Model K.

By 1939 the car which was destined to become a legend in its own lifetime appeared – the Lincoln Continental. It was the direct result of the setting up of a styling studio at Edsel Ford's instigation in the early 1930s. Eugene Gregorie, joint head of the studio, began work designing a sporting car of European type (which Edsel called 'continental') in 1932, but it was the introduction of the Zephyr that gave him the opportunity he really needed. He promptly suggested that a distinctive car could be produced from the standard body components of the Lincoln Zephyr Convertible Coupé by a little judicious customising.

In November 1938 Gregorie arrived at his design; the long, low, 'continental' look was achieved simply by cutting a four-inch strip out of the doors and body. A Continental was completed in March 1939 and shipped down to Edsel's holiday retreat in Florida where the sleek, grey, coupé created a furore of excitement, and in October that year the first production Continental came off the line, and although based on standard Zephyr components, each one of the subsequent cars was virtually hand built to traditional Lincoln standards.

Altogether 5322 of the original Lincoln Continentals were produced in the 1940–42, and 1946–48 periods, all with a close resemblance to Eugene Gregorie's original conception, the hallmark of which was the spare tyre vertically mounted at the rear of the car.

The Lincoln Zephyr itself reached its sales peak in 1937, went into a gentle decline, ceased production in 1942 when the USA entered World War II, and was not revived after the war.

When Edsel died in 1943 the Lincoln division lost its creative guiding light and thereafter built cars with less individuality but no less luxury, although the Continental name was revived in 1953 and again in 1961 to denote the absolute top of the Ford range.

Marmon

Too ambitious for the age

In its earliest days the Marmon company of Indianapolis produced simple yet durable cars; in 1907, however, they broke away from utility conveyances in the form of the V8 60hp model known as the Marmon Sixty.

Following the Marmon Sixty, the company was determined to build the more interesting kind of car, but the V8 was discarded in favour of conventional T-head fours from 1909, in the 40/45 and 50/60hp models. In 1906, Marmon started a racing programme to help publicise their cars, and in fact enjoyed some success – it was a Marmon for example that won the very first Indianapolis 500 in 1911.

The postwar pattern of Marmon output was laid down in 1916 in the guise of an advanced 5.5-litre six-cylinder, with aluminium cylinder block and overhead valves, designated the Marmon 34. Lightweight construction was the outstanding feature of this handsome car, and it was retained up to 1927.

After toying with an overhead-valve eight of just over 3 litres in 1927, to back up the well-established but costly 74bhp six, they went over to the straight-eight configuration, commencing with the model 68, followed by the more successful, cheaper, Roosevelt in 1929.

The Roosevelt was renamed the 'R' in 1930, and it was supported by three more such cars, in the form of the side-valve model 69 and the fine 4.9-litre, and 5.2-litre, overhead-valve, four-speed eights.

The model 79 was capable of some 75mph, and when cruising the 4965cc engine was virtually inaudible. Its four-speed gearbox, unusual on an American car, enabled it to accelerate from 10mph to 30mph in 4.6 seconds despite a weight of 36½ cwt. It was this kind of effortless performance which sold the Marmon both in Britain and the USA.

If they had kept to this sensible policy of manufacturing successful straight-eights, Marmon might have survived until the present. As it was they became obsessed with the multi-cylinder configuration in its most expensive and complex form, bringing out the 9.1-litre light-alloy V16 model 16, for 1931. Developing an alleged 200bhp, it was a magnificent machine, but it was too expensive to survive in the Depression years.

A three-speed gearbox was deemed adequate for this smooth and powerful model, but the car did not appeal as had the 3.4-litre model 70, and the effective 5.1-litre model 8/88, and the company struggled. With their sights set on a V12, which might have bridged the gap between the well established eights and the big V16, Marmon were forced to admit commercial defeat in 1933.

Above: elegant, efficient, and technically perfect, the Marmon V16 was a car of the highest class. Unfortunately it was marketed at the depth of the Depression in 1931. The Marmon V16 engine, built in alloy, displaced 9.1 litres and produced 200bhp. The usual Marmon coachbuilder was LeBaron, but others were used from time to time; this is a 1931 phaeton by Waterhouse

Packard
Pioneers of V12 extravagance

The Packard Motor Car Company was founded in 1900, having grown out of James Ward Packard's New York and Ohio Company, makers of electrical equipment.

The first Packard car, in fact, predated the company, it was completed by James and his brother, William Doud Packard in 1899. Called, appropriately enough, the Model A, it had the single-cylinder engine mounted under the seat, high wire wheels and tiller steering that were typical of early American cars, although in 1901 Packard was one of the first makes to go over to the steering wheel.

In 1901 a wealthy Detroit manufacturer, Henry Joy, bought a controlling interest in Packard, and hired the designer of the first four-cylinder Packard Model K, a Frenchman called Charles Schmidt.

Schmidt produced the Model L in 1904, noteworthy in that it was the first Packard to feature the yoke-shaped radiator that was to become characteristic of the marque, which was already becoming prominent as a maker of luxury cars.

The first six was added to the Packard line in 1912, even though the fours had been showing sparkling pace in competition, starting with the special Grey Wolf built on a Model K chassis in 1904. This clocked 77.8mph that year to set records at Daytona, and was placed fourth overall in the first Vanderbilt Cup Race in 1904.

In 1915 came the car that was to put Packard on the motoring map for all time, the sensational Twin-Six. While others were debating over four, six and eight cylinders as the proper number for a luxury car, Packard leap-frogged them all with their twelve-cylinder engine. introduced in May 1915 for the 1916 model year. Although not the first such engine, the Packard twelve was the first of its

Left: a Packard 526 convertible coupé of 1928, with a 6.3-litre, 106bhp, straight-eight engine

Opposite page, top: a Packard 525 Single-Six tourer of 1927 from the Marga Pozzato collection. *Middle:* a Packard 645 phaeton of 1929, and, *bottom,* a 1930 tourer from the Sylvester collection

type to be built in large numbers for cars. So successful was it that almost half the firm's 1916 output of 18,572 was accounted for by twelves; sales and profits doubled with the Twin-Six launching.

Built through the 1922 model year, the 6950cc, L-head twelve-cylinder, although it had only three main bearings and a slender crankcase, had roller tappets and could rev smoothly to 3000rpm, which was its maximum. It hardly needed its three-speed gearbox as it could accelerate smoothly from 3mph in top gear. Prices ranged from $2600 for a touring car, to $4600 for the long-wheelbase Imperial Limousine. During this first incarnation of the Twin-Six, Packard made 35,056 such cars, beautiful big automobiles that were favoured by tycoons, by royalty, and by Presidents; Warren G. Harding was the first US President to be driven to his inauguration – in a Twin-Six Packard.

After World War I Packard's first postwar model, the first to issue from an improved and expanded plant in 1921, was a six. This was the Single-Six, followed, in June 1923, by the most important Packard of the 1920s, the Single-Eight. This replaced the V12, and brought into production the classic straight-eight, a type which Duesenberg had pioneered in the US in much smaller numbers. The eight had a displacement of 5860cc and an output of 84bhp, only 6bhp less than the Twin-Six in its final form. It had a cast-iron block, with side-valves opened by short rocker levers, mounted on an aluminium crankcase that was fitted with nine main bearings. The otherwise conventional chassis featured four-wheel brakes with a mechanical linkage, being among the first models from a major

Above: a model 833 cabriolet of 1931 from the Bruce Cole collection. *Below:* a model 900 roadster of 1932. The roadster style body was a particular favourite in America, and is typified by the dicky seat and external luggage compartment

Left: a close-coupled, two-door coupé of 1913 on a Packard 1003 chassis. Note the movable windscreen (Kalervo collection)

In 1915 Packard introduced the first American touring car with a twelve-cylinder engine. The V12 engine featured aluminium pistons, and the car could be bought for only $2650. *Left*: a V12 roadster coupé of 1934 (Edward G. Blend Jr collection)

Left: another 1934 Packard, this a two-door opera coupé from the Heinmuller collection. Note the fully chromed radiator grille, compared with the partially painted example immediately above

Left: a 1932 V12 with Victoria convertible body by de Dietrich from the De Forest collection. Some of the greatest American coachbuilders of the time built on the Packard V12 chassis, stylists such as LeBaron, Brunn, and Rollston, in addition to de Dietrich

Above: a convertible Packard cabriolet of 1940, styled by the American coachbuilder Howard 'Dutch' Darrin, and known as the Packard Darrin

Left: a twelve-cylinder sports coupé of 1934 from the Du Monte O. Voight collection. Note the partially painted radiator grille and the rather strange mascot on top of it

American maker to have braked front wheels. A four-speed transmission also came into use with the new Packard eights.

After the business slump of the first years of the 1920s, car sales rose again by the mid-decade and Packard consolidated its position as the number one luxury car in the United States. By the standards of the day, Packard's straight-eight was smoother running than the V8s that were favoured by Cadillac and Lincoln, and was thus quieter in the enclosed bodies which came into use during the '20s.

Output kept climbing, and was up to the 50,000 car per year level in 1928. This was the year Packard stopped building six-cylinder cars and placed all its confidence in straight-eights of different bore sizes to suit car weight and price classes. This policy was inaugurated on 1 August 1928, when Packard chose to launch what it called its Sixth Series, showing, like Pierce-Arrow, by this designation its contempt for the conventional model changes engaged in by other manufacturers.

In the late 1920s Packard came dangerously close to building a sports car, with the Speedster Eight models of the Sixth and Seventh Series. They had large-bore engines with enlarged manifolds, a higher compression ratio and a high-lift cam, delivering a sporting 145bhp at 3200rpm in 1929–30 trim. Only 220 Speedsters in various body types were built, showing that the type's guaranteed 100mph top speed held little appeal to the traditional Packard buyer.

At the top of the range at the beginning of the 1930s was a completely new 67 degree V12 of 7292cc; it had four main bearings and a deep-sided iron block with aluminium cylinder heads, and delivered 160bhp at 3200rpm. On this Twin-Six chassis, the finest coachbuilders of the day, such as Dietrich, LeBaron, Brunn and Rollston, made some of the most handsome cars of all times, automobiles that served to epitomise the 'classic' era in American motor history. The market for cars like these, priced as they were from $4000 to $6000 in the Depression years, was not great, and only 5744 were made before Twin-Six production ended in 1939.

Early in 1932 Packard had introduced another 'economy' car, the Light-Eight. Although a pretty car, with a unique curved-bottom interpretation of the classic Packard grille, the Light-Eight failed to catch on and was discontinued in 1933.

Packard was still the sales leader by a clear margin among the luxury car manufacturers (although in a shrinking market) when it decided to protect the heart of its range with a completely new car, moderately priced for Packard, and in the medium price range for the industry at large. This car, announced in 1935, was the Packard 120, so named because of its 120-inch wheelbase. It was the first Packard to have independent front suspension, from a design by research engineer Forest MacFarland.

With four-wheel hydraulic brakes, a genuine Packard straight-eight engine, fresh teardrop-fender styling and a price tag, in its cheapest business coupé form, of only $990, the 120 had a powerful appeal to the many who had only dreamed of owning a Packard before. When a six was added to the line two years later, Packard production set the all-time record figure in 1937, when 109,518 cars were built.

Between the 120 and the Twin-Six, the straight-eight Packard tradition had been kept alive during the 1930s, against tremendous economic odds, by the Senior Series models carrying 160 and 180 designations. One of the most attractive and memorable bodies built on this chassis was the graceful Convertible Victoria styled by Howard 'Dutch' Darrin for the 1940 and '41 seasons, best known simply as the Packard Darrin, a worthy contemporary of the first Lincoln Continental. The lifetime of the Senior 180 Packard in the West was ended during World War II, when dies for its body and chassis were sold, at modest cost, to the Soviet Union, which had always shown a liking for Packards. Made to cement wartime relationships, this deal accounted for the postwar appearance of Russian ZIS models that looked identical to the pre-war Packard Senior 180 models which had been so successful.

Packard introduced a very handsome new body for its Clipper model, unveiled in March 1941, on a 127-inch wheelbase as a competitor to Cadillac in the upper-medium-price class. Its tapering forms were subtle and delicate, flowing back from a high, narrow grille. This was the style with which Packard resumed production after World War II, with both six and eight-cylinder engines.

In June 1955 Packard lost their independence following a merger with the Studebaker company. This take-over was a result of Packard's having lagged behind in styling and design in the years after World War II, and although Packard were rejuvenated briefly in 1955 when the whole range sold well, 1956 turned out to be the last year in which genuine original Packards were made. Although the marque name was used by Studebaker on later models, the final nail in the coffin came in 1962 when the Studebaker-Packard Corporation dropped Packard from the name. Thus ended the Packard story; from the first Packard of 1899 until the last, the company produced 1,610,890 automobiles not to mention over 43,000 trucks up to 1923.

Left: a typical late-1930s American design, this is a 1938 Packard sports coupé. Models such as this emphasised the ostentatious use of sheer size to impress, then in vogue. This large, although admittedly very elegant, coupé is merely a two-seater (Couron collection)

Left: a Victoria model convertible of 1939, one of the last Packards built before World War II. At that time, of course, the USA had another two years of peace before the emphasis turned to military production, and in 1941 Packard introduced the first of its famous Clippers (H.W. Kranz Jr collection)

Pierce-Arrow
A glamorous victim of the Great Depression

The car which symbolised an atmosphere of sybaritic snobbery in 1920s America sprung from the very humble origins of George N. Pierce's wire products business of Buffalo NY. Pierce moved up from bird cages to bicycle spokes, complete bicycles, and eventually cars.

The first Pierce car appeared in 1901, designed by an Englishman, David Fergusson. Known as the Motorette, it was a 2¾hp De Dion-powered stanhope buggy which seemed to have borrowed design points from nearly every popular vehicle of the day.

In 1905 Fergusson introduced his classic Great Arrow four-cylinder, a 24/28hp, 3770cc model on the fashionable Mercédès lines. The Great Arrow Roi-des-Belges tourer, in fact, had body panels cast from aluminium, a method of construction that was to be a distinctive feature of the company's products for the next fifteen years. Although a wood framework was used the manufacturers claimed that the cast panels resulted in a lighter, stronger body – it also facilitated the production of elaborately curved contours without panel beating. By this time Pierce were already a major power in the American motor industry.

In 1913 Pierce-Arrow decide to adopt a new marketing strategy: from that point on there were no annual model changes. Instead a 'Series' designation was introduced, which changed only when radical alterations to the specification were made. Pierce-Arrow claimed this move was made because their cars were so nearly perfect that there was no point in introducing a new model each year.

The last of the model 66s – the biggest production car built in America, which at one time had an engine of 13,514cc – were produced in the spring of 1918 after that model's best year in production, in which 301 had been turned out. At the same time, the 38hp was dropped, and a new 47hp introduced; it was known as the Fifth Series, and had four valves per cylinder, with cylinders cast in pairs. This lasted little more than a year, and then a revised series with monobloc power units appeared.

Left: a Pierce-Arrow model 81 of 1928 in runabout version, with a six-cylinder engine. This example is now in the Harrah collection

Left: a Pierce-Arrow model 845 of 1935 in club sedan form, powered by a V8 engine, and belonging to the Harrah collection

Below: a 1701 model club sedan of 1937, also from the Harrah collection. This was one of the last Pierce-Arrows built by the Buffalo, New York, company which ceased production the next year

By 1920, however, there were ominous signs that the policy of aiming at the upper crust market alone was losing its potency. Sales began to slide, and in an effort to reverse the trend the company brought out a 'cheap' model, the Series 80 which introduced four-wheel braking to the Pierce-Arrow range. Its moderate price (starting at $2895) and refined engineering combined to make it a best seller, in Pierce-Arrow terms. A more powerful engine was available from the end of 1927, and this was used in the Series 81 which succeeded the 80 for 1928. Unfortunately the styling of the 81 did not go down at all well with the Pierce-Arrow clientele, and the model, its sales slipping, was hastily interred.

As work proceeded on a straight-eight successor to the Model 36 which was beginning to show its age, the shareholders, frightened by the company's falling revenues, voted for a take-over by the then prosperous Studebaker Corporation. It was a disastrous mistake with serious consequences.

While Studebaker ownership did not diminish Pierce-Arrow quality, it demeaned it: to the typical Pierce-Arrow owner, accustomed to buying his car from a bespoke dealer, it was as though he had gone into a cut-price grocer's to buy champagne. This was a pity, for the new 5998cc straight-eight of 1929 was an excellent car, a fact reflected in sales of 8000 for the season.

Next, Pierce-Arrow began development work on a radical new model, a V12, which made its bow in 1932, in 6522cc and 7030cc forms, with prices starting at only $3900. The Mormon Meteor, Ab Jenkins, took a 1932 roadster with a prototype 7571cc V12 engine on Salt Lake Flats for a record attempt, and set up an unofficial American 24-hour speed record of 112.9mph. The following year, he took a stock V12 on to the flats and made the record official with a 117mph average, breaking fourteen international and 65 other records for Pierce-Arrow. He subsequently upped the 24-hour figure to 127.2 mph with a modified Pierce-Arrow, but even the excellent publicity accruing from these record runs could not help revive Pierce-Arrow sales.

A consortium of Buffalo businessmen had bought Pierce-Arrow back from Studebaker in 1933, but they might as well have saved their money. The addition of hydraulic tappets to that year's V12 made no difference to the sales graphs, nor did the exciting Silver Arrow, designed for the Chicago World Fair of 1933, with futuristic full-width styling and a streamlined rear end with a tin rear-view 'dormer window' cause more than a ripple of excitement. Ten were built, with a $10,000 price tag but, although a 'production' Silver Arrow was subsequently offered, it was only a fastback version of the standard sedan.

After only a year of regained independence, an achievement of dubious value in view of the company's crumbling reputation and status, there were rumours that Pierce-Arrow was seeking new mergers, and some financial reconstruction was already being undertaken. Sales for 1935 were down to 1000 cars, yet at the end of the year, three outstanding new models, which were advertised as 'the safest cars in the world', were launched. These were the Model 1601 eight and Models 1602 and 1603 twelves, and their advanced specification included huge vacuum-servo brakes, strong X-braced frames, anti-roll bar at the rear, quadruple headlamps, reversing lights, dual tail-lights, tinted safety glass, overdrive, crankcase emission control, freewheeling and many luxury items. It was too good a package to offer at $3195, and the company began building trailer caravans as a sideline to try and bolster its finances. However, it was too late. Pierce-Arrow struggled on through 1937 and into 1938, and then a creditor demanded that the company should be liquidated to pay back the $200,000 he was owed. The firm was declared insolvent and its assets auctioned . . . to realise only a paltry $40,000.

It was a sad end for a marque which in its heyday could count on orders for cars with diamond-studded tonneaux and gold-plated brightwork.

Pontiac

'Chief of the Sixes'

The name Pontiac, after the famous Indian chief of the mid-eighteenth century, was revived by the General Motors consortium in 1926 for use on a car made by the member Oakland company.

'The Chief of the Sixes' as the first Pontiac was known, was an all-new design, and sales of the popularly priced side-valve, 3064cc six totalled 76,742 in the first year of production, 140,000 in 1927 and 210,890 in 1928. For 1930 the Pontiac was redesigned and fitted with an overhead-valve, 3277cc, six-cylinder unit also used in the Buick Marquette.

In 1932 the first Pontiac straight-eight appeared. It was also the first American straight-eight to sell at less than $600. Its 3654cc power unit developed 77bhp, giving a top speed of almost 80mph. The straight-eight featured, in common with other General Motors models, hinged quarter-lights in front and rear windows – a simple innovation which was none the less hailed as a great technological breakthrough.

1934 saw a slightly more positive technical advance in the adoption of Dubonnet-type independent front suspension. This system used a horizontal coil spring for each wheel, activated by a trailing arm link from stub axle to the spring; the Americans termed it 'knee-action springing'.

All-steel 'turret-top' bodywork was another feature of the 1934 Pontiac line, while for 1935 the cars acquired 'Silver Streak' styling with radiator grilles which followed the vulgar contemporary vogue. Underneath the bodywork the Pontiacs were quite straightforward; the Dubonnet-type front suspension was retained, with semi-elliptic springs at the rear. The engines were side-valve, and the gearbox a three-speed unit.

There were no major changes to the Silver Streak's specification for some years, but even so sales doubled in the 1935–36 season, calling for further enlargements of the factory to meet demand. For 1938 there was the option of a column-mounted gearchange (which was standardised on the following year's cars), while the coupé had a curious sideways-on rear seat which folded away into a cubbyhole in the passenger compartment when not in use.

There was, however, a new look for 1941 in the shape of the new Torpedo range, which had twin-choke carburettors allied to larger engines than the previous year's models. Apart from the cheaper Torpedo, there was also the Streamliner and Streamliner Chieftain, all available with six or eight cylinders, it was basically this range with which Pontiac resumed production after World War II.

Below: a curious Pontiac model of 1929, this is a six-cylinder landaulet. *Right:* a Pontiac two-door cabriolet sports of 1933 with a V8 engine

Stutz

The all-American speedster

The first Stutz car, an unremarkable 6.3-litre machine, was built by the Ideal Motor Car Company of Indianapolis in 1911; the Stutz Motor Car Company *per se* did not appear until 1913.

In 1914 the archetypal Stutz, and one of motoring's most legendary models, was born – the Bearcat. The original Bearcat aped the Mercer Raceabout formula of massive engine, minimal coachwork (bonnet, wings, two seats and a fuel tank were deemed adequate) and proved remarkably popular, with sales rising to 2207 in 1917. By 1920, however, the Bearcat was becoming emasculated; the last Bearcat, the 4.7-litre Speedway Six of 1924, had little to offer.

In 1925 the Belgian designer Paul Bastien created a car intended to exemplify 'safety, beauty and comfort', but the new Vertical Eight could not shake off the sporty image of its forebears that easily. Its 4.7-litre straight-eight was endowed with a single overhead camshaft, and developed 92bhp at 3200 rpm, enabling the car to achieve 75mph. The Safety Stutz, as it was known, had a worm-drive rear axle, which permitted the car to be built very low, while an advanced feature was the use of hydraulic four-wheel brakes.

Altogether, the new Stutz was one of the outstanding American cars of the day, and the Black Hawk speedster versions were entered in a wide selection of races from 1927 onwards, which they duly won. The great sporting year of the Stutz was 1928; one of the new 4883cc Black Hawks was driven at 106.5mph at Daytona, to set up a new American stock car record. Several times between 1928 and 1932 Stutz raced at Le Mans, coming second in 1928 and fifth in 1929.

The design of the straight-eight was improved for the 1931 season, and there was a new model in the form of a cheaper overhead-cam six, marketed as a Black Hawk, in the hope of revitalising sales.

The American market was now becoming dominated by the ostentatious V12 and V16 giants from Cadillac, Packard and Lincoln, and in response the last great Stutz power unit was introduced, the eight-cylinder DV32, to power the new Stutz Bearcat of 1931.

The Bearcat's double-overhead-cam engine featured four valves per cylinder, and produced 155bhp at 3500rpm. Not surprisingly, each Bearcat was guaranteed capable of 100mph.

The single-overhead-cam straight-eight and the Black Hawk Six were continued alongside this splendid new model, which rather eclipsed them with its technical specification, but it was excessively expensive and the days of the DV32 and the SV16 were numbered. In 1935 Stutz ceased production.

Above: Stutz will always be remembered for their impressive sports models, an example of which is this 1923 Bearcat – very different from the rudimentary Bearcat of 1914 (Ford Museum)

Above: the superb 4.9-litre Stutz Black Hawk Speedster of 1928.
The Black Hawk was introduced in 1927, and in the next year a
special version was placed second at Le Mans (Harrah Collection)

Wills Sainte Claire

Traditional cars from a revolutionary spirit

Childe Harold Wills worked with Henry Ford from 1902 to 1919 on the design of both the Model A and the famous Model T, designing the Model T's planetary pedal-operated transmission, and in fact Wills even originated the famous Ford logo.

Wills gradually became disenchanted with Henry Ford's conservatism in retaining the Model T unchanged as long as possible, and the final break came in March 1919 when Wills walked out with severance pay of $1,592,128. He bought 4400 acres at Marysville, Michigan, near the picturesque Lake St Clair, and set out to build a car 'ten years ahead of its time'.

Wills used all his considerable skills in metallurgy in developing a new car, as different in concept from the ultilitarian Model T as it was possible to imagine; he named it the Wills Sainte Claire.

It was the first car to use molybdenum steel in its construction, and the connecting rods were made from aluminium. In its engineering it reflected the latest European thinking, particularly the work of the Swiss Hispano-Suiza designer, Marc Birkigt. The power unit of the Wills Sainte Claire, which made its debut in 1921, was a sixty-degree V8, with a single overhead camshaft for each bank of cylinders. Swept volume was 4343cc, and thus it was somewhat surprising that the power output was a modest 65bhp at 2800rpm.

Nevertheless, the engine bristled with refinements; its massive crankshaft ran on seven main bearings, and drove the single vertical kingshaft which controlled both the overhead camshafts and the cooling fan (which had an automatic clutch which disengaged the fan at speeds of over 40mph, when it was not needed).

There was a choice of two wheelbases at first, though by 1924 only the longer (127in) was available. On its radiator, the Wills Sainte Claire proudly bore the image of a Michigan Grey Goose flying over a lake and pine trees (some said that the bird had been chosen as a subtle homage to Marc Birkigt), and the cars were named Grey Goose, too.

Though its engineering was so sophisticated, the Wills Sainte Claire fell down badly in the styling department; maybe all those years working on the utilitarian Model T had dulled Wills' critical faculties, but the Grey Geese were really ugly ducklings whose somewhat ponderous lines were not enhanced by the use of massive and clumsy disc wheels with protruberant hubs. One ingenious touch featured on some Grey Goose models was a 'courtesy light', a small spotlight fitted in the scuttle on the left side of the body and aimed backwards to cast a pool of light in the area of the rear wheel and thus enable

oncoming drivers to gauge the width of the Wills Sainte Claire.

Priced at only $2475 in two-seater form, the Wills Sainte Claire Grey Goose Traveler represented excellent value for money, and the 1923 sales figures of 1500 units must have seemed encouraging: that was, however, the marque's high spot, and thereafter the factory's output tailed off slowly but surely.

A new model was announced in 1925 as a replace-

ment for the V8; this had an overhead-cam straight-six engine of, again, around 4½ litres. Like its predecessor, this new Wills Sainte Claire was capable of reaching a terminal velocity of around 75mph, despite a weight of 30cwt, even in two-seater form, and several record cross-country runs were recorded, culminating in a coast-to-coast dash from New York to San Francisco in 83 hours and 12 minutes in 1926.

The change of model failed to avert the inevitable, however, for the Wills Sainte Claire was just too good for the market: maintenance was difficult and expensive, for few mechanics understood how to repair such a car. So in 1927 the Wills Sainte Claire died, though Childe Harold Wills himself lived on until 1940. One wonders, however, whether the V8 configuration in the Wills Sainte Claire had any bearing on Henry Ford's decision to launch a V8 Ford in 1932. . . .